Edward J. Murphy

THE FINAL CONCLAVE

The Final Conclave

MALACHI MARTIN

STEIN AND DAY/*Publishers*/New York

First published in 1978

Copyright © 1978 by Malachi Martin
All rights reserved.
Printed in the United States of America
Stein and Day/*Publishers*/Scarborough House
Briarcliff Manor, N.Y. 10510

SIXTH PRINTING, 1978

Library of Congress Cataloging in Publication Data

Martin, Malachi.
The final conclave.

1. Popes—Election.   I.   Title.
BX1805.M39   262′.13   77-16145
ISBN 0-8128-2434-2

For the deliberations of mortals are timid,
  and unsure are our plans.
... who ever knew your counsel, except you had given Wisdom
  and sent your holy spirit from on high?
And thus were the paths of those on earth made straight
                                        Wisdom 9:14, 17–18

Author's Note

The heart of this book, beginning on page 113, is the description of Conclave 82. The participants are fictional. But in every other respect it is a scenario based upon the factual material preceding it and upon all available accurate knowledge of the issues and factions at work in the choice of Pope Paul's successor.

Contents

THE BEGINNING

Up on the flat rock perched between Mount Hermon's three peaks, Jesus and the "Prince of this World," as Jesus sometimes called him, had met head-on some years before. Mount Hermon's 9,232-foot head is forever lifted above everything, visible to the naked eye from everywhere around this land: southward from Syria, eastward from the Mediterranean, northward from the tip of the Dead Sea. And, so the Bedouins say, westward from the middle of the Great Desert.

"All you can see from this rock," the Prince had cajoled, grandiosely sweeping in the vast horizon of kingdoms and sea lanes at their feet, "all these will I give you, if you will kneel down and adore me—be my servant!" Power for power. That was the deal. Between Satan and Jesus it has always been a dispute about power. The Prince had lost that round.

Now, near Hermon again, and some three years later, Jesus rubs salt into the wound of that defeat. It is not hard to picture. The scene is somewhere outside the Syrian town that is today called Baniyas, at the foot of the triple-peaked, snow-capped mountain of Hermon. Close by, the River Jordan springs up and flows down the length of Palestine, filling village wells, giving life to olive plantations, vegetable gardens, to fields of melons, to orchards full of oranges, figs, apples, pomegranates, and to fields enameled with wild flowers. The blue skies above the immobile face of Hermon host the brilliant noonday sunshine; even the slate-grays and browns and yellows of sand and stone force eyes to squint against reflected glare. The wind ruffles hair and clothes. The Jordan waters chatter behind the voices of the small band of men making their way up toward Hermon.

Jesus, in the lead as usual, flings an apparently innocent question over his shoulder, as he sometimes does about local gossip: "Who do *you* say I am?"

The impetuous Simon blurts out the first sentiment he feels: "You are Christ, the Son of the living God."

Jesus stops abruptly. One imagines his eyes riveting Simon's gaze. "You are blessed, Simon! No mere human told you that. It is my father in Heaven who revealed it to you. Now I tell you solemnly, *atta kefa:* You are rock! Upon you, as on a rock, I will so build my Church that all Satan's force will not destroy it. I will give you the Keys to the Kingdom of Heaven. Whatever you

3

forbid on earth will be what Heaven forbids. Whatever you allow on earth will be what Heaven allows."

These are the words that reveal the endless course of God's power among human beings, and the endless struggle joined against it by "all Satan's force." Jesus reassures Peter and all that belong to him that they will finally enjoy a special Triumph and Blessing. The Triumph will be Jesus' triumph and that of his Church over Satan. The Blessing will be the universality: All men and women will accept Jesus' salvation and believe in him. But neither the Triumph nor the Blessing will be won by Jesus alone. He binds himself to Peter, to his Church, to all Peter's successors, and to all men and women.

John and James and Judas and the others respond to Jesus' symbolism immediately, glancing up at the rock of Hermon, then back to Jesus' face. They know him well enough! He is saying and doing something significant. But they do not understand. "It was hidden from us," Mark would write years after the event, "and we were afraid to ask him about it all."

Of all the choices Jesus might have made for the first leader of his Church, Simon had to be the least likely. In his betrayal of Jesus by public perjury, Simon would be second only to Judas Iscariot who would actually sell Jesus to his enemies for money. At the first onrush of difficulty, this "rock" would run for cover like a scared rabbit. Yet, years later, he would be martyred and would not flinch in his love or devotion.

Even on that day near Hermon, Jesus knows of what Simon is capable, as clearly as he knows the sneering contempt of the Prince for this "rock" of a man. For it is within his unique *memory* that Jesus speaks to Simon as head of the Church, about the Church, about Satan's endless, tireless threat. And it is within that all-encompassing *memory* of Jesus that what he says to Simon, he says as well to Pope Paul 6 as to every Pope who will come after.

The very key to understanding here is Jesus' *memory*. For this is not memory in the puny way we understand it:

"... The Board of Ed. has abolished memory lessons as a waste of the pupils' potential. ..."

"Scratch your memory, dear: Where did you put my cufflinks? ..."

"Forget I ever gave you this money, pal. ..."

"For a simple fee of $500, we guarantee you a photographic memory at the end of our five-week course. ..."

"The IBM 3033 carries eight megabytes in its capacious memory. ..."

In the reduced state of our twentieth-century thinking, we see memory merely as a miniaturized electronic computer, singsonging facts and figures along nerves and synaptic joints. Yet, in some way, most of us still realize that when we give rein to our hates, our fears, our loyalties, our hopes—feeling areas where our total selves are involved—we exercise *memory* in some greater sense. Facts and figures perhaps. The past as well. Also, the future. All made present within our conscious selves. Only sleep, weariness, the close presence of evil, or our own choice, seem to make that full *memory* opaque, dormant.

In Jesus, that *memory* is an ever-awake consciousness of spirit that never sleeps because never tired, because never only mortal. Nothing past. Nothing simply in the future. All present.

So, at this moment, near Hermon, the ordinary dimensions of existence are transcended. Time past is as if it never expired. Time to come is already accomplished. All for this instant. Simon, now *kefa, Petros,* Peter, the rock, is the current head of the Church—in every age. The 11 others are multiplied into the millions and billions of all other men and women and children. And the narrow piece of desert scrubland where these 13 men stand is a kaleidoscope not only of the earth, but of the universe—the planet Earth as well as the stars and endless galaxies. And Judas is there. And the Prince.

Everything about this occasion is symbol as well as reality. The mountain called Hermon. The Jordan. Rock. Water. Permanence and life. The rock on which the Prince dared to tempt Jesus, Jesus has taken as the symbol of his own power and of his own constancy in the world forever. Above all, the choice of Simon: always, victory over Satan through the weakest elements. "God has chosen the weak and the foolish to confuse the wise of this world," Paul would write some 40 years later. And so Simon with his dull mind and weak determination is God's answer to the Prince whose brilliance of intelligence and unbreakable will is thus diametrically opposed. Humanly, we can almost hear God answering Satan's defiance:

"You say that your wisdom and strength entitle you to pride of place? Very well, then. Your humiliation will be complete. I will beat you down and destroy you ultimately and forever precisely through what is weakest, what is almost stupid, what is despicable in your eyes."

As if the rabbit killed the snake. As if the starving prisoners of Gulag overthrew the Red Army. As if a trainload of whipped Jews on the way to Auschwitz brought Hitler and all this power to nothing.

But there is more. The affront to the Prince at Hermon is magnified. In the face of this Enemy, Jesus is relentless. Puny Simon is not only the rock for Jesus' Church. Puny Simon will personally have the power to represent Jesus. Personally! This pygmy will have greater power than the fallen Archangel ever had. Concrete power. The Keys to the Kingdom. The secret of eternal bliss. Whatever this Simon allows is what Jesus allows. Whatever this Simon forbids, Jesus forbids. Jesus can and will make sure that in all matters concerning entry into Heaven Simon cannot err. Puny Simon. "I will be with you all days, right up to the end of the universe." Simon will be Jesus' personal representative and the source of guidance for all subsequent believers.

That day in Jesus' *memory* up on Mount Hermon all those believers hear his words, "You are Peter." And he hears those believers centuries later as they coin the responding phrase: "Where Peter is, there is the Church of Jesus."

That day, Simon does not understand. But even that will not destroy the course Jesus has set. Looking into Simon's eyes squinting back at him in the brilliance of the sunlight, Jesus sees it all. All the mistakes and the blundering adaptations Simon would try to fashion from Jesus' message of universal salvation. And as with Simon's gifts, so with his mistakes: They would be shared down the centuries.

First: the mistake of political domination. Simon would understand the peculiar power of Jesus in terms of conquest and empire. "Isn't it just now, Lord?" Simon will ask crassly, even after Jesus rises from death, "isn't it just now that you are going to restore the Kingdom of Israel?" Most of Simon's successors in Rome for nearly 2,000 years would make the same mistake. It is an idea whose attraction dies hard. The Triumph of Jesus translated into imperial triumph.

Then: ethnic domination. Simon would fail to understand the universal nature of Jesus' intention. Even shortly after he receives the Holy Spirit, Simon will insist that Christianity is an ethnic privilege. He will stubbornly refuse Baptism to non-Jews. When Jesus must send Simon a special message to make him bend on this point, even then Simon will tell the others—Paul and people like him—to baptize non-Jews. But he will not.

And a third: geographical domination. Toward the end of his life, as a prisoner in Rome, Simon would tie Jesus' salvation to one place. He would remain a Palestinian. In his own persistent hatred of Rome, his hard-headed idea would exclude the love and the reality of Jesus. Jesus would come back soon at Armageddon near the Plain of Sharon in Palestine, Peter believed and taught. He would take Jerusalem and destroy Rome and its empire.

In that destruction would lie the Triumph of Jesus and of all who believe in him. In the survival of the believers, according to this view, would be the Blessing of Jesus. But if that were so, that Blessing would be translated into a temporal blessing of an elitist people; and the Triumph would merely be the setting up of a special heartland. How many would seem to be excluded by these mistakes repeated down the centuries!

Still, Jesus will work even with these limitations of Simon's. As he will work with the limitations of each one of Simon's successors. As he will work through all the complaints and wars and strifes and schisms that will center upon the lack of understanding of and by these weak men through the painful centuries.

Peter did not understand things any better, perhaps, than the throngs who deserted Jesus in bitter disillusionment, when Jesus did not, as they expected, restore political power to Israel upon his triumphant entry into Jerusalem three days before his death. But in all his confusion, Simon would never finally desert Jesus, never forgo his love for Jesus. And, in the end, what matters to Jesus is that a man not renounce love. No Peter would. And Jesus would never desert Peter.

Late one night, a few months after that dazzling day on Mount Hermon, Jesus walks with a much smaller group in the darkness toward the Garden of Gethsemane. Again, Simon walks behind Jesus. Again, he hears Jesus speaking to him. "Simon, Satan has claimed power over you and intends to make you his plaything and instrument." So, Simon is warned again: He will be fair game for Satan.

But then, in that power-based assertiveness, that commanding supremacy that was unique to him, Jesus goes on: "But I have prayed for you so that your faith does not fail or falter. When, therefore, you fail ..." the insistent realism of those words must have cut at the heart of the emotional Simon, "... when, therefore, you fail, you will be able to repent your error. And you will be able to give all associated with you fresh grounds for continuing belief."

That is all Simon is told. Jesus maintains the mystery of his ultimate intentions and deep purposes. It is only his methods he reveals. For the rest, Simon must make do with the limitations of his own character. As must each of his successors. Until one last moment for each. ...

On another night some thirty years later in Rome, Simon Peter at last sees it all as Jesus saw it all from the beginning! Even then, Simon sees it from a topsy-turvy angle. He and some two-thousand other Christians have been tied to crosses stuck upside down on the grassy embankment around the Imperial Gardens on Vatican Hill. They have been daubed with pitch. Tonight, they are to be living, screaming, dying torches. Emperor Nero, his lovely concubine Poppaea, and their guests will have light to eat by and sights to joke about. Each Christian will die in the classical sign of Satan—the upside-down cross.

Down the Vatican Hill and across the River Tiber, a slave called Linus stands silent, watching. Simon Peter had once baptized him. And then, this morning when they came to take Simon Peter to die in the Gardens, he had called Linus and appointed him as his successor. "You are the rock now, Linus." Simon Peter told Linus this in the presence of all Christian leaders. "You are Peter. . . . Lead them, as I have led them. In the name of Jesus. My death doesn't matter. The Lord is coming soon." From where he stands now, Linus can see slaves running among the crosses setting the bodies on fire with quick jabs of blazing torches to each head.

Out of Linus's hearing, Simon Peter keeps mumbling the last words he had said to Jesus: "Lord, I love you. You know I love you. I love you." Through the smell and the smoke and the Roman laughter. "You know I love you, Lord." Simon Peter awaits his turn.

Then, through the haze, Simon Peter can make out the bulky figure of a centurion standing in front of him, legs wide apart, red cloak hanging down the left side. In the light of the flames, Simon Peter catches the flash of the short sword held in the right hand, motionless, but at the ready for thrusting.

"By the grace of Afranus Burrus, Jew," the centurion mutters quietly and dutifully, as he tenses for the strike. Simon Peter is not for burning. Burrus, a Christian convert with influence in high places, has obtained as last favor for Simon Peter that he die by the sword.

Amid all the horror, the fire and smoke, the screams of the dying, the music, the laughter of the guests, there is an instant of light for Simon. All is clear. The cold smile of that blade. The tightening of the centurion's fingers around the haft. The muscles stiffening in the wrist and arm. The bracing of those two legs. The right side of the body drawing back measuredly. Simon Peter's consciousness is flooded with memories. *Forgive them. . . . Bless them. . . . Pray for them. . . . Love them. . . . Do good to them. . . . Whatever you allow on this earth will be what Heaven allows. . . . Whatever you forbid on earth will be what Heaven forbids. . . . You are Peter. . . .* He sees the face of his beloved Jesus once again, as every Pope does at death's hour, and now for the first time he enters Jesus' *memory* where all is achieved—the full Triumph of Jesus, the full Blessing of Jesus—all in a flash as the blade bites between his ribs and goes through lung and heart. *All men and women. No Jews. No Gentiles. All one. Not Palestine alone. Not Rome merely. But all lands. The earth. The skies. The beginning. The end. The sin. The Prince of the world sneering. Jesus on Calvary. Jesus in glory. . . .*

As the sword comes out, it draws blood after it like a waving crimson ribbon. A clean cut done by an expert. The centurion sees a wasting mask of agony and terror fall momentarily like a pinching claw over Simon Peter's face, drawing every feature together in a knot of suffering. A moment when the body grows rigid, stiff, straight, as taut as the pole holding it, vibrating within itself from the toes down to the head in a last inner effort. Then it collapses, twitching, eyes rolling, the face relaxing in that expressionless resignation and helplessness only death confers, blood and phlegm pouring out from the mouth in the low groan of one last breath, urine and excrement dropping to the ground.

In the following week, the body of Simon Peter is recovered by Linus and the other Christians. In the darkness of night, they hurriedly dig his grave in a spot toward the north end of Vatican Hill. Among Christians the spot over Simon Peter's grave will be known as the "memory" of Peter.

The word goes out via the Christian grapevine to the small Christian communities in Milan, in Marseilles, in the Greek cities, in Syria and Palestine and Africa: "Peter is dead. Linus is his choice."

Today, on that same north side of Vatican Hill, the "memory" of Peter is now in the central crypt of a huge Basilica, Saint Peters's, built around the spot where Peter died during Nero's banquet. Beside the Basilica, there is an elaborate 1,000-room building, the Apostolic Palace.

On the fourth floor of one wing of that Palace, about 400 yards from Peter's "memory," the death of Pope Paul takes place. Paul's waning hours and days are assiduously watched by the powerful Vatican bureaucracy and followed over radio and television by hundreds of millions of people in every land on this earth.

Paul has some comfort. He, like all Popes, has made his adaptations of Jesus' message. And, now, with death closing in on him, the vision of Jesus is also his lot. Paul's entry into the *memory* of Jesus, his moment of utter, timeless clarity.

As far as the *memory* of Jesus goes, it is the same for Simon's death and Linus's appointment as it is for the death of Paul 6 and the appointment of Paul's successor. Only for us, as once for Simon Peter, the details are confusing.

About 600 yards from the "memory" of Simon Peter, the successor to the dying Paul 6 and to Simon Peter will be appointed by the votes cast in a special meeting called a Conclave. Up to 120 Cardinals of the Roman Catholic Church, each one over fifty and under eighty years of age, will meet on Vatican Hill in the Hall called "Nervi." Not in the Sistine, whose walls enclose centuries of Roman history, whose frescoes speak in silent tints of past genius and eternal faith. Not in the Sistine. In the Nervi, its cement poured into place not 15 years ago, its four walls bare, its undulating ceiling and sloping floor opening like a maw ready to receive thousands as though they were few. No frescoes. No oil canvasses speaking of God, Heaven, Christ, eternity. Only embedded in one wall the eyeless booths for TV and radio crews. The Nervi. Just outside the colonnade surrounding Saint Peter's Square. It flanks—but does not touch—the 1400-year old Leonine wall surrounding Vatican City. It does not touch Saint Peter's. Or the Apostolic Palace.

The Nervi. So Paul 6 decreed before his death. This sudden break with the tradition of the Sistine is no quirk of chance, no trick of time out of kilter. The entrance of these Cardinal Electors into this hall, with no roots and no parallel in time past, makes visible the break with history that these Cardinals, and all the people on earth, are living and cannot escape.

○

When some historian comes later to write an account of this Conclave, it will surely be called the Book of the Bet. But, unless he is Christian, he may not understand that what these men did, they did in spite of their worldly power and personal ambitions, and because of their trust in the promise of Jesus that "all Satan's force will not destroy my Church," and because they heard Jesus saying "You are Peter." In terms of worldly wisdom and practical politics, they bet on the impossible. In terms of their faith, they could do nothing else.

When the next Pope is elected here in the Nervi, he will know that he will rule over a Church, once unified and monolithic, but now split from top to bottom and sideways in a zigzag fashion on issues of fundamental beliefs, religious practice, and personal morals. The Church he will head finds itself already in a world totally changed from the world his predecessors knew.

When the next Pope is elected here, he must know by then that he can no longer expect to live permanently in Rome. He and each of his successors will always claim to be the Bishop of Rome, the successor to Peter, and the personal Vicar of Jesus among humans. But his role will take on the aspect of a journey, a pilgrimage; in part freely chosen, in part forced upon him.

The break with the long past is already complete. And he will know it.

He will dwell in places no Pope ever saw. He will take steps no predecessor ever contemplated. He will decide on issues and acute problems no Pope before him even dreamed of ever. For in no other way will he be able to be Pope. And he will end up understanding his Papal role in a manner so different from past Popes, and so disconcerting to believers, that many will cease to believe. On his pilgrimage, the weakest will never start with him. The weaker will never make it. Only the strong will go along with him to the end.

Put in simple terms, it is now recognized that the Roman Church, its Vatican and its hierarchy throughout the world, has accumulated a political, diplomatic, and financial baggage that must be discarded: its financial investments, which amount to some billions of dollars; its wealth in real estate and concrete valuables, which provide collateral that rises well into the hundreds of billions; its tenacious and effective stance in the world of diplomacy, establishment politics, and corporate power; and finally—most poignantly, indeed—its working concept of "Church," Church government and authority and power over the salvation of all human beings.

Only a few times in the history of 263 Popes has such a moment arisen; perhaps never has so bold a choice been imminent. Those few Roman Popes who might have taken such a leap refused this choice as blindly as Simon Peter refused to baptize non-Jews. Each clung to the idea of temporal power as stubbornly as Simon Peter expected Jesus to establish a political kingdom in Palestine. But, unlike Peter who received a special message from Jesus to admit non-Jews to Baptism and to salvation, there was no special message for those Popes.

Only today has there been another kind of message from Jesus to his Church: It has come in the irresistible force of a revolution now unmistakably visible to Vatican realists. On the basis of that revolution they are making new plans.

This revolution they see already well on its way is not political in nature, but it will affect the politics of all nations. It has nothing directly to do with Marxism or Western democracy, except that it appears to spell the end of both as we have known them. The revolution, in Vatican thinking, has its origins on that level of life and value where Jesus and Satan battle and have battled for all the ages of man and for the soul of humanity.

This sort of Conclave and this kind of thinking is the direct legacy of Paul 6. Despite his shortcomings and earlier failures, he finally understood the revolution; and, in his last days, he did his best to prepare his Church for it.

Not everyone will agree that he came down on the right side. Indeed, by the end of his life Paul 6 became unacceptable to all four factions among the Cardinal Electors of his Church, the 118 or so men who would set the policies and elect the Pope after Paul's death.

All the problems in the closing days of Paul 6 stemmed from these factions that make up a pretty spectacular array of thought and opinion from far Left to far Right. Neither of the two farthest extremes among these groups represents a majority in Church thinking. But even so, one extreme seriously threatens schism, while the other threatens revolution—even violent revolution. These factions that faced Paul will be the factions in Conclave.

The Progressivist faction is made up of three groups: Christian Marxists; the "new theologians"; and a goodly number of Charismatics.

The Christian Marxists advocate a close alliance, political and otherwise, between Christians and Communists. Between them and Pope Paul 6 there burned always an undying enmity.

The "new theologians" and intellectuals hold that practically everything in the Roman Church—from Papal authority, male priesthood, the ban on homosexuality and abortion, the idea of God, the belief in Jesus' resurrection and divinity, down to the idea of a parish church and infant Baptism—all is out of date and must be revamped. These "new theologians" think that only with a fresh-minded, Progressivist Pope can the Church be saved from total disintegration.

The Charismatics, going on a fresh interpretation of the Bible, and relying on the exercise of new gifts—called the gifts of the Holy Spirit—insist that only by the exercise of those gifts can the faith be saved. They would therefore introduce Charismatic practice into every phase of church life. But this in itself would be a disruptive force. For a central persuasion of Charismatics is that the Holy Spirit communicates directly and personally with each one. The overall authority and teaching power of Bishop and Pope is bypassed. Charismatics, of course, claim that they represent the spirit of the primitive and early Christian Church.

The Traditionalist faction is at the opposite extreme from the Progressivists. Traditionalists protest that the Roman Church has been corrupted in the last twelve years, mainly by the Christian Marxists and the "new theologians." They denounce Paul 6 as a heretic. They insist on reversing all the changes effected in the Church since the sixties under Paul's direction. They regard Paul, at his worst, as a traitor and, at his best, as misguided and deceived by the wiles of Satan. There are powerful men in this camp and it is from this quarter that the serious threat of schism has menaced Paul and the Church for over a decade.

The Conservative faction in Rome and throughout the Church decries the Progressivists—whether they are Christian Marxists or the "new theologians"—and they also decry the Traditionalists. The Conservatives wish to steer a steady course with some gradual adaptations, but with no profound change in the basic structure of Roman Catholic government and belief. The Conservatives do not think Paul erred in allowing change, but they think that Paul went too far and too fast.

Finally, the Radical faction believes that the Roman Church must take one step in one specific direction: to divest itself of all sociopolitical and financial interests, and actively to take up and use solely the weapons of spiritual power. The radicals blame Paul for not taking bold, imaginative steps to free the Church of all entanglements with political and financial interests whatever their color or stripe. Their being called "Radical" recalls the saying of a sixteenth-century Pope, Alexander 6, who should have known what he was talking about. "The root (radix) of all the troubles besetting the Throne of Peter today is our temporal power together with our wealth and our international prestige."

It is a considered judgment on the past 263 Popes to say that, although most of them filtered the power and the teaching of Jesus through the prevalent mentality of their times, none of them finally *identified* the salvation of Jesus with territorial sovereignty and political influence. Their fault has lain in *allying* the two. But even in the perfumed garden of worldly success, the tradition of Peter that is the legacy of every Pope has enabled them to hear the slightest click of barbarity sharpening its knives. And, when all around them has become a howling parliament of pain, men have usually found the chief citizen of Rome already standing at some as yet unopened door, his hand on the knob. "When, therefore, you fail," Jesus said to Peter, "you will be able to repent your error, and you will give all associated with you fresh ground for continuing belief."

So it has been with Paul 6. And he communicated his judgment and feeling for the future to the principal Cardinal Electors who gather behind the locked doors of Conclave 82—a Conclave that would be like none before it.

For the Electors themselves, as for us who picture them in Conclave, there is required a special effort. To understand in belief. To believe with understanding. Jesus will not reveal his ultimate purposes, not even the details of our near-future history to these Electors. He did not reveal the near-future to Simon Peter and his companions near Hermon. Yet we, as children of a much later generation than Peter, know something more than he did at Hermon. We know, for instance, that Jesus saw far beyond Palestine, beyond Judaism, beyond Imperial Rome, and beyond what we see even now, when he said: "You are Peter."

We realize that now. Even so, today it takes humility and faith for Electors and for the rest of us to see, as Jesus does, far beyond even the extremes of the vast *mixtum-gatherum* of Catholicism and Christianity: beyond Greek monks on Mount Athos; Benedictine monks in England; Mexicans on their knees before our Lady of Guadaloupe; Polish Blessed Bread; Australian aborigines singing Mass; Irish shamrocks; Arab golden domes; beyond Eskimos scratching the Ave Maria on whalebones and Chinese gongs sounding the Angelus; beyond German Advent wreaths; African tomtoms tolling a Requiem; Russian ikons in Mrs. Gromyko's luggage; Scandinavian girls wearing Saint Lucy's crown; Japanese Zen-like Catholic chapels; Maltese Crusader Crosses; Dutch Girl Guides catechizing Amsterdam prostitutes; California nuns cleaning lepers in Seoul; Cardinals signing checks in Rome for the gnomes in Zurich; nuns dying as guerrillas in Guatemala; and, beyond, Lutherans, Presbyterians, Baptists, Adventists, Methodists, and the thousand and one other Christian sects. It takes humility and faith to see beyond all this delirium and chaos—and to move beyond all this, even as Jesus contains it all in his *memory* and transcends it all.

For these Electors, it is the evening of the Conclave, as indeed it is a certain evening for the institutional Church of Conclave, for Rome and its Vatican. The sunlight of human glory and power that lit its former days has ceased. Great frescoes do not look down on this Conclave from Sistine walls and ceiling. Many of the ancient songs are, like the Latin it once imposed on all, muted and no longer heard. In our modern world, there is a feeling of disquiet, of life narrowing down, of grace being eroded from every day's hours, of charm disappearing, of sensations being bleached in the glare of modernity with modernity's shamelessness. All Christians experience this today. But throughout the Church of Jesus there is audible the voice of Jesus' salvation speaking of his love for all human things and his irrevocable decision and promise that nothing would undo that salvation or quench that love.

With the authority of Jesus, these Cardinals will choose one of their own number as the 264th successor of Simon Peter. And, as at Simon Peter's appointment near Hermon, the same principals will be present: Jesus repeating: "You are Peter"; the Prince, watchful always, bent on making the Cardinals and their particular choice of Pope "a mere plaything and an instrument."

The battle goes on.

THE FIRST
OF THE
PILGRIM POPES

The men and women of the twenty-first century will be fascinated by the figure of Giovanni Battista Montini who became Pope Paul 6 in June of 1963. Our faces are flattened against the glass and we see but darkly. They will be at a sufficient distance to judge what he has done.

They will look back to see what sort of men were his intimates, his trusted helpers; what his driving motives were; whether his theology was as wise as his piety was genuine; whether he played secular power-politics using the authority of Jesus; whether he compromised fatally with those he considered lesser enemies of his faith in order to outwit those he thought greater ones; whether he allowed personal friendship for a few to interfere with his judgment on life-and-death issues that involved believing millions.

They will see, as we cannot, whether Pope Paul's vision of the twenty-first century was correct—so brilliantly correct that they, our descendants, will marvel at his foresight—or so dismally incorrect that his name and his Pontificate and his ideas will be hated and cast in infamy. It will be either one or the other. Because it was Montini, with two or three other individual men of our age, whose stubborn will swung his 715-million member Roman Church around officially to face in a direction the vast majority did not want and did not understand.

For our descendants he may well be seen as an innovator as gigantic as Peter the Great of Russia or Mao Tse-tung of China. They may say of him: He saw over everybody's head, he saw beyond their limited horizons, and he was a great among the pygmies. And he may be the fourth Pope in history to be dubbed "great." Paul the Great, like Leo the Great, Gregory the Great, and Nicholas the Great.

Those twenty-first-century people, not we, will understand the double role we have seen Pope Paul playing. They will see him as the last of the old-time Popes firmly rooted in the 1800-year-old Papal tradition, as querulously imperative and as insistently monarchic as any Pope who came before him. And they will see him as the first of the Pilgrim Popes, men who acted as if their Church had been exiled from human society and they wished to do the ancient penance of pilgrimage—in the name of all Christians—in order that

17

once more Jesus, his Vicar and his salvation, be accepted within the human regime.

Paul was never really welcomed by the Romans, by that Vatican bureaucracy that an irritated Pope Pius 12 once described as "like the Bourbons who learned little and forgot nothing." Paul was a northern Italian who had made his name as a churchman in Milan for nine years. As far as the Romans were concerned, the man born and baptized in northern Concessio as Giovanni Battista Enrico Antonio Maria Montini could just as well have remained up north with the other barbarians where Pope Pius 12 had exiled him from the Vatican.

But Montini returned as Pope Paul 6 on June 21, 1963, and he brought with him a whole train of northerners; architects, financiers, clerics of various callings, publishers, designers, art people, and the hangers-on whom every successful Cardinal acquires. The "Milan Mafia" according to Roman clerics, adulterated the exclusively Roman character of the Vatican which Pacelli (Pius 12) fomented during the almost 20 years of his reign.

During the Milan years and then in Rome, outsiders remarked on the reverence, almost awe, in which members of the "Milan Mafia" held Montini. There had always been a special camaraderie among them and the hostility they met in Rome only united them more.

A notable fact about Paul's Papal court and the Vatican administration in his time is that it shared the "horizontal" character of most modern governments. The personnel was mediocre. No giants jutted up above the level of the general mass.

Yet Montini had around him men as colorful and as clever as any Pope in history. Secretary Don Pasquale Macchi, not always wise in his choice of friends, but loyal to Paul throughout; the Stakhanovite Benelli, brusque in his faith, avid in his zeal for supernatural immaterialism; the hard-smoking Cardinal Villot who had developed a bureaucratic competence through a lifetime of petty bargaining; the stolid, retiring Willebrands, man of peace, perpetually surprised by his own success, afraid to move in any direction, and who, as the Romans joked, got anxious only about German Lutheran reaction to anything Roman—even a breakdown in Vatican plumbing; the quick-witted, sure-footed Cardinal Vagnozzi whom Paul always felt had "said 'Good Morning!' to the Devil and got away with it"; veteran Cardinal Ottaviani, gnomic as though conserving evergy, hoarding old truths, always warning Paul of dangers; Cardinal Wright, of torrential egocentrism, ubiquitous, gourmand, eloquent, who in the hope of inheriting the earth had declared himself meek, but who eventually rose to heights of faith his contemporaries never thought possible in him; Archbishop Casaroli, Paul's traveling salesman of Vatican Ostpolitik, the man of the future who knew everyone's secrets.

The key to the character of the Papacy of Paul 6 lies in Paul's reaction to, and his decision about, the vision Pope John 23 had of the Church. In the minds and according to the policy of the Cardinal Electors who made Giovanni Battista Montini Pope in Conclave 81 in June 1963, Montini was supposed to implement that vision.

The newness and peculiarity of John's vision lay in its superiority to anything we find before him in the Popes. In fact, in one sense, no Pope ever had John's vision.

John's immediate predecessor, Pius 12, came nearest to it. After his earlier mistakes and fantasies about *Romanità*—the power of Rome as the center of the Church—and about the continuing power of the ancient Roman Catholic "heartland" in southern Europe, Pius 12 did come to a vision of the chessboard of history. He finally transcended petty details of geography and local histories, so that his gaze locked into the basic struggle between Jesus and Satan. But he too readily identified the enemy as Marxism. Thus far, Pius's vision. And at that point, he died.

Angelo Roncalli, as John 23, did not suffer from that narrow focus. Opposed as fiercely as Pius 12 ever had been to Marxism, Roncalli's focus was wider. Although he did believe in the Satanic origin of Marxism, John did not accept Pius's view that implied that an outside and opposing force—Marxism—was trying to change society, and Jesus' Church. John's main contribution was his simple intuition that a change had taken place *already*, and that only the surface of previous things remained, like shells of buildings ready to collapse. John saw that the world of Pius 12, of Pius 9, of Clement 7, of all past Popes was dead and gone. The struggle against Marxism John classified as one minor skirmish, soon to be over, in a much more profound and cosmic struggle.

The essence of the change John saw was this: All the social, political, ideological, ethnic, and intellectual boundaries that had divided human beings for centuries had lost their validity. No one could explain it, but it was certain that gone from the human scene was some root persuasion, some deep conviction. Because of that conviction, men had preserved those boundaries up to John 23's very moment in history. But now a new unheard-of and frightening human unity was emerging. And all the old boundaries, all the things men and women had understood and lived by, were disappearing.

For John, as for Pius 12 and Paul 6, the essence of the cosmic struggle lay in the plans and counterplans of two personages: Jesus and Satan. It was a deadly game played on the chessboard of the human universe. The chessboard was cosmic. The issues were cosmic. The players were cosmic.

The intuition of John told him that in the wake of the vast change that had taken place, religion in general and Christianity in particular were in danger of being bypassed; that Satan had made his move to nullify all that God had accomplished. And, in fact, it was plain to see that Christianity *was* being bypassed, that it was increasingly isolated and cut off from the political, civil, intellectual, and cultural life of men and women.

As his intuition was simple, so was John's practical solution: open windows and doors; knock down barriers; let the spirit, already here, fly out across the face of humanity. Hence, his Council—Vatican Council II. Hence his paternal and loving attitude. And hence the spontaneous and universal feeling that this 77-year-old Roman Pope, John, created within a span of only three years and six months: a feeling that no good was impossible any more, and that no evil could not be overcome; a feeling that, somehow and unexpectedly, grace had been poured out, that all hate could be melted by that grace, and that the best of things could be hoped for. "All has been changed," John told his generation. "Come to our Council and celebrate and make plans together with us." And then John died.

When Paul 6 stepped into the Pope's sandals, he translated John's cosmic vision of change, and developed his own new policies, according to his own abilities and his own vision.

As far back as the 1930s Giovanni Montini as a young ecclesiastic had been profoundly influenced by a single attitude that would, thirty years later, go a long way toward making him a Pope unlike any Pope before him. It was an attitude first made popular and then repudiated by a French philosopher of great popular appeal, Jacques Maritain. Montini, in fact, willingly wrote an introduction for the Italian edition of Maritain's *Integral Humanism.*

"Be a witness by service," runs the idea, "but do not think that any other initiative is possible, practical or called for." In practical terms, what integral humanism has to say is that all men and women are naturally good; they will respond to the good and reject the evil *if* they are shown the difference. The function of Jesus' Church at this stage in human history is merely to bear witness to that difference, not to make superhuman efforts at Catholicising politics, economics, literature, science, education, social life, or any of the other aspects of human society. Only to witness by service to men and women—without any distinction of creed or race—this is the task of the Church in today's world where a new unity among human beings has emerged; a world which of itself excludes Christianity and the central authority of the Pope as the Vicar of Jesus and the center of world unity.

So, in Paul's view, the Papacy and the Church had to set out once more to attract men and women to the faith, but in a different way. They had to break out of their isolation; an isolation that was, in large part, owing to their own deficiencies. There must be a new effort to find men and women again, to be with them and become acceptable to them.

When Paul spoke of himself as a pilgrim and of his Papal reign as a pilgrimage, he was referring to this effort. He saw it as part penance for the failures of past Churchmen, and part search for those human beings who did not yet know Jesus, Jesus' Church, and Jesus' salvation.

This integral humanism of Paul 6 permeated the entire policy of his Pontificate. How far Paul has been able to direct his Church on to that pilgrim path remains for a subsequent generation to judge. In the meanwhile, we can take our own measure of his success by examining how Paul acted on three occasions of capital importance that intimately concerned Church diplomacy, Church finance, and Church belief.

October 4, 1965.

Paul's Alitalia Flight #2800 touched down at Kennedy International Airport carrying Pope Paul 6, seven Cardinals, ten Vatican aides, sixty newsmen, commentators, light and sound technicians, and 200,000 covers bearing new Vatican commemorative stamps.

Paul motorcaded at about 12 m.p.h. in a black, bubble-topped, flag-flying, fluorescent-lighted, leather-upholstered, seven-passenger, 1964 Lincoln convertible. He was watched by a hundred TV cameras and more than two million New Yorkers who lined the 24-mile-route to Saint Patrick's Cathedral in Manhattan.

The way was guarded, prepared, and facilitated by 15,000 New York City policemen, the Fire Department, the Pickpocket and Confidence Squad, plain clothes detectives, 5,000 barricades, 40 bullhorns, 27 tow-trucks, 13 ambulances, 1 bomb truck, 2 motor-launches on the East River and 2 helicopters overhead.

He spoke to 11 Cardinals, to Archbishops and Bishops, and 4,000 people in the Cathedral. He met and talked with President Johnson and, at the Waldorf Astoria Hotel, had Mrs. Johnson and teen-age daughter Luci presented to him, lunched with Cardinal Spellman and his associates, and conferred with a score of visitors, officials, and well-wishers.

Finally, Pope Paul proceeded to the United Nations. That was the reason for his pilgrimage. "It offers the occasion to further the cause of peace, so close to Our heart, and at the same time to promote a greater understanding among the nations of the world," Paul had written to U Thant on March 1, 1965. "It would," U Thant replied to Paul on April 16, 1965, "give a new and vigorous impetus to endeavors of men of good will everywhere to safeguard and strengthen world peace ... bringing humanity closer to the fulfillment of its legitimate aspirations."

U Thant greeted Paul at 3:13 in the afternoon that day in October 1965. He led Paul first to the Meditation Room: a windowless, unfurnished, trapezoidal chamber, 30 by 18 feet, its symmetrical walls blank but for a fresco by Swedish artist Bo Beskow, depicting geometric patterns in blue, yellow, gray, brown, white. In the center of the room, a waist-high solid block of stone and iron ore. The only illumination, a shaft of dim, yellow light striking the shimmering surface of rock.

Then U Thant led Paul to the General Assembly for its 1,374th meeting.

A color photograph of the General Assembly was taken during Paul's address at 3:45 P.M.: The Assembly Hall is a sloping whirlpool of 11 ordered eddies arrested for one still photographic instant in inevitable movement downward to the place where Paul, white-clad Priest, stands. The weight of the Hall bears down on his diminutive figure as on a fulcrum. Three thousand listeners, necks craned, are watching him. There is no apparent movement except Paul's head and shoulders. It is a moment of electric attention, a vigil of nations.

"We have a message to deliver to each one of you."

Paul has the ears of the world. His message has willing translators into over 35 languages, is heard—even seen—literally all over our planet. One almost expected to hear Paul address the human race: "Children of men! Nations of the Earth! Peoples of every land! This is now the way of *your* salvation. ..."
In this almost universal attention Paul could have stated blandly without unduly surprising anyone: "On the 29th of June, Feast of the Apostles Peter and Paul, the Lord Jesus Christ told Us personally that this is what men must do to solve their problems ..."; or, "We propose to solve the continuing deadlock of East and West, of haves and have-nots, of black and white, in the following manner ..."; or, "We men can now arrest the lethal arms race, reconcile Arabs and Jews, bring China to reason with the family of nations, dispel the clouds of nuclear holocaust, feed, educate, and console the world's billions by ..."

But there was none of all this. Paul as Pope, as Apostle, had no alternatives to offer. He did not preach or announce the Gospel message as Peter and Paul had done 1900 years before to Roman, Greek, and Semite. Christ either crucified or resurrected was not the burden of his words.

Paul said, "We wish Our message to be a moral and solemn ratification of this high institution ... as an expert in humanity We bring to this organization the voices of Our late predecessors, those of the whole Catholic episcopate, and Our Own, convinced as We are that this Organization represents the obligatory road of modern civilization and of world peace."

The motionless silence of a few seconds ago is ended. The magic moment is over. Now, the rest of Paul's words will be, all feel, a benign testimony endorsing their existence, acknowledging their difficulties.

All the principal participants and protagonists of mutual hate and predictable wars are sitting in semicircular rows before Paul. Webs of intrigue and opposition and self-interest clothe them as surely as do their dark suits and national costumes.

To them Paul says, *"You give sanction to the great principle that relations between the peoples should be regulated by reason, by justice, by negotiation; not by force, fear, or fraud."*

In the coming year of 1966 alone, for causes foreseen and excluded by the United Nations Charter, there will be suppression of human liberties in Haiti (2nd row) and South Africa (6th row); civil and guerrilla warfare and strife in both Congos (10th row), India (2nd row), the Dominican Republic (11th row,) Guatemala (1st row), and Indonesia (2nd row). Blacks will riot in 43 American cities protesting discrimination. Refugees from war and oppression will be many: 12,000 Cubans in Spain and 200,000 in the United States, 15,000 refugees from Portuguese Guinea in Senegal; 700,000 in Western Europe from the Iron Curtain countries; 50,000 Tibetans in Nepal and India; 1,100,000 Chinese from the Communist Mainland in Hong Kong and 80,000 in Macao; 800,000 Arab refugees in Lebanon, Syria, Iraq, and Jordan; 12,000 South Vietnamese in Cambodia; 575,000 Africans displaced by civil wars and rebellions. By September 1966, 300,000 will have been killed in the Indonesian civil war. By December, 6,644 Americans alone will have died in the Vietnam War.

Yet Paul says, *"there is no need of long speeches to proclaim the finality of this institution."*

Before Paul sit the representatives of nations that will bring the accumulation of armaments, with a view to future violence and death, to new levels. In fiscal 1966, the United Kingdom (7th row) will have a defense budget of $6.081 billion; France (1st row) $4.465 billion; Japan (3rd row) $946 million; U.S.S.R. (7th row) $14.208 billion; U.S.A. (8th row) $57.718 billion. Both the latter will supply Arab nations and Israel with the material that would make possible the War of June 1967. Pakistan (5th row) will accept arms from Communist China to fight India.

Paul continues, *"Suffice it to recall that the blood of millions of men, that countless and unheard-of sufferings, that useless massacres and fearful ruins have sealed the pact uniting you, with a vow which must change the future history of the world: Never again War! War, never again!"*

After his address, Paul stood at the head of a 300-man receiving line in the north end of the delegates' lounge facing a huge chocolate-colored map of the world. All walked up to him willingly, greeted him pleasantly, some reverently: the Great Powers; Nationalist China; Soviet allies and satellites; the uncommitted Third World. For all of them, Paul had a word. Observers noted the extra moment he spent with Gromyko; the reverence of Mrs. Gromyko; Paul's affectionate, two-handed clasp for Arthur Goldberg; the Africans and Asians who kissed Paul's ring; his gentleness with Jacqueline Kennedy.

Finally, Paul gave a last glance at the assembled guests. More non-Europeans than Europeans. More non-Christians than Christians. That was the lesson in his memory.

When the plane carrying Paul with his entourage and his gifts and 52 reporters arched through the sky over Manhattan and the United Nations, Paul was barely over two years into his reign. Yet at the heart of the lesson he had learned was the eerie intuition of the finality of the new condition of his Church that Popes had resisted for a thousand years. Paul would speak about the intuition to many in the years to come.

A new mentality of humankind was in the making, as yet barely appearing in the motley United Nations crowd. And the sooner the Church prepared to divest itself of all it had acquired by way of regionalism, nationalism, and culture, the more ready and adapted it would be to survive, to flourish, and finally to prevail among humans as the unique portal of divine revelation.

But to the casual observer the fundamental message of Paul's visit was not very grand: "We the Church, are on the sidelines," his visit seemed to say. "As an organization we know we have no say in your business. We want to remind you, however, that we are here."

This was the first concrete and hard-headed expression of Paul's integral humanism.

Spring 1969

It is late at night in the Papal study on the third floor of the Apostolic Palace. No more secluded and secure and private time and place has been found by many previous Popes for ultra-secret meetings.

The meeting concerned Vatican finances. Such meetings have been part of Papal business for over a thousand years.

Pope Paul is alone with the financier, Michele Sindona. Popes, more often than not, have preferred to conduct such high-level affairs alone.

There is no official entry about the meeting in Paul's appointment book, and there never was. In each week of each year in the history of Popes, just as in the history of premiers, presidents, kings, and corporation heads, we know there have been such "nonmeetings."

Paul comes to an agreement, affixing his signature as Pope to a contractual, bilateral document. Vatican archives are full of such documents.

In virtue of that signature, Paul binds and obliges a goodly part of Vatican finance and Papal monies. Popes have always—and rightly—considered themselves the solely responsible stewards of what has always been called in Rome "the patrimony of Peter."

The scene is unique only in one respect. By his signature, Pope Paul authorized the financier to sell the Vatican's controlling interest ($350 million) in the huge conglomerate, *Societa Generale Immobiliare.* By that signature Paul also allowed Sindona access to other Vatican funds for further investment.

The money centers of Europe and the United States will be filled for years with half-finished stories, garbled accounts, wild reports, and incomplete versions of what turned out to be a financial loss of apparently huge proportions for the Vatican. *Il crack Sindona*—the Sindona catastrophe—is not a simple affair. That the signing took place in those circumstances between Pope Paul and Michele Sindona is now an admitted fact. Initially, the Vatican denied it, stating that the signing was between Sindona and Cardinal Guerri, a senior Vatican member.

Paul's memories of Sindona reached back well before the spring of 1969 to his own first few years as Archbishop of Milan. His preoccupation with Vatican financial administration and general policies went back even further.

As pro-Secretary of Vatican State for Pius 12, Montini had already agitated for reform in Vatican financial administration. He knew firsthand the abuses and the abusers. In 1954, he drew up a report citing the names and activities of Pius 12's own nephews (Carlo, Giulio, Marcantonio Pacelli) whom Pius had put at the head of Vatican finances. Pius's reaction to the report was violent and swift. Montini found himself on a train for Milan, for exile, and for disfavor. One of Paul's bitterest memories on that long, one-way train journey was of a day shortly after the end of World War II when he had listened to Pacelli speaking from the public balcony of Saint Peter's in Rome, denouncing a certain Dalmatian priest, Ernesto Cippico, as having "brought scandal in the Church." Cippico had embezzled some thousands of dollars from the funds of Eastern European refugee groups. Even as he listened to those words, Montini had known that over on the Quirinal, out in the magnificent country villas, and within the Vatican behind Pacelli's back, there were men and women who dealt every day in millions of Church dollars—the "patrimony of Peter"—buying war, selling peace down the river, cynically, scandalously. Cippico lacked only protectors in high places. Montini could almost see a Satanic rictus behind the whole affair.

Later, as Pope, one of Paul's first major pronouncements, in 1967, was

Populorum Progressio in which he attacked laissez-faire capitalism and castigated the "international imperialism of money" whereby in the end "the poor always remain poor and the rich become ever richer." The Vatican, as an international trading partner, was included in his attack. In his heart, Paul wished to take radical action, to give back to those poor what was theirs. When "we do help the poor," he stated (quoting St. Ambrose), "we never give to the poor what is ours; we merely return to them what belongs to them." Paul's Papacy lost many friends in high places in the Vatican, in Europe, and in the Americas, when *Populorum* was published.

By the time of that publication, nevertheless, Paul had decided on the broad lines of a reform in Vatican finances and on an ultimate goal: divesting the Church of its financial clout, thereby expelling that element of the "Prince of this world."

In the late sixties, according to the most reliable reports, the annual budget of the Vatican lay between $25 and 40 million. Its investments ran to more than $4.8 billion. Managing these huge investment sums were two main financial administration departments.

The first, the *Institute for Religious Works* (IRW), at that time under the direction of venerable Cardinal di Jorio, had been set up during World War I. It paid the salaries of the Vatican bureaucracy and held Vatican accounts and investments for other Catholic institutions, for about 1,000 Vatican citizens, and for "a few limited and chosen friends (Italian and non-Italian) of the Church," as one official states. Its assets were estimated conservatively to be upward of $3 billion. Paul found, however, that no balance sheet was ever produced. The IRW moved huge sums around the world money markets, operating freely of any national exchange control regulations. It had even transferred monies back and forth between the belligerents during World War II. Obviously the IRW had built up considerable foreign exchange dealings and confidence. Whenever Paul needed money to cover Vatican expenses, di Jorio simply drew it from Paul's account (#16/16).

The *Special Administration of Holy See Property* (SA) dated from 1929, the year Mussolini's government paid $2.4 million in reparation for the Italian Papal states seized by the Italian Republic in 1870. It was run by some competent lay bankers (with cleric assistants by their sides), and was advised by J.P. Morgan of New York, Hambros Bros. of London, and Rothschilds of Paris.

By the late sixties, monies from both IRW and SA were invested in every sector of Italian industry and commerce. On the boards of directors of companies in which the Vatican had an interest, there always sat a Vatican "family" man, somebody like Massimo Spada or Luigi Mennini.

One business venture in which the Vatican developed a controlling interest was the giant, multinational *Societa Generale Immobiliare* (SGI). Its president was Count Galleazzi, former governor of Vatican City and relative of Pacelli's personal doctor, and four of its key Board members were Vatican "family" men. SGI was highly diversified, holding property such as office buildings, construction companies, real estate, residential areas, etc., on both sides of the Atlantic—the Rome Hilton, the Pan Am building on the Champs Elysees in Paris, the Watergate complex in Washington, D.C., and the Stock Exchange in Montreal, Canada, figured among the real property.

Paul, persuaded that Europe was heading for a total eclipse of its autonomy, decided that it was time for a change. Apart from geopolitical considerations, there were other reasons: he was advised of a coming recession and inflation period; the running expenses of the Vatican had increased enormously since the Vatican council, mainly because of new Secretariats and Commissions with large expense accounts; some Vatican-controlled companies were losing heavily (the flour and pasta company, Pantanella, lost $2.5 million and required refinancing of $4.8 million); the Vatican work force had risen by one-third since 1963 and had tripled since 1948; Vatican pensioners ran to about 1,000. And to cap this picture, the Vatican was engaged in a losing battle with Italian fiscal authorities over the Vatican's claim to be tax exempt for its 1962 dividends by virtue of the 1929 Concordat with the government.

As in the situation when Paul visited the United Nations, the reasons for action were there.

Paul's first overt move in the major financial areas of the Vatican was to establish a new administrative arm in 1968. The *Prefecture of Economic Affairs,* PECA as it is known, was set up to coordinate investment policies, check on expenditures, and prepare the hitherto unheard-of Vatican balance sheet. And, sure enough, by the seventies, PECA produced budget estimates and a consolidated balance sheet.

For a short time PECA was governed by Cardinal Angelo Dell'Acqua. Then Paul confided PECA to the care of a career diplomat, the 62-year-old Cardinal Egidio Vagnozzi, back from nine years as Vatican representative in Washington. Vagnozzi was an arch-conservative and ally of such powerful old-time hands as Cardinals Ottaviani and Siri. Assisting Vagnozzi were Cardinals Cody of Chicago and Martin Höffner of Cologne, Germany.

Paul also installed a new head of the IRW, Father Paul Marčinkus, a priest of the Chicago archdiocese. A native of Cicero, Illinois, born of a second generation Lithuanian family, ordained in 1947, postgraduate student in Rome's North American College, subsequent member of the English language section of the Vatican's Secretariat of State, six-foot-three (the Italians nicknamed him *il gorilla),* and very personable, Marčinkus became a friend of Macchi, Paul's secretary. He accompanied Paul on his trips around the world. Marčinkus became a bishop with basic salary of $6,400 as head of IRW.

The first aim of Paul and his advisors was to extinguish the Vatican's system of controlling interests in Italian companies, to pull out of Italian money markets, and to go "foreign" into the promising world of Eurodollar blue chips and offshore profits.

Among all the men available to make such a vast shift of such vast sums, no one seemed so suitable and so adapted as a man already known to Paul: Michele Sindona.

Michele Sindona had, indeed, made himself adaptable for such a major job. Ever since he had bought a truck and with it had begun a lucrative trading business with the United States armed forces in wartime Sicily, he had spent a little over 20 years preparing for that triumphal, nocturnal signing. Born in 1917, in the town of Patti near Messina, Sicily, educated by the Jesuits, successful law student at Messina University, Sindona left Sicily in 1947 carrying with him glowing recommendations from the Bishop of Messina (who only knew Sindona's generous donations to the Church) for the archdiocesan authorities in Milan. There he opened an office specializing in tax consultancy in relation to the dollar market.

By 1959, Sindona was well on his way, with signal successes already behind him. To date he had acquired the *Banca Privata Finanziaria* (BPF) and a steel foundry (which he sold to the American Crucible Company); he had established a holding company, *Fasco AG*, in the tax-haven of Liechtenstein; through *Fasco* he had obtained controlling share in *Finabank Geneva;* he had founded a foreign exchange brokerage, *Moneyrex,* headed by Carlo Bordoni; had knit close relationships with Luigi Mennini, top official in the Vatican's IRW, with Massimo Spada, Vatican "family" man (who became a director of Sindona's BPF), and with Don Pasquale Macchi, Archibishop Montini's personal secretary and confidant.

By the time he came to Montini's close attention, Sindona was already legal counsellor to the textile group, SNIA-Viscoa (Spada was one of its directors), president of Keyes Italiana, Mediterranean Holidays, Philips Carbon Black Italiana, managing director of Cheseborough-Ponds, and board member of Remington Rand Italiana.

What cemented Montini's esteem of Sindona as early as 1959, was the $2.4 million Sindona raised for Montini from Milanese business circles in order to finance an Old People's Home (the Casa Madonnina).

In 1968, the Vatican lost its 6-year battle with the Italian fiscal authorities and it was penalized. The time had come to take the jump. And Sindona was ready to help the Vatican jump.

Within those seconds toward midnight in the spring of 1969, when

Sindona, and then Paul, bent over and signed their names to the agreement, Sindona was given control over vast foreign exchange resources. In all foreign money markets he now carried the Vatican imprimatur on all his dealings.

As Sindona bowed to kiss Paul's ring and depart into the dark Roman morning with as much financial power as many a nation on earth, for one moment Paul saw him, as it were, transfigured—his dark suit, black tie, white shirt, urbane manner, smiling deference, obvious satisfaction—all the details seemed to mirror another power alien to the power Paul wielded because of that Fisherman's Ring Sindona had just kissed with so much ease. It was not so much that Sindona reportedly belonged to the Freemasons. It was, rather, that Paul felt Sindona was an instrument in the hands of unknown powers. From then until 1977, the impression was to grow as news filtered back to Paul.

Sindona quickly moved on several fronts. He transferred $40 million to the Luxembourg Bank, Paribas Transcontinental (subsidiary of Banque de Paris et des Pays-Bas); $15 million of this was acquired by California-based Gulf and Western (Paul shuddered a little when he learned that Gulf and Western owned Paramount Pictures Corporation) whose 44-year old president, Charles Bludhorn joined the board of SGI. Under Marčinkus, the IRW took a large block of shares of Sindona's Finabank. The Vatican retained 5 percent control over SGI, but it proceeded to divest itself of Italian companies like the Condotte d'Acqua (in 1969), Pantanella (in 1970), and Serono (in 1970; a maker of contraceptive pills). It also diversified into foreign companies: General Motors, General Electric, Shell, Gulf, IBM, and some airlines.

Sindona became president of seven Italian companies, vice-president in three banks, and bought a controlling block of shares in the Vatican-linked Banca Union (BU), thereby at least tripling his Roman banking operation. He was later to fuse his old BFP and the BU into *Banca Privata Italiana* (BPI) Through Sindona's maneuvering of funds, the Vatican acquired a participation in BPI (20 percent), thus enabling Sindona to forge links with Hambros (25 percent) and the Continental Bank of Illinois (15 percent). Continental's chairman, David Kennedy, who was Secretary of the United States Treasury under President Nixon, later became a board member of Sindona's *Fasco AG.*

Everyone was surprised when, in 1972, Sindona suddenly transferred himself and his family to the United States where he had taken a cooperative apartment at the Pierre Hotel in New York in the name of his wife, Katerina. He bought controlling interests in the 20th largest United States bank, the Franklin National. He offered $1 million as an anonymous election contribution for the reelection of President Nixon, but Maurice Stans refused it.

Barely one year later, the first crack in Sindona's empire became apparent to all. The American Securities and Exchange Commission (SEC) halted all trading on Vetco Offshore Trading Industries when it found out that Irving

Eisenberger, a Los Angeles investment counsellor, had acquired 25 percent of outstanding shares in Vetco (in violation of Federal Security regulations). It also came to light that 20 percent of Vetco's shares and options were acquired by Eisenberger on behalf of the IRW through the Liechtenstein-based Fiduciary Investment Services (FIS) which had an office in Sindona's Roman office complex. The IRW had many shares and options in FIS. In mid-March 1973, IRW had acquired 454,000 Vetco shares which were part of 714,000 Vetco shares sold by FIS, the largest block ever traded on the American Stock Exchange.

The Vatican paid $320,000 in penalty compensation for that illegal transaction, and the Italian authorities started a long inquiry into Sindona's dealings. Another crack in Sindona's empire.

When Villot informed Paul of the enquiry, and he learned from Vagnozzi about the penalty, Paul's papal memory stirred with the age-old unease: Had he left the Church defenseless? Had he involved the Church more than ever with the power of this world?

In 1973, and for two agonizing years, Villot and other officials brought Paul news of disaster after disaster in the Sindona affair. Sindona's BPI sustained foreign exchange losses of $48 million in 1973, and another $150 million in 1974. Then it was discovered that the Franklin National Bank had a minimal $43 million in losses hidden as "phony profits" in foreign exchange dealings with Sindona-controlled Swiss banks.

Other Sindona-controlled or Sindona-linked banks started to collapse—Wolff, Herz, Herstatt, Aminot—with consequent Vatican losses. By October 1974, Italian authorities were ready to move against Sindona, Spada, Mennini, and other unnamed persons involved in the crack. The charge: falsification of BU accounts in 1960. The possible penalty: 15-year jail terms for each of them.

On January 9, 1975, Swiss authorities closed Sindona's Finabank. It had sustained foreign exchange losses of at least $82 million. Sindona made a last fruitless attempt to raise capital (about $300 million) by offering for sale new capital shares in a small holding company, Finambro. But Guido Carli, Governor of the Bank of Italy, scotched that idea.

Vatican losses were huge. In January 1975, Spada declared that the Vatican had by then lost 10 percent of its total worth. Swiss banking sources speak of something in the region of $240 million. Despite Vagnozzi's public statements in April 1975 that Vatican investments in the affair amounted to $500 million (he did confirm a heavy Vatican shift of investments from Italy to the United States), and that Vatican losses in il crack Sindona were minimal, reports persist that those losses may have gone well over the billion-dollar mark.

Paul's memory of the Sindona affair continued to be bittersweet all his remaining years. It showed him more clearly than ever the extent to which the institutional and hieratic Church was chained to an international monetary system that belonged in principle and in practice to the spirit of the "Prince of the world." But with all its disasters, the entire Sindona venture had not served to rend those chains.

Two things are certain about Paul's venture with Michele Sindona. He wished to align Vatican and Church finances with United States interests. He also wished to detach his Church in Europe from its involvement in the ancient heartland where it had occupied a predominant position and played the role of chief potentate ever since the Roman Emperor Constantine converted to Christianity in the 4th century and, by his enormous gifts and benefices to the then-Pope, Silvester 1, set the footsteps of all succeeding Popes on the path of political and economic power. Silvester had been the *"first* rich father" of Christianity. In Paul's mind, he himself would like to have become the first poor Pope in a long time.

But in Paul's lifetime this was not to be. "Perhaps," Paul remarked in February of 1977, "perhaps only the hand of an oppressor can free Us and the Church from it all. Satan may overleap himself. The dowry of Constantine is too much to carry in today's world." Paul, the well-read humanist, knew his Dante too well not to recollect the lines that end the *Inferno:*

"Ahi! Constantin, di quanto mal fu matre,
Non la tua conversion, ma quella dote
Che da te prese il primo ricco patre!"

"Alas! Constantine, how much misfortune you caused,
Not by becoming Christian, but by that dowry
which the first rich father accepted from you!"

December 8, 1965, was the closing day of the four-year Ecumenical Vatican Council. In a cafe near Saint Peter's a French Archbishop, Marcel Lefebvre, was seated with two of his own priests and some guests. Lefebvre was explaining to them the legal grounds on which he considered the decisions of the Council to be invalid and nonobligatory. Nowhere, Lefebvre observed, did any Council document state that to disobey the decisions would bring on *anathema* (the ecclesiastical condemnation par excellence for a breach of the true faith). Besides, Lefebvre argued, the council had erred ... it had embraced "neo-Modernism and neo-Protestanism."

Lefebvre was convinced that the Council had been hijacked by Bishops and theologians who were acting in a spirit of Protestantism and neo-

Modernism. At the turn of the century neo-Modernism had been a movement among theologians and intellectuals who declared that belief and dogma had to change with the changing nature of mankind. But the neo-Modernist Bishops and theologians at the Council in 1965 were out for something else: a new kind of Reformation. "We are not going to have another Reformation" was a frequent phrase on the lips of the Progressivist theologians of the Council. Paul and others had always understood this to be a repudiation of Luther's revolt in the sixteenth century. But Lefebvre insisted there was another interpretation. Luther, Lefebvre said, had decided to revolt, to leave the Church of Rome, to go out and found his own church. But the new theologians were really saying, according to Lefebvre, "We have no intention of doing the foolish thing Luther did—to try to found another church. We are going to stay and burrow deep within the Church and change it into the image we have of what it should be."

Son of a textile manufacturer from Tourcoing, France, a scholarly priest, member of the Holy Spirit Missionary Order, former Bishop of Dakar, Senegal, a former Superior General of the Holy Spirit Missionary Order, then Archbishop of Tulle, France, the 60-year-old Lefebvre had been one of the more powerful and active Conservatives during the Vatican Council. As the Conservatives lost ground, and the Progressivists gained victory after victory, a hardline resistant mood set in among the Conservatives. "We," said Cardinal Siri of Genoa to a friend, as they came out of one Session of the Council where Progressivist views had triumphed: "we are not going to be bound by all those decrees."

But Siri kept his revulsion under control. He did not act as he had threatened. It was Lefebvre who would translate Siri's defiance into a public campaign that would finally present Paul's Church with its first threat of real schism in over a century.

The first eruption of pro-Lefebvre sentiment occurred four years after the Council. It was 1969. Paul promulgated a new official text for celebrating Mass—the *Mass Ordinal*. Paul's Ordinal consisted of an *Introduction* followed by the new text of the Mass and ceremonial instructions to replace the ones that had been published and authorized by Pope Pius 5 in the year 1570 and had been used ever since.

Two Italian priests, both Lefebvre's followers, wrote a critique of Paul's new *Ordinal*, condemning its *Introduction* as opposed to traditional Catholic belief. The critique was leaked, of course, to the Italian and French press, so the fight became public. People began to range themselves on the two opposing sides: those for Paul's Mass and those for the old Mass of Pius 5. Pressured by the powerful Cardinal Ottaviani and others, Paul did the only thing he could: He asked his *Congregation for the Faith* (formerly the Holy Office) to examine the *Introduction*. The *Congregation's* answer: Everything is all right, except certain elements of Article 7 in the *Introduction*. Ottaviani, at least publicly, declared himself satisfied.

But Lefebvre was not satisfied. He obtained permission for his own Institute and Seminary at Ecône in Switzerland. It was from here that, from 1974 onward, he launched devastating attacks on the established Church in Europe and the United States. On November 21, 1974, came Lefebvre's first public manifesto declaring the Vatican Council false, the Pauline Mass illegal, and the teaching of the Bishops erroneous.

By Autumn 1976, still operating out of Ecône, Lefebvre had become an international figure not only in reputation, but in holdings. He had acquired five chateaux in France which he used as new Seminaries to train over 100 new recruits in what he characterized as the true Catholic doctrine. He published a biannual newsletter and his book, *J'Accuse Le Concile*. He founded more seminaries in other countries, including the United States. Everybody involved in the affair became progressively bloodied.

It was Villot, to his credit, who warned Paul early in 1975. Lefebvre must be suppressed, Villot insisted, and his movement discredited and liquidated. The Church had an extreme Right that had been successfully contained. There was an extreme Left—in all Latin American countries, in the United States, and in most European countries—that the Church authorities had hitherto contained successfully. It had been decided upon long ago as official policy that both extremes were necessary so that the Church might move the majority at the center in the direction judged best for the Church's future existence.

Paul's treatment of Lefebvre and the Lefebvre mentality was dictated primarily by the basic premise of Paul's integral humanness: Present the face of your Church to all men with as little emphasis as possible on what separates the Church from other groups. The principle was one of openness, of seeking similarities and correspondences, of eliminating what really repelled outsiders. A majority in his Church may be Traditionalist in tendency. But in Paul's estimation, the vast majority outside it were Progressivist and could not accept a Traditionalist Church.

Hence Paul encouraged the Third World group. He sided with imprisoned terrorists. He allowed the most extraordinary aberrations in doctrine and behavior to go unpunished and even uncorrected. He abolished—against the will of the majority of the Bishops in the Second Vatican Council—the Latin Mass. He allowed a Lefebvre, a man of the Right, to be attacked, condemned, ostracized, and ridiculed, while not doing anything to restrain those men of the Left who published and lectured on Catholic doctrine in a way diametrically opposed to Paul's own teaching. He made no attempt to prevent the disappearance of the intricate network of Catholic devotions to the saints, to Christ, to the Papacy as such. He went more than the symbolic extra mile in accommodating Communist regimes in Eastern Europe.

Without any real opposition from Paul's Vatican administration and Paul's Rome, the Rosary, the devotion to the Eucharist, the Stations of the Cross, devotion to the Sacred Heart of Jesus and to the Virgin Mary, the value of pilgrimages to the holy places of Christendom, fidelity to the Pope, conformity to Canon laws, the Catholic interpretation of the Bible, the sacrosanct character of the priesthood, the vocation of nuns, the practice of religious meditation and asceticism—and all the other visible sources of enthusiasm and initiative in the Catholic Church—were snuffed out as officially approved and propagated elements of Roman Catholic life. There can be no doubt about it: Paul's policy was to favor the Left and extinguish—not even tolerate—the Right.

For Paul, the danger was that the Church as the official presence of Jesus had once more become relatively unknown and comparatively insignificant in the ever more complicated affairs of the human race, which in the foreseeable future would increase to six or seven billion. The Vicar of Jesus—no longer a fixed and accepted resident in a central, venerated shrine, but a peripatetic pilgrim in a new order of human things—would have to seek throughout that world a fresh mode of representing Jesus.

In that case, the salvation Jesus won in his battle with the "Prince" would once again have to start with humble beginnings, to create a new civilization among humans of many generations later than Paul's own; a race for whom humanness will have ceased to carry any connotation of genetic characteristics, of geographical origin, of skin pigment, of social status, of linguistic difference, of foreign economic trade, of past historical associations, even of earthly birth.

Now, if Lefebvre were allowed to continue, he would draw heavily on the extreme Right and on the center where a majority of Catholics stood, thus disrupting Paul's policy by emphasizing the differences between Catholics and non-Catholics. Lefebvre spelled catastrophe for Pauline policy. He must be stopped.

So, Paul pressed on. A commission made up of Cardinals Garrone, Tabera, and Wright interviewed Lefebvre early in 1975. Garrone, alas, treated Lefebvre as if he were a dangerous and negligible madman. Tabera vented his full fury on him: "What you are doing is worse than what all the Progressivists are doing." Finally, under Villot's instructions, they issued a condemnation of Lefebvre on May 6. Further, they instructed Monsignore Mamie, Swiss Bishop in whose diocese Lefebvre's Ecône Seminary lay, to withdraw canonical approval from the seminary and to order Lefebvre to surrender it to the Church. Lefebvre turned to the Vatican Court of Appeals, but its Prefect, Cardinal Staffa, under instructions from Villot, refused to review Lefebvre's case.

From spring 1976 the battle went public, and nastily so. Major newspapers and many magazines in Europe and the United States began to carry headlines and articles about the Archbishop and his cause. By March, Lefebvre was the object of a continual stream of demands, threats, and orders from the Roman Ministries. The general message: *submit or else.*

Of course, Lefebvre did not submit. In May he toured the new Society of St. Pius 5 Institutes in the United States—at Houston, Texas; San Jose, California; Armada, Michigan; and elsewhere in Oklahoma, Virginia, Minnesota, and Arizona—conferring the Sacrament of Confirmation on children, preaching against the Ecumenical Council.

On the same Lake Albano where the Pope's summer retreat, Castel Gandolfo, stands, Lefebvre's sister founded a novitiate where new sisters (five Americans, five French, and one Austrian) went into training.

Once back in Europe, Lefebvre announced that he would ordain 26 young men at Ecône on June 29, 1976. On May 24, at the suggestion of Cardinal Villot, Pope Paul spoke openly, at a public Concistory, of Lefebvre's revolt. Paul appealed for unity. It was the first time in over 217 years that a Pope had publicly attacked a prelate of his Church. For Paul was now faced with a real danger: Lefebvre might consecrate a whole series of bishops, establish his own dioceses in competition with existent dioceses. He was already ordaining priests. And those priests were real priests!

Between June 22 and 28, 1976, Jesuit Father Dhanis, sent from Rome by Villot, had several interviews with the Archbishop, trying to stop him from going through with the proposed Ordinations. Dhanis' message: You face suspension (that is, he would be forbidden to say Mass or exercise any or his priestly functions) and possible excommunication. Still Lefebvre would not yield.

On June 28, Cardinal Thiandoum went as Paul's special emissary. His message: If you go through with this, they will strip you of everything. Pause and reconsider.

On the morrow of that conversation, June 29, Lefebvre ordained his 26 priests and deacons, and preached a bitter sermon against "the traitors of our faith." Nobody present doubted that he was referring to Pope Paul as well as to Villot and others.

On July 10, Villot sent Archbishop Ambrogio Marchioni to Ecône with a letter demanding Lefebvre's submission. Lefebvre again refused. On July 22, Villot had Lefebvre "suspended." Lefebvre dismissed the suspension as a bagatelle and preached a sermon on the "confusion through bastardization" that the Vatican was creating. We have, he said, "a bastard rite (the Pauline Mass), bastard sacraments, bastard priests." And he added: "If the Pope is in error, he ceases to be Pope." At that point, Lefebvre had stepped over the line. He was on his way to open schism and to excommunication.

All churches were now barred to Lefebvre. On August 20, in an abandoned hall formerly used for wrestling, he celebrated his Saint Pius 5 Mass. He preached to his congregation of over 6,000 people: "The Council has bastardized the Faith with neo-Protestantism and neo-Modernism." The same day, at Castel Gandolfo, Paul himself spoke sorrowfully to 7,000 gathered in the courtyard beneath his study window: "Help Us to prevent a schism in the Church. Our brother prelate has challenged the Keys (of authority) placed in Our hands by Christ." He also stated: "We will not answer the Archbishop in the tone he uses with Us."

But the battle continued. On September 5, in the presence of 2,000 people in Besançon, France, Lefebvre said his Mass of Saint Pius 5, and preached: "Catholics who want to keep the tradition of their ancestors and who want to die in the Catholic Faith will flock to us."

But the counter-attacks came at him. Cardinal Garrone condemned Lefebvre's mixture of "liturgical rigor and reactionary policies" (Lefebvre praised the military regime of Argentina), and said "Change is necessary. False steps during that change are damaging. But immobility is lethal."

Five bishops—German, Austrian, and Swiss—appealed to their Catholics not to have anything to do with Lefebvre. French theologian Yves Congar appealed to both sides: "Let us have a moratorium on mutual injury. Over 28 percent of French Catholics support the Archbishop's views." Both Lefebvre and Paul would have liked to see a moratorium on the entire matter. But only at the beginning of fall was any real effort made to call a halt.

Earlier in the year, Lefebvre had twice asked Villot's office, as protocol requires, to arrange an audience for him with Paul in the Vatican. Each time Villot refused. Paul heard about it all only much later. Paul did agree to a request made on Lefebvre's behalf by Cardinal Bernardin Gantin, a black African, that Lefebvre have an interview with Paul. But Villot would not allow the meeting. "The Pope will not see Lefebvre," he told Gantin. "He (the Pope) might change his mind, and that would only create confusion."

On September 8 Paul sent another letter to Lefebvre. Lefebvre replied through mutual friends: "I want to work under your authority . . . but I must speak to you personally. . . ." Archbishop Benelli sent a message to Lefebvre which said summarily: Come to Castel Gandolfo with a letter petitioning an interview with His Holiness. On September 11, Lefebvre did just that. The *Osservatore Romano* would report, tongue in cheek, that the Archbishop "unexpectedly presented himself at the Pope's villa." And he talked with Paul for over an hour.

When Paul came down that day to see Lefebvre in the Reception Hall, he was surprised: He remembered the Archbishop's appearance; the long, slightly aquiline nose, the thin lips in the wide mouth, the determined chin, the wary look in his almost almond-eyes. But it was now Lefebvre's attitude that struck Paul, or, more accurately, the vibrating atmosphere that surrounded his diminutive figure. Not arrogant. Not resentful. Not servile. Not sulky. Lefebvre, in short, seemed possessed by some devouring idea that haunted his face, his words, his gestures, even his dutiful act of kneeling and kissing Paul's ring.

Paul let Lefebvre pour out all his complaints and express all his fears. And when Lefebvre had finished, Paul returned to his basic position: "As you are now going, you will be destroyed. And all your work will be for nothing."

Lefebvre's words were clear to Paul. "Holiness! I am willing to do anything for the good of the Church."

"Without obedience to the See of Peter, without our unity in Christ, the Church cannot exist," was Paul's answer to Lefebvre.

The Archbishop went on to ask for his "rights": the right to celebrate Mass in the old way; the right to train his priests in his own seminaries. He was ready to do anything for the Church of Christ, Lefebvre went on to say, but the faithful who feel threatened should have an alternative to the new-fangled practices and teachings launched by the "new theologians." At present false teachings are given them, and their Faith is in danger of being destroyed.

"Does the Archbishop intend to consecrate new bishops?" Paul asked. This was a nightmare thought; Lefebvre *could* validly consecrate new bishops. That would be a classical schism, another splinter church, more disunity.

If good bishops were needed, he would do his duty, was Lefebvre's answer. He also said that His Holiness had been misinformed about the faithful. A big minority in every Catholic population yearned for the old Mass and for the old teachings.

Paul was well aware of the trouble. Many found it hard to go along with his changes. In a sense, Paul's pilgrimage had begun; and not all the faithful could begin it with him. There was serious unrest in the Church. There was disobedience among Catholic Leftists as well as among Catholic Rightists who followed Lefebvre. Already a Bishop Dozier of Memphis, Tennessee, in the United States, wanted to hold irregular "Confession and Absolution" mass meetings. On August 20, 1976, Paul had had to consent to release an entire Convent of Dominican nuns from their religious vows: They, like Lefebvre, abhorred Paul's new Mass form. Father Gommer DePouw in Long Island, New York, celebrated only the old Mass, and had developed a congregation of over 10,000, some of whom came from miles away each Sunday. DePouw probably had a couple of million secret sympathisers.

To his recollection Paul lost his temper only at one point in the conversation. Lefebvre was asked why he personally attacked and condemned Paul. His answer was maddening: "Someone must keep the truth before the eyes of the faithful."

"What am I supposed to do when you condemn me?" Paul turned on him. "Resign? Is that what you want? Is it my post you want?"

But Lefebvre calmed him down. "You have the solution at arm's reach," continued Lefebvre. "One word from you to the Bishops and they will allow us Traditionalists to use their churches for worship. Isn't that our right?"

Paul had done his best to win Lefebvre to his own point of view. He had explained that he, more than the Archbishop, was extremely troubled by the zigzag split that ran from the College of Cardinals down through the Bishops, through the Priests, and into the people all over the Roman Catholic population in Europe and elsewhere. There is an actual de facto schism in the Church, Paul explained to Lefebvre. But nobody has been condemned. And it should stay like that. The losses would be irreparable for generations to come if Rome had to condemn thousands of Catholics.

Paul had gone on to explain how he saw his own function: to preside over his divided Church; to bring the mass of Catholics to a central position and attitude; to admonish all and sundry when they erred; and to launch a series of statements over a period of time in which the traditional doctrine concerning basics—the Eucharist, priestly Ordination, Papal infallibility, the ethics of abortion and sexuality, and so on—would be echoed. Thus there would ring out in his Pontificate, and beyond into the dark age facing Christianity, a clear bell-like voice stating and restating against all opposition within and without the Church the traditional doctrine in its barest outline.

All his attempts, however, to convince Lefebvre had been in vain. "What can be wrong with at least having a trial-run with forming priests the way you and I were formed? In the traditional way? What can be wrong with it?" Lefebvre pleaded.

One part of Paul's brain told him: Nothing. Nothing at all. Another part said: Too dangerous! Lefebvre will attract a large minority—perhaps a majority!

Still, the interview had not ended too badly. As they walked to the separation point, Lefebvre made one last try: "But can't you do something to protect us, to ease the pressure on us, Holy Father?"

"I can't answer you now. The Curia must be consulted. We will see.... We will think about the whole thing." Then, with his usual gentle smile: "We should end our conversation now. But let's pray a little together." They said an Our Father, a Hail Mary, and the traditional prayer to the Holy Spirit, the *Veni Sancte Spiritus*. Both of them spontaneously recited the prayers in Latin. It was more natural and had a greater savor for them than any other tongue.

For Lefebvre, it was not as bad as he had expected, so he explained to the press. "The Pope spoke to me like a father . . . he opened his arms to me. . . . It is the beginning of dialogue. . . ." Nor had it been as good as he had wished. "We reached no conclusion. . . ."

But for Paul, it was disturbing. Lefebvre could not be stopped by threats nor by entreaties. Pushed mercilessly by Villot's downright treatment, the least Lefebvre might do would be to cause an ecclesiastical schism. He might (the thought caused Paul to shudder) set himself up as anti-Pope. . . .

In the end no good result came from the interview. Paul could not relent and allow an alternative style of worship and belief. That, too, could end up in schism and doubt among the faithful. He could not approve of Lefebvre, because his authority was at stake. And he could not allow the Traditionalists in his own Papal Curia that sort of a triumph. The struggle would go on.

Lefebvre received a long private letter from Paul dated October 11, 1976, in which Paul again demanded Lefebvre's submission. Early in 1977, Villot published Paul's October 11 letter to Lefebvre. It was an attempt to discredit Lefebvre. But the Archbishop was still not to be stopped; and his movement continued. In January of the same year, 31 French intellectuals signed a manifesto in support of Lefebvre and asked the Church to return to the "authentic tradition" which Lefebvre represented. Still excluded from local churches, he and his followers continued to celebrate their Mass in make-do locales: a garage in Indianapolis; a rented VFW Hall in Hicksville, Long Island; a barn in Surrey, England; a disused dance-hall in Bonn, Germany. Then, taking another step toward schism, Lefebvre and his followers, growing in number each day, started their own churches in Europe, North America, and Latin America.

Lefebvre publicly denied that he was "anti-Vatican" or unfaithful to the Pope. He kept on saying meekly but firmly that he had no intention of creating a "Tridentine Vatican"—that, he insisted, was just another lie spread about him. He denied any desire or intention to become an anti-Pope or to build a basilica "to rival St. Peter's in Rome"—another calumny. All I want, Lefebvre kept saying, is to "keep options open for bewildered but faithful Roman Catholics."

When Paul is dead, Lefebvre's followers will still be active, and the Traditionalist movement will have a new status in the Roman Church. And it will be up to Paul's successor—the man elected Pope in Conclave 82—to decide what to do about the Traditionalist movement which now cannot be snuffed out.

Paul's decision about Lefebvre, his speech and attitude at the United Nations, and his venture with Michele Sindona, were each part of his more basic decision about his Church. Nothing, Paul maintained, but a complete change in Church attitudes could assure the Church's future.

And this basic conclusion came to Paul from a lifetime spent in Vatican service, all wreathed in a complicated web of recollections, lessons, regrets, joys, successes, failures, speculations, theories, and interpretations about men and women and children, about cities and nations and communities and continents, and—very late in his life—about Planet Earth in relation to other planets and other galaxies. The miracle of Paul 6 is that, given his background, he did reach such openness of mind. The fateful question about him is: Did he go too far?

What outsiders saw as contradictory in his decision-making was, in fact, the result of his scrupulous caution against losing all balance in the nerve-wracking tightrope walk that he was called upon to perform almost from the day he became Pope, between the Traditionalist majority and the Progressivist minority. The world into which Paul was born was the world of Croce's "infinite absolutes." It had been formed by a long list of geniuses unknown today to a majority of men and women—Aquinas, Bonaventure, Dante, Petrarch, Giotto and Signorelli, Raphael and Titian, Michelangelo and Bramante, da Vinci and Galileo, Vico and Manzoni, Vivaldi and Verdi, the warrior Pope Julius 2, the feisty Pio Nono, the intransigent Pius 10, and that incarnation of *Romanità*, Pacelli. Paul came all the way from that dead world to where he could envision an end to the civilization and culture and Church structures made possible by such a litany of past geniuses. This is the true measure of Paul. Pius 12 did not achieve that, nor even beloved Pope John 23, much less any previous Pontiff. Most of today's leaders have not achieved it. Paul saw the end. He acted accordingly. In doing so was he wise? Only time will tell.

Where Paul certainly failed and where he left an unenviable inheritance to the Cardinal Electors of Conclave 82 was on a capital point. Within Paul's policy framework, the Church had no alternative to the forces let loose around it. The Ship of Peter was, in Paul's view, simply supposed to flow with the tides and currents. Opening his Church to all outside influences, he created no initiative within his Church. In all this he allowed, sometimes caused, the traditional sources of Church initiative to be quenched so that at the end of his reign it was the semidarkness of twilight time.

And so the Cardinal Electors of Conclave 82 must ask themselves first, not who of their number shall be Pope; but whether there is any initiative left them in the modern world. Must they now just flow with the tide? Should they adopt a new policy for an active and an actively Roman Catholic Pope? Or is it their duty to opt for a holding policy and for a caretaker Pope, a Pope of transition?

Whatever they decide, Paul's admonition to them has been clear. He sometimes called himself the Pilgrim. He did see himself poised on the threshold of the ancient Roman Catholic dwelling that would shortly be abandoned as incompatible with the changing world scene. There he beckoned to the faithful, and to those he prayed would come to have faith. And he called on "men of thought, men of power, men of labor and fatigue ... once again to find meaning for their efforts in Jesus and in His Sacrifice."

In the twenty-first century, whether men and women remember Paul as great or ignoble, they will look back and remember him on the rainy Easter morning of 1977, a slight, slow-moving, limping figure in white, carrying a wooden cross through Roman streets, standing under an umbrella to speak his message again in the deep, unfaltering tones of an old man who believed with all his heart.

THE TIME
BEFORE CONCLAVE:
THE PRE-CONCLAVE
BULLETINS,
1970–1977

Series One—*1970*

FIRST RUMORS POPE PAUL WILL RESIGN

Rumors of Pope Paul's resignation fill the air by 1970. As early as 1966, visiting the grave of Pope Celestine 5—one of the last Popes to resign (in 1294)—Paul spoke of abdication. By then, he was already embroiled in troubles: a bitter clash with the Jesuits; looming problems with Vatican investments; difficulties in post-Vatican Council developments; Vatican involvement in the United States' intervention in Southeast Asia. Paul spoke of "having been deceived by those around me."

In 1967, he ruled that all Bishops in the Church, on reaching their 75th birthday, must offer to resign and be prepared to have their resignation accepted. By 1972 Paul himself would be 75. Cardinal Parente, in fact, spoke in his rancor over Paul's new ruling: "... if a 75-year old Bishop is not capable of ruling a diocese, please tell me how can a 75-year-old Pope be capable of governing the universal Church!" Parente had a point. And, indeed, Paul considered resignation.

POPE PAUL FORESEES END OF AMERICAN AND EUROPEAN DEMOCRACY—MAKES FIRST MOVES TOWARD RADICAL CHANGES IN CHURCH GOVERNMENT AND PAPACY

"We bear the responsibility of ruling the Church of Christ because we hold the office of Bishop of Rome and consequently the office of successor to the Blessed Apostle Peter, the bearer of the master keys to the Kingdom of God, Vicar of the same Christ who made of him the supreme shepherd of his world-wide flock." So Paul said in one of his first encyclical Letters,° on August 6, 1964.

° *Ecclesiam Suam* (His Church) was the title of this Letter.

But by the opening of the seventies, Paul's thinking has changed radically. He is thinking of a more open Church, another mode of Papal government, and a different kind of Papacy.

He wants to abolish Conclave altogether. That is the only way he sees to break the hold of the all-powerful "club" of Vatican officials and their lay supporters around the world who have, for centuries, decided who will be Pope—frequently before the Conclave took place. Of course, the Pope was no less Pope, no less Bishop of Rome and Vicar of Christ, for the way he was elected. But he was less effective. Paul sees Conclave as a product of the Middle Ages, of Southern Europe, of the old European establishment, the ancien regime. That is past. Finished. Eighteenth- and nineteenth-century style democracy as it exists in the United States and some Western European countries also is finished, in Paul's view. The future, he thinks, lies in the Third World of Asia, Africa, and Latin America.

He begins to prepare an encyclical letter to point out all this, and to open new paths of thought—to plough the ground for extreme change. He is willing to resign by 1972 provided that he will have achieved two goals. First: Total revamping of the method of electing a Pope. Second: the election of the man he chooses for next Pope; a man who can be trusted to follow through with all of Paul's changes, and with whom Paul will be able to work.

Paul, by means of conversations and correspondence, begins a discrete probing of opinions about changing the Conclave system, about his own abdication, and about the identity of his successor. Word of his attitudes and plans spreads through the main chanceries, to the Cardinals and to the Pope-makers among the bishops, all over the world.

Meanwhile, Paul begins to key other major actions to his plans. He has to make a huge transfer of Vatican finances. And, through the Commissions set up by the Second Vatican Council, he has to try to change the attitude of the mass of Catholics. That mass is Traditionalist by habit and not open to vast change, at least not to the vast changes that Paul judges necessary in this day and age.

LIST OF CANDIDATES FOR NEXT POPE BEING FORMED

As of now, the majority of *papabili* are Italian: Cardinals Dino Staffa, Antonio Samoré, Sebastiano Baggio, Paolo Bertoli (all Vatican-based), Giuseppe Siri of Genoa, Corrado Ursi of Naples. Jan Willebrands is Dutch, but he too is Vatican-based. The only black African whose name is mentioned now and again is Lauren Rugambwa of Dar-es-Salaam.

But these names will change according as death and disfavor overtake the Cardinals in question, and according as other more ambitious and/or more promising candidates come to the fore. Paul intends to create more Cardinals anyway. There is some talk of seeking a non-Italian, but still European, candidate in order to make a transition from the custom of electing an Italian. The second-next Pope could then conceivably be a non-European.

Series Two—*1971*

DECLINE OF RELIGION IN THE UNITED STATES

The surveys of pollsters George Gallup, Jr., John O. Davies, Jr., and the American Institute of Public Opinion have sent shock waves through Paul's entourage. The results indicate that 89 percent of Protestant ministers, 61 percent of Roman Catholic priests, and 63 percent of rabbis think that religion on the whole is losing its influence in the United States. And they should know. When the newly born Jesus movement is cited as counter-indication, it is dismissed by Paul and his advisers as transitory and "faddish."

PRIESTLY CELIBACY ATTACKED

Another factor against Paul's ideas of an early resignation is the nascent anti-celibacy opinion. Already, 40 percent of priests in Italy favor abolition of celibacy. In Spain, 33 percent of priests have voted for optional celibacy. The Conference of Latin American Bishops (CELAM) has called for optional celibacy.

PAUL'S PROPOSED UNIVERSAL LAW FOR THE CHURCH AND HIS OWN INFALLIBILITY ATTACKED

To cap all this, the first savage attack by a Roman Catholic in modern times on Paul's Papal infallibility is published. It is a book by Hans Küng, the German-born theologian, of whom the world will hear much.

When Paul has a draft law for the whole Church drawn up by a secret group of his own Canon lawyers, over 220 theologians from German-speaking lands condemn it unreservedly. Cardinal Leo Josef Suenens of Belgium attacks, ridicules, and condemns it in a public interview. The Canon Law Society of the United States does the same. Thus Paul has some preliminary sign of what the "new theologians" of Progressivist views wish to do with Church doctrine. If he can only guide all these eruptions and rebellions, he may bring his Church to a more open position and thus attract non-Catholics. His policy will be to restrain, not condemn, these attacks.

PAUL ADOPTS POLICY OF CONCILIATING THE LEFT-WING AND MARXIST MOVEMENTS

Paul's openness to the Left becomes evident in a series of moves all over the globe. Paul receives President Tito of Yugoslavia on a state visit. The Hungarian Minister of Foreign Affairs also pays a visit to Paul. Paul sends Cardinal König of Vienna to Budapest and has him persuade Cardinal Mindzenty to leave his asylum in the United States Embassy. Paul's promise to Mindzenty: "We will never, as long as you are alive, appoint another Cardinal Primate in Hungary." Mindzenty's removal from Budapest and his exile to Vienna, where he is to live in the old Austro-Hungarian Seminary, is a boon for the Communist Government of Janos Kadar. Mindzenty has been a thorn in the living flesh of the Marxist state. Paul also sends Archbishop Agostino Casaroli, an official of the Vatican Secretariat of State, and Father Pedro Arrupe, General of the Jesuits, to Moscow for talks. He arranges for talks with the Communist Government of Czechoslovakia.

Paul is criticized for the one-sidedness of his policy. While Marxist governments get concessions from the Pope, those governments do not ease up on their own ferocious anti-Catholic and antireligious attitude. And this goes as much for Tito's Yugoslavia as for Russia and elsewhere. Paul is further attacked for his removal of Cardinal Angelo Rossi from his post as Archbishop of São Paulo, Brazil, because Rossi supports the right-wing government in its strong-arm measures against left-wing terrorists, Marxist guerillas, and propagandists; and for his, Paul's, support for the bishops and priests who revolt and riot against the right-wing government of President Stroessner in Paraguay.

Paul does not disapprove of the friendship and association of Cardinal Silva Henríquez with the Chilean Marxist dictator, Salvador Allende. Silva joins Allende on the public platform at a mammoth meeting of socialist and Marxist cadres at May Day celebrations. And when the White Fathers Missionary Congregation decides to withdraw all its personnel from Mozambique in protest against the colonial rule of the Portuguese, Paul approves of their action.

Paul reveals his mind most significantly in his Apostolic Letter published in

May. In it he calls for a new regime in the near future. The Letter echoes the theme of liberation theology; no progress by religion can be made unless a new economic regimen is installed, a regimen which transparently will mean the transformation—really the termination—of classical capitalism.

HUGE NEW AUDIENCE HALL INAUGURATED
BY POPE PAUL

Pier Luigi Nervi is one of the most famous twentieth-century engineer-architects who specialize in what reviewers of avante-garde architecture call "the Atlantic style," or the "Atlantean style." Nervi was the master architect of the Roman Catholic Cathedral in San Francisco.

Atlantean buildings are not symbolic of anything, nor blueprints of any sacramental presence of Divinity within this human universe. They do not evoke the supernatural or the trans-human, or echo in their stark lines any traditional grace and beauty.

Atlantean buildings are masses of undulating architecture that express the engineering dynamism of their own creation, not any goal or aim of ideal outside or above them. They always seem about to erupt, or take off as gigantic wingless things driven by their own self-contained strength. But their thrust is horizontal, not vertical.

At Pope Paul's request, Nervi completed plans for such a hall. In 1964, he presented the plans to the Pope, and Paul approved them. On May 2, 1966, workmen began demolishing the buildings that stood in an area east of Saint Peter's Square, between the Holy Office Building and the Leonine Wall of the Vatican. This would be the site of Nervi's huge Hall of Audiences.

On June 30, 1971, the "Nervi," as it has come to be called familiarly, is inaugurated and blessed by Pope Paul in a public ceremony. Here Paul will hold his Papal Audiences. Here future Synods of the Bishops of the Church will be held.

The Nervi is a long, more or less trapezoidal, building. Its main doors face eastward, as do the doors of Saint Peter's Basilica. Its roof is undulating. On each of the two long walls of the trapezoid, there is one oval, stained-glass window, set like eyes in this protean mass. The windows are by Giovanni Haynal. Marc Chagall was first asked to propose designs for them, but Chagall's art with its note of confusion and incivility was finally judged unsuitable for a place that should express the sacred serenity of God and the harmony between God and man.

Inside the Nervi, the Main Hall is gargantuan. Its floor slopes downward, like the floor of any theater, from the entrance to the stage at the western wall, nearly 2,756 feet away. The undulating ceiling is like the roof of some giant mouth swallowing the visitor. That vaulted ceiling is constructed of 42 prefabricated, white, geminate arches. The Main Hall holds 6,900 people seated, or 14,000 people standing.

On the stage, the Pope's throne is placed on a raised dais. Behind the throne will be placed the biggest bronze sculpture in the world, commissioned by Pope Paul in 1965 from the 64-year-old Pericle Fazzini, one of Jacqueline Kennedy's favorite artists. There were some reports that Pier Luigi Nervi was disturbed that the commission had gone to Fazzini, and by Fazzini's plans for the sculpture. "Two primadonnas singing in the same opera will not sing well at all," Nervi was reported to have quoted another Atlantean, Le Corbusier.

But Paul likes Fazzini's plans, commenting: "I want a work that will last." His Holiness will have it.

It is in the Main Hall that Paul has his General Audiences. Here he will celebrate his 80th birthday in 1977—the day many expect he will resign.

Apart from the Main Hall, the most important room is the Synod Hall, or "Upper Room," as it is also called because of its location above the Main Hall, tucked neatly under the Nervi roof. That nickname, "Upper Room," brings to mind echoes of the upper room in the house in Jerusalem where the Apostles waited, after the Resurrection and Ascension of Jesus, for the coming of the Holy Spirit at Pentecost. The floor of this modern Upper Room, is formed by the sloping outer curve of the huge ceiling of the Main Hall below. The Upper Room is reached by ample staircases and by elevators. It seats upward of 280 people and is equipped with every modern device necessary for simultaneous translation, and for instantaneous radio and television broadcasting. The quasi-official description of this room speaks of its "perfect efficiency in holding large numbers of people and providing technical services . . . which will make this Synod Hall ever more useful—and used—for important meetings of a religious character. . . ." In fact, the Third International Synod of Bishops, set for the coming September 30, will be held in this Synod Hall, this Upper Room. And there is already a rumor, poohpoohed by many Vatican officials, that Conclave 82 may be held here, and not, as in centuries past, in the Sistine Chapel.

Paul, in his inaugurating speech, stresses one aspect of the Nervi: It was built to be the special place where "the Holy Father will welcome the people and which will express a spirituality suitable for the sovereignty of the Pope and the faith of believers. . . (The Nervi) will be a visible symbol of the unity of Pope and people."

Rumors or no, the Nervi, with its Main Hall and its Upper Room, is destined for fateful and historic meetings.

Series Three—*1972*

POPE PAUL'S RESIGNATION THIS YEAR
IMPOSSIBLE

None of Pope Paul's plans for altering Church government has come close even to marginal success. His proposed resignation would be catastrophic for his plan of extreme change.

First, the College of Cardinals. Paul's new ruling that barred Cardinals of 80 and over from Conclaves has eliminated the old guard chieftains: Ottaviani, Parente, Roberti, Tisserant, Zerba. But a good majority of the Electors would still be Traditionalist: Cardinals such as Samorè, Siri, Traglia, Vagnozzi. A whole host of Italians and most of the Cardinals from the United States, Germany, Spain, Portugal, Ireland, England, Austria, and Poland, are Traditionalist. The very same holds for Yü Pin of China and Kim of Korea, Razafimahatratra of Tananarive, and all the African Cardinals.

The results of Paul's probings, though still incomplete, convince him that he could not persuade enough Traditionalist Cardinals to accept his plan. Resigning in those circumstances would be certain, swift death for his Papal policies.

On top of that, there have appeared this year the first genuine signs of serious revolt among clergy and lay people against Paul's new "liberal" laws of worship that have changed nearly every aspect of Catholic religious life. The spearhead of the revolt is one Archbishop of the Traditionalist mind that Paul felt it so essential to change: Marcel Lefebvre. Archbishops don't make headlines much these days. But this one proves to be an exception.

Lefebvre preaches that Paul's revised version of the Roman mass is an inspiration of Satan. He charges that the Vatican has been infiltrated by Communists and atheists, and corrupted by Protestants. He gives voice and focus and new muscle to the Traditionalist faction of the Church. And he is setting out to create a backlash movement in the Church of Europe and the Americas.

Paul, for his part, is as aware as Lefebvre that most Roman Catholics do not like his new forms of worship or the way theology is going.

At least two extraordinarily powerful Cardinals hate Lefebvre: Villot, the Secretary of State for the Vatican; and Cardinal Garrone, a Frenchman, as are Villot and Lefebvre. These two urge Paul to stay on as Pope, in order to combat Lefebvre and the entire Traditionalist movement.

On top of these matters, small straws in the wind begin to make Paul uneasy about how his plan is proceeding for the massive transfer of Vatican investments. Both Cardinal Vagnozzi, head of the Vatican's *Prefecture of Economic Affairs* (PECA), and Bishop Marčinkus, head of the Vatican *Institute of Religious Works* (IRW), bring disturbing reports of the management of Vatican funds in the hands of Italian financier, Michele Sindona.

PAUL PROPOSES NEW DEMOCRACY

For the moment, the only way for Paul to further his vision of radical reform is to remain on as Pope and try to effect a reform himself. He issues another Encyclical Letter, known by its first two words, *Octagesima Adveniens* (the Eightieth Anniversary). It concerns the state of democracy and its future.

His message about Western democracy is put in a negative way: "It is necessary to invent fresh forms of democracy," he says. And it becomes clear in his message that what he means are democratic structures as different from American style democracy as America's democracy is from the Democratic German People's Republic.

Paul's letter greatly encourages many in the Roman Catholic Church who regard democracy as an outworn system and as a pest. Paul's letter stimulates such men to think of a wholly new departure in the next Pontificate, and even of the possibility of a real rapprochement with Marxists in Europe and Latin America. For, while Paul rejects Marxism as an ideology, he does not completely reject Marxism as an economic system, or as a political structure, or as an intellectual framework.

PAUL LOOKS TO NEXT POSSIBLE DATE FOR
RESIGNATION AS HIS APPOINTMENTS OF NEW
CARDINALS SWING BALANCE OF POWER AWAY FROM
OLD GUARD. THE PAPABILI *BEGIN TO EMERGE*

The next date when Paul could willingly resign would be on his 80th birthday, September 26, 1977; or, if the Sindona Affair and Lefebvre problems are laid to rest, possibly sometime before that date. Always provided that Paul is confident that he has attained his two main goals of revamping the Conclave system and the assurance that his successor will be the man of his choice with whom he can work, even in retirement.

At this time, only one name stands out for Paul on his list of possible *papabili*: Sergio Pignedoli, Vatican career man, Assistant to Secretary of State Villot. He is not yet a Cardinal. But Paul will soon be making some Cardinals; and those appointments must, as far as possible, reflect his new policies.

Since becoming Pope in 1963, Paul has made more Cardinals than any Pope in history—150 in all. The first group in 1965 contained due and expected appointments, as did the second group in 1967.

His 1969 appointments already marked a change. Out of 32 new Cardinals, 11 belonged to the Third World of Africa, Asia, and Latin America. Two Frenchmen are appointed, Gouyon and Marty, together with the Dutchman Willebrands, and the United States's Deardon.

Meanwhile, the Traditionalist Curia has fixed on two Vatican career-men as its candidates.

The French, the Germans, and the others have not yet made up their minds.

CARDINAL VILLOT QUIETLY BEGINS
PRE-CONCLAVE ACTIVITY

The Secretary of State for the Vatican or some other senior member of the College of Cardinals will be the Camerlengo of the Universal Church when the Pope either dies or abdicates. He will be in charge, so to speak, until a new Pope is elected, and he will be responsible for the organization and the functioning of Conclave 82.

He has not ignored the possibility of Pope Paul's resignation. Or of his death. It is not too soon to begin the huge task of taking stock of the status quo of the world and of the Church on every issue and in every area.

Nowadays—and differently from past ages—it is issues, not personalities, that dominate the Conclave election.

Accordingly, the first task of the Cardinal Electors in the Conclave will be to formulate and adopt the *General Policy*—a Papal policy to be followed by the next Pope. That *General Policy* will be based on the conditions, changes, and developments in religion, politics, and economics, and on the current evolution of nations and of the community of nations.

Villot, as Camerlengo of the Conclave, begins the process of gathering the vast amounts of information required and of organizing that information into what are called *Position Papers* and *Special Reports*.

Position Papers will, on the basis of extremely accurate and up-to-date information, describe the condition of: Roman Catholicism; Eastern Orthodoxy; non-Catholic Christian Churches; non-Christian religions; Europe; Russia; the United States; Latin America; the Near East; Africa; Asia. These *Position Papers* are drawn up with the aim of giving the Electors a comprehensive view of the state of religion (Christian and non-Christian), the evolution of world politics, and economic projections for the next ten years. Under all headings, of course, the emphasis is on the position of the Roman Church in relation to religious conditions, politics, and economics.

There are three *Special Reports*. These deal with the Pontificate of Paul 6 (his politics and achievements and failures); the results of the Second Vatican Council; and the social revolution around the world.

Finally, on the basis of the facts and analyses contained in the *Position Papers* and the special Reports, a summary of the condition of the world as seen by the Roman Curia, and a blueprint of a general policy, are supplied in the *General Policy Paper*.

All of this will be the subject of discussion, debates, and exchanges by the Cardinals in the Conclave, until they reach a consensus on a *General Policy* that is accepted by a vote of two-thirds plus one. Only after adoption of a *General Policy* will the Conclave proceed to elect the next Pope.

Series Four—*1973*

AMERICAN AMBASSADOR MARTIN DISSUADES
POPE PAUL FROM GESTURE TO THIRD WORLD

Paul's Papal policy carries him in the direction of being open to all comers and all shades of opinion, especially from the Left. That policy suffers a rude shock in January 1973. A delegation of American anti-Vietnam War activists arrives in the Vatican asking for an audience with the Pope and carrying as a gift for him some fragments of an American bomb dropped on Hanoi.

Paul's policy has been to receive such anti-war groups and Vietcong representatives.

But American Ambassador Graham Martin succeeds in persuading Paul not to receive this delegation. Increasingly, United States authorities are realizing how Paul's mind is working, and what could happen if Paul's policies should affect the mind of the next Conclave and the policy of Paul's successor.

PAUL EFFECTS FURTHER CRUCIAL SHIFT
IN TRADITIONAL POWER BLOCS

On March 5, Pope Paul creates 29 new Cardinals. Only seven are Italian—Sergio Pignedoli is among them. Twelve are Third World Cardinals. With these appointments, Paul has upset still further the Traditionalist balancing power of large European groups: the Italians alone, or the Italians and the Spaniards together, or the French with the Italians and the Spaniards. No European bloc can ever dominate a future Conclave.

With this last change in numbers, Paul is ready to move on to the next part of his plan for reform of the Conclave system—and of the Church.

PAUL'S FIRST FORMAL PROPOSAL FOR
REVOLUTION IN WORLD-WIDE CHURCH GOVERNMENT

On the same March 5, at a secret Consistory of his Cardinals, Paul asks the College about the possibility of "utilizing in the election of a Pope the contribution of the Oriental Patriarchs and of elected representatives of the episcopate, that is to say, of those who make up the permanent Council of the Secretariat of the Synod of Bishops."

Apparently simple words! But this is "Romanese" for one of the most far-reaching changes proposed in over twelve-hundred years of Roman Catholic history.

Paul's idea concerns more than merely slicing up the pie of Papal elections among more Electors. He wants more than a mere democratization of Conclave by the inclusion of a few men who aren't Cardinals. He is aiming for more than an increase in the number and the diversification of Electors. He is asking his Cardinals to approve two measures that would have effects neither Paul nor they can foresee.

First, he is asking them seriously to weigh the feasibility of reforming the relations of Papacy and bishops so that, *as they now are,* non-Catholic Churches such as the Eastern Orthodox Churches and the Anglican Church can achieve de facto union with the Roman Catholic Church. This is a huge change. Always, up to now, Rome has said that the non-Roman Catholic churches would finally have to submit and "return" to the fold of Catholicism.

Second, he is asking the Cardinals seriously to weigh the feasibility of electing the Pope, after his own abdication, on the very broad basis of Electors drawn both from the Catholic Church and from non-Catholic Christian churches. If they consent to that, it will mean that the Pope they elect will be handed, as the mainstay of his Papal policy, the principle of governing in conjunction with all those Catholic *and non-Catholic* Electors.

In all of this, Paul has taken seriously the admonition of non-Catholic churchmen: "Peter (meaning the Pope) must give up his imperial power in the Church, in order to gain authority in spirit and in moral stance."

It will take a couple of years for all the opinions and reactions to be gathered in, analyzed, and brought to a conclusion. But Paul's efforts along these lines will fail.

Series Five—*1974*

*RETURNS SUGGEST THAT CHANGES PROPOSED
BY PAUL IN 1970 ARE REJECTED BY CATHOLIC
AND NON-CATHOLIC CHURCHMEN*

"Extremely negative"—this is the nature of the responses so far received to Paul's earlier probings, begun in 1970, when he made his first tentative public overture at abdication, tied to his pet reforms.

Many responding point out that, if Paul's ideas are adopted, the Pope will become the equivalent of the elected chairman of the Roman Catholic Episcopal, Inc. And that, in effect, would only place the Roman Church in the same helpless position in which the Anglican and Episcopal Churches find themselves today.

Others observe that the very system Paul now proposes has already paralyzed the Eastern Orthodox Churches—Greek and Russian. Those Churches have failed to expand. They have become nothing more than national Churches. They have not healed the differences between themselves and other Christians. And most of them have sunk into a ghetto of their own ossified traditions.

The Internationalists—those who earnestly want a non-Italian Pope—object that, in all probability, in Paul's new system the Pope would always be an Italian. Maybe he would be a very honored and honorable member of an international board of Bishops. But his chief title would still be Bishop of Rome—and, for all its glory, Rome is and always will be an Italian diocese. Just as the Bishop of a French diocese should be French and the Bishop of a German diocese should be German, so the Bishop of Rome will be an Italian. Now, the Internationalists add, no Italian Pope has ever made the Vatican truly international—opening out the "Roman Club" to others. The last Pope to promise to do that was Martin 5. But once he was actually elected in 1417, he concentrated more power than ever in Rome. So the Internationalists see the whole proposal as a trap.

The response to Paul's proposal from various governments is also negative. General Franco of Spain, right wing regimes in Latin America, the United States Government: none wants to see local Bishops have autonomy, and thus be placed beyond the control and veto of the Vatican when it comes, for example, to hairline election battles between Communists and non-Communists, both in Europe and in Latin America.

In spite of the fact that his Papal policies do not seem to go well—or perhaps because of that—speculation never dies that Pope Paul will resign. Most Cardinal Electors still have their eyes fixed on September 26, 1977, Paul's 80th birthday. But when Paul made his rule excluding 80-year-old Cardinals from Conclave, he had no thought of himself at 80. He thought only to exclude the core of the Traditionalist old guard in the Vatican from any direct influence on the future of the church.

MORE PAPABILI BEGIN TO EMERGE
FACTIONS DEVELOP

For the moment, under the prodding and persuasion of the powerful Bishop of Marseilles, Roger Etchegaray, the French Cardinals and their foreign friends have rallied around the figure of a German Cardinal as a prime pan-European candidate, one who is in favor of slow, gradual change.

There is another group of Electors who are seeking a Third World candidate. Their choice would be somebody who is a true Progressivist, and in favor of a totally "open" Church: easing up on all the official differences maintained between Catholics and other Christians; adaptation of all Church activity—theology, liturgy, piety, social performance—to modern conditions; cultivation of Marxists as people trying to effect suitable changes in the regimen of nations and individuals.

The Italians are slowly splitting up into three groups: the Conservatives (who advocate slow, gradual change—but change); the Traditionalists (who want a strong reassertion of all pre-Vatican Council II Church beliefs and practices); and the Radicals.

The Radicals decry both Conservatives and Progressivists as two sides of the same coin. They accuse both of them of advocating no initiative specific to the Catholic Church, but of merely allowing themselves to be pushed— whether slowly (the Conservatives) or at breakneck speed (the Progressivists)—by outside events and interests. The Radicals accuse the Traditionalists of being out of touch, of trying to set the clock back, and of being blind to the vast change that has taken place already.

The Radicals would uproot the entire system of Church government and religious activity—all that savors of a former age when the Church was immersed in politics and wielding temporal power. They would repair the damage done since the Vatican Council by the liberal Progressivists—especially in doctrine and Liturgy. They would oppose the slow changes of the Conservatives as being merely pale, hesitating imitations of the Progressivists. But they would not try to restore the old order of things—as the Traditionalists often seem to wish to do.

Series Six—*1975*

FINAL RESULTS OF POPE PAUL'S PROBES:
NO SUPPORT FOR HIS POLICY OF
PLANNED REVOLUTION

Whatever the rumors—and they persist—of his resignation, and whatever the public response to those rumors, it is now quite unfeasible for Paul to contemplate resigning.

First, again, the Conclave. The Eastern Patriarchs will not participate, they answer, in the election of a Roman Pope. Their response mirrors the old Eastern anti-Roman prejudice: "As long as the Bishop of Rome claims sovereignty as a temporal ruler and absolute authority over all the Church, we cannot appear to endorse such an unapostolic and uncatholic position by participating in a Papal election—even as observers." They appear to want the chicken, but are unwilling to hatch the egg.

And, for a great variety of reasons, most Europeans and Americans consulted fear Paul's proposal. Some, because his successor would be another Italian. Some—a surprising number, in fact—want no change in the status quo of Conclave. Some—quite a large minority—are in total disagreement with Paul's theology of the Church, and with his obvious leaning to open every door and window in the Church. "Too much, too fast, in too many directions, with too little thought as to the aftermath," is how one person summarized the gist of the comments.

TRADITIONALIST THREAT GROWS

At the same time, the revolt of Traditionalist Archbishop Marcel Lefebvre is obviously becoming much more, not less, dangerous. Lefebvre's support is growing around the world. He could possibly even spearhead a revisionist movement throughout the Church, negate many of the changes Paul has already made, and make further development of Paul's plan even more difficult. In volatile times, such a movement could even lead to schism of the Church.

FINANCIAL DISASTER IN THE VATICAN

The Sindona affair, about which Paul had been worried but still hopeful, now has assumed disastrous proportions. Before it is over, the Vatican will, by some reliable estimates, lose well over a billion dollars and much credit in this huge failure that the Italians have come to call *il crack Sindona.* It is now reported to Paul that Michele Sindona is a member of the Masonic order. Villot's advice to Paul is firm and clear: Before our losses go beyond all our power to measure and control, before they turn and destroy us, let us get out of this miserable affair.

It will take another two years before Paul can rearrange everything. Meanwhile, this mess alone makes Paul's resignation impossible for now.

PAUL SHIFTS HIS TACTICS, REMAINS FIRM IN PURPOSE OF REVOLUTION AS HE REVISES CONCLAVE RULES

Having had no encouragement at all for his early probings of 1970 with regard to changing the Conclave system, or for his more recent attempt in 1975 to open up the Papal election in a radical way, Paul contents himself now with getting out a new revision of the old Conclave rules. This much he can do, even over the objections that he knows will come from many quarters.

In his new rules, Paul repeats his edict barring Cardinals of 80 and over from Conclave. He limits the total number of Cardinal Electors to 120. To avoid long Conclave discussions, he sets a limit of three days on voting. If, at the end of three days, voting is fruitless, there is to be one day of prayer and free discussion, then back to voting for another three days, and so on.

One of the chief preoccupations in the new Conclave rules is to exclude interference by any person or group of people outside the Conclave: "There has emerged as more relevant than ever," Paul legislates, "the need to safeguard the election of the Roman Pontiff from external enterprises . . . and the interference of groups and form of pressure characteristic of modern society. . . ." It is forbidden "absolutely," Paul now directs, "to introduce into the Conclave technical instruments of whatsoever kind for the recording, reproduction, or transmission of voices and images. . . ." Conclave officials accompanied by two technicians equipped with electronic detection devices must make periodic checks in order to uncover any bugging devices or any other violations of Conclave secrecy.

Further, Paul abolishes a decree of Julius 2 going back to the early 1500s against buying the Papacy with money or promise of jobs and favors. Paul's new rule means that, while it is still the grave sin of simony to buy votes in order to get oneself elected, the man elected even by such means is nevertheless validly elected and must be accepted. The two rules—one about electronic surveillance, the other about the validity of simoniacal elections— are obviously connected in Paul's mind.

The centerpiece of Paul's new Conclave rules is his reformulation of the very character of the Papal Conclave. Paul has not been able to get an "open" church by moving directly toward radical change. His new tactic is to stress the localization of the Pope so that the Church at large can be more de-Romanized. The Conclave, Paul asserts, is "the act of a local Church within the Church of Christ." The "local church" is Saint Peter's in Rome and its Roman diocese. The Conclave is primarily for the election of a new Bishop of *that* local Church, and of the diocese of Rome. That election has been performed for over a thousand years by the Cardinals of the Roman Church. As Bishop of Rome, the new Pope is automatically the successor of Peter who was the first Bishop of Rome. It is in this way that the new Bishop also becomes all that Peter was: Vicar of Jesus and head of Jesus' Church.

Further, "the right to elect the Roman Pontiff belongs solely to the Cardinals of the Roman Church." Paul thus reasserts the privilege of the Romans as the holders of a special deposit of faith, to elect Jesus' representative on this earth.

CONTINUING SPECULATION ABOUT PAUL'S RESIGNATION AND PRE-CONCLAVE ELECTIONEERING SPAWNS NEW POLITICAL INITIATIVES

Paul now realizes that his talk of resignation and of dying, together with the general interest of the Cardinal Electors in the coming Conclave, has set in motion several pre-Conclave enterprises. On the part of some United States Cardinals, there is an initiative—which Paul does not yet understand, except that it is at variance with his own plans—to forge an alliance with Polish and German Cardinals.

There is already a working pact between some Latin Americans and some Eastern European Cardinals. This agreement is sometimes playfully termed the "Latin American–*Ostkardinalaat*" pact.

And there is the New Alliance formed around Cardinal Leo Suenens of

Belgium. Its motivation stems from the very Progressivist theologians who have emerged since the second Vatican Council. It is supported by many Bishops. They, in turn, derive much encouragement from the heads of the major non-Catholic churches. They would like to open the Church to all sorts of influences—Church government, Church activity, Church doctrine, and Church commitment to solve socio-economic problems.

Of course there are still the Traditionalists, centered mainly in Paul's own house, the Vatican, who lay claim to the allegiance of many Bishops and Cardinals around the world.

All these factions—the American Initiative, the Latin American–*Ostkardinalaat* members, the New Alliance group, and the Traditionalists—share one common trait: opposition to Paul's plan for reform of the Conclave and to Paul's favorite *papabile*, Cardinal Sergio Pignedoli.

PRE-CONCLAVE ELECTIONEERING PROCEEDS— "OFFICIAL" LIST OF SUITABLE CANDIDATES AND POLICY OF NEW POPE BEING FORMED

At this point pre-Conclave activity is mainly confined to the higher echelons of Church bureaucracy. It does happen, however, that some ordinary bishop who is head of some powerful regional or national conference has more to do with the choice of the *papabili* than many a Cardinal and many a vested interest in the financial and political worlds. Such a bishop, for instance, is Roger Etchegaray, Bishop of Marseilles. Such also is Archbishop Augustine Casaroli, Vatican expert on Soviet Eastern Europe. Such men exercise considerable power even in the ultimate election of the Pope. The process does not usually extend itself much lower than regional Bishops' Conferences.

The process essentially consists of a leisurely sifting of the names of possible candidates in the light of the issues presented in the *Papers* and *Reports*. For it is issues that decide who can be a viable candidate. The Vatican's Apostolic Delegates (16 of them), Apostolic Nuncios (70 of them), Vicars General (32 of them), local Cardinals residing in countries around the world, plus special emissaries and the permanent Vatican representatives in international organizations, are expected to and do, indeed, find out discreetly the attitudes of the various governments to the various possible candidates for election as Pope.

There are two ways one can become a possible *papabile*: you declare yourself willing and able and desirous to be a candidate and, if elected, to accept the Papacy; or, those who admire you and/or think you suitable decide that you should be on that list.

The list is never officially promulgated or, say, "typed on office stationery." It comes into existence quietly, and mainly by word of mouth. But gradually, without any brouhaha, the names of anywhere from six to ten Cardinals occur and recur whenever the subject of the next Pope's identity comes up for discussion. These are the possible *papabili.*

To go from the status of possible *papabile* to being a real *papabile* on the primary list is a subtle process. That primary list is very restricted and, with only a few changes, it will determine most of the voting and politicking within the Conclave itself.

THE AMERICAN INITIATIVE—AMERICAN CARDINALS DEEP IN VATICAN POLITICS FOR FIRST TIME IN CONCLAVE HISTORY

As far back as 1972, the publication of Paul 6's encyclical Letter *Octagesima Adveniens,* with its negative attitude toward democracy as we have known it, with its recommendations that men should seek "new democratic structures," and its apparent encouragement of Marxists, started a violent reaction in the United States among prominent churchmen and financial circles. With a Democratic victory at the polls in 1976 already predicted, and with even greater commitment of the Democratic Party in the United States to "social democracy," it was feared that the basic capitalistic character of the United States would be seriously affected if the prestige of a new Pope increasingly supported such a thrust of "social democracy." "Already 43% of the working sector is employed by the U.S. Government," went one report sent to Rome from New York. "We are on our way to some form of socialism. Why push farther?"

The so-called American Initiative was born at the end of 1974 but began to take on form only in 1975. It had its origins primarily in the will of the United States Cardinals. At the very least they recognized that a Pope with an inclination to favor socialistic structures for his own reign and for that of his successor, would mean policies inimical to the interests of the United States and of the society to which the U.S. Cardinals belong. By 1975 they know that the one central question to be decided about the next Pontificate concerns Marxism, alliance with Marxists, and the attitude of the Church to Marxist governments.

The first aim of the American Initiative is to break the so-called Latin American–*Ostkardinalaat* working pact, the Marxist-oriented bloc. If most Latin American Cardinals and their supporters succeed in forming an alliance with Eastern European Cardinals, the appeal of such a faction in Conclave will be enormous. The Latin Americans could then advocate peace and collaboration with Marxists and Marxist governments, and virtually parade the Cardinals from the countries of Eastern Europe already living under Communist rule as quite able to survive and flourish—even collaborate—with Marxist regimes at home. If they can do that, then the Latin Americans and their supporters will have a powerful appeal for Italian Cardinals faced with the possibility of a Communist regime in Italy—not to speak of the French, Spanish, and Portuguese Cardinals, faced with the same possibility in their respective countries. That would bring in all of southern Europe.

Further, the strength of the working pact lies in the Polish Cardinals, and particularly in the prestigious and formidable Cardinal-Primate of Poland, Stefan Wyszynski of Warsaw. He, together with Cardinal Wojtyla of Krakow, has untold influence with the German and Austrian Cardinals. In sympathy they are close to Hungary and Czechoslovakia. That northern bloc together with the Eastern Europeans could form a governing majority in the Conclave. And the Eastern European Cardinals stand high in the estimation of the Asiatic and African Cardinals. If all those should stand together with the Latin Americans, and draw in the southern Europeans as well, there would be an absolute majority to be expected in the Conclave, a majority that would wreck any plans or projects of other groups.

The American decision to break that working pact, therefore, has a definite, an urgent, strategic purpose.

The idea is to detach the Poles—and with them, the Germans—from the Latin American–*Ostkardinalaat;* working pact. Cardinal Krol, himself of Polish extraction, extends an invitation to Cardinal Wojtyla to come to the United States on a formal visit. And already Cardinal Krol has started one of those Cardinalitial tours that will mark the pre-Conclave electioneering period from now until the Conclave takes place. This one takes him to Poland.

Both *papabili* and Pope-makers among the Cardinals and Bishops now undertake such tours. You will find Cardinals crisscrossing the Atlantic and the Continent of Europe, appearing in Africa, Latin America, and various parts of Asia. Wherever they go, they must go with the complaisance, if not the connivance, of the local Cardinals. For between brother Cardinals, unwritten but rigid laws forbid them to encroach uninvited or unwelcome on each other's ecclesiastical territory. Other occasions, too, are provided by chance events when an important number of Electors can get together, ostensibly for some ordinary reason, and communicate face-to-face about the pre-Conclave electioneering process and its various twists. The American Cardinals will not be the only ones making crucial strategic visits.

AMERICAN CARDINALS SEEK ALLIANCE WITH
EASTERN EUROPEANS AND GERMANS

The deal offered by the Americans is a complex one and their arsenal of arguments is formidable. All the Eastern Europeans and most of the Germans (as well as many Africans and Asiatics) are against the election of a Curial Cardinal, a Roman of the Romans. The Americans, who lean toward that view themselves, advance the idea of a pan-European *papabile*, a candidate chosen from one of the old Christian nations of Europe outside Italy.

The proposal is tempting for both Germans and Poles. The Poles suspect the inclinations of those who have been advocating an alliance with Latin American Cardinals. And the West German Cardinals do not want to see the Russian zone of influence extended further than East Germany.

Others set out to persuade the Poles also that any working alliance with the Latin Americans will result only in a softening of the Church's line toward Marxism. Such a softening would have a very damaging effect on the already harsh rigors that the Church faces in Poland, Czechoslovakia and in the Baltic countries. The Churches there have won some mitigation of persecution because of the previous hardline stance of the Vatican.

There is, in addition, the threat of backlash. The possibility of such an alliance in the Conclave might well polarize all the other factions and unite them behind a really reactionary Traditionalist candidate—and there are still many of those.

Finally, the Americans are in possession of certain reasons of State derived from their associations at home, reasons which make it imperative that Russia not be any further facilitated in its "Finlandization" of Western Europe. What would happen, they ask the Poles, if the United States really followed a policy of isolationism and hands-off in regard to Western Europe?

As this American Initiative is pursued with success, in Rome Paul 6 and Villot are baffled, each for his own reasons. Paul knows that the genuine tendency of a man like Cooke of New York or Krol of Philadelphia is more Traditionalist (with some Conservative tinges) than anything else. Why then are these two pursuing a pan-European candidate? And both Paul and Villot resent the intrusion of politicking American Cardinals in Northern and Eastern Europe. Paul and Villot share the old Roman horror of the *Anglo-Sassoni* and the policy of divide-and-conquer that has always marked their dealings with Europe for over one hundred and fifty years.

This Papal reaction results in a cooling of relations between Cooke of New York and the Roman authorities. Meanwhile, Cooke and others make no move to heal the breach with Rome, for they suspect that Paul may already be a lame-duck Pope—he may have to resign on his 80th birthday in 1977.

LATIN AMERICAN CHURCH FIGURES COORDINATE "OPEN TO MARXISM" PLAN

Many Latin American Electors have coordinated their Conclave strategies and choices of Papal policy and of Papal candidate under the principle of an open-to-Marxism attitude. They have at their command an infra-structure of priests' councils and organizations of layfolk that runs through most of the major countries of Latin America—Chile, Brazil, Argentina, Venezuela, Bolivia, Colombia, Peru, and with deep ramifications in Mexico.

The tone of this Latin American infrastructure runs from light pink to deep red—from priests and bishops and layfolk enthusiastic for "democratic socialism," all the way to priests, bishops, and layfolk rooting for outright Marxism—Marxism by any means, fair or foul.

The American Cardinals are kept au courant with all of this.

EUROCOMMUNIST THREAT AFFECTS RIGHT-WING ITALIAN CARDINALS

The rise of the Eurocommunist threat (the possibility that Communists will enter government in significant and even decisive numbers in France, Spain, and Portugal) has begun to work on the hitherto monolithically right-wing Italian Cardinals, and the effect is helped along by the sympathies of those Cardinals who are already "open" to the Marxist dialogue. In particular, Cardinals Pellegrino of Turin and Pironio of the Vatican are disposed to consider the advent of a Communist government in Italy as not the ultimate disaster.

But it is the general trend of affairs at the Vatican that has really begun to divide the Italians. It is an open secret that the bulk of Vatican investments are being put within the North American continent, safely out of the reach of any European disaster. This is a sign of "pulling out" that is not lost on the Cardinals and Bishops in Italy.

There is also the fact that, actually, in the 36 localities where completely Marxist governments rule locally in Italy, there is no real friction between Communists and Catholics. On the contrary, the very twist of public events helps their friendship. Due to the deterioration of the Italian economy, the rising unemployment, the inflation, the soaring prices, the dislocation of public order, the kidnappings, murders, robberies, both the Communists (who stand for strict law and order) and the Catholics (who have no other rule to live by) are drawn together. In fact, they become the joint targets of the neo-anarchist groups and of the terrorist factions that model themselves on the Baader-Meinhoff gang in West Germany.

Besides all this, the Communists in the Italian Parliament have shown themselves to be political "gentlemen"; *borghesi*, in fact. They come to an agreement of *non sfiducia*, the "non no-confidence" pact, with the Democristian Government. This means that the Communists, who command a majority in Parliament, will never introduce a no-confidence motion. And the Communists keep their word. The government, which is a minority government, does not fall thanks to this kept promise of the Communists.

Besides all of these signs and portents that Italian Churchmen see, Archbishop Casaroli, Vatican expert in Communist politics and Vatican Emissary to Russian satellites as well as to Moscow, appears drinking cocktails in the Kremlin and dining in Bulgaria and Prague with Communist officials. It is observed that he has cordial relations with *all* Communist governments in Eastern Europe. Further, Pope Paul himself has not hesitated to receive Russian government representatives and to bow to Russian pressures in matters such as the Mindzenty case, where Paul thrust the Hungarian Cardinal into obscurity at Russian insistence. The mood, all sense, is of certain detente.

An additional and increasingly important factor influencing many Italian Bishops and some Cardinals is the existence of several Italian-born organizations that openly proclaim as their purpose the formation of an alliance between Marxists and Christians. These organizations, begun about seven years ago, have flourished, and now their influence runs through dioceses and universities and professional groups all over Italy.

Series Seven—*1976*

BY HIS NEWEST CARDINALS POPE PAUL ENSURES FURTHER POWER SHIFT FROM EUROPE AND WESTERN INDUSTRIAL NATIONS

On May 24, Pope Paul announces the creation of 21 new Cardinals; over half are from the Third World. There are only three Italians. There are three new Eastern Europeans: Poland's Filipiak, a Traditionalist; Hungary's Lekai, a Progressivist; Czechoslovakia's Tomašek, a Traditionalist. There are what are called obligatory appointments (either because the diocese occupied by a Bishop or Archbishop is traditionally headed by a Cardinal, or because some Bishop or Archbishop has secured the promise of a "red hat" by one means or another): Baum of Washington, D.C., a Conservative; Hume of Britain, a Progressivist. All will be eligible to vote in Conclave next year or the year after.

HEAVY PERSONAL POLITICKING BY CARDINALS ON INTERNATIONAL SCENE— PIGNEDOLI VERY VISIBLE

There are more Cardinalitial tours, and there are further fortuitous events facilitating face-to-face discussions between future Conclave Electors.

Cardinal Conway of Ireland dies in April. At his funeral in Ireland there are six Cardinals, two from the United States. Cardinal Pignedoli goes on an extended tour of the United States. It is part of a worldwide tour during which he listens to Tibetan monks in Switzerland, Hindus in England, Muslims in the Philippines and in Libya, Saudi Arabians and Egyptians in the Middle East—all this ostensibly in function of his role as Prefect of the Vatican Secretariat for Relations with non-Christians. But the trip is a *papabile* tour on his own behalf.

In the United States the highlight of Pignedoli's trip is a convention at the

Maryknoll headquarters at Ossining, New York. Many—not all—Maryknoll priests and nuns are known now throughout Latin America as being deeply and actively involved with, and committed to, Marxist guerillas and political activists.

On July 15, Pignedoli preaches a special homily. Presiding there is Newark Archbishop Peter Gerety, who keynotes the convention with his statement that the Gospel must be integrated "with the socio-economic, political, and global structures which are becoming increasingly important." And Pignedoli, in agreement with two Archbishops—one of whom is Marcos McGrath of Panama—half a dozen bishops, 75 priests and nuns and lay people, challenges the Roman Catholic Church "to make social justice and human rights integral parts of the Gospel." This is Pignedoli's expression of Paul's plan for "opening up the Church decisively in love for all mankind."

The Eucharistic Congress at Philadelphia in August provides another occasion for a big gathering of Cardinals, domestic and foreign. The main word from Rome is that a Papal resignation by Paul is quite possible next year, 1977, at his birthday on September 26. A galvanizing thought!

The American Initiative is advanced somewhat in private discussions.

Lekai of Hungary, accompanied by a layman, attends, but is rather isolated from all the others, as nobody feels quite sure of where Lekai stands or in what he is implicated.

When the Congress is over, and after a tour of the United States, Cardinal Wojtyla of Poland is the personal guest of Cardinal Cooke in New York. There is now a strong feeling of agreement in favor of the American Initiative between the Poles and the three Americans, Krol, Cooke, and Manning of Los Angeles. But Cody of Chicago, Carberry of St. Louis, Shehan of Baltimore (retired but eligible to vote in Conclave until the end of 1978), and O'Boyle of Washington (also retired), all Traditionalists, are opposed to the American Initiative.

The Poles agree to communicate with other Europeans.

CONCLAVE EXPECTED TO BE COMPLEX.
HÖFFNER OF COLOGNE EMERGES
AS POSSIBLE CANDIDATE

The coming Conclave 82 promises to be much more complicated than any remembered Conclave of this century. As the views of future Electors and present Pope-makers come in with recommendations concerning the Papal policy that the next occupant of Peter's throne should follow, they are analyzed and put into a general précis. There seems to be no way of reconciling the different factions—so divergent are their views and so unsure are the political and economic conditions envisaged for the next ten years.

Gradually, the reactions to *Position Papers* and *Special Reports* are reduced to a *General Policy Paper.* To everybody's amazement, and to Villot's satisfaction, the general consensus seems to run in the direction of having an Italian Pope who will not be a Curial man. All tend to think that the next Pope should be projected for a ten-year pontificate. This conclusion determines more or less that the choice will be of a candidate with that age and health expectancy.

In spite of this apparent concordance of view, there remains a feeling at the center of things, in the Vatican, that the subterranean rumblings and movements of which the Vatican is aware, will only come to a head at the Conclave. The possibility of a real breakthrough on the part of the "open-to-Marxists" and Third World mentality, has evoked from the Conservatives a stand-by plan for a pan-European candidate. And, indeed, all those pushing the idea of a pan-European candidate are, in the main, Conservatives, with a sprinkling of Traditionalists.

More than one Conservative Elector, unwilling in principle to be nominated as a *papabile,* has disclosed that he would be a willing candidate in two circumstances. First, if thereby he would offset the candidacy of someone put forward by the Progressivists; or, second, if he could foil an attempt by the Curia to get a really Traditionalist Italian elected. There is a third circumstance: Although he is not yet a Cardinal, Archbishop Benelli, present Under-Secretary of State and close collaborator of Pope Paul, will be a Cardinal before Paul dies; to block the candidacy of Benelli, More than one Conservative would be willing to be put in nomination.

AMERICAN INITIATIVE BOTCHED—LOSES CREDIBILITY WITH EUROPEAN ALLIES

An unexpected factor has put the American Initiative in supreme danger: the meeting of the *American National Pastoral Council* at Detroit, October 21–23, supposedly part of the United States's Bicentennial celebration. Entitled a *Call to Action* (CTA), and at the cost of some hundreds of thousands of Church dollars, the meeting is organized by Cardinal Deardon of Detroit with the very active help of Archbishop Peter Gerety of Newark and Monsignor John Eagan. The late professional agitator and chaos theorist, Saul Alinsky, would have been pleased with the way the CTA was managed.

Gathered at the meeting are 1,340 delegates from 152 American dioceses, and 1,100 observers from around the nation. The delegates from each diocese should be chosen by the Bishops—it is their Lordships' duty. But, it is reported, the Bishops leave the choice to various sublevel diocesan committees. It is not unusual for Bishops to sign papers of approval with no fuss and not much attention when they are placed beneath their pens by diligent secretaries. Now, those committees are, to a large degree, peopled with Catholic radicals who are left-wing in politics, liberated in their views of sexuality, culturally separated from the past history of the Roman Catholic Church. Of course, the left-wing of the Catholic Church should be represented among the delegates. But the way in which their Lordships acted ensured that the overwhelming number of the delegates belonged to the left-wing.

Forty percent of those attending the CTA are clergy. Another forty percent are women, mainly nuns. Special groups present and very active are ex-priests, ex-nuns, homosexuals, proabortionists, Christian Marxists, Christian Socialists, Christian pacifists. As yet to be explained is, how is it possible for the Bishops and Cardinals of the Roman Catholic Church in the United States not to see what is coming?

The Apostolic Delegate, Archbishop Jadot, is also present. The Delegate acts as would have been expected from someone who is a poor theologian. He furthers the impression he has given since his arrival in the United States as he traveled widely around the country. His greatest determination before and during the CTA appears to be the cultivation of the same kind of popularity as of his predessors, Amletto Cicognani, enjoyed. Cicognani, universally popular with American Bishops, eventually retired to Rome to become a Cardinal of the Church. Jadot's attitude to the entire "Call to Action" meeting is, in short, one of urbane permissiveness more often found in schoolteachers on holiday.

The CTA meeting becomes an object-lesson in Alinsky-style parliamentary tactics: All opposition to liberal ideas is cut off, silenced, steamrollered; all unwelcome motions from the floor are tabled; any opposing group action is met with a vociferous claque. And it all works. The CTA issues over one thousand resolutions and 182 specific demands. Some examples: that abortion, homosexuality, women priests, married priests, all be legalized in the Church; that Marxism be freed from condemnation; that the Church propose and labor for a classless society: and so on.

Cardinal Krol of Philadelphia, supposedly the prime Churchman in Catholic America, tries to explain all this in the *Detroit Free Press* of October 23. He speaks of "rebels taking over the Conference," and he makes light of the whole thing by speaking of "a few manipulators who had received the support of a naive group of little ladies." It is too little, too late, too crude, from too important a man, in too important a crisis. The damage has been done.

On November 9, Cardinal Deardon tries to pooh-pooh and whitewash it all in the report about the CTA which he makes to the Bishops' meeting in Washington, D.C. None of his Episcopal colleagues lay the blame where it should be laid.

At the same time, Krol defends the CTA meeting as "the most diversified assembly in our history"—a statement so inappropriate with regard to a religious gathering that any unknowing stranger who had walked in at that precise moment of the Bishops' meeting could easily have thought that Krol was talking about the American economy, World War II in the Pacific Theater, or the Vatican's portfolio of investments. He tells his colleagues that "the intelligence and commitment of those chosen to attend is a testimony to the discernment of the Bishops who appointed them." This is more subtle than a mere whitewash. Krol knows as well as anyone that the Bishops did not appoint the delegates. And he knows they should have. But this appears to be Krol's way of saying to his fellow-Bishops: Well, without thinking, you signed the papers creating them delegates officially; so, you are in this as deep as I am.

This remarkable performance of the American Cardinals has, from beginning to end, seriously injured the American Initiative in the minds of the Polish and German Cardinals. They already regarded the French Cardinals as dangerously left-wing—which they are. And now the Americans! The Poles and Germans suspect that Gerety and Deardon might represent the majority stand of the American Bishops. And Krol is compromised in their eyes because of his role in CTA and his subsequent defense of it. Fencemending is going to be necessary if the American initiative is to get off the ground again.

Series Eight—*1977*

ON THE INITIATIVE OF PAUL 6 AND SECRETARY OF STATE VILLOT, THE VATICAN STARTS TO PREPARE MINDS FOR COMMUNIST PARTICIPATION IN EUROPEAN GOVERNMENTS

The first inkling of this initiative comes in June of this year. It starts in France. For the Vatican as for Moscow, France is the linchpin of Europe's political evolution, just as Germany is the linchpin of Europe's economic and military evolution. As France goes politically, so will go the rest of Western Europe—this is an axiom of Vatican geopolitics. Looking to the French national elections in March of 1978, Vatican officials reason that if the Communists, in alliance or not with the socialists, emerge as participants in government, this will be an example and a stimulus for Italy, Spain and Portugal.

The French Bishops publish two documents in June of this year: on Marxism and Christianity, and on the condition of Christians in the world of the worker. Both are of Villot's (and ultimately of Paul's) inspiration.

The Bishops speak quite clearly. "Of course," they say, "Marxism and Christianity as philosophies are incompatible." But this incompatibility, they go on to say, does not allow us to refuse to welcome Marxists in government and elsewhere in public life. We must of course be vigilant and ask the right questions of Marxists. In sustained dialogue. And avoiding all rupture with them. But then we should leave them go to it. Why? Because: "We cannot ask religious faith to play a role which does not belong to religious faith. Now, religious faith is not supposed to inspire our actions."

Then, in the September 9 edition of the Vatican's *Osservatore Romano*, Vatican spokesman and mouthpiece for Paul 6, Federico Alessandrini, comes right out with it:

"It is obvious that even a mere participation in power by the Communist parties in some Western countries such as Italy, France, and

possibly Spain would mark a substantial success for the Soviet Union. ....
But as things stand, the hypothesis does not seem remote from reality. Nor
can one see how the United States could oppose an action carried out in
line with the self-determination of peoples."

This is a clear warning to the United States that the Vatican has made up
its own mind; that the United States should respect the democratic ideal of a
free vote in Italy bringing Communists to power, and should not interfere
with the internal affairs of Italy.

On September 19, Paul receives a delegation from the Czechoslovakian
Communist regime headed by Karel Hruza, Director of the Religious Affairs
Secretariat of the Czechoslovakian Council of Ministers. Together, Paul and
Hruza go over new agreements between the Vatican and Czechoslovakia.
Paul is on his way to obtaining greater freedom for the 11 million Roman
Catholics in that country and removal of the ban on the 540 priests who have
been under a law of silence and inactivity imposed by the Communist
regime.

When President Jimmy Carter's personal envoy to Paul, Miami lawyer
David M. Walters, meets with Paul for an hour's discussion on October 6,
Paul's replies and remarks to Walters are diplomatically couched but clear:
We are not against Marxist participation in government here or elsewhere.

When President Carter's human rights program comes up as a topic in
Roman conversations, authorities are cautious. After all, they point out,
Carter has just received Julius Nyerere of Tanzania and greeted him as "a
superb politician who holds the key to the future of peace and equality of
treatment and freedom in Africa." The United States Government knows, of
course, that Nyerere has: relocated half his peasant population, burned their
homes, beaten and killed them when they resisted; allows no right to strike,
no free press; holds over 7,000 political prisoners in filthy jails; and uses
torture and assassination to maintain himself without an effective opposition.

If there is any doubt still about the Vatican's position, Monsignore Virgilio
Levi, Vice-Director of *Osservatore Romano*, writes on the front page of the
October 27 issue:

"Marxism seems to be changing and Catholics must be taught by the
Church to evaluate when they ought to collaborate with Marxists for the
common good. ...." Catholics must be instructed in such a way as to be
"sensitive to socio-political evolution where such an evolution is taking place,
to be capable of appreciating that which is valid in what is proposed, but
able to be firm in measuring what deviates from Christ and from the
Christian attitude toward life and behavior. ...." So, with a view to
collaboration with Marxists, the Church must develop Christians who are

"ready to collaborate with frankness and clarity where collaboration is demanded for the common good."

The brutal fact is that in the parliamentary elections of last year, Italian Communists won 34.4 percent of the vote. The Democristians won 38.7 percent. Communists offer stability in a country where the people have long since abandoned the Christian view of government as defender and promoter of the common good. Political power in Italy—as elsewhere—is seen as a vehicle to promote their own economic good. "So let's take government with Marxists," the people conclude. Paul's Vatican goes along with all this. There is no other way.

CARDINAL BENELLI APPEARS SLATED FOR MAJOR ROLE AS POPE PAUL PREPARES FOR COMING MARXIST DOMINATION OF WESTERN EUROPEAN GOVERNMENTS

Pope Paul's actions appear to reveal a serious uncertainty in his mind about the ultimate success of the revolution he wants in Church government. He has, to be sure, done all he can through his appointments of new Cardinals to increase the chance of a Third World Pope. At the same time, in his revision of Conclave rules, he has emphasized the status of the Pope as Bishop of Rome, apparently to make it possible for the future Pope to sit with the heads of other Christian Churches as a specially honored equal with his equals—first among his peers, a Bishop among bishops.

He is still convinced that a full revolution is coming. But by now Cardinal Vagnozzi, among others, has convinced Paul that a pan-European candidate is the best he can hope for as an interim move in order to stave off worse. Worse, in this case, could be a stampede of a majority of the Electors in favor of a complete Traditionalist. And, if there is a pan-European candidate and Pope-elect, at least that may serve to rope in those Cardinals who are tending to ultra-Progressivist solutions—something Paul does not favor within the Church itself, even though he is willing to accommodate Marxists in other ways.

By early 1977, Paul has revised the rather freehanded way in which he has regarded the possibility of a Eurocommunist government in Italy and elsewhere. There have, of course, been pressures from outside the Vatican on Paul to change his original stance on this point. One example: At a meeting held in April of the previous year at the *Center for Strategic and International Studies* at Georgetown University, the participants—people such as Horace Rivero, William Colby, John Connolly, Clare Boothe Luce, Ray Cline, among others—made clear the disastrous effect a Communist government in Italy would have on vital United States interests.

Paul's continuing revision of his previous stance is in large degree due to the work of American officials, disturbed by the "open" policy Paul has been pursuing. In addition, Vagnozzi, who is Vatican finance expert, and others as well, have pointed out that, despite the Sindona losses, Vatican finances now depend vitally on the United States and its favorable attitude to the Vatican.

Paul, therefore, reverts somewhat to an idea he had back in the sixties: a united Europe capable of once more becoming an economic and political force in the world, even if it may have to go through a period of "Finlandization" by Russia. "In the final count," Paul would remark in August of this year, "nothing new is coming out of Russia or China—culture is dead, their technology is borrowed from the U.S.A. And the U.S.A. is over the hill. Europe still has the resources spiritually and intellectually and culturally to blaze a new path."

It is with this in mind that, on June 27, he proceeds to make his trusted aid, the 56-year-old Archbishop Giovanni Benelli, a Cardinal. He has of course other reasons fo doing so. Benelli, faithful to Paul, is hated by certain other powerful Vatican figures. If Paul were to die, say, and leave Benelli as a simple Archbishop, Benelli could very well end up as resident Bishop of some seven-parish, walled town in distant and mountainous Calabria, or finish his days copying documents in an obscure office of the Vatican. He has to be protected. And he has to have a voice in future Conclaves—possibly be elected Pope at some future date.

But chiefly, Benelli's Cardinalate will give him the standing with which he can undertake a new role: that of organizer of a "new soul" for Europe. Benelli will seek to galvanize political, religious, economic, and cultural interest in, and support for, a new unity in Europe. As Cardinal, Benelli, together with a group of Catholic Bishops, is to meet this Fall with various European political leaders.

Casting an eye over the prospective roster of Cardinal Electors in the next Conclave, Paul also decides that the tendency toward "openness" requires some brake. Besides Benelli, he creates three other Cardinals who, he is sure, will constitute that sort of a brake: Father Luigi Ciappi, Dominican priest and theologian to three Popes—including Paul; the 55-year-old Archbishop Bernardin Gantin of Benin, already a member of the Roman Curia; and Josef Ratzinger, Archbishop of Munich. Of these three, Gantin and/or Benelli could one day be Pope.

PAUL REVIVES RUMORS OF HIS EARLY
RESIGNATION—DRAWS ELECTIONEERING MOVES
INTO OPEN. MAJOR WORLD POWERS RESPOND

Fed by Paul's own statement on at least three occasions that "the end is near," rumors of his resignation run wild for the first nine months of 1977. Some chanceries begin to prepare for an Autumn resignation; many chanceries proceed to act as if Paul's entourage no longer has the power or the prestige of the Pope's entourage.

The United States, the United Kingdom, and Russia make official enquiries of their Vatican contacts about the possibility of Paul's resignation. For, no matter what various factions within those countries may think, the happenings at the Vatican have a deep import for the various powers.

Meanwhile, just before Paul leaves for the Papal Villa of Castel Gândolfo, Vatican Radio and the Vatican newspaper *Osservatore Romano* come out with scornful denials of Paul's impending resignation.

There are, of course, ample grounds to suppose that Paul has allowed—and even has fed—such rumors. His motive: to bring electioneering moves out into the open—to tie as many opposing hands as possible, as far before the fact as he can.

At the same time, he displays a *vitalità*, as the Italians delightedly call it, quite ill-suited to a Pontiff supposedly on his last legs and about to die or crawl away helpless. He goes to Pescara by train in the September heat; he preaches in the rain to those who come for the Eucharistic Congress; then, to top all that, when saying goodbye to one group of Spanish pilgrims, he cups his hands and shouts in hearty good humor: *"Tornate! Tornate! Vi trovarete ancora all'appuntamento!"* (Come back again! Come back again! Be here for your next audience!)

This old and infirm Pope, a "solitary Atlas" in the words of Cardinal Suenens, is playing a much cleverer end game than many of his younger colleagues.

AMERICAN CARDINALS TRY TO RETRIEVE
AMERICAN INITIATIVE PLAN. SURVEILLANCE,
HARASSMENT, PERSECUTION, ISOLATION ARE
ORDER OF THE DAY FOR CHURCH IN EASTERN EUROPE.

The first major move to mend fences and repair the hopes of the American Initiative is made on August 1 of 1977 with Cardinal Cooke's trip to Poland. He engages in talks in Warsaw with Church officials in the chancery of the

Cardinal-Primate of Poland, Stefan Wyszynski—notably with Bishop Zbieg-
niew Kraszemski, who will certainly be a Cardinal. He makes an extensive
tour of dioceses in north-western Poland for five days. He participates in the
national Polish pilgrimage to the venerated shrine of the Virgin at
Częstochowa where he prays with 80,000 Poles.

At Częstochowa, also, he goes into the matter of Papal candidates with
Cardinal Wyszynski, as also with Roman-based Cardinal Nasalli Rocca (also a
pilgrim at Częstochowa). Rocca is a Traditionalist.

After that, Cooke proceeds to Krakow for similar talks on the same topics
with Wojtyla.

The second major move for the restoration of the American Initiative
begins when Cardinal Krol, Archbishop Joseph Bernardin of Cincinnati (the
President at this time of the American Conference of Bishops), and Bishop
James S. Rausch of Phoenix, Arizona, leave together from Philadelphia
International Airport on September 20 for a week's visit with Cardinal Lekai
of Hungary. They are going on the heels of Billy Graham who is just
concluding a visit there and will come home saying he found religious
freedom in Hungary. A fond dream, that, but not one that blinds many men's
eyes—and certainly not Cardinal Lekai's.

On the face of it, this is a churchly visit by one Cardinal and two Bishops
to a fellow Churchman. After all, Paul 6 himself had received the Communist
head of Hungary, Janos Kadar, in the Vatican, earlier in the year. How
natural then for these important prelates to celebrate a High Mass, as Krol
and Bernardin do, in Budapest's St. Stephen's Cathedral before a congregation of 3,000 that includes the entire Hungarian hierarchy of Bishops and the
Honorable Imre Miklos, chief of the Government Office of Religious Affairs.
Appropriate too for them to baptize 60 infants, and to attend a festive music
celebration at Matthias Coronation Church in honor of Paul 6's birthday.
This visit is filled with many such appropriate churchly rounds.

Privately, the Americans check out the progress of Vatican-Hungarian
diplomatic discussions. Things are progressing slowly, and nothing promising
is being achieved. The Hungarians are only interested in gestures that will
have great propaganda value: public normalization of relations, so that
Communist officials can be photographed with clerics; the return of St.
Stephen's crown to Hungary (the United States Government has possessed it
for many years), something the American prelates can easily arrange with
Jimmy Carter; and so on. The American prelates are interested in substantial
matters such as freedom of worship and freedom of publication.

The Americans make their mind clear on other points to Lekai. And they
have a complex message to deliver to the Cardinal of Hungary: The most
feasible *papabile* now is a pan-European. The stand being taken by a growing
majority of the Cardinal Electors favors a policy hewing closely to the

weaving United States policy of allowing Eurocommunist governments to accede to power in European countries, but not to express even tacit approval of such a change in ideology.

None of the Americans come away totally reassured that the safety of Hungarian Churchmen's families and friends will not be used as a means of ensuring that those Churchmen hew to a pro-Marxist line in their activities and public utterances. Nor can the Americans find out exactly how far the sympathies of Hungarian Churchmen extend towards a Marxist-Christian alliance. On his way home from Hungary, Krol stops for two days—September 29–30—in Prague, Czechoslovakia, to speak with Cardinal Frantisek Tomašek. The picture is bad for the Church in this country—the bleakest picture apart from North Vietnam and Albania. It is the subject of unremitting persecution, harassment, and isolation. "What's the main problem?" Krol asks at one point. "To be or not to be," is Tomašek's grim answer. Tomašek does not entirely appreciate Pope Paul's Hamlet-like indecision regarding Marxism. "Doesn't His Holiness realize that we are being throttled here?" Tomašek exclaims.

Tomašek's attitude is clear, if finally a little disappointing. He will stand with the Poles in the matter of a *papabile*. He thinks Lekai is under too much surveillance and control and is totally isolated. Although Tomašek will stand with the Poles, personally he would rather wait and see in the matter of a pan-European *papabile*. He is not sure if, after all, the Church doesn't need a Traditionalist Pope—at least for a period of time. "Well, what about a pan-European Traditionalist?" is the burning question.

PAUL HAS REVIVED HOPES OF EFFECTING REVOLUTIONARY CHANGE

Paul, actually, has no intention of resigning in September 1977. Again, circumstances forbid it. Currently, there are delicate behind-the-scenes negotiations with Communist governments in Prague and in Budapest. Discussions with intermediaries of Russia continue intermittently. And the very subject of the talks gives Paul some hope that his idea for a reform of the Conclave system (and, with it, of the method of government in the Church) can be achieved. For one of the chief subjects under discussion is the fate of the Moscow Patriarchate and its relations with the Papacy.

The flow of intelligence and events this year adds to Paul's interest. Jesuit Father General Pedro Arrupe takes a trip to Moscow and other places as a contact man and to pick up reports of a delicate kind. Arrupe's statement on his return—that he saw signs of relaxation in religious persecution in Russia—is flatly contradicted by Father Casimir Pugevicus, Director of Lithuanian

Catholic Religious Aid. In his letter, smuggled out of Russia, Pugevicus blasts Arrupe's statement as a "time-serving Soviet manoeuvre" used in order to create a false impression.

At home in Italy, negotiations of a new agreement between the Italian State and the Vatican are almost completed. The new agreement will replace the Lateran Concordat of 1929 and will place the Church where Paul thinks she should be: Catholicism will no longer be the official religion of Italy, and the Church's teachings and laws about marriage, divorce, and such matters will no longer be binding on Italian citizens. At the same time, quiet discussions continue about the entry of Communists into the Italian Government.

In Paul's view, there is new hope, therefore, that he might yet attain his goal: reform of Roman Catholic governing structures; in particular, the method of electing the Pope and the relationship of the Pope with the heads of other Christian Churches. If he were to reach these goals, then Paul would resign. Otherwise, he would die in Peter's sandals. The probability is that he will, indeed, die as Pope.

But still he hopes.

NO 80TH BIRTHDAY RESIGNATION BY PAUL

In the August 30 edition of *Osservatore Romano*, associate editor Reverend Virgilio Levi has protested against what he called the "uncivil" campaign in the Italian press which, "without any factual basis," has been spreading "imaginary and eccentric news" about Paul's resignation. Vatican spokesman, Reverend Romeo Panciroli goes on Vatican Radio to strike the same note.

On September 26, his 80th birthday, Paul gets up at the same time as usual (6 A.M.) and goes to bed at the same time as usual (2 A.M.) There is no resignation. Nor will there be any during the coming Synod of Bishops which starts in four days' time. Paul receives congratulatory messages from world leaders, and unveils a new set of bronze doors to St. Peter's Basilica.

The celebration of Paul's birthday culminates in the Nervi. Here, sitting on his Papal throne before a packed audience, Paul listens to a concert in his honor. Behind him, finished and installed for the occasion, is the bronze sculpture by Pericle Fazzini, commissioned by Paul 12 years before.

Reportedly, the materials and castings cost half a milliard of lire; further work expenses cost one million lire and Fazzini's personal fee was fifty million lire.

It is huge. Fazzini's theme is Resurrection. The sculpture's central figure rises, leaning forward dynamically as if in motion. Splayed around it are masses of branch-like arms and fingers, and masses of bronze, flailing, rising, rising, leaning forward. Fazzini has almost achieved the impossible. For that zareba of dynamic bronze reminds onlookers both of the branches of an olive tree—the symbol of peace and resurrection—as well as of an atomic explosion and world disintegration.

BISHOPS MEET IN ROME—
DRESS REHEARSAL OF CONCLAVE 82

Pope Paul opens the 5th international Roman Synod in Rome on September 30. There are 204 Delegates, including Bishops, Cardinals, and Patriarchs. There are prelates here from Eastern European satellite countries—Poland, Czechoslovakia, Bulgaria (but not from Hungary)—as well as from Africa, Asia, and the two Americas. There are two from Vietnam: the Cardinal of Hanoi and the Archbishop of Ho Chi Minh City (Saigon). There are also some observers—Protestant and Jewish—and a group of Charismatics invited to Rome by Belgian Cardinal Suenens. Average age of the Delegates this year is five or six years younger than the average age of those who were at the last Synod in 1975.

The topic of the Synod: Catechetics—that is, the teaching of religion—in the world today, with special reference to children and youth. But the subject occupying the attention of anybody important at the Synod is the next Pope and the Conclave. In many ways, this Synod is almost a dress rehearsal for Conclave 82.

Catechetics are discussed from the various points of view that the Delegates bring to the Synod.

The Africans are interested in how to adapt Catholicism to local native ways and mentalities.

The Latin Americans are divided: Some are pushing liberation theology (they are rebuffed severely); some are pushing "democratic socialism" either as a political solution or as a military-political solution (they are also rebuffed); and some are pushing Traditionalism (they do not find very many to support them). But one problem *all* Latin Americans are talking about is how to deal with rising Marxist movements.

Delegates from developed countries bring up problems created by technology and by living conditions higher than are found elsewhere: their countries are in danger of atheism and secularism.

The Eastern European and Asian Delegates are concerned about the lack of freedom of worship, of schooling, of the press.

And most European Delegates are concerned with the specter of Communism hovering on their near-future horizon.

The opening ceremonies, which take place in the Sistine Chapel, are televised and transmitted overseas by satellite. Pope Paul tells the Delegates: "We have been chosen, called and invested by the Lord with a transforming mission. As Bishops, we are the successors of the Apostles." Observers are struck by Paul's use of the term "transforming." This is straight out of Paul's mentor, the late philosopher Jacques Maritain, from whom Paul learned all of his ideas of "integral humanism." It is also a term very much in use by the "new theologians" and the Marxist-minded in the Church, who speak of "transforming human society"—meaning the installation of Marxism in place of capitalism. They no longer speak of "converting" people to their Catholicism or of "preaching the salvation of Jesus"—just "transforming society."

Those acquainted with Paul's proposed reform of Conclave and Church government realize what he is saying: "From now on, our function is to witness, to evangelize ourselves, to stay with all men and women, to become part of their world, to perform services in the social and political field. And just wait." All the Delegates feel complimented at being included with the Pope in Christ's commission to "transform" the world. None of those who come from the Communist dominated nations of Eastern Europe like Paul's address.

Symptomatic of Conclave attitudes and of the deep factional divisions among the Electors is the choice (by vote of the Delegates) of group moderators for Synod workshop discussions: Archbishop Bernardin of Cincinnati (Conservative); Archbishop Denis Hurley of Durban (Progressivist); Archbishop Dermot Ryan of Dublin (Traditionalist); Archbishop Roger Etchegaray of Marseilles—the Pope-maker of Europe, as he is called (Progressivist); Cardinal Marty of Paris (Progressivist); Cardinal Felice of Rome (Traditionalist). Charismatics—some Americans are among them—are to be "available for private meetings between Charismatics and Delegates."

Cardinals and Bishops with left-wing leanings are tremendously encouraged and enlivened in their pre-Conclave electioneering hopes by the address given by Archbishop Van Binh of Ho Chi Minh city. Says the Archbishop trenchantly: "The Vietnamese Catholics are determined to co-exist and flourish with Communists. The Communist regime is seeking to unite all our Vietnamese citizens in the rebuilding of our country. And, thus, we Catholics of Vietnam refuse to live in a ghetto and to remain on the margin of society." Binh concludes: "We Catholics expect shortly to be impregnated with Marxist-Leninist doctrine. But we will remain true Catholics."

Archbishop Franic of Spalato, Yugoslavia, caps all this when he asserts loudly that "Communist atheism is not the real danger." The real danger is: "the moral permissiveness, the eroticism, the drug-addiction, the decadent music, and the violence of Western culture." Words that could have been taken from the proceedings of the 25th session of the Soviet Praesidium. And he adds: "Since 1950, the population of Latin America has increased from 164.4 million to 341.9 million in mid-1977. Is capitalism going to feed them?"

Such speeches have a profound effect on the Italians, Spaniards, French, and Portuguese, faced as they are with the possibility of living under Communist governments in the near future—or at least faced with the choice of such governments.

AMERICANS CRITICIZED, SCORNED
AT ROMAN SYNOD

During the Synod Sessions and informal discussions, many Delegates speak frankly. Cardinal Deardon's behavior over the October CTA meeting at Detroit is called "criminal." Archbishop Bernardin's behavior is called "feckless." The urbane negativity of Archbishop Jadot, Apostolic Delegate to Washington, is termed just that, "urbane negativity," with the motive ascribed "for the sake of his career." The American Bishops as a whole are blamed for not having supervised the election of delegates to the CTA, and for allowing the meeting to fall into the hands of "irreverent ex-nuns, lesbian nuns, unfaithful priests, ignorant layfolk, and crypto-communists."

In addition, the Americans are embarrassed over things such as the resolutions of the Brooklyn, New York, Diocesan priests' Senate (calling for married priests, optional celibacy, etc.) and the survey of Chicago diocese priests (a majority no longer hold with traditional church teaching on birth control, masturbation, and homosexuality). And, then there are documented reports with lists of names of nuns, priests, and some bishops who already belong to the Communist Party in the United States or to front organizations of the Communist Party.

In general, Americans are criticized for being interested in everything: the neutron bomb, the Panama Canal Treaty, national health insurance, environmental pollution, the disposing of atomic wastes, energy consumption—everything, that is, except the things that should be their prime concern, such as the living faith of the people and the soundness of doctrine. One Polish prelate asks: "Now, how could we consider an American *papabile* when most of you don't know any theology and some of you are organizing a little *putsch* of your own?" "From their politicking for the Panama Canal Treaty, you would think that the American Bishops were interested parties in helping U.S. banks retrieve the $2.77 billion in outstanding loans to Panama," was one complaint uttered.

Further, no one can explain to many Europeans and Africans why the American authorities have not yet dismissed Roman Catholic missionaries in

Latin America and Africa who proclaim Marxist revolution—such as Sister Janice McLaughlin, only recently expelled from Rhodesia, who stated: "I support the freedom fighters ... it's impossible to bring about change without war."

And the Africans have a further grumble. Why the strong political stand by the United States Bishops against South Africa? Do they not know, it is asked, that in Africa there are 21 one-party regimes, 13 dictatorships, 6 military dictatorships, and only 12 multiparty states (some of which are de facto one-party states; some of which are in an endless process of "drawing up a new constitution"), and that throughout all these countries, blacks have less liberty and economic well-being than in South Africa? Why grandstand for a political policy that is obviously dictated by purely political motives?

After all is said and done, the Americans proceed to put their feet in it, and display how deep goes their lack of sound doctrine, even on basics. When the revised and final draft of the Synod's conclusion is distributed to the Delegates, some of the Americans object to several elements. They object to speaking of catechesis as a "conversion process." They object to the fact that the draft presents a historical notion of Jesus rather than one of Jesus experienced daily. They object to the short shrift given to social justice and ecumenism—the two planks on which many American Bishops spend their episcopal life and activity.

PRE-CONCLAVE ELECTIONEERING AT SYNOD

The Delegates, Cardinals, and Bishops are busy about the Conclave and Paul's near-future plans. "The Conclave has already started," was one constant comment by observers. Indeed!

High on the *papabili* list stand three Italians (Baggio, Pignedoli, Felice), one Argentinian of Italian extraction (Pironio), and more than one non-Italian.

One Dutchman, Jan Willebrands, the Primate of Holland who also works in Rome, has been on an early *papabili* list. The Primate of England, Cardinal Basil Hume, has also been mentioned. At the present time, both are probably good "straw men"; that is, their names can always be used as outside alternatives, but only as the least of many evils.

Willebrands has his hands full in Holland where Catholicism is less vibrant than it is in the Congo. Besides, Willebrands has not got the breadth of mind required in a Pope. And he seems to be fascinated by anything that non-Catholic Christians do. Many Conservatives cannot abide his type of ecumenism.

The 55-year old Basil Hume's attractiveness as a *papabile* lies uniquely in his background. Born of a distinguished Protestant father, Sir William Hume, and of a French Mother, with a brother-in-law who is Secretary to the British Cabinet, Hume was educated at Oxford and then in Fribourg, Switzerland. As a noted Benedictine Abbot, he became well-liked by Anglican ecumenists. Given Britain's reduced status as a world power, Hume's ecumenical standing gives him a certain stature and appeal: he does not come from "a colonialist super-power." But again, and for different reasons, he will not move onto the primary list of *papabili*. As the doughty Cardinal Ottaviani remarked: "To go from an Italian Cardinal to an Anglo-Saxon would be too much for Europeans and too little for non-Europeans."

The "Pope-maker of Europe," Archbishop Roger Etchegaray of Marseilles, is reportedly seeking a suitable left-wing candidate among the Italians and Europeans. Most of the French Electors now stand on the left.

The American Bishops have rallied with Höffner and the other German Cardinals (Bengsch of Berlin and Ratzinger of Munich) and thus made temporary allies of the Poles as well in their stand against any really left-wing candidate. But the Germans fail to rally the French Cardinals.

Paul is quite active throughout the Synod. He lets it be known that he intends to create more Cardinals shortly. Some will be traditional and therefore obligatory appointments, such as the Irish Archbishop of Armagh; some will be rewards for work well done (as Archbishop Casaroli for his work in Soviet eastern countries); but some, obviously, are meant to create additional Conclave votes in favor of Paul's policies.

SYNOD ENDS DELIBERATIONS ON A NOTE OF UNITY

In spite of deep differences, this 5th International Synod closes on a note of harmony and unity between Pope and Delegates, and between the Delegates themselves.

Cardinal Baggio, himself no mean *papabile*, holds a press conference and tells the journalists that "it is grotesque to have to defend an ecclesial assembly against the charge of having finished its work in harmony." Baggio's remark is aimed primarily at the "new theologians" and the Catholic left-wing intellectuals who continually represent the Bishops of the world as in total contention with the central government of the Church in Rome. They had expected the Bishops and Delegates to revolt during the Synod. They did not.

True, two main thrusts have emerged: one Rightist, that includes Traditionalists, Conservatives, and Radicals; the other, Leftist, that includes Progressivists, "new theologians," and the Marxist-inclined. But the dispute was kept between Delegates and behind closed doors. A compromise was arrived at between the two. The Delegates drew up a 3,000 word message to the People of God. They also submitted 34 propositions to Paul. These described the methods to be employed in instructing Christians in their faith. Paul will use them and the message to produce a Papal document on the whole subject of catechetics. The Americans submitted their own revisions, but they have had no effect.

Between Left and Right, one dispute concerns the meaning to be given to the terms "authentic and complete" doctrine. The Progressivists insist it includes socio-political theory and activism. The others refuse this. The "new theologians" and the liberation theology of the Latin Americans finally get no pride of place. But, there is still no agreement on what "authentic and complete" Christian doctrine means.

CARDINAL ELECTORS HAVE GRAVE DOUBTS ABOUT PAUL'S JUDGMENT AND POLICIES

Several Latin American Cardinals, together with Delegates from Europe and Asia, let Paul know that they cannot back his political outlook on Latin America. It is now clear that, while Paul acts as if he stood with the centrist-reformist position (those who stand here seek to reform abuses in the economic and social systems of Latin America, without replacing the system), he has given a green light to the leftist-reformist position (those who seek to replace capitalism with "democratic socialism"). Paul has no answer to those who point out that the leftist-reformists always side with the "violent terrorists who include guerrillas and terrorists, and who seek total Marxization of Latin America by violent means." This reaction must tell finally in the general pre-Conclave attitude of the Electors.

Among many prelates at the Synod there is a note of profound questioning: Has Paul 6 gone too far? Will he go too far yet? Has he pushed the Church too fast? Who really helps him make decisions that shock the majority of the faithful? Has he let go of too much too suddenly?

As of the end of the Synod, the College of Cardinals had 118 members eligible to vote as Electors of the next Conclave. Of these, only 4 (Siri, Wyszynski, Léger, and Gracias) participated in the election of John 23 at Conclave 80 in 1958; 12 of them (including Rugambwa, König, and Bueno y Monreal) were in Conclave 81 which elected Paul 6 in 1963. So the vast majority of Cardinal Electors in Conclave 82 will enter it without any experience of Pope-making or of Conclave politics. The only stratagem of ecclesiastical politics that most of the Electors know, and will bring to bear on Conclave 82 is the stratagem many of them employed at the Second Vatican Council: Before the event (in this case the Conclave), say "yes" to everything; then proceed to Rome, into Conclave, and overturn all commitments and promises, and by sheer weight of numbers carry the day in favor of what they really want.

CARDINAL ELECTORS AND CONCLAVE PERSONNEL AS OF NOW

The 82-year old Cardinal Luigi Traglia is buried on Thursday, November 24. Pope Paul is present at the funeral. Traglia's death reduces the College of Cardinals to 132. This number includes 34 Italians, 32 Europeans, 23 Latin Americans, 16 North Americans, 10 Africans, 12 Asiatics, and 5 Oceanians. Of these, 118 are eligible to enter Conclave within the calendar year of 1978.

Cardinals may not bring any personal assistants, secretaries, or aides into Conclave with them, except when grave illness necessitates such extra help. The Camerlengo and his Committee are the final judges in each case. Non-Cardinals officially admitted to the Conclave include the Secretary of the Conclave, who is in charge of Conclave documentation; the Vicar of Rome, who is a Bishop and who must witness the Election as the representative of the Pope's diocese; two or more assistants to the Vicar of Rome; the Papal Master of Ceremonies with his assistants in order to ensure due observance of all Conclave and Election rituals; one or more assistants to the Camerlengo to aid him in his duties; about three to five ordinary priests to hear confessions in different languages; two doctors with their assistants; an architect; at least two technicians and, as present plans for Conclave 82 are going, probably three times that number for electronic surveillance and security; two alternating teams of translators to ensure simultaneous translation at the Sessions of Conclave; and whatever other service personnel (carpenters, electricians, plumbers, barbers, a dentist, etc.) are judged as necessary and fit after careful consideration and scrutiny by the Camerlengo and his Committee. In addition to all these there are a couple of laymen who always enter Conclave with the Cardinals. Their duties belong to the secret of the Conclave. All in all, the total population of Conclave comes to something around 200–250 persons.

PRECEDENT-SHATTERING BREAK WITH TRADITION
IS DECIDED UPON ALREADY

It is now certain that with the consent and advice of Pope Paul 6, the decision has been taken not to hold Conclave 82 in the Vatican locale where all Conclaves but one have been held since the sixteenth century.

Traditionally, the Cardinal Electors in Conclave live in the Apostolic Palace overlooking St. Peter's Square, their rooms or "cells" clustered around the Sistine Chapel where all Conclave ceremonies and Sessions were held. There in the Sistine, beneath Michelangelo's long ceiling frescoed with scenes from Creation and Salvation, in full view of Michelangelo's *Last Judgment*, surrounded by paintings from the hands of Botticelli, Pinturicchio, Roselli, Perugino, Signorelli, Della Gatta, Ghirlandaio, Pope after Pope has been elected, usually by direct balloting and sometimes by unanimous acclamation. The history that has been lived in the Sistine overpowers its painting, its fresco, and its sculpture. There tradition was molded, adapted, preserved, asserted, and handed on faithfully.

Now all this is over and done with. In Conclave 82, only pre-Conclave exercises and ceremonies (swearing-in of Cardinal Electors and Conclave participants) and the Preliminary Session of the Conclave will take place in the Sistine. From then on, the working Sessions of Conclave 82 as well as the actual election of the new Pope to succeed Pope Paul 6 will be held in the "Upper Room" of the Nervi. The Cardinal Electors will be bussed morning, afternoon, and evening from the *Domus Mariae* where they will have their living quarters. The *Domus* stands in its own grounds at a distance of a mile or so from the Nervi, is surrounded by a high wall, and has all the conveniences. Security is going to be a problem.

The change, the decision to make the change, and the new locales chosen are just more clues to the anticipatory outlook of Paul 6 and those who today wield Vatican power and who are guiding the Vatican and its Church into the world of the twenty-first century and beyond.

They willingly say goodbye to the ancient setting of Conclaves in the Sistine. The Election result will not be signaled to the outside world by puffs of white smoke from a stove fired with the ballot papers of the Electors. It will be electronically communicated by radar and television image. And the new Pope will give his blessing, not from the front balcony of St. Peter's Basilica overlooking Vatican Hill and the Square and Rome, as has been done up to this time. He will stand on the stage of the Nervi in front of Fazzini's *Resurrection* and, televised instantly to the four quarters of the globe, he will give his blessing and say some short words that will crackle out over the airwaves in simultaneous translation into 14 languages.

"For future elections of Popes, we need an ample space," was Paul's enigmatic reply, when asked why he made this change. The fact is that Paul was acting in this matter as he had acted in previous years on other matters. He banned the Latin Mass, although the Bishops at the Second Vatican Council declared themselves *for* the Latin Mass. He insisted that the priest face the people while saying Mass, although neither Bishops nor people wanted the change. Paul envisions a wholly new way of electing Popes; if not the next Pope, his own successor, then at least the Pope after that. Some who talked with Paul came away with the impression that he was thinking of the earliest Roman elections when all the Christians of Rome gathered in one place and chose their Bishop by acclamation and a primitive voting method.

At a still later date, so Roman rumors run, another candidate for Pope will stand on that stage in the Nervi and be chosen not in Conclave, but by a new, and as yet untried, global system which will be the twenty-first century version of the ancient Christian Roman Church practice when a few hundred gathered to choose their spiritual leader. *Vox populi.* The voice of the people.

Special Bulletin

HOW THE VOTES FALL ON THE EVE OF
CONCLAVE 82

As of late fall 1977, there seems to be a clear majority of Cardinal Electors in favor of what has come to be known as the *General Policy*. In essence this seems to be more or less identical with the Conservative position. It calls for an Italian, but non-Curial, Pope who will admit slow changes in the Church.

Of the 118 Cardinal Electors, there are 28 Italians, 31 Europeans, 18 Latin Americans, 14 North Americans, 10 Africans, 12 Asiatics, and 5 Oceanians. They range in age from 49 (Ribeiro of Portugal, Sin of Manila) to 79 (Shehan of Baltimore, Violardo of Rome). There are 22 in their fifties; over two-thirds are between 63 and 75. If Conclave 82 were not held before December 1978, two (Shehan, Violardo) would be ineligible.

Conclave 82 promises to be one of turmoil for many reasons. The United States Cardinals, for the first time in history, are going to use their weight. There is, for the first time in history, a minority of Italian Cardinals. Apart from anything else, some very powerful personalities of opposing views will participate in the Conclave. Each exercises powerful gifts and commands a strong following.

Luigi Ciappi, the 69-year old Florentine, has spent most of his life in theological studies and the spiritual direction of souls. Indeed, all know he is, before all else, a theologian, a confessor, one of the last real old-time "spiritual directors." All trust him. A member of the Dominican Order, former dean of the theology faculty at the Pontifical Angelicum University of Rome, made a Cardinal only in 1977, the 85th Dominican priest since 1213 to be named Master of the Sacred Palace—the Pope's theologian—Ciappi is also spiritual advisor to Pope Paul 6, a consultant at Villot's Secretariat of State and at the all-powerful *Congregation for the Faith*. Ciappi is ever ascetic, calm in demeanor, prudent in words.

The favorite candidate for the Traditionalists is Pericle Felici. Aged 65, a Vatican career-man, Felici made his name as Secretary-General in the Second Vatican Council. Most people fear Felici. Only some really like him.

97

Not that he is not likeable. But Felici is the oldest and the most experienced Vatican man at dealing with international meetings of Bishops and Cardinals. As Secretary of the Second Vatican Council, and in the teeth of a highly organized, intelligently deployed, and always unscrupulously liberal bloc of Bishops, Felici almost outwitted them all. Not quite! But almost. He wields "the fine Roman hand," as the saying goes. He has many "friends." He is all satin and no visible steel, all sibilance and no gutterals, all peace and hope, no war and no desperation. Even in defeat, Felici rarely loses his coolness of judgment. If the idea of a Traditionalist Pope successor to Paul 6 is seriously entertained, the prime *papabile* will be Felici.

The Conservatives claim for themselves a forward-looking position: gradual and careful change in order to adapt to the changes in modern society, a brake of sorts on the pell-mell changes Pope Paul 6 allowed and imposed. The front-line Conservative *papabile* is Cardinal Sergio Pignedoli, with two runners-up, Cardinals Paolo Bertoli and Sebastiano Baggio.

Sergio Pignedoli, 68 years old, Vatican career-man, has been a Cardinal since 1973. A former Navy Chaplain in World War II, Apostolic Delegate in Africa and Canada, now Prefect of the Vatican Secretariat for Relations with non-Christians, Pignedoli is multilingual, widely traveled, deeply acquainted with Muslim, Buddhist, and Hindu leaders. Pignedoli is considered to be unacceptable to the Traditionalist bloc: They find him too popularity-seeking, too willing to compromise with non-Catholics. The Progressivists do not like him because he will not change fast or furiously enough. But Pignedoli has let everyone know that "adjustments" can be made to accommodate enough of the Traditionalists and Progressivists to achieve a working compromise within the Conservative framework. Pignedoli himself, meanwhile, is more than willing to be elected Pope. And he has been the favorite *papabile* of Paul 6.

The 70-year old Paolo Bertoli is an enigma for most Romans, and quite unknown to most foreign Cardinals. A Vatican career-man, former Papal Nuncio to Paris, Cardinal at the age of 61, Bertoli is only known really for his downright decisiveness. Once, when a preferred employee in Bertoli's Vatican office was replaced with someone not of his choice, Bertoli simply slammed the door and walked right out of his position as head of a powerful Vatican ministry. He now holds several important posts in the Vatican and is a dark horse as Papal candidate. Few people know that Paolo Bertoli is an intensely zealous student of piety and mysticism, and that he enjoys the confidence of statesmen on both sides of the Atlantic. Bertoli could not care less what people think.

A Conservative runner-up with far less chance is the 64-year-old Baggio. Former Papal Nuncio to Chile and Brazil, former Apostolic Delegate to Canada, and former Archbishop of Sardinia, Baggio is now head of the powerful Vatican ministry, the *Congregation for Bishops*. The stocky, square-faced, charming, shrewd, Venetian Baggio, has an incomparable acquaintanceship with the Bishops of the Church, because each Bishop has to pay a visit to Rome every five years, and each one must pass through Baggio's office. He also has wide acquaintance with Latin America and its problems. Baggio is distrusted by the Traditionalists, has a weak reputation as a theologian, and would probably follow through on the policies of Paul 6.

The present working majority behind Pignedoli as the front-runner Conservative is rather formidable and, as of Fall 1977 it somewhat exceeds the two-thirds plus one majority needed for a valid Conclave election of a Pope. But that majority is not arrived at in a simple, direct way. For, in themselves, the Cardinal Electors are divided into four main groups, none of which commands the needed majority. The Conservatives could assure themselves of a working majority in the Fall of 1977 on the basis of foreseen and much discussed compromises.

Before any compromise and working alliance, the Traditionalists are 50 in number: far short of the two-thirds plus one majority.

Conservatives, in themselves, are no better off, with only 35 basically guaranteed votes, the Conservatives also lack a commanding majority.

The remaining Electors are divided into 26 Progressivists and 7 Radicals. Schematically, therefore, the blocs are:

Traditionalists	50
Conservatives	35
Progressivists	26
Radicals	7
	118

The catalyst for this no-win situation is the ever-rising pressure from the Progressivist Roman Catholic Bishops and priests in Europe, in Latin America and, to a far lesser degree, in the United States. There is the possibility of an alliance between Conservatives and Progressivists, giving a simple majority of 61. In the backing-and-forthing of Conclave electioneering, it would be relatively easy for a simple majority of 61 to pick up the remaining 18 votes required for a two thirds plus one majority.

To offset this possibility, Traditionalists (50) would be willing to make a compromise with Conservatives (35), thus producing more than the absolute majority needed for election. The chief point on which Traditionalists are willing to compromise is the ecclesiastical character of the next Pope: He would be an Italian but a non-Curial man (i.e., not a member of any Roman Ministry), and a non-Roman (i.e., not pro-Curia in his sympathies).

If necessary, the Conservatives will consent to back a non-Italian European—the so-called pan-European *papabile*. Such a candidate would split the Progressivists, reducing their number to at least half its present strength. Only in dire straits and in real danger of seeing the Conclave swing violently to the Left will the Traditionalists support a pan-European candidate.

The most likely pan-European candidate is a Dutchman, Cardinal Jan Willebrands. He is a 69-year-old, round-faced, bespectacled, balding Dutchman who is trusted by Traditionalists, Progressivists, Conservatives, and Radicals—mainly because he offends none. He can be a guarantor of Progressivist orthodoxy while a permissive father for the experimentation of far-out Progressivist ideas. For 15 years he headed the Vatican's Ecumenism center, the *Secretariat for Christian Unity*. A Cardinal of nine-years' standing, appointed Primate of Holland in 1976, he has been nicknamed the "Flying Dutchman": He still functions at Rome's Ecumenism center, while commuting as Primate of Holland. Willebrands has balanced delicately between his functions as Primate of the Dutch Church, which is in practical schism from Rome, and his function as Vatican insider enjoying the confidence of Pope Paul and many Progressivist Italians.

Coming up more and more frequently in conversation as a possible dark horse is Giovanni Benelli. Nicknamed by his enemies the "Gauleiter," the "Cossack," "Il Duce," "the Hangman," Benelli had been extremely powerful as sub-Secretary of State under Villot, and had axed many a hotbed of political patronage, feather-bedding, and cronyism in the Vatican bureaucracy. It was Benelli who was responsible for the removal of Monsignore Bugnini, once a strong hand in Vatican affairs concerning Liturgy and worship. Even then, Bugnini's friends were so powerful and Benelli's enemies so strong, that Pope Paul could take no stronger action against Bugnini than to send him as Apostolic Delegate to the Shah's Teheran, a plum in the diplomatic job-list. But, at least he was banished from any sensitive Vatican post.

This proved to be the beginning of Benelli's downfall. Vulnerable as a known sympathizer of Archbishop Lefebvre, in opposition to Villot, and vulnerable as the one who had brought down Bugnini, Benelli as simple Archbishop and Vatican aide finally fell prey to his persistent and powerful enemies. There was no way even the Pope could protect Benelli's position in Rome. In fact, only the Pope's unilateral and unexpected action prevented Benelli from being exiled and nullified forever. Paul made Benelli Cardinal and Archbishop of Florence. Benelli, Paul reasoned, still had a chance to come back. He was near Rome, and he would have a vote in Conclave. "Benelli will have his day, of course," Paul had told Villot.

Benelli, at Paul's instigation, set out to recreate the idea of a unified

Europe. Success in this effort may be Benelli's last milestone on his way to the Papacy.

The formation of the Progressivist and the Radical blocs is of such a recent date that no one Cardinal Elector has emerged as the leader of Progressivist or of Radicals. Reports in Rome would seem to indicate that a "dark horse" is the prime organizer both of Progressivists and Radicals. Although no one is sure, the name of one African Elector is mentioned as the Progressivists leader, while the name of an Anglo-Saxon Cardinal is brought up as the true organizer of the Radicals.

Special Bulletins—
From the Death of Paul 6 to the
Opening of Conclave 82

WHEN THE POPE DIES

When Pope Paul 6's doctors declare him medically dead, the interim government of the Vatican falls to one Cardinal who from then on is addressed as the Camerlengo of the Universal Church at that moment. He will remain in charge, organizing a caretaker government, until the next Pope is elected.

As Camerlengo he approaches the cadaver lying in the Pope's bedroom. He is accompanied by two other Cardinals, flanked by other Vatican officials, and watched by representatives of the Italian State and international diplomatic corps. He taps the dead Paul's forehead three times with a silver hammer, and asks each time: "Giovanni Battista, are you dead?" When he receives no answering sign, the Camerlengo intones the phrase: "Pope Paul is truly dead." This is the age-old ritual at a Pope's death.

He then removes the Fisherman's Ring from the fourth finger of Paul's right hand. It is broken, together with all of Paul's seals of office, so that no one can use them to authenticate a false document.

An official death certificate is drawn up by a Papal secretary. The Cardinal Camerlengo locks the private apartments of the dead Pope. With a small committee of Cardinals, he assumes charge of all Vatican affairs. He arranges the burial of Paul and the Conclave at which Paul's successor will be elected. Summonses are sent out to all the Cardinal Electors, announcing the death of the Pope and declaring the official opening date of Conclave 82 at which Pope Paul's successor will be chosen by the Electors. The Conclave must begin, at the latest, 20 days from the day on which the previous Pope dies.

During nine days of official mourning, all Vatican flags are flown at half mast. The five bells of St. Peter's take up a traditional mourning cadence, tolling for hours on end each day and into the night. Vatican attendants prepare the body for burial, washing and embalming it. It is then taken to St. Peter's Basilica where it lies in state in the nave of the Basilica on a crimson-trimmed bier watched over by Papal Swiss Guards. Later it is brought to the apse where the triple Papal coffin (one of cypress wood inside one of cedar wood inside one of bronze) awaits it.

When nine days of official mourning are over, a Requiem Mass is sung in St. Peter's attended by all Cardinals in Rome, by the diplomatic corps, by government representatives, and by tens of thousands of Roman Catholics. "Eternal rest grant unto him, O Lord" is the refrain of the obsequies. One Vatican official pronounces a public eulogy. The dead Pope's broken ring and seals, and three velvet bags containing samples of all coins issued during his Pontificate, are placed in the coffin with the body. The *sampetrini,* the attendants at St. Peter's, close the three coffins with gilt nails. The Camerlengo and his assistants seal the last coffin. It is then lowered by pulleys to the crypt beneath the marble floor of the Basilica and placed in the sarcophagus that already carries the dead Pope's name. Some yards away, in the same crypt, is the tomb of Simon Peter.

CLOTHES FOR THE NEW POPE

For the new Pope who will be elected at the Conclave, Vatican tailors prepare three sets of vestments: large, medium, and small sets of white cassocks, white slippers embroidered with a gold cross, white skull caps, red rochets, red cloaks, and red stoles.

THE CARDINAL ELECTORS OF THE CONCLAVE TAKE OATH TO EXCLUDE ALL OUTSIDE INTERFERENCE OR INFLUENCE ON THEIR VOTE FOR POPE

On the opening day of Conclave 82, the Cardinals assist at the morning Mass of the Holy Spirit in the Pauline Chapel, which is part of the main Vatican building adjacent to Saint Peter's Basilica. Afterward they disperse, some back to their hotels or their apartments in the Vatican, some to meetings and caucuses, some to go sightseeing.

In the afternoon, they again assemble in the Sistine Chapel, together with the service personnel of the coming Conclave. Alone, without any outsiders in the Chapel, they listen while the Cardinal Dean reads Part II of the *Special Constitution* drawn up and promulgated by Pope Paul 6 on October 1, 1975. Its title: *Concerning the Method of Electing the Roman Pontiff.* The seven chapters of this Part II contain approximately 5,600 words in Latin. The Cardinal Dean reads every word of it to the Cardinals.

When he has finished the reading, the Cardinal Dean reads out loud in Latin the fixed formula of the solemn Conclave oath:

"Each and all of us, Cardinal Electors, gathered in this Conclave, promise, vow, and swear a solemn and sacred oath that each and all of us will observe all prescriptions and laws which are contained in the Apostolic Constitution of the Supreme Pontiff, Paul 6, which was promulgated by him on October 1, 1975, and which begins with the words 'In Electing the Roman Pontiff. . . .'

"We also vow and swear that whoever of us, under God's providence, shall be elected, we shall vindicate and protect for him the spiritual and temporal rights and liberty of the Holy See. And, if necessary, that we will keep on for ever vindicating those rights and liberty.

"Moreover, we particularly promise and swear that we will maintain secret from everyone, including all Conclave personnel and Conclave aides, all matters pertaining in any way whatsoever to the election of the Roman Pontiff; also, all matters which directly or indirectly concern the voting in Conclave or in the place of election; and that we will never in any way violate that secret, either during the Conclave or even after the election of a new Pontiff—unless that same future Pontiff gives a specific permission or a certified dispensation from the secret.

"In the same way, we will never accept the task of proposing a veto or an exclusionary clause against any candidate, in any shape or form—even in the form of a simple wish—on behalf of anybody else or of any civil or political or other authority. Nor shall we ever disclose that we have or know of a veto or exclusionary clause, no matter how we come to know of it. Nor shall we give any help to any such intervention or request or wish, or to any other move by worldly powers and authorities of any grade or status or to any group of people or to any individual who would like to be involved in the election of the Pontiff."

When the Cardinal Dean has finished reciting this solemn Conclave oath in a loud voice, each Cardinal stands up, comes forward, and states in an audible voice: "And I, Cardinal _____ so vow and swear." Then, laying his right hand on a copy of the Gospels, he adds: "So help me God and this Gospel of God which I touch with my hand."

*CARDINAL ELECTORS ARE TOLD WHAT THEY ARE
EXPECTED TO DO IN CONCLAVE 82*

The Electors and Conclave personnel are then joined by members of the diplomatic corps, invited heads of State, invited guests. They all listen to a special sermon—the *Exhortation*—concerning the duties of the Electors in this particular Conclave 82. The Cardinal who gives the *Exhortation* is chosen for his speaking ability as well as for the reputation he enjoys among his brother Cardinals for holiness, learning, and understanding.

The *Exhortation* preceding Conclave 82 will proceed somewhat in the following fashion:

"My Most Eminent and Most Reverend Lord Camerlengo! My Most Eminent and Beloved Brothers, My Lord Cardinals! Most Reverend Bishops and Monsignori! Beloved Priests and Brothers and Sisters! Most Distinguished Gentlemen and Ladies! My dearest Christian brothers and sisters!

"Just twenty-one days ago, the Universal Church and all of us enjoyed the presence of Our Most Beloved and Eminent and Holy Lord, His Holiness Pope Paul 6 of most gracious memory. And, since then, the good Lord Jesus has seen fit to call His Holiness home for judgment, for reward, and for eternal peace.

"Your humble servant was privileged to be with His Holiness in his last hours. And whatever I here communicate of His Holiness' last thoughts, I do so with the sure knowledge that such was His Holiness' will and desire.

"His Holiness wished most of all, to most humbly beg pardon of all Your Eminences, of all Your Reverences, for any hurt or pain His Holiness may have caused any one during his pontificate, either by thoughts, by words, or by actions. And, when expressing this sorrow, His Holiness asked that you remember, not the pain or disappointment or hurt caused you, but the forgiveness of our Lord Jesus, which—I can assure Your Eminences—Pope Paul humbly sought on his deathbed, and which, I am sure under God's providence, His Holiness received. So? Why should we not imitate Our Lord Jesus in this matter of forgiveness—as indeed we are supposed to imitate Him in everything?

"This is not the place or the occasion to speak in praise or appraisal of His Holiness. Others will do that at future times. If his Holiness enters into the theme of my *Exhortation,* it can only be in so far as His Holiness is bound up with that *Exhortation*'s proper theme—the duties of the Most Eminent

Cardinal Electors—of whom I am, unworthily, one, in this Conclave 82 which is about to begin.

"In one respect, My Brothers, we enter this Conclave both clear-minded and unconfused. We know our duty: to choose a worthy successor to Peter the Apostle and to Pope Paul of happy memory. To choose him so carefully and with such personal detachment that, at the end of our labors—for labors they shall be, I think—we can truly announce to the Universal Church and to the world of men and women and children around us: 'It has seemed good to the Holy Spirit and to us to choose a Vicar of the Lord Jesus. ... We have a Pope!'

"But in other respects, we are just as confused as any of our contemporaries. For, like them, but with a bitter sharpness they never undergo, we are buffeted by cruel winds and harried by ill-tempered events that brook no delay and threaten to carry us and our beloved Church off in directions we know must surely lead to shipwreck of our hopes and extinction of our precious faith.

"My own small contribution as the one chosen to give this pre-Conclave *Exhortation* is intended to help Your Eminences in our difficult task. It is the fruit of my study and reflection on our long, laborious history. And if there is one lesson that leaps out at me over and over again from the pages of that history, it is that, time and time again, this institutional Church, which was founded by Jesus, which survived the catacombs, which was placed on a pinnacle by the Emperor Constantine, and which has survived for all those centuries, that this Church has been brought by uncontrollable human events to a very dangerous brink, to a sheer, steep cliff of decision on more than one occasion. Unfailingly, each time, the Churchmen at the head of affairs shied away from one stark decision. But still, time and again, the Church is brought back to face that decision. Until now, in Conclave 82, we may face it for the final time. And, believe, me, all that I say of those good men who have come before us, and who have all gone to God, I say without any intention of reproach or of condemnation.

"But, let me give you some ordinary examples. Pope Leo 3 in the eighth century was, for a variety of reasons, brought to the point that he no longer could exercise any temporal power at all; any financial power, any military power, any diplomatic power, any political power. Did he then renounce all claims to his temporal power and rely solely on the power and authority of Jesus? That power Jesus promised when he said to Simon: 'You are Peter. To you I give the Keys of the Kingdom of Heaven,' as the Gospel relates? Did he?

"No. His Holiness, Leo 3 of happy memory, did not. He fled as a fugitive on horseback to Paderborn, knelt and kissed the hand of the Emperor

Charlemagne who then proceeded to reinstall Pope Leo in even fuller exercise of all that worldly power.

"The hard decision—to rely solely on the power of spirit and of Jesus—that hard decision had been refused.

"A little over six hundred years later, at the Council of Constance, the representatives and rulers of six major European nations gathered to reform the Church which had been wracked and ruined by the disputes of Popes and anti-Popes. But the main proposal in front of everybody's mind was simple: Let us once and for all rid the Papacy and the Church of Jesus of its temporal power, since it was precisely through that power that the Church has been wracked by a series of devastating wars, diseases, famines, massacres, cruelties, desecrations, anti-Popes, anti-Synods, anti-Cardinals, hate, bloodshed, torture, infidelities, and the believers of the Church have been scandalized and confused.

"What happened?

"No sooner was Pope Martin 5 of happy memory elected Pope than he and his Curia of Cardinals dissolved the Council—in virtue of his supreme power as Pope. And in spite of the general wish for reform, Pope Martin of happy memory returned to Rome where he again reassembled all the elements of Papal temporal power. Remark well! At this time, there had been no Reformation, no Martin Luther, no revolt, no splintering of Christian unity! If a harsh decision could have been faced, think of the greater harshness—the pain, bloodshed and suffering—that would have been avoided.

"But the hard, hard decision was refused once more. The Pope could only envisage his spiritual authority within the framework of land, money, diplomatic prestige, and political clout.

"Almost one hundred years later, in the middle of Luther's revolt, Pope Clement 7 found himself stripped completely of all that temporal power, and under siege in Castel San Angelo together with a few weeping Cardinals. Their tears were for the loss of their grandeur to the conquering Imperial Armies that had occupied the Vatican and Rome and Italy and Europe. The Vatican with its Treasury, the states and properties of the Pope in Rome, in Italy, in Sicily, in France, and elsewhere, were all in the hands of an irresistible sacriligious, armed enemy.

"Again, it was suggested that all would be well if His Holiness and his Curia would renounce all the temporal power they had lost.

"What happened?

"Pope Clement signed an agreement to pay for his own ransom and thus to escape from San Angelo. From outside Rome, he again assembled enough money, prestige, and armaments—in short, enough temporal power—so that eventually he was restored to his throne. And he handed on to his successor a Church whose spiritual authority again relied on temporal power.

"The hard, hard decision was again refused. No Pope could bring himself willingly to rely for his authority solely on the promise of our Lord Jesus.

"I would tire Your Eminence and all my dearest listeners if I were to go over in great detail the other examples. But did not His Holiness Pius 6 of happy memory and His Holiness Pope Pius 7 of happy memory face the same decision? And did they not fight tooth and nail, and successfully, for that temporal power? And was not that a refusal on their part—all in good conscience, of course—to take that very, very hard decision?

"And when His Holiness Pius 9 of holy and happy memory refused to leave the Vatican in 1870, thus becoming instead its famed 'Prisoner,' was he not also refusing to take that hard decision?

"And, even when in 1929, His Holiness Pope Pius 11 of blessed memory signed the Lateran Concordat with the Italian Government, renouncing the Papal power lost in 1870 and accepting huge financial indemnities for those losses, was he not also refusing the same hard decision?

"In sum, insofar as Popes and Churchmen have insisted on wrapping the exercise of their spiritual power—that power of Peter—in the panoply and panache and might of money, diplomacy, political influence, and vested interests, have they not all of them refused that hard, hard, very, very hard decision?

"And, My Brother Cardinals, have not we, each one of us, tasted that power one way or another? And is it not sweet to the taste? And is it not difficult to relinquish? And is it not very easy to rationalize it, and to conclude that it is a felt necessity for our spiritual mission—when in reality we know in our heart of hearts that it degrades, makes impure, and finally divagates our spiritual intentions? Eh? Is it not so?

"A difficult question, My Brothers! And a painful question, My Brothers! But a question we must ask. A question we must answer. Without any denigration of that long line of illustrious men, all 262 of them—for I omit the Blessed Apostle Peter from my remarks—who were called by Jesus to be his Vicars, and who died with the vision of the Crucified in front of their eyes and in their spirits. No! No denigration!

"But let us hear their voices now speaking to us with all the wisdom of centuries' hindsight, and with the unflawed illumination from the Light of the eternal God's own face. For, My Brothers, we have very few alternatives today, surrounded as we are by new structures and unheard-of adjustments in our modern world.

"New forms of life are coming into existence around us—all of them shot through with a new mental, psychical, and spiritual outlook. And, as they take their place in the skein of human society, the dark-faced angels of despair, of rage, of impotence, of atheism, of mercilessness, wrap each one of them in gloom and threat, so that they are confused at each juncture by double knots of doubt and fear.

"For us, Electors, our common task is to strip off those wrappings, unravel those knots, discover new resurrections for the Church, and reveal new joys for all the sons and daughters of our common and Universal Father, God the Awesome, God the Loving.

"The voices of all past Popes and Saints say to us now, surely: 'Listen not to the voice of the banker, not to the voice of the broker, not to the voice of the prince-bishop or the ambitious Cardinal, not to the dynastic family, not to the money-changers, not to the monopoly-managers, but to the voice of Jesus speaking from the masses of our human family. You, our descendants in spirit, have compassion on the errors we made, and imitate us in what we should have done, and not in what we did.'

"Make no mistake, Most Eminent Brethren! That very hard decision so often offered, so often refused, comes up once more today. It stands stock still on the doorstep of Conclave 82, ringing insistently, demanding to be allowed in, to be answered.

"If we do not allow it entry, then we leave the great God Himself standing on time's doorstep, where He will wait patiently for another generation and a subsequent race of men and women. For this has been God's decision in the Lord Jesus: to be with us humans and to remain with us until He finally splinters the husk of time in which our Church's history and the whole human story has been wrapped, and this world ceases.

"But, if we were to act in that way, we would have failed. We will be forgiven surely. But we will have failed. For, more than any of the superpowers, more than any other institution on earth, we have to answer those devastating queries human beings are now asking us: 'Are you people *really* the messengers of the Holy Spirit? Have you people your own weapons of *spirit?* Your own *moral* power? Or are you merely more than ordinarily clever power-brokers, preying on our hopes, capitalizing on our broken dreams? We know whom you say Jesus was. But tell us: Who are *you? What* are you?' Thus, the hard, hard queries of our contemporaries.

"If, however, we open the door of our Conclave, and admit that hard decision among us, if we allow it entry in our midst, we will most certainly have hard thoughts to think, hard words to exchange with each other, hard actions to discuss and contemplate.

"If we persevere, My Eminent Brothers, in the mystery of innocent trust, and with the power of enthusiasm, we will be able to turn to our world in all its confusion of peace and war, of birth and death, of love and hate, hope and despair, of joy and sorrow, of youth and old age, turn to it and say: 'We have the Good News for you and for ourselves! Listen to us, please!'

"And we will tell them in accents they will understand and in words they will not doubt: 'Whatever Jesus touches has meaning. And he has touched us all. Each one of us. And our Church. And this Vatican. And this Rome. And Italy. And this human universe. We are not sown into time like so much corn. And this universe is not adrift on seas themselves adrift in ever vaster oceans that wallow in their turn among fathomless deeps. For the Word was made Flesh and dwelt among us. And all Flesh has seen His glory.'

"May the good Lord bless us all. I have finished.

"Amen."

FINAL CEREMONIES CUT CARDINAL ELECTORS OFF FROM OUTSIDE WORLD

After the *Exhortation,* everyone moves from the Sistine to the Pauline Chapel. There, the service personnel of the Conclave are sworn in. Their oath of office concerns the secret of the Conclave and the performance of their duties. In the presence of all the Cardinal Electors, and of the visitors, each one of the personnel and participants comes forward singly and swears:

"I _____ promise and swear to perform my duties diligently and religiously, according to the rules laid down by the Supreme Pontiffs and the norms drawn up by the Sacred College of Cardinals."

Then, laying his hand on the Gospels, he adds: "So help me God and this Holy Gospel which I touch with my hand."

The Cardinal Electors and Conclave personnel then remain in the Pauline Chapel while all visitors and guests are asked to leave. The Camerlengo, with three other Cardinals at his side, makes sure that no unauthorized persons remain. At the same time, across St. Peter's Square in the "Upper Room" of the Nervi, and at the *Domus Mariae* about a mile away, the same precautions are taken by officials delegated by the Camerlengo and his *ad hoc* Committee of Governing Cardinals. The electronic surveillance officials also check all three locations.

The Conclave is not officially and legally in existence until all three places are secure and the Camerlengo has personally received word from the Nervi and the *Domus Mariae* confirming that no unauthorized person or persons are within the limits of the Conclave area in the Nervi and the *Domus Mariae*, and that the surveillance teams are satisfied that all is secure. The Cardinal Electors may then leave the Chapel to await a warning bell announcing to them that within twenty minutes the Preliminary Session of Conclave 82 will be held in the Sistine.

THE FINAL CONCLAVE

The Opening Evening

On the first evening of Conclave 82, as soon as all the Conclave personnel have taken the oath to preserve the secrecy of the Conclave, the Camerlengo has a few short words to say to them before they gather in the Preliminary Session. In quiet, distinctly pronounced Latin, he says simply: "My Lord Cardinals, we have about twenty minutes before our preliminary meeting which, as you know, will be held in the Sistine Chapel. Let us commence our work with trust in God's blessing and guidance. I hope that your accommodations are to your satisfaction, and that our daily assemblies in the Nervi Hall will be fruitful and rapid." He glances at the young Monsignore at his side. "Monsignore will be here constantly to help you in any way possible."

Except for rare occasions in Conclave Sessions, that measured and quiet tone of voice is the unwritten rule of Conclave talk and behavior. Low-key. Unhurried. Confident. Dispassionate. Understated. In contrast, outside the Sessions, Electors will communicate as they wish—vehemently, passionately.

Now, as the Camerlengo finishes, the Cardinals start to leave the Chapel and gather outside its main doors. As they do, the Conclave bell rings with a sharp middle-pitched tone; it is now 6:45 P.M. In a quarter of an hour the opening gathering of Conclave 82 will take place.

Outside in the wide corridor, flanked by high frescoed walls and ceiling, the Cardinals tarry a while. Most of them have studied their schedule. One or two ask a neighbor what the bell means, but mostly as a means of relieving tension or breaking the ice. Cardinals Kand, Franzus and Ni Kan move up to the Camerlengo who has stopped to chat with Delacoste and Borromini. The three have something to ask the Camerlengo. Delacoste and Borromini leave. Bending down from his gawky height to listen to the three Cardinals, the Camerlengo nods vigorously. Then he bows in the general direction of all, gives a quick look of recognition to a few better-known faces, nods to his young assistant Monsignore who will stay and answer queries, and then disappears down the corridor to his own quarters, followed by Kand, Franzus and Ni Kan.

Two or three small groups of Cardinals stay chatting. Calder and Eakins of

115

the United States are with Bonkowski of Poland. A group of Latin Americans—Lynch and Ribera among them—are talking excitedly with the Spanish Cardinals. Over in one corner, Hopper of Africa and some British Commonwealth Cardinals—Hartley and Copley—are listening to Coutinho and the other Indians, Chera, Desai, Constable. The Italians are in small knots of six or seven around two or three key figures—old, battlesome Riccioni, the ebullient Lombardi, and Domenico of Rome.

Gradually, as everyone drifts off, the young Monsignore is left alone there, the silence growing around him. When all are gone, he opens one of the doors into the Sistine Chapel to check once more that all is ready. He smiles as he notices the slight figure kneeling at the righthand side of the Altar. "Domenico!" he murmurs to himself. "Who else!"

He closes the door quietly and walks off down the corridor to the Camerlengo's office.

Outside in the Courtyard of San Damaso, two guards on duty walk back and forth in front of the main doors that lead to the Sistine Chapel area. At the Courtyard entrance, Prince Chigi, Marshall of the Conclave, gives final instructions to his aides. The white and yellow Papal flag has been lowered since the death of Paul 6, and will not be raised again until the new Pope is named some two or three days from now. The Chigi family flag flies in its place. Prince Chigi enters a limousine waiting nearby and departs through the arch of the courtyard gate, across St. Peter's Square, over the Tiber by San Angelo Bridge, and on to the Chigi Palace and dinner.

At the upper end of the Square, near the steps of St. Peter's, a crowd of tourists—sightseeing Romans, nuns, priests, some TV camera crews with their equipment—still linger as though unwilling to see the end of the excitement and the pomp of the Conclave opening. High up in a rented apartment on the Via della Conciliazione, which leads directly into St. Peter's Square, two men sit at a table console, now and again turning a knob, and listening to the radio transmission. After a few minutes, one of them rises, goes to the telephone and rings a number. When he gets an answer, he says merely: "Contact is established and continuous. Control is exact."

In the city, nightlife is starting. The restaurants in the Piazza Navona and along the Via Veneto are filling up with people. Up around the Spanish Steps and along the Corso, the boy pickpockets and the teenage prostitutes mingle with the strolling crowds. Abroad, Papal Nuncios and Delegates in Washington, London, Paris, Buenos Aires, and other capitals inform their host governments that the Conclave has begun. Radio, television, and newspapers around the world announce the same message.

Quiet envelops St. Peter's and the Apostolic Palace. Cardinal Domenico prays in the Sistine. "Lord Jesus, look on us all mercifully. You promised to be with us for all days and that all the forces of Satan would not destroy your Church. Help us now. Help your Church. We cannot help ourselves. We do not know what to do. We lack the insight of love and the greatness of humility. Those who should be our brothers are our enemies. Those we should shun are our allies. Help us, Lord Jesus. Help us all. Help our brothers. Help those whom we do not help but merely use. Help us, Lord Jesus. ...."

The young Monsignore reaches the Camerlengo's office. Kand and Ni Kan have already gone. They and Cardinal Franzus had all arrived in Rome barely in time for the start of Conclave and, unlike most of the other 118 Cardinal Electors, had not received all the *Position Papers* before their arrival. Kand did not receive them because the Vatican knows it cannot depend on anything remaining confidential in his Communist country; Ni Kan, because of a prolonged absence from Hong Kong and Taiwan during which he could not be reached—the rumor is that he undertook a secret mission to Peking for Pope Paul; Franzus, because the Vatican did not trust him wholly.

Kand and Ni Kan have taken their copies of the *Position Papers* from the Camerlengo and gone to heed his advice: "Go and read them with some other Cardinals who have had time to peruse them carefully; in this way you can get the bones of each *Paper* before the First Session in the morning."

Only Franzus has remained behind. As he enters the room, the Monsignore detects a little heat. Franzus is asking the Camerlengo for "the other reports." Heat in the grave decorum of the Conclave is detectable by the rigid politeness of extreme formality and the unsmiling eyes of adversaries.

The Camerlengo regrets he has no other reports to give the Most Eminent Cardinal.

In that case, what the other Most Eminent Electors are saying must be inaccurate.

"Well, then, if we understand each other. ..." There is no need for the Camerlengo to finish the sentence, except to give his smile, well-known in Rome—it speaks volumes and conceals volumes.

Franzus does not smile. But his tone is always measured. "I understand exactly and precisely."

The Camerlengo knows that this is only a preliminary to round one with Franzus and others. "It has started already," the Monsignore hears him mutter after Franzus has left.

The 6:55 P.M. warning-bell rings. The young Monsignore goes out. He will signal the Camerlengo when all the Electors are present in the Chapel.

The Sistine Chapel is well-lit by six extra lamps introduced for the occasion. As the Cardinals take their seats, there is a quiet but very apparent sensation of excitement and gusto. Most have never been in Conclave before. The few who have had that experience undergo a certain foreboding. The stakes are high, much higher this time than before.

The lines of seated Cardinals beneath the huge ceiling of the Sistine are not dwarfed by the enormous height but rather seem set there as if all the beauty and dignity and awesomeness of that Chapel were made to encase them forever. Each Cardinal Elector settles down, gazes quietly around, now and again looking up toward the High Altar, gesturing in recognition to some friend or glancing at the walls. The purple and white robes that each of them wears seem the most natural accompaniments to the cascading hues and tints of Michelangelo's frescoes of God creating Adam, of the Deluge, of Eve's Creation, of the Last Judgment, and of Godhead.

The Preliminary Session

Shortly after 7:00 P.M., the Camerlengo enters accompanied by two Cardinal-Assistants. All stand. The young Monsignore remains outside, closes and locks the doors, and sits down at a small table to wait and watch. He can hear nothing of the proceedings inside.

The Camerlengo goes to the center of the sanctuary at the far end of the Chapel, kneels for a moment before the High Altar, then rises and goes to his seat at the center of the Presidents' long table placed facing the Cardinals.

More than one Camerlengo emerging from earlier Conclaves has told of this moment: of the effect that first glimpse of the assembled Cardinals has had on him. All eyes are upon him. He has arranged this Conclave. He, as no other man, knows the interests, the passions, the issues at stake. He has made necessarily arbitrary decisions that will affect the course of the Conclave, and so of the Church of Jesus, in many ways.

The Camerlengo's Conclave is unlike most recent ones in some important respects. The robes of the Cardinals are the same. It is the faces that are different. Black, white, yellow. And their minds are different. But even in ordinary Conclaves, it is the concentration of responsibility that suddenly strikes the Camerlengo, as he faces "his" Conclave in its first moments. In 1939, when Cardinal Pacelli, as Camerlengo, turned to face the Cardinals, they saw beads of perspiration forming on the forehead of that experienced, arrogant, and utterly self-confident Vatican diplomat.

Odd, one would think, for men so used to power. But Conclave is different, even for such men as these. "Nothing, for that moment," wrote Cardinal

Antonelli in the nineteenth century, "nothing stands between us and the Lord Jesus. All our lives we have someone above us—our parents, the priest, the Superior, the Cardinal, the Pope. But now, nobody. Until we have a Pope, this is it. And we are it. An appeal from us for help can reach no higher authority. We stand at the brink of the chasm between what is human and what is divine."

The Camerlengo stands now before the Cardinals who, as they wait for him to speak, see above his head the figure of Jesus coming in the *Last Judgment* as Michelangelo painted it. The Camerlengo betrays his feelings only by a little tic at the left corner of his mouth. He now has a maximum of fifteen or twenty minutes to get things moving. This preliminary meeting is not a Conclave Session. It is meant to introduce the Conclave, its issues and its main candidates. The Camerlengo goes through the documents, schedules, and the list of *Position Papers* already in the Electors' possession, quickly noting for the assembly any minor changes, apologizing for any inconveniences in their living quarters, and going over some practical matters such as provision for special diets, the names of the priest-confessors at the Electors' disposal, the activities of the surveillance technicians who will be found at irregular periods checking the security.

There then follows his formal presentation of this Conclave 82 and its issues. It is in part a review of what most Cardinal Electors know already. And, in part, it is an expression of his own conclusions as Camerlengo.

"Within the last few months, Most Reverend Lord Cardinals, there has been general agreement on some important headings, all of which makes our task perhaps a little easier here." He glances down at his agenda page. "As you can see from the *Position Papers* on the state of the world and from the *General Framework Paper,* we have what we can call a common outlook based on a relentless and reliable analysis of the Church's condition. Where we differ—divided in no less than five ways, unfortunately but not irreparably—is how to deal with this condition. No agreement has been possible on this point, hitherto.

"Now, as Your excellencies know, there are three *Position Papers* drawn up exclusively by us here in Rome, outlining my own recommendations on the basis of our information and experience. One of these Papers concerns the events and the major consequences of the Pontificate of my Reverend Lord, Pope Paul 6. The second sums up what we see in hindsight is the total effect until now of the Second Vatican Council and its decrees. This second is naturally, logically I might say, intertwined with the first *Paper* on Pope Paul's reign, since His Holiness presided during the years just following the Council. The third *Paper* details what we in Rome see as the dominant movement of our age. I would wish all of us, Reverend Brothers, to have read these *Papers* thoroughly before the First Session tomorrow. Back-up documentation may be had on request.

"As for candidates, we are acquainted with the initial listing of nine candidates as of 1975. That list has been reduced—reasonably, I think—to five. And my Lord Cardinals Masaccio, Vasari, Yiu, Ferro, and Lowe are the names the majority of you agreed should be put forward as most likely to obtain the necessary majority for election. All this without prejudice to the possibility that the Holy Spirit will inspire us all to elect still another as the next Pontiff. For, in our present condition of mind, even if we took six ballotings right now, you all know as well as I do that we would not reach an agreement. Again, that fundamental point divides us: how to deal with the present crisis. For crisis it is." He pauses, then corrects himself. "At least for a large majority of Electors." His eyes light for a brief second on Cardinal Thule.

"Our points of agreement are as follows.

"A large majority hold the next Pontiff should be Italian. Some wish a Pontiff of non-Roman, non-Curial character. But this can be settled by compromise.

"All are agreed that ideally his pontificate should be at least ten years in duration—although on this point, we can only do our best. Life and death are usually beyond our reach." The Camerlengo grins slightly, then continues. "And, finally, all agree that he should be theologian, teacher and leader, not so much a politician, an activist, a chairman-of-the-board.

"Beyond that we begin to disagree on the type of Pontiff who is best fitted to lead in the midst of the turmoil and danger now besetting the Church. And we differ on this point because we cannot, finally, agree among ourselves on what is happening to the Church, on what type of Churchly organization we ought to develop. We therefore cannot make up our minds and agree on what role the next Pope should play. And, hence, our deadlock. For, as our habit of acting dictates, first we determine the policy lines of the next Pontificate. Then, we elect the next Pope."

The Camerlengo stops here. He would sorely like to continue. But the rules of his role as Camerlengo forbid him to do more than present the issues. He has, however, one unusual step to take. He looks long and hard at his notes, then lifts his eyes and runs a quick glance around: "I crave your indulgence, Excellencies, while I humbly make a suggestion. In view of the deep importance of the situation, and of our own disunity on this grave point of policy lines, after having consulted with the Preparatory Committee of Cardinals, I decided that at this initial meeting it would be advisable to let one spokesman for each of the major groups have a word with you, so that none of us be in the dark as regards our central point of disagreement." The Camerlengo gazes around the Chapel. Most heads nod in agreement. Some faces are staring at him, impassive, some brooding, some puzzled, one or two in obvious revolt. But he has the majority. He continues.

"The spokesmen are, in order of cardinalitial seniority, My Most Eminent Lord Cardinal Riccioni of the South; My Most Eminent Lord Cardinal Thule; My Most Eminent Lord Cardinal Lynch; My Most Eminent Lord Cardinal Bassano; and My Most Eminent Lord Cardinal Domenico." As he names each one he looks at them. The Camerlengo is known to be able to convey diametrically opposite sentiments with the same smile. "Each one of My Most Eminent Cardinals will confine his remarks to a period of ten minutes. After eight minutes have elapsed, the Reverend Cardinal will be notified that he has yet two minutes to wind up his remarks. Please, My Most Eminent Cardinals! Please! Ten Minutes!" Then—with a smile—facing toward the Cardinal: "My Most Eminent Lord Cardinal Giuseppe Riccioni!

Riccioni walks down past the long table of the Presidents, kneels a moment at the Altar to say a short prayer, as all the speakers will do, then turns, advances to the table at which the Camerlengo sits, and faces the Electors.

"What I have to say, Most Eminent Brothers, will not take ten minutes.

"I represent a solid number of you from Europe, Africa, and the Americas. We are of the opinion that the next Pontiff must be a man of iron discipline who knows how to command, how to punish, how to maintain order, how to cut off the rotten branches, how to hold on to the deposit of faith."

There is at this point a certain rustle among the Electors—feet being shuffled as the Cardinals straighten up in their places, papers up to now held in the hand being laid down on the little tables in front of each throne. Riccioni has their ears. All sense the battle being joined between the old Church represented by Riccioni, and the new Church of the Progressivists.

"I have read the *Summary Report* on the late Pontificate. I have only one point of disagreement. *We*, I should say, have only one point of disagreement with its authors. The paper concludes that the policy of Pope Paul vacillated between two extremes: rigid adherence to certain doctrinal points like priestly celibacy, contraception, the Devil; and openness on certain other more pragmatic circumstances—the Vatican *Ostpolitik*, the innovations in the Liturgy, challenges to the teaching authority of the Church.

"I do not agree that the Pope merely vacillated." Riccioni's voice hardens and his eyes narrow. "I think that we have had some fourteen years of destruction, of permitted decay." Riccioni pauses. He wants to shock people out of complacency. "I think," he goes on, his voice deepening in disgust, "I think we may speak of the Devil let loose in the vineyard of the Lord."

A low murmur becomes audible—remarks are passed from one Cardinal to another.

Riccioni raises his voice, still calm and now almost dispassionate: "I know. I know. But look at the conclusions in the *Position Papers*. I remember! All of you remember what His Holiness Paul 6 did say: 'The Church seems destined to die.' Those *Position Papers* show a bleak picture. And even though they are not with us today, I want to remind you that those trusted watchdogs of the faith, My Lord Cardinals Ottaviani and di Jorio, are with us in our fears."

Those Cardinals, both over eighty years of age, can no longer participate in Conclave. But their influence is still huge over many younger Cardinals in Conclave 82. A short time ago these older men held all power. And Riccioni is reminding everyone that within Vatican life they still have to reckon with these powerful men.

"None of us, none of these experienced Churchmen, think the Church is destined to die, or even seems so. My Lord Cardinals, we need a Pontiff who will hear the Lord Jesus saying: 'All the force of Satan will not prevail against my Church,' and: 'I will be with you all days, even to the end of time.' And we need a Pontiff who will act so as to preserve the life of the Church." This is the closest anyone dares come to an open condemnation of Paul 6. All realize that whatever candidate Riccioni recommends will be expected to clamp down on all the changes made by Pope Paul, and to restore the Church to the way it was before Pope John 23.

"It is for this reason that I and others propose as candidate My Most Eminent Lord Cardinal Vasari. And I beg Your Eminences to consider his record, hear his advices, and examine his candidacy carefully. I am delegated to deal with any adaptations and commitments in his name and in the name of this group. I have spoken. I thank Your Eminences."

Riccioni turns to step away from the table, then pauses, glances at the Camerlengo as if to say, one more word, if you please. He speaks with intensity and feeling—looking steadily in the direction of Cardinal Thule now—"Neither lives nor ideas nor ambitions—even if we have identified our own ideas and ambitions with the Church's condition—nothing matters but the Church. I thank Your Eminences."

With a solemn face, Riccioni makes his way to his place.

"My Most Eminent Lord Cardinal Otto Thule of the East!" The Camerlengo almost grimaces in his effort to smile at Thule. All the years, Thule's piety has interfered mightily with the Camerlengo's plans and his almost geometric approach to theology and religion and faith. In whatever post, the Camerlengo was, Thule was sure to be the opponent of the policies the Camerlengo espoused.

Standing now not two feet from his powerful enemy, the Camerlengo, and facing his fellow-Cardinals, Thule gives the impression that there is absolutely no trouble, no discord, between him and the others. This is Thule's hour—if ever. He has worked hard days and long months for it, traveled, lectured, written, engaged in discussions. The craggy, leonine face is utterly serious. Thule's heavy-lidded eyes, normally unsmiling, fully staring, are now sharply illuminated. His look is one of deep reverence, the awed expression of a man who sees the chasms of destruction opening at his feet on either side, but keeps his eyes on the shining mountain top ahead.

As he speaks, those who have not known Thule are surprised that such a bulky, heavy-faced, broad-shouldered man can exert such softness to temper the steel in the tones of his voice. "My Lord Cardinals, I bring you today the tidings which millions of Christians in our Church, in every Church, even those outside the Churches, our Jewish brothers, our Buddhist and Hindu and Muslim brothers, have already heard. Never before were so many diverse people of our globe willing to confess that 'Jesus is Lord.' The gentle, overpowering voice of the Spirit!"

This is enough to keynote all Thule will say. Many of his listeners need to hear only one overtone in Thule's voice—it is the faintest trace of a rasp—and to catch the persistent gleam in his eyes—it is the spark of the dedicated fanatic—to be reminded of what the late Cardinal Tisserant said of Easterners: "If we Latins have fire, it is in our hearts. But the Easterners have fire in their brains." Thule is an Easterner. His brain can burn and explode.

Whether they remember Tisserant's words or not, everyone quickly understands the deep commitment this man has made to all he is saying. "All over the world we know there is a vast revolution. As the Most Reverend Camerlengo pointed out, we differ only as to our interpretation of it. Many, especially those I speak for today, believe—or, better still, *know*—that this is the hour of the Spirit. Old walls are coming down. Old prejudices are disappearing. We are all in malaise, like voyagers about to step willy-nilly onto the deck of a strange ship for a journey on uncharted seas toward an utterly new and completely unknown continent. The very skies are opened up to man; and, some suspect, alien voices are trying to speak to us from beyond our galaxy.

"Now, what Christians have lacked is being accomplished. Unity! My Brothers! I myself am of the center. But some years ago, I decided to exert special care for our non-Catholic brethren and also for those Catholics who no longer felt at ease within our institutional Church. Somebody had to walk on the waters. With trust. And not sink. The institutional Church—what *we* represent—*and* all believers are one and the same. God forbid that we should abandon any part of the Church."

Thule pauses, gazes around at all the faces. He has touched some chord in Makonde whose eyes are shining. Others, Riccioni among them, are looking askance at Thule. A majority are plainly fascinated.

"Trust, Most Eminent Brothers. Trust. We must trust the Spirit. It is no longer a question of whether we break with the past. The Lord himself has broken us away from it. We must open our hearts." His tone rises with excitement. "Our hearts! And our minds. Our minds! We need to take a vast step. One vast gigantic step! In tune and in step with men and women across our cherished world. No one of us wants a repetition of the Papal captivity that Pius 9 chose in 1870. No one of us can. No one of us wants the Church of Constantine." His right hand pushes away some invisible obstacle; the voice is categoric. "That is all done and finished. Pope John 23 said: 'We must return to the simplicity the Church had when it left the hands of Jesus Christ.' No doubt about this!"

Then, lowering his voice for the drama of the contrast, and saying each word very slowly and distinctly: "With Your Eminences' permission, I humbly propose as candidate My Most Eminent Lord Cardinal Lowe." A pause. Then, still calmly: "You have his documents. You know his history. You know what he thinks on the subjects of our discussions. He is a foremost ecumenist. He is in favor of an utterly open Church. You know how high he stands in the esteem of Asians and Africans. You know the appeal of his voice and name for the Protestant Churches in Europe and America. His motto is 'Unity in Christ.' And we need unity. Unity based on unanimity. Absolute unanimity. The oneness of one concordant voice.

"In recent years, my Venerable Brothers, we have seen the possibility even of an anti-Pope. Yes! An anti-Pope!" This reference to the rebellious Archbishop Lefebvre is completely understood by every man present.

But many also remember how Thule made his own bids to outflank and out-Pope Pope Paul 6—once through his efforts to obtain the powerful post of Secretary of State; another time by his tremendous but unsuccessful effort to assemble a gigantic international congress of the Church and thus out-maneuvre Pope Paul in that way. Even now, there are some here who see the frequent international meetings of Thule's religious movements as a new and escalating effort to call a People's General Council of the Church. And what, some have asked behind closed doors and in private letters, would the Vatican do if Thule presided over an international meeting of Bishops and Cardinals, with priests and laity from all over the Roman Church? Supposing they took some weighty decisions—say, to ordain some Catholic women. Would that be schism? Would Thule then in effect be an anti-Pope? Supposing they elected an "international" People's Pope?

But all know that Thule's warning of the danger of an anti-Pope is directed at Lefebvre—and at Cardinals Riccioni and Vasari and their Traditionalist supporters here and in the Vatican. Thule's horror of Lefebvre is almost pathological. The entire Traditionalist movement spearheaded by Lefebvre bodes death for all Thule stands for.

Lowe looks at Thule, throws a look to a few friends who smile back, then folds his lower lip over his upper lip—a characteristic trait of his that, some say, indicates his stubbornness.

Thule ends swiftly now, on a simple note: "My Lord Cardinals! There is much to discuss, much to explore. I and those who stand with my point of view are ready to enter into the deepest discussions with any of you. We feel strongly we have the voice of the Holy Spirit with us. We feel that the Church is just about to be born again in a new guise before all men!" He stands for a moment's silence. Again, the soulful look. "I thank Your Eminences!" As he strides back to his place he nods to some colleagues. He is flushed with exertion, satisfied. Apart from anything else, Thule is one of the best orators among the Cardinals. He knows this, feels his power. He touches Lowe lightly on the shoulder, and they both smile pleasantly. The Camerlengo's face is a study in expressionlessness.

Now his voice rings out as he announces the next speaker: "My Most Eminent Lord Cardinal Paul Lynch!" The Camerlengo announces the name without a trace of effort or emotion in his voice; and he is not smiling—even conventionally; he stares at Lynch, at the bland face of the man moving forward now at a leisurely pace. Only some here today know the behind-the-scenes struggle the Camerlengo has waged with this man, how Lynch supported the Marxists, how he has opposed the present right-wing regime in his own country, and how the Camerlengo nearly went berserk over the endless stream of telegrams and dispatches between Rome and the Cardinal's home town as Rome unsuccessfully tried to curb Lynch, and as the previous Pope, Paul 6, defended Lynch and curbed the Camerlengo.

The Camerlengo had placed a watch-dog on Lynch: a veteran Vatican diplomat, experienced churchman, a genuine Roman, the Papal Nuncio in the area. But the Nuncio turned out to be impotent in this situation. Lynch had too many contacts; and, anyway. a Papal Nuncio could do very little against a Cardinal in the Cardinal's own territory. "What can you do when he has a majority of Jesuits and Dominicans, priests and nuns, as well as government officials and lay people, fighting his battles for him?" the Nuncio had once complained to a reproving Camerlengo during one of his periodic visits to Rome.

Lynch's prayer at the High Altar is brief and he appears uneasy. When he turns to address the Conclave, his normally pale face seems deathly white. Not the white of fear but the bloodless expression of severely felt emotion.

Contrary to what many expect, Lynch's tones are calm, his language slow and deliberate. "Eminent Brothers," Lynch says as he turns his head from side to side to take in both rows of Cardinals, "an ancient Roman once lifted the fold in his cloak and said to Rome's enemies with whom he was discussing the future relations of their two countries: 'I hold peace and war, life and death, in this fold of my Roman cloak. Which will you choose today? You can have either.' We know from history that his enemies chose war. And they perished." The very Hispanic accentuation of his words seems to create a peculiar silence of attention.

"Today, the people of this world are mired in the deep fold of their misery and pain, their want and insistence on justice. Men and women and children, all ask us the same question. Three-fifths of them go to bed hungry every night, get up in subhuman living conditions, die from malnutrition and disease, have no permanent work, much less a glimmer of real hope for economic betterment. They certainly have no visible alternative to back-breaking, unrewarding work, to hunger, to suffering, and no alternative to a painful death. And everywhere, they are saying to us with one voice: 'It is too much suffering and injustice to bear.' And further they say 'Within this deep fold of our poverty and misery and helplessness, we in our vast numbers and in our suffering, we hold an invitation to peace or to war. For we must have justice. We must have hope. If these precious things shall not be ours in peace, we will have them by war. Choose! You! And we will give you what you choose. But we will have justice and hope!' This is the voice of the majority of men and women and children today."

The Camerlengo shifts in his chair and begins to take notes. There is a heavy pause, but no stirring among the Cardinals. They are held, as they measure Lynch's words.

"As Pontiff, we do need an efficient, learned and pious man. True! But he must also be one who can be a symbol of hope. And more than a symbol! We need someone who will not be afraid to accept what His Holiness, Pope John 23, said: 'The substance of our doctrine is one thing. The expression of that substance is quite another.' And, again, as the Pope said: 'Philosophical theories remain sometimes. But the economic and political conditions which they spawned change and develop.' We need a Pontiff who is not afraid to ride on the present tide of democratic socialism. . . ." There are a few murmurs. The Camerlengo raises his head but keeps his eyes on his notes, a characteristic habit of his. "Oh, I know the term 'democratic socialism' needs defining. How ever you define 'democratic socialism,'" Lynch insists with a slight touch of anger in his voice, "this does not mean we forsake the Church. For neither I nor my colleagues will take second place to anyone here or throughout the Church in love for that Church and for Christ's Gospel.

"There is a tide in human affairs today; and it cannot be turned back. All who do not ride with it will be swept away and destroyed by it."

The Camerlengo is signaling the two-minute warning.

"My Lord Cardinals, without further explanations and in the hope that we will all discourse peacefully, fraternally, and come to an understanding of the seriousness in all these matters, I wish to propose My Most Reverend Lord Cardinal Yiu as candidate for Supreme Pontiff. May God help him, help you all, all of us, to see what is happening."

Youthful looking fifty-six-year-old Lazarus Hou Lo Yiu, a candidate for Supreme Pontiff, a Cardinal at age fifty, is neither theologian nor master politician. A simple man imbued with the history and culture of his beloved homeland, he is known throughout Asia as a dedicated anti-Marxist and anti-Communist, an admirer of American democratic ideals, and a resourceful tactician in the struggle taking place between the government of his own country and the Leftist groups led by clergy. Nobody really knows what Yiu thinks, or so the feeling about him goes.

Yiu's nomination has made some Cardinals restive and has set off a buzzing of whispers throughout the Chapel. Why Yiu? Some Cardinals throw looks, askance or approving, in Lynch's direction. Others, hunched in their seats, are taking rapid notes. Yiu, as Lynch's nominee, is openly unpopular with the Conservatives and Traditionalists who see him as an unwilling pawn, a sop even, drawn by his Third World status into a symbolic stance that smells more of world power politics than of compassion for the poor and starving.

Lynch's final two minutes are running out. He does not want to let this occasion get away quite yet. He speaks again, trying to recapture full attention for his remarks. "Without wishing in any way to instill an undue emotion into this august Conclave of Most Reverend Electors, or to impugn the independence of the Conclave and of Holy Mother Church, I have a message to communicate. . . ."

The Camerlengo interrupts, his little silver bell ringing insistently. He knows the message. The guts of Lynch's proposal is a working alliance between Marxists and Roman Catholics, a sort of de facto agreement to live and let live, even to aid each other, and to settle their own personal scores later on. This is what Lynch has talked up during the last months. The Camerlengo has more than one reason for hoping that such a discussion will never arise.

The Cardinals who have understood the Camerlengo's move have broken out into open conversation, some have stood up as if to stretch their legs. Lynch's initiative has been taken away.

Lynch flushes slightly, regains control of himself, then walks slowly toward his throne. As he passes, he glances quickly at the Asiatic. Yiu's face is immobile, his eyes cast down, his hands folded on his lap.

Even before Lynch reaches his throne, he hears the Camerlengo: "My Most Reverend Lord Cardinal Bassano!"

The Camerlengo cannot announce the name fast enough—anything to redirect attention totally. All he needs now is for some revered and irresistible figure to stand up and demand his right of "a sentence of rejection." A lengthily expressed opinion by one member can always be met with a short sentence of rebuttal by some opponent. It is then understood that at a later time a full rebuttal will be heard. But the point of a "sentence of rejection" is that more often than not it provokes a public outcry among all the Cardinals rejecting then and there what has been exposed at length.

The Camerlengo does not want any such public outburst. Not that he shares Lynch's viewpoint. But he fears that such a violent rejection could provoke a swift reaction among Lynch's supporters. Franzus, Buff, others, would be on their feet demanding equal time. Order would be disrupted.

Passions would be naked. Real, open, factional infighting could ensue. Positions harden, compromise becomes difficult or impossible. And that could mean trouble, a lengthening Conclave, and other possible dangers. Indeed, the Camerlengo's plans as Camerlengo do not include any prolonged public discussion of Lynch's main proposal. In such a discussion, inevitably everyone would learn of the behind-the-scenes dealings with the U.S.S.R., of Franzus' involvement in it all, and of many more delicate matters.

As Cardinal Bassano makes his way forward, the Camerlengo seeks out Cardinal Franzus with his eyes. Yes, Franzus has got the point. Franzus is looking steadily through those thick spectacles at him, his eyes shining with understanding but not with satisfaction. The Camerlengo coughs and looks down again at his notes. Franzus knows too much. Who told Franzus about those "others reports"?

Bassano kneels a moment and prays. Now he begins: "Most Reverend and Most Eminent Lords, my Brothers in Christ, Illustrious Cardinals of the Holy Roman Catholic and Apostolic Church—" Bassano's mellifluous Italianate voice oozes in around the Camerlengo's thoughts. Cardinal Calder of the U.S. looks over at his friend, Cardinal Artel, and then settles down on his throne as if to escape the cascade of calming rhetoric he expects. Artel smiles, as only Artel can smile.

Bassano's words are brimming with piety and faith and dignity. In his heart of hearts, he is a Traditionalist. But for a while now, he has been at loggerheads with his own faction. His common sense tells him that change is necessary. He has thrown in his lot with the Conservatives.

"We serve an all-powerful Lord Jesus," Bassano is saying, "who can at any moment command the winds and the waters around this Ship of Peter, so that they be still, so that the Ship be in safety to proceed on its eternal course of destiny as God's source of salvation for all men." Cardinals sit back and relax and look at each other, at Bassano and the Camerlengo. This is going to be predictable. The Camerlengo, however, shows the slightest trace of that tic: He must be controlling some lively emotion.

"Many are afraid," Bassano's voice is lowered still further, becoming more confidential in tone. "And why not? Many say: it is the catacombs again for the Church. And there are reasons for their fear. Many say: Let us go back and reform. Others say: Quick! Let us go and walk with the sons of men. Let us be nearer to them. And, in each case, they have their reasons. And their persuaders." This last reference is the nearest Bassano will come today to touching on the Marxism of some Cardinals and their friends on the other side of the Iron Curtain.

Then with a soft upswing to his voice, as if leniency in thought were needed: "And, probably, all are correct to some degree. Certainly . . . " an indulgent smile, "all are sincere.

"What we do need, however, in my humble opinion—and I speak for many others here and throughout the Church—is a *careful* policy. The time is not ripe for sudden change. The Spirit of God blows gently, pointing the way quietly and in peace, not by fits and starts. We need mature development— perhaps more mature than any displayed recently." For the moment, Bassano will not sharpen this criticism of Paul 6. "Slow change, gradual adaptation to circumstances. Otherwise . . . " the voice drops again to a quiet bass, "we may fall into the traps of our Enemy and of our enemies, the enemies of the Church of Jesus.

"Some of those enemies we can outwit. Some of them we can convert. Some of them we can defeat directly . . ." just a touch of Roman triumph- alism in that last remark. "But all of them, I repeat, all of them, we—the One, Holy, Catholic, and Apostolic Church—we will outlive, and eventually see them descending to the compost-heap of history, while the Church goes on in strong tranquillity." The Camerlengo is signaling gently, with a smile. Two minutes. Bassano pauses, smiles back, continues:

"Those for whom I speak—and you know their names, they are numerous— think that we need a Pontiff who will know how to lead the Church throughout all the gradual phases of development and adaptation. While we could support My Most Reverend Brother and Eminent Lord, Cardinal Masaccio—provided that adjustments and agreements are settled—we wish to suggest that there is more than one other candidate among us today who can fill this all-important functon. The names can wait. This is a matter for further discussion, for balloting, for fraternal tractations, for mature medita- tion, and for the Holy Spirit's guidance. These are my words to you, Most Eminent Brothers today. I thank the Camerlengo and you, Most Reverend Lord Cardinals!"

On Bassano's lips, the terms "adjustments" and "agreements" refer to the conditions favorable to this group or that individual, conditions to which a *papabile* must agree in order to win the Papal election. Conservatives, because they balance between Traditionalists and Progressivists, have to be extremely punctilious about "agreements" and "adjustments."

The Camerlengo waits until Cardinal Bassano has regained his seat smiling, waving to some of his friends down the rows. Then he rings his silver bell to capture the attention of those Cardinals who are talking together. It is just after 8 o'clock by now.

"My Most Reverend and Eminent Lord, Cardinal Domenico!" the Camerlengo calls. Domenico takes his time responding. He has been consulting with Cardinal Angelico and Cardinal Azande, his next-door neighbors. A small, gaunt man and somewhat uncomfortable in his cere- monial white and purple, he gets up slowly, unhurriedly, gathers his robes about him, and proceeds to the High Altar where he too prays for a moment. The silence grows. Domenico begins.

"The Most Reverend and Eminent Camerlengo does not wish any of us to be late for supper." Domenico shares his own sense of ease with his Brothers. A small ripple of quiet laughter comes from the Cardinals: "I for one am hungry. Besides, it is a long time since I sat and listened for so long to other men speaking." No surprises to be expected. No jolts. Not tonight anyway. Domenico is at ease, all can feel easy. . . .

Domenico, they say, knows more secrets about everybody than anyone else, not excepting even the Camerlengo. But he has the discretion of a confessor-monk, and the face of an ageless angel. Not bland innocence. And not the old man's jollity and contentment, or the "I've seen it all" attitude, which is sometimes one step away from the beginning of senility. No. Domenico's face is ageless for some deep inner reason of soul. And his look is innocent, because of time purged and space cleansed within him during long years of obscurity and quiet work as a scholar.

"In just a few words, Most Beloved Brothers, let me say this: We have grave difficulties. We have been offered four different approaches to these difficulties by Brother Cardinals. These approaches were offered us in all loyalty and truth." Domenico then administers a series of gentle but deliberate slaps.

"Of course, we must hold onto our deposit of faith. But we cannot, any of us, presume to hold onto the actual sociology and very politics of Peter the Fisherman—now, in this day and age!" Domenico does not have to look in the direction of Riccioni and his Traditionalist nominee, Vasari. All understand the criticism, and other eyes seek them out.

"On the other hand, it is also true that change must be serious and planned. And, yet, we cannot hang back, while real opportunities slide past us, while we give mere token acknowledgement to profound changes taking place in the world around us." Conservative Bassano seems unperturbed by Domenico's remarks.

"As for our Marxist Brothers, I am reminded of what an American commentator once said—the Lion may, on invitation, lie down with the Lamb. But the Lamb won't get much sleep.

"I agree with my Venerable Brother"—a glance to Thule—"that an anti-Pope looked likely in these last few years. But His Eminence knows that Archbishop Lefebvre is not the only one suspected of heading in such a direction." Thule reddens as Domenico so easily pinpoints for all the weakness and the threat to the Church, of Thule's position.

"The group I speak for is not numerically great," Domenico continues blandly. "We feel that all four approaches should be examined. For each one has something to offer. But we also feel all four can be radically criticized. Frankly, we have no particular candidate in mind—in keeping with the General Policy—nor do we right away exclude any candidate. We would not whole-heartedly support the candidacy of My Most Reverend and Eminent

Lords, Cardinals Vasari, Lowe, Masaccio, or Yiu, at least not for the reasons adduced by my most esteemed colleagues who preceded me in speech here this evening."

Domenico, as leader of the Radicals, knows the Conclave and Papal mechanism better than most. It is policy that matters. As the Conclave phrase goes: "Policy is the Pope-maker." And Domenico wishes to exclude no *papabile* at the beginning, nor fix on one from the start.

Domenico looks over at the Camerlengo. His time is almost up. "The watchword therefore," he continues, "in my opinion, is loving collaboration. Loving frankness. No haste. No panic. Let us love. Let us pray. Let us trust. Trust the Lord Jesus, that is to say, Whose Church needs a Pontiff, and Who will not desert His Church. Jesus is among us. This we believe, don't we? I thank Your Eminences."

A little murmur of applause follows Domenico as he returns to his place. Such applause is unusual. But Domenico's place of honor in their minds is special. He nods to one or two of his colleagues. As he sits down, Angelico leans over and touches his arm. Some words pass between them. Then Angelico leans back on his throne and nods to Azande. The black Cardinal returns his look somberly and impassively, only his eyes expressing his understanding.

It is very close to 8:30 P.M. Now that the general positions and attitudes of the five major factions have been laid out, there is a general restlessness to move out of this formal atmosphere and to begin the night's work. There is much to be done between the time this preliminary meeting ends and the convening of the First Formal Session of the Conclave at 10 A.M. tomorrow. There will be private meetings. Electors will be sounded out and wooed. Some will study and rehearse their positions.

The Camerlengo announces the end of the meeting. He thanks all present, then rises and goes to the locked doors. He knocks three times on them. The young Monsignore outside unlocks the doors and stands aside to allow the Camerlengo to precede him, and then falls into step behind.

As he leaves, the other Cardinals begin to emerge. Some are silent and alone. Some are talking quietly in small groups with others. Franzus and Lynch and Thule have found each other. Buff catches up with them. Behind them come a number of Italians. Yiu, with Azande and Lotuko, is joined by Lohngren. Yellow, black, and white, they walk away together. Coming up at the rear are the Polish, French, and Spanish Cardinals.

Domenico is the only one who remains, even when the service personnel enter and start tidying and dusting the Chapel. He sits alone and quite still. Then he rises and leaves. The bus will be waiting for him.

NIGHT: 9:00 P.M.—1:00 A.M.

Once in the *Domus Mariae* where they are quartered, not all the Cardinals go in to supper—which is optional in any case. Groups begin to form in the corridors and rooms. The arduous business of this long night begins to get under way. Franzus disappears with Thule and Lynch and Buff into Thule's apartment to hammer out their strategy. Kand is buttonholed by Garcia the Spaniard; Karewsky of Eastern Europe joins them. They enter Kand's apartment. Ni Kan is seen with Motzu the Asiatic entering Yiu's apartment. There is a meeting of German Cardinals in the rooms of Cardinal Hildebrandt of Latin America. The Mexicans and some of the other Latin Americans have split up in various rooms.

By 9 P.M. the personnel has left the Chapel. The Chapel is quiet. One lamp is still on. And a little red light indicates the Tabernacle where the Eucharist stays.

By 9:15 P.M. supper is over. More Cardinals join those already gathered in various rooms, holding meetings and sending out to other groups for information, for visits, for explanations.

At about 9:30 P.M. the Camerlengo goes with his young assistant to inspect the house Chapel and to make sure that the surveillance technicians have done their work. As the two of them enter the Chapel, they see a kneeling figure just visible in the light of the flickering red lamp in front of the Tabernacle. It is Domenico. He is kneeling without any support, his head raised, his eyes closed. The Camerlengo stops.

Then they both notice that one other person is in the Chapel. It is Cardinal Henry Walker. He is still seated in his place, bolt upright and motionless, his huge girth filling the seat, his back straight, his head flung back, his Rosary passing bead by bead through his fingers. Everyone knows the Cardinal hates to be found praying and, much more, to be looked at while he is praying.

"Later," the Camerlengo whispers to the Monsignore. "Come, we have work to do." They leave Domenico and Walker in peace. "The Eminent members of this College of Cardinals never cease to amaze me," the Camerlengo says to no one in particular as he reenters his office with the Monsignore.

The calmest and least involved in the evening's activities and discussions are the Cardinals from the British Commonwealth countries: Krasnow, Hartley, Moore, and Reynolds; Oceania's Copley and Dowd join them all in Reynold's apartment. There they are joined by Hopper and Morris the Anglo-Saxon.

Morris has worked in and out of Rome for years, is a good theologian. He brings along with him a young Oceanian Cardinal who betrays a stutter as he greets them all.

None of these men, except for the young Cardinal with the stutter, is closely allied with any faction or group. The young Cardinal has become a friend and confidant of the Camerlengo. The others have not been privy to much of the pre-Conclave electioneering. Only one of them, Krasnow, has been in previous Conclaves; but he has stayed away from Church politics for a long time. So, most of these Cardinals, including Krasnow, have more questions than opinions about the Conclave. Their interest is obviously less in strategy or persuasion than in scorekeeping.

It is natural that Cardinal Morris's young friend with the stutter becomes the target of questioning. And, when asked the meaning of this evening's preliminary meeting, he has much to say. "As far as the Office is concerned" (everyone understands that for the young Cardinal "the Office" means the Vatican Secretariat of State), "up to this afternoon, there were only four groups. Nice and tidy, you know. In each group, one major candidate all vetted and approved, and each with one fall back candidate. Vasari for the Traditionalists, with Canaletto in tow; Masaccio for the Conservatives with Ferro of the Vatican in tow; Lowe for the Progressivists—the "Third World-ers and Ecumenists—with Lombardi of Latin America in tow; and Yiu for the Christian-Marxists, with Lamy of France in tow. And, among these, there was only one group that could command the needed majority. Even at this evening's meeting, I don't think Domenico was speaking for a group—even though he did speak of sympathisers. Rather he was speaking for various members of four different groups and for some of the uncommitted and the undecided. But he is powerful and persuasive. Not political power. Something else. He didn't stand up there without some reason. . . ."

"What was the general line up of votes among those four main groups as of, say, yesterday or this morning?" Hartley asks.

"Well, that's the problem. The Camerlengo had it all worked out. He showed me the final—or what he thought were the final—lists last week. A clear picture. As far as we were concerned, a strong man like Domenico would acquiesce in a general consensus and, with him, would go Angelico and his followers."

"As you say, Eminence," Cardinal Moore comments, "nice and tidy. Germanic nice and tidy." Someone laughs a little. The Camerlengo's one-time nickname was *Akribei*, so keen is he that every subordinate in his Office should have "accurate and clear" ideas of his policy and wishes. The Camerlengo had his leg pulled at times about his desire for clarity of thinking. But he took it all in good spirit.

"But now the picture has changed, eh?" Reynolds pursues the line up of votes.

"Well, at least the picture is no longer clear, not clear at all. You see, there's this Thule movement, and the Franzus movement. We didn't expect it, although we should have. The problem is: If Thule and Franzus get together, that becomes a real threat. And, then, there will probably be a fifth group, possibly a sixth."

"Why a fifth, let alone a sixth?"

"Because the only way to stop a Thule-Franzus *demarche* would be to go for a non-Italian, pan-European candidate—somebody like Cardinal Lohngren, if the Thule-Franzus thing became really feasible. In that case, Domenico or Angelico might head still another group."

"Do we know exactly how strong the Thule-Franzus thing has become or is likely to become?" Moore asks.

"We are just in the process of finding out right at this very moment," the young Cardinal says with a glance at the door, as if he could see through it down the corridor and into the office where the Camerlengo sits. "Whoever the new Pope is, whoever is backing him, whatever his background, there is a solid, conventional wisdom to the election."

"You mean, my friend," Moore breaks in, "there are priorities?"

"Ah yes! Priorities! In fact, mainly four priorities. At least in the Conclaves I have heard about. First on the list is always the relationship between the Vatican and the State of Italy. Clearly the Pope must be acceptable to the Italian Government in its present form and in whatever form is anticipated during his projected pontificate. He is, after all, the Bishop of Rome.

"The second big priority on the list is very closely linked to the first: the multiple business interests with which the Vatican is closely linked through its investments, starting with Italy—mainly in Rome and Milan—and then taking in Europe and the Western Hemisphere. For, if any proposed candidate's name sends tremors through important segments of banking or industry, the odds are heavy against such a man making even the primary list of *papabili*.

"And the third priority concerns the whole complex of politics and diplomacy. Without putting a veto power over candidates into the hands of any government, the Conclave has to single out those candidates who would definitely not be acceptable or favorably looked upon by any major or any middle-level national power."

"Does this apply to the U.S.S.R. also?" Reynolds asks.

"Of course! Of course! And that is also a sign of the power of the Papacy even today. Statesmen realize that whatever moral unity they rely upon in areas of vital interest to them depends to a large degree on religious leaders. The Soviet experience has shown—as the Romans, long before it—that you cannot suppress religion. The Soviets may not say that out loud. But they know it well enough.

"The last big priority is constituted by the national and international Conferences of Bishops or, rather, I should say, the preferences of such Conferences." The young Cardinal is referring to the seven regional groups (Europe, North America, Central America, South America, Africa, Asia, Oceania); the eight international plenary Reunions of Bishops; the ninety-eight national Bishops' Conferences that take place everywhere from Angola to Zambia; the fourteen Oriental Rites that mainly inhabit the Soviet Union; the six partriarchal Synods and five Bishops' Conferences that function in the lands of Islam.

"Cardinals preside over the workings, the deliberations, and the consensus achieved in each one of these branches of international Church government and administration. Few people realize what a complicated but useful mechanism these Conferences represent," the young Cardinal continues. "It is by means of these that Rome knows the current problems in each region and each nation. And thus, also, those working at the center of things in the Vatican have a hand in the solutions offered, because the proposals for solution usually have to be referred to Rome. So there is a non-stop, two-way flow of traffic. There's the constant action of Rome, and the reactions of regional Conferences, and *their* subsequent actions. So there develops a very keen local consensus about Papal policies, about how the Vatican implements those policies, and about how it treats local bishops.

"Consequently, when a Papal election comes around, these Bishops' Conferences are the first groups to know what sort of a Pope *isn't* needed—at least in their opinion—which of the proposed *papabili* should be given a chance, and which should be excluded without a second thought.

"It is the Secretaries General of each Conference—men like Archbishop Bernadin of Cincinnati, Ohio, former head of the North American Conference, and Bishop Etchegaray of Marseilles, France, for the European Conference—men like that who wield power over the Conclave from the point of view of outsiders. For they, in turn, can usually deliver the Conference vote to the resident local Cardinal or Cardinals on ordinary Church matters. Thus, foreign Cardinals, together with the Secretaries General, become in this sense Pope-makers."

"In the light of all that," Hopper asks, "how would you answer the question: which of the three leaders has the best chance of being elected? Ferro, Masaccio, or Vasari?" The young Cardinal does not answer.

"What, in your estimation, is the central issue in this Conclave 82?"

"The old, old question: power. Among men and women today, throughout our whole human society, two types of power are struggling for victory. The power of the Marxist revolution. And the power of the old world, of world capitalism. Can you imagine what influence either of those two powers could wield if they succeeded in infiltrating the Church of Rome at the top—if, say, the new Pope gave orders that everywhere Catholics were to look kindly and with favorable eyes on Marxists? Or, vice versa, if he took a very, very strong stand against Marxism?"

"Is it possible to imagine the mind of a Pope or of a Vatican which would take up such an open attitude on the Marxism question?"

"Quite easy. Most easy." The young Cardinal laughs. "For instance, in what other way do you think it would be possible to re-Christianize Europe, undo all the bastions of anti-Catholic and anti-Christian feeling? The quickest way would be to liquidate all those bastions. And, tell me, Reverend Brothers, tell me as far as you know, what is the one socio-political power that makes it its first business to liquidate all such bastions?" The answer to the young Cardinal's question is obvious to all.

"One last question, Eminence. If you were a *papabile*, would you be inclined to such an open mentality?" There is a short pause as the young Cardinal draws in his breath and his lower jaw shakes a little. For the first time in the conversation he is having difficulty in overcoming the stutter.

"Nnn-nn-no question bbbb-bbbbut I would side with Mmm-mma-mma-artians!" Everyone laughs. The young Cardinal has already stood up. "I promised to drop in and see the Camerlengo after the preliminary meeting." He gives a playful wink. "As the Americans say, tune in to tomorrow's Session. . . ." He gets a pleasant laugh. When he leaves and closes the door, more than one of the older Cardinals in the apartment has a speculative look in his eyes. The young Cardinal is very, very intelligent.

"Has he always had that stutter?" Reynolds is mildly curious.

"Oh no. Only since five or six years ago. The result of an accident," Morris answers. Then he turns to Krasnow. "Eminence, you have been in Conclaves before. Give us some of your ideas!"

Back in his office, meanwhile, the Camerlengo works silently over lists of Cardinals and candidates, while his Assistant types up memoranda in the outer office. Suddenly, he throws down his pencil and rings for the Monsignore.

"Go over and see if Lohngren is free for a few minutes. Discreetly, of course. Be careful! But before you contact Lohngren, tell Ruzzo I want to have a word with him." Ruzzo is the chief of security, and should have already made his rounds for the night.

Ruzzo arrives, shaking his head in a gesture of disbelief. There is some transmitter working within the Conclave, he tells the Camerlengo. But he cannot locate it. It appears to be a recording-transmitting device, automatic, turned off and on by remote control, and going on and off irregularly, Ruzzo tells the Camerlengo. The curious thing he says, is that whenever he gets close, or seems to be getting close to the carrier of the bug, the device stops working.

"Try and find it, Ruzzo," the Camerlengo pleads. "I want that bug; we still have time."

When the Monsignore returns with Lohngren minutes later, the Camerlengo gets right down to business. "Your Eminence, eighteen months ago as a result of talks with your Brother Cardinals in Germany and with the Bishops, you informed me that you did not wish your name to be submitted under any foreseeable circumstances as an active candidate. I must ask you now: Is this still your Eminence's attitude? Or has Your Eminence had second thoughts." Then, as if to emphasize the importance of the question: "For any reason, any reason?"

Lohngren looks steadily through his glasses at the Camerlengo. "I said at that time to Your Eminence that, given the complexity of our situation and the qualifications of many widely appreciated candidates such as Masaccio, Ferro, and *especially* since there was no danger either *within* the College of Cardinals itself"—Lohngren emphasizes the words—"or within the traditional heartland of Europe—given these two conditions, I did not want to be put in nomination." Lohngren pauses. Then, "You see, Eminence, I could not foresee any really feasible contingency by which such a danger could arise."

The Camerlengo nods. "None of us could have," he says tersely to the German.

"Well then, am I to understand now that your statement at the preliminary meeting about the *General Policy Framework* and the agreement about it was for public consumption?" Lohngren asks.

"Yes and no," the Camerlengo hesitates. "There is agreement, so far. When they get to know the facts—well, that's precisely the problem we have. The danger. . . ." He breaks off helplessly, looking at Lohngren.

The danger he and Lohngren are discussing arises from two factors. One is the future of Western Europe as foreseen by the Secretariat of State. This is the political and economic domination of the Continent by the U.S.S.R.—sometimes referred to as the "Finlandization" of Western Europe. The other factor is the rising star among Christians of that faction that favors a very positive approach to Marxists—not quite an alliance, perhaps—at least not now—but a working agreement.

Since the beginning of the decade, the Camerlango has known about the "Finlandization" idea and understood the danger. Indeed, he has known that Pope Paul 6's financial policies for the Vatican—the entire Sindona affair included—were gauged to this danger: settle in for a long-range siege, while the financial sinews of the Church are safe across the Atlantic. The *General Policy Framework* was part of that long-range siege strategy.

But the birth of the "openness-to-Marxist" mentality complicated things; it was a clear and direct threat to the *General Policy Framework*. An Electors' faction now existed that wanted to throw the fortunes of the Vatican and the Papacy in with a "Finlandized" Western Europe, as opposed to alliance with the United States.

On top of all this, the foreign policy of the United States itself, was no longer trilateral—with the United States, Europe and Japan as the three cornerstones. Black Africa would offer alternate markets to the ones the United States itself contemplated would be lost, with a Finlandized Europe.

So, the United States may well bypass Europe, hold and nourish its association with Saudi Arabia. Without Saudi Arabia, the United States could be forced to stop functioning for a sufficient length of time for it to be crippled. Saudi Arabia was vital in its way, as Japan was for the Pacific defense of the Continental United States.

The specific and immediate danger which both Lohngren and the Camerlengo now face is the possibility that the next Pope will be the candidate of the "openness-to-Marxists" Electoral group.

Lohngren sits down heavily. His head is bowed, his chin on his chest. He thinks for about a minute. Then raising his eyes to the Camerlengo's: "But now, I do not think I'm exaggerating, Eminence. I'm convinced that the danger is real." Lohngren breaks off, as if the words he is about to say have sunk out of view and he cannot find them.

The Camerlengo waits a while, then: "Have you been talking with Tsa-Toke . . . ?"

"Yes," Lohngren says. "A short conversation. But enough of course." He raises one eyebrow and looks at the Camerlengo quizzically: "Now I know why Paul made Tsa-Toke a member of the College."

"He is fully alive to all the eventualities," the Camerlengo comments. "Always was."

Cardinal Gabriel Joseph Tsa-Toke, Archbishop in Asia, one of Paul's surprise Cardinals, had come to Rome lately and blandly stated that it was possible and feasible for Christians not merely to coexist with, but to be involved in a fully Marxist-Leninist state and still remain good and loyal Catholics. He was, in effect, what Paul intended him to be: a showcase Cardinal for the new outlook. Tsa-Toke's behavior was shattering for the Italian Cardinals—and it immediately started them speculating about how they might behave under the "Eurocommunists" of Italy. It was devastating for the Americans, and alarming for the East Germans and Poles who already knew what it was to live in a fully Marxist-Leninist regime.

Tsa-Toke's attitude was John's and Paul's: "We can outlive Marxists, change Marxists, but we cannot keep them out—of Asia, of Europe, of Latin America. And, anyway, who wants American capitalism? Isn't it, in the final analysis, as unacceptable as Marxism? And isn't that capitalism being slowly transformed—in England, in Ireland, in Canada, in the United States itself—into 'social democracy'? And isn't that half-way house to the 'democratic socialism' which the Latin Americans have been proposing for the last dozen years?" These were the few comments that could be gleaned from Tsa-Toke. The "openness-to-Marxist" Electors love Tsa-Toke. He is their showcase Cardinal, too.

Lohngren continues. "But more important than my conversation with Tsa-Toke—after all, we all heard him at the Synod of Bishops some time ago—more important than Tsa-Toke are the *Special Reports*, especially the *Latin American Report*. I've read them all."

"So now?"

"So now," Lohngren answers with a small sigh of admission, "I suppose ... yes ... all right ... I now am a ... perhaps, should be a possible candidate. But Your Eminence understands, a candidate under certain specific circumstances."

"Well, then," the Camerlengo answers slowly as he smiles, "Your Eminence, I think we should discuss the *Reports*. And those circumstances. Now, I mean. I really think so. Now, eh?"

The Camerlengo rings for his young Assistant who has been seated in the outer office: "Monsignore, it's going to be a late and long night. Why don't you take some time off for a cup of coffee and a nap. I shall ring for you. Say, in half an hour? Very well."

As Lohngren begins to talk, the young Monsignore closes the door of the outer office and strolls down to the rooms where the priest-confessors are lodged. They are there, all five of them in their shirtsleeves, talking about the day's events and tomorrow's eventualities. The young Cardinal is there too, just finishing a cup of coffee.

A fellow German looks up as the Monsignore enters the sitting room: "*Gott!* What a face! They don't want to make you Pope this time do they, Gerhard?"

The Monsignore sits down and remarks to no one in particular: "So now we have at least five groups. ..."

In the Secretary's office the Camerlengo reassures Lohngren, but always with the master statesman's tactfulness. "Eminence, put your mind at rest. If the candidate of choice is to be non-Italian, Your Eminence can be sure—of course, I speak under correction by my Brother Cardinals, but still—that there will be sufficient support to make that a general decision."

"First and foremost, Eminence," Lohngren replies, not looking at the Camerlengo, "I must ascertain the status of Your Eminence's own plans. Remember, when we had our conversation some months ago, all seemed to be set."

"Well! All was set, mind you, Eminence," the Camerlengo answers quickly. "But it took time for all the information about United States policy details to arrive and be analyzed. And, then the Office takes its own good time to inform us of what is going on. I only got full details on the Moscow-Kiev conversations quite late." The Office, part of the Secretariat of State, had been conducting top-level talks with U.S.S.R. officials. Subject: detente between Rome and Moscow.

"These talks went very far, before I heard the substance of them," the Camerlengo goes on. "Then there was Tsa-Toke. And then, *Gott in Himmel!* there is Thule and Franzus and Buff and Lynch. It all has come as one huge, indigestible lump.

"Now at the preliminary meeting this evening, I still hewed to the *General Policy Framework* mainly because a majority of the Electors haven't all the facts. It is worth a chance that the *General Policy Framework* candidate may yet be viable."

"But then, Eminence," Lohngren retorts testily, "in the face of a rising crisis from the Left, I simply don't understand why you and Lamennais were so rabid and poisonous about Lefebvre." Cardinal Lamennais, German like the Camerlengo and posted to the Roman Curia, shared with the Camerlengo an undying hatred for Traditionalist Archbishop Marcel Lefebvre. "Your attacks on him misfired. As Witz said to me last month, your method of dealing with Lefebvre was as good an idea as importing rabbits into Australia in the nineteenth century. Fine at the start, maybe, but when they multiplied in their millions—as rabbits like to do. . . ." Lohngren was obviously not sparing the Camerlengo in fixing blame for the encouragement and strength Rome itself had given the Marxists in attacking the Rightist Traditionalist faction, but leaving the Leftists untouched.

"The fact is," the Camerlango defends himself, "the policy agreed upon by Pope Paul called for a shifting of the mass of Roman Catholics from the extreme Right—where they have always been, by the way—from the extreme Right over toward somewhere near the Center. You know as well as I why we wanted to do that, of course. Without such a shift toward the Center there would be too much disruption in the Church of the 'eighties and 'nineties:

the people had better get used to some dislocation and confusion. Anyway, the implementation of that policy of moving away from the extreme Right, required some precipitate—er—some new element. The Progressivists were designated as just that. So they were allowed to flourish. Then along sails Lefebvre and repolarizes everybody all over again! *Mein Gott!* Right back to where we were!"

"And in the meantime," Lohngren says drily if not quite accurately, "the Progressivists multiply—like those rabbits in Australia. And we have the danger of a Marxist Church!"

"Exactly, precisely! Impossible to foresee," the Camerlengo completes the comment. "But this office *does* except the cooperation and understanding of the College."

"Nevertheless, cooperation or not, I take it now that there is a real feasibility of a rush vote for a Thule candidate? So much so that, as a viable alternative, Your Eminence thinks we should provide for the choice of a pan-European candidate?"

"Correct and. . . ."

"And the considered opinion is that I would be an acceptable candidate under this rubric?"

"Your Eminence can see the logic of it all quite clearly," the Camerlengo says crisply. "It's just that we did not count on any groundswell for the Left among either the Italians, the Africans, or the Asians."

"But the basic idea and purpose of a pan-European candidate—will it—can it work?" Lohngren's query is genuine.

"Well, Angelico's been working on it, y'know. Montini's idea was that if he could breathe some new life into the 'one Europe' idea—Angelico's been speaking of a 'new soul' for Europe, but that's his way of talking—then, even with 'Finlandization,' we would have a chance of changing the political situation and even changing the color of Marxist ideology and economics. This could be our only hope finally of offsetting the ultimate victory of the U.S.S.R."

"I don't know." Lohngren is musing. "I don't know. A socio-political solution for a religious problem has always been the Vatican answer. And it hasn't worked." He breaks off and looks at the Camerlengo. "But then there is Thule and Company. . . ."

"Yes," the Camerlengo's eyes are gleaming. "Thule *et al.*"

"I never really thought," Lohngren says as a general comment, "that the Italians would waver, or that the Thule idea would catch on." He pauses and looks up at the Camerlengo. "But, then, these are strange times, times when the unexpected is already real, and when none of us really knows what's going on among our own people, do we now, Your Eminence?"

"I daresay!" the Camerlengo is curt in word and glance. "Now, three questions: First, how feasible do you think the recommendations are in the *Special Report* about Latin America? Second, what does Your Eminence think is the strength of the groundswell of support for the view expressed in that *Report*? And, finally, you mentioned 'specific circumstances' surrounding your possible candidacy. The Curia, of course, has its own specific circumstances. But first let us hear Your Eminence's."

"Naturally. Naturally." Lohngren answers easily, as one used to power and power-moves. "Your Eminence has read the *Latin American Report*. As far as I am concerned, the essential of the *Report* lies in its documentation of a deal between some of the Latin American and European Cardinals. And then, the Argumentation of the *Report* is very persuasive. With what we already know of Thule and Franzus, the proposal in the *Latin American Report* becomes all too 'feasible,' as you say."

The evidence cited in the Vatican *Report* on Latin America consists primarily of an exchange of letters between some two or three Cardinals in Europe and Latin America, and some memoranda that had been circulated. The "deal" will purportedly come first through Cuba's Fidel Castro and, later, through Cardinal Franzus.

The evidence provides solid reasons for thinking that a majority of Latin American bishops have been sold on the idea of so-called "democratic socialism." As far as the Camerlengo and Lohngren are concerned, "democratic Socialism" is merely a window-dressing title for a Marxist state connived at by churchmen. The *Report* shows that those bishops have influenced many of their Cardinals—Lynch is not at all alone among his brother Cardinals. The *Report* shows further that the Africans are wavering; that a good bulk of Europeans, certainly including Franzus from the East, but also a share of the Italians, are open to changing their minds. Even some of the Curial Cardinals could be affected.

But there is another aspect to the Report—the so-called "Chinese Schedule." The "Chinese Schedule" purported to be a program that had originated in Red China, was drawn up in Spanish, and was intended as a plan for infiltrating the Catholic hierarchy and the whole Church in Latin America by "progressively replacing the religious element in Church teaching with a Marxist element."

"No doubt, I suppose," Lohngren asks, giving a sidelong glance at the Camerlengo's desk covered with papers and documents, "that the 'deal' is official?"

"If not *officiel*," the Camerlengo answers, resorting to the nice difference in the French expressions, "then certainly *officieux*. More than 'inspired.' No doubt. Moscow's offer. And that goes for the Argumentation too. Of this there can be no doubt. Now, do not presume the same authenticity for the 'Chinese Schedule.' "

"Authentic or not, self-fulfilling prophency or a genuine document and plan, it matters little," Lohngren answers. "What's outlined in the 'Chinese Schedule' is what's happened! And on top of that, we know Franzus *has* been approached. *With* a deal. *By* the Russians. Although the Secretariat has apparently precious few details. . . ."

"Franzus has been extraordinarily taciturn—to use a mild word," the Camerlengo gives a wintry smile. "As Your Eminence says, we have precious few details. But it is the Argumentation in the *Report* which I find. . . ."

"Yes. Yes. That Argumentation. And the proposed deal. A very nearly global plan, if you play it out in your mind. Precisely that has persuaded me we have a real danger."

The news of a deal, of connivance and planning to 'deliver' the Church, with its powerful popular influence, in key areas of the world into Marxist hands, the Camerlengo and Lohngren take as the facts of the case. They are old hands and have dealt with matters on a global scale before. For them, the important decision now is whether the *Latin American Report,* with its analysis of the future and its recommendations of what to do, can carry the Conclave.

In substance, the Argumentation of the *Report* says that the prospect of Soviet "Finlandization" and even the Marxization of most of Western Europe, and the Marxization of the most of Latin American, does not undo the soul of the Roman Church with fear.

The *Report* points out that historically the Christian mentality guiding the Church has never accepted any political theory or any practical, working institution that made anybody but God the source and regulatory agency of power—of any power, but particularly political power.

In this framework of Christian attitudes, the *Report* goes on, modern democracy and Marxism are on a par—at least democracy as it has been presented theoretically and installed politically from the eighteenth century onward in Europe and the Americas. For despite the protestations of democracy's many professional defenders and the outlook of many nations thus democratized, the modern concept of democracy is one in which the people are the *source and* the regulatory agency of all political power. No genuine Christian and Roman mind was ever seduced by that idea of democratic humanism, a bastard offspring of the seventeenth century Enlightenment, that beckons toward a haven of confidence in the nature of the world and in human nature—without reference to the prior power of God.

In this framework of Christian attitudes, both democracy and Marxism are inevitable consequences of the view that reality is only of the senses—that reality is locked into the visual, solid, touchable, measurable world. The *Report* quotes Einstein on this point: "People slowly accustomed themselves to the idea that the physical states of space itself were the final physical reality."

In the Christian mind, the *Report* argues, modern democracy and Marxism obviously are merely two variants of a "closed-in universe" outlook; an outlook that says the universe itself is all; and God is closed out of, or identified with, the universe. Democracy appears much more tolerant than Marxism. But it is not really, and therefore is not itself the solution of human problems.

When the Church denounces Marxism, it does not intend to defend democracy or capitalism against Communism, or even to defend liberty against dictatorship. Because, the *Report* argues further, we moderns have all arrived at the final moments of a civilization that has declined into an exclusive servility to the senses, to an inevitable totalitarianism that will be just as complete whether it claims modern democracy or Marxism as its father.

The *Report*'s conclusion after all of its analysis and Argumentation is that between Communism and modern Western-style democracy, there can be only one practical choice—Communism together with its accompanying ideology—or, as the *Report* prefers, "democratic socialism." Why? Because, the *Report* concludes, Communism as a political system and Marxism as an ideology show all the evidence of being open-ended to the future, of marching to a future of some kind or other. But democracy and capitalism are both revisionist and retrograde.

It is for all these reasons, the *Report* states, that the liquidation of the democratic structures of Western Europe is not and cannot become a source of terror for the Roman mind, or for the really Christian mind. *But*, the *Report* concludes, the *certainty* of its liquidation is the occasion for a completely new departure in Vatican policy, in the attitude with which the next Pope must be elected, *and* in the kind of Conclave "mandate" he must be given as a condition of being elected.

It is nothing less than that, that the Camerlengo and Lohngren weigh between them now. And they must, in additon to the weight of the *Latin American Report*, take into account the Report summarizing the secret discussions between the Vatican and the U.S.S.R. about detente between the two. And, on top of all that, everyone can see the strength and appeal of Cardinal Thule. The Camerlengo is aware that Thule and Franzus and Lynch are meeting now. All of these elements may be more or less separate, but they are all powerful elements tending in the same direction. Do they present an irresistible tide?

"I suppose we must face the hard fact," Lohngren is still weighing possibilities in his mind, "that a candidate of the Curia is bound to be Italian, if not Roman, and is bound to be Curial minded, if not a working member of the Curia. And if the Argumentation of that *Latin American Report* is correct, the election of such a man would provoke a very severe, very deleterious reaction in the Soviets. And, if they will soon hold sway over most of Europe and in Latin America—however indirectly—then the Church could only suffer more."

"Eminence, there is one more fact we have learned quite recently. And it complicates everything. There appears to be an alliance, or at least one in the making, between Thule and Franzus."

Lohngren raises his eyebrows. "Eminence, we in Germany have known about the Thule-Franzus alliance, or anyway a proposal of alliance, for quite a while. Thule tried to get our German Cardinal Kiel into the affair. I really began to think seriously again of the pan-European candidacy as a means of offsetting the Thule-Franzus thing. Then Lynch got involved, and the Latin Americans—the *Ostkardinalaat* and the *Westkardinalaat,* as we in Germany described them. What I couldn't gauge until now was how much support they might pull away. But if we could still offset their moves. . . ."

"That's it," the Camerlengo replies. "That's it exactly! We offset any possibilities of the Thule-Lynch-Franzus wave. The idea is that we avoid the issue altogether. We enter the First Session tomorrow as if the *General Framework* still held. Most of the Electors don't have the information in the *Report,* and don't see the Marxist alliance as a force in the Conclave yet. Most will enter the Session supporting the *General Framework.* With a short Conclave, the *General Framework* position might hold. If it fails, then we must quickly put forward a pan-European candidate, a non-Italian, a non-Curial man, a man who will represent the 'one Europe' idea and hold the line against the Marxist plan. No Frenchman will do: they are all over seventy, except Gellee of the East." The Camerlengo looks up and gives a hint of a smile. "Gellee would not be the best choice." He looks down, still speaking. "We can forget Buff—already burned his boats. And forget all four Spaniards, and the Eastern Europeans—they all hold key positions in their own countries and cannot be replaced easily. Da Gomez, the Iberian, is only forty-six; and Witz won't accept—thank God! That leaves the Germans. Kohl and Kiel are both too young. All key Electors agree that the proper candidate should be over sixty. Kirchner is Curial; and, besides, we both know his gifts are definitely not pontifical. Lohfink is eighty-two and that's too old. Munch is seventy-eight, Borlach is seventy-seven and Eck is seventy-nine. They would end up too old too fast. We can't make do this time with an interim Pope. There's too much at stake and events are going very fast. That leaves"—the Camerlengo looks up steadily at Lohngren—"Your Eminence."

The Camerlengo straightens up in his chair and gazes at the man whom he may be acknowledging as Pope in a few days' time. "Besides, my Venerable Brother, you happen to have an unparalleled popularity with European

Bishops and Cardinals. I know, or knew, Bishop Marsellais as your good friend." Roger Marsellais, Bishop of Lovon and Secretary to the Conference of European Bishops, is the all-powerful king-maker among European Bishops, and a former supporter of Lohngren. "I also know his support has left you. But, please, go and talk to him. He's not immovable. A good man, Roger."

There is a pause. Almost a rest after their long discussion. Then the Camerlengo becomes the practical dealer. They have discussed the crisis, he observes to Lohngren. And they have seen that Lohngren is the only viable answer if the *General Policy* position does not hold. So now, the conditions! Lohngrer said he had his conditions.

Lohngren is direct. "Well, first there is the question of European investments. Then there is the post of Secretary of State—he must be a German. And, lastly, there is Angelico." The Camerlengo stiffens in his chair at the mention of Angelico's name. He swivels around to face Lohngren directly and watch every expression in his eyes as he speaks.

During this long interview with Lohngren, at the other side of the Conclave enclosure, three Cardinals are seated in Kand's apartment: Kand himself, Karewsky, and Garcia the Iberian. They are rapidly going through the *Position Paper* which Kand has not yet seen.

The seventy-eight year old Kand is a veteran of Nazi persecution and Stalinist prisons. A Cardinal since 1975, a pawn in the desperate game the Vatican has played with the Communist regime in his home country for a dozen years, Kand has weathered it all; and, at home, his diocese is even now weathering a most vicious anti-Catholic persecution. His drawn face, the deep lines around mouth and eyes, his frail figure still active but in constant pain, and the tones of his voice, all tell of deep suffering and continued confrontation with bitter enmity.

Though Kand is a Cardinal, the Communists will not allow his official appointment as Archbishop. Kand's task is to lead his millions of Roman Catholics and give them some hope and some direction.

Jan Karewsky, sitting with this group, is a different sort of man. Just sixty-one, cheery, subtle, active, quick-witted, well-read, resourceful, humorous, a Cardinal since 1966, he heads a major diocese, is completely alive to the issues confronting the Church, both East and West, and has no illusions. Between him and Kand the difference is more than one of age. It is a difference in personal experience and in basic character. Karewsky has never been in prison. Nor has he suffered at the hands of the KGB operatives. Kand has been a living martyr. The atmosphere for Catholics in his country is quite different from that in Karewsky's country: one is relatively easy. The other is deathly. And over and above personal experience, Karewsky is naturally an optimistic person and insuppressible. Kand is a quiet man, not a fighter, but intensely loyal.

The third man in the group, José Garcia, a seventy-four-year-old Archbishop, has been a Cardinal for seven years. He is a powerful character set in a solid frame. Progressive in thought, but cautious in matters of dogma and belief, conservative in questions of moral practice, open to new ideas, Garcia has no tolerance for wishful thinking. He has all the explosive pride of his country, the downright frankness characteristic of his grandee ancestors, and an ability to sympathize with weakness and to go along with compromise. He is free of any taint from the Falangist Party, has never flirted with Communists or Socialists, and has an unblemished personal reputation. "If Garcia were Italian," Pope Paul was once supposed to have said, "he would surely be Supreme Pontiff."

"Supposing we start with the *General Framework Paper,*" Karewsky says to Kand. "It draws on all the other *Position Papers.* And we will refer back from the *General Framework* to particular passages in individual *Papers* when this is helpful or necessary to fill you in. I have marked my own copies heavily in red. I've underlined the paragraphs of the first chapter of the *General Framework* that concern the internal condition of Roman Catholicism, and prospects for near-future expansion in the world. Just glance at them, as I run through them quickly with you.

"As far as the present condition of Catholicism goes, the analysis can be summed up in two words: decline and fragmentation. Within the decade since the Second Vatican Council, there has not been merely a serious decline in the *number* of priests and nuns. It is rather that the *practice* and *profession* of traditional Catholic doctrine has ominously declined, in some places disappeared.

"On tell-tale points of practice: the use of contraceptives, of abortion, of hysterectomy and vasectomy as contraceptives, of divorce and remarriage, of common-law marriages, of tolerance in matters of pornography; in the practice of voting against the Catholic conscience and law; of accepting other religions as equal in validity to Catholicism; of refusing the teaching authority of Pope and Bishops; of neglect of the Sacraments—particularly of Penance and the Eucharist—in all this, there is no country in the whole world where the picture is bright. But what is most symptomatic is the obvious decline of really active religious belief on the part of the clergy—cardinals, bishops, and priests."

From time to time, Karewsky's eye returns to the well-marked *General Framework* Paper before him. But he knows all too well what it says.

"And even that is not all of it," he goes on summarizing for Kand. "The

Report analyzes at length the new and well-embedded movement tending to erase all and any distinction between priest and lay person; between Church and ordinary social grouping; between the sacred and the profane; between psychological therapy and religious devotional practice. This tendency, this confusion, is spurred powerfully by a new generation of theologians, the so-called theologians of liberation, who equate the Church's mission with social activity and her religious ideal with material betterment. These new theologians seem to have deserted the main principles of traditional Christian philosophy. Cardinals Lynch, Manuel, Marquez, and many ordinary bishops are deeply a part of all this.

"What you heard in Lynch's remarks this evening was only the tip of the iceberg. Men like Gutierrez, Küng, Schillebeeckx, Laurentin, have been working and worrying away skillfully from within the Church for the past dozen years or so. They have been so effective that such basic doctrines as the divinity of Jesus, his Resurrection, the forgiveness of sin, the privilege of Mary the Virgin, the teaching power and authority of the Pope as Peter's successor, and life after death in another dimension of existence called the supernatural, all this seems to have disappeared from the mind and outlook of these theologians! And from the minds of many—thousands upon thousands—whom they have influenced.

"This mass of change and decay is shot through with some powerful forces of disruption. There is a vast movement of selfist philosophy according to which the ego of each one is the final and the only acceptable norm of what is true, and of what is right and wrong, for each one. The prime Roman Catholic example is the Catholic Charismatic movement. Not only does the Charismatic movement tend to tear the institutional Church apart. Their very narcissism makes them suitable adepts for the wiles of these Christians who seek to identify the Christian effort with Marxist aims. Now that is not true of each Charismatic. But it is true of the *movement* as a whole.

"Next to this selfist philosophy there is the overall subversion by the new theologians of priestly seminary training. The whole training of young priests now is completely away from the traditional doctrines, and over to an outlook that stresses urban problems, population problems, political rights, ethnic development, and an ambiguous type of belief and religious devotion that allows for any form of religious faith. But with one big 'kicker': In all this so-called freedom, belief *must* hew to the specific political theory generally called 'democratic socialism.' Küng, Lynch, and that crowd move back into the picture here. The authors of the *Papers* see no inherent difference between that socialism and the structure of any work-a-day Communist regime. As Santiago Carillo, the Spanish Communist Party leader, said in November 1977, there is no fundamental difference between a Eurocommunist and a socialist. And you and I, my dear Kand, can see better than most what lies ahead, if such a trend wins out in the end." Kand raises his eyebrows and shrugs.

"As for the near-future expansion of Roman Catholicism, the *General Framework* briefly states that there is no visible hope, now or in the near future—as far as they can humanly judge—of any rapid or widespread expansion of Catholicism—or even of Christianity—in Africa, China, Southeast Asia, India, or in the countries of Islam. *Nobody* disagrees here. The conclusion is unanimous. *Position Papers* 9 through 11 make that clear." Karewsky searches out a phrase in the *General Framework* Paper and quickly finds it:

" 'While missionary efforts continue, they will be merely and foreseeably token. No vast conversions, no wholesale take-overs are in sight.' "

Kand continues reading: " 'If then we continue to speak of the coming Kingdom of Christ and of going forth to preach to all nations, we must not delude ourselves. The days of vast missionary expansion are over for now. They were, in their day, always accomplished on the back of some Imperial or Colonial power. Such powers—except one, the U.S.S.R.—have ceased to exist. And the Church lacks any other dynamic in the social and political and cultural orders with which to explode in the bright light of Christ before the nation.' "

Kand puts the papers aside, muttering, "the bright light of Christ before the nations." He looks at Garcia: "What's the alternative, my friend? Thule?"

"That would be, in my humble opinion, to invite total adulteration of the faith!" Karewsky breaks in before Garcia can answer.

"Then what?" Kand takes up the puzzle. "We can't just acquiesce and wait. We'll just wait and wait and wait and wait and be picked off one by one by our enemies, or perish by attrition."

"You think *that* is bad!" Garcia cocks his head to one side. "Wait until we've finished briefing you on the rest of the *Papers.*"

Neither Karewsky nor Garcia has any doubt as to where Kand stands on the issues. But their purpose is to gain him positively to their side—to the Radical position. They need his witness to what life under a Marxist regime is like. And they also need to have access to his intelligence sources. In his home town, even watched and monitored by the Secret Police, Kand is at the center of a network that takes in the Soviet Union and the Western arena.

"But didn't Pope Paul realize what the situation is like?"

Garcia is the one to reply this time, "Oh yes! Yes indeed! He himself spoke of the self-destruction of the Church—a strange expression, don't you think? And he alluded to 'the smoke of Satan which has entered the Church.' And, I think, you both heard him say in 1975 that 'the Church seems destined to die.' And he meant every word of it. No metaphors. Paul realized the danger, saw how far things had gone. He had one policy: foment a united Europe, witness to the truth, pacify all factions—*integral humanism!* But it did not work. And when he woke up to that icy-cold fact, it was too late to change it." Garcia's voice is not hard; rather it has a regretful, compassionate tone.

"All right," Gracia grunts as he turns some pages. "Now look at the next section of the *General Framework*. These pages summarize *Position Papers 2 through 4*. Namely, the condition of non-Catholic Christians—the Eastern Orthodox and Protestant Christian Churches."

Skimming the paragraphs, Kand learns that, in the general opinion of the Cardinals and Vatican consultants, the condition of all non-Catholic Christian sects is deteriorating at an even faster rate than that of Catholicism.

First, some so-called Christian Churches are Christian in name only, but not in their official stances and beliefs—notably the Unitarian, the Christian Scientist, the Mormon Churches. Kand reads:

> If to be Christian means professing and maintaining belief in a divine creation of the universe from nothing, in the efficacy of Christ's death as the unique redemption for all mankind from sin and from Hell; and, further, in belief in the Sacraments, in the divinity of Jesus, in his Resurrection, in life after death, in the existence of the soul as immortal and really distinct from the body, then such churches or sects are not Christian at all.

> Further, run the conclusions of the *General Framework*, most of the major Protestant Churches incur the same criticism of being non-Christian to some degree or other. This is applicable to the large majority of Anglicans all over the world—including the Episcopalians of the United States—to a small minority of Lutherans and large majorities of Presbyterians, Methodists, and Baptists.

> We can say that effectively, these vast numbers of self-styled Christians profess beliefs either at variance with basic Christian beliefs or totally contradictory of basic Christian beliefs.

"Can it be as bad as that?" asks Kand. "What about this—I admit, volatile—enthusiasm in the United States, for instance. The—what do they call themselves—the born again people? And all that flurry of enthusiasm for renewing the Liturgy?"

"Let me give you one instance of Protestant liturgical renewal," Garcia rejoins quickly and heavily. And he tells of an Easter celebration organized some years ago in Cambridge, Massachusetts. It was a "Byzantine Mass," he recalls, or so its organizers claimed. It was celebrated by ministers of four denominations in a Boston discotheque; it was enlivened by body-painting, jumping, hugging, moaning; punctuated by the Hallelujah Chorus, Hindu Mantras, and the Kiss of Peace; and it ended when the "worshippers" rushed out to greet the sunrise chanting the Beatles' hit record, "Here comes the Sun!"

"They are, you see, in quite a frenzy of ridiculous and pathetic despair," Karewsky comments.

"That's not renewal," Garcia concludes. "It's ribald nonsense."

"Am I to understand then," Kand is surprised, "that the much vaunted ecumenical movement is a dead letter?"

"Yes. But all that is a separate section," Garcia says quietly, "and is included in the *Special Report on The Pontificate of Pope Paul 6*. We'll get there in due course. First, let's go ahead with the *General Framework*."

But Kand is hungry for news. He has heard only bits and scraps, and tonight is a feast. "Before leaving this point," he says, settling back in his chair, "tell me briefly about Suenens and the Charismatics' born again movement."

"You won't believe how serious it all has become, my friend," Garcia shoots a quick glance at Karewsky, as if to seek his agreement. "Suenens was heard speaking in tongues. In tongues, if you please. Glossolalia."

"Glossolalia? When?"

"Last year, in Kansas City, in the State of Missouri, where there was a major gathering of Charismatics at an international meeting. . . . 'Ad gallum hum . . .' That's reportedly how he began, or something like that."

Kand stares at Garcia then slowly turns to look at Karewsky, then back to Garcia in disbelief. "You aren't serious?"

"I assure Your Eminence I am serious. And His Eminence is quite serious. The report," Karewsky assures him, "is very explicit. Paul knew as we all do, that the born again syndrome is just another stage in the declining day of Protestantism. Luther and the other reformers of his time proposed justification by faith alone without good works. They almost did away with any need for Baptism or personal repentance. Now, the born again business means that you don't need Baptism with water. Or the Mass. Or the Eucharist. Or confession. Or the priest. Or the Pope. Or a historical Jesus, for that matter. They all come down to the same thing finally. Religious economism—my own word for it: You take what you *feel*, what you *feel* you want, what you *feel* you like. And you forget the rest."

"What has Thule to say to all that?" Kand asks.

"That you will hear tomorrow, I am sure."

"Now," Garcia interrupts, "let's get on with it or you will not be ready for the First Session tomorrow. The next section on Eastern Orthodoxy is tragically simple to summarize: Orthodoxy is in the catacombs and will stay there, perishing slowly. What emerges into the sunlight on a later day will be tattered remnants. Official Orthodoxy in the U.S.S.R. has been bastardized through faithful service to their political masters in the Kremlin. Unofficial Orthodoxy—among the ordinary people—will continue in the U.S.S.R. and Greece and elsewhere. But it has no prospect of any near-future prosperity or expansion.

"As for non-Christian religion," Garcia goes on summarizing the *Paper*, filling out the picture Kand must have in order to be able to judge the condition and prospects of the Roman Church, "Buddhism and Hinduism are being eroded according as modern life invades the countries and the peoples they most dominate. For them, there is no compromise possible that will let them live in their essential purity. They are doomed to the refuse-heap. Probably," Garcia winds up, "as the *Paper* says, 'probably isolated parts of each may develop into a sort of social feeling, a kind of Ethical Culture by Orientals for Orientals.' But essentially, we can dismiss them as negligible."

"Now, Islam." Karewsky takes up now. "According to the *Reports*, Islam is only a slightly different case. The *Reports* state that in certain sectors of Islam there is a chance it can evolve out of its ghetto. But, overall, the picture looks bad for Islam. In the principal Muslim countries, it is being slowly transformed into a political ideology and merely cultural way of life. The nearest parallel, ironically enough, is with the vast majority of Jews, who remain attached to something they call Judaism, but which is really no longer a religion so much as an ethnic and cultural outlook, or 'identity,' now based on the sovereign state, Israel, as its mainstay. It's the impact of modern life, as usual. The mainstay of Islam is Saudi Arabia and the House of Saud in particular. All, in other words are in trouble."

As Kand goes on with his briefing, and as the Camerlengo continues his dealings with Lohngren, in another apartment close by the Camerlengo's office Cardinal Angelico has just received eight visitors.

"Your Eminence," Cardinal Azande of Africa bows to Angelico. "Please pardon this vast intrusion! But all of us," he indicates with a graceful little gesture the seven other black Cardinals standing around and behind him— Duala, Salekê, Kotoko, Lotuko, Chaega, Bamleke, Makonde—"wish to get counsel from you." Angelico bows to his visitors; he is unsmiling, pleasant-faced.

"Why don't you all find a comfortable place to sit. If I can be of any help. . . ." He turns away for an instant. Azande notes that Angelico lifts his eyes to an image of the Sacred Heart of Jesus framed and hanging on the wall.

Azande smiles at the others. Angelico's habit of instant prayer on all occasions is known to all the Cardinals.

"Your Eminence. We are on our way to a consultation in the apartment of my Lord Cardinal Thule. We have an approximate idea of what we will be asked to do and to accept. But there is one gap in our knowledge—or perhaps, it is in our judgment. And you are the most fitted to enlighten us on the matter."

"None of us, Eminence," Makonde, the oldest black Cardinal, takes up, "have been near enough to the subject. Yet it is capital. Frankly, it is the previous Holy Father and his Pontificate. There are two *Supplementary Position Papers,* as you know, that deal with Pope Paul. And we have read those *Papers.* But it is not enough. We know you had something to do with drawing up both *Papers.* Since you worked closely with Pope Paul, and since you were such a good friend of his, we would like to hear from your lips not simply the substance of those two *Papers,* but rather how Your Eminence thinks they should influence our judgment in the choice of candidate."

The *Supplementary Position Papers* were curiously laid out. In dealing both with Paul's financial and political policies, as well as with the Pope's implementation of the decrees of the Second Vatican Council, the authors of the *Papers* contented themselves with expounding the facts; the decline of religious obedience; the revolt of clergy; the spread of Marxist thinking among theologians and philosophers; the vast decline in vocations to the priesthood; Vatican financial losses; Vatican concessions to the Soviet satellite regimes; the persecution and suppression of the Church in those countries. These *Papers* add up to a long jeremiad of failures and mishaps and deficiencies. But, unlike the other *Papers,* no final judgment is passed on it all. There is not even a general summary of the meaning of what Paul accomplished.

Paul's overall policy of accommodation to nearly all left-wing, liberal currents, and his violent rejection of the Traditionalist movement are both described. But, again, no final judgment is made. Instead, both *Papers* end by saying, in sum, that Paul's entire policy as Pope represented an "open judgment" on the vast changes that the world of the sixties and seventies has been undergoing.

"The fact is," Saleke observes, "we have been satiated with one type of judgment—if you can call it a judgment. We need a balance."

"I know." Angelico understands the problem. "Balance is often the hardest thing to come by these days." He looks at Makonde, the most conservative among the blacks. "Your Eminence was present at the Second Vatican Council. You realize, perhaps. . . ."

"I have given my point of view," Makonde says stoutly. "My Brothers have heard me explaining that the Council was hijacked by liberal theologians. But we still need a balance." In Makonde's mind, as in Angelico's, much of what happened in Paul's reign, and much of the present trouble in the Church, was caused by the way Paul went along with what Makonde has bluntly called hijacking.

"What I have to say about these matters is what I personally think." Angelico is avoiding any semblance of leadership or spokesmanship or "inspired" opinions. "You all know my history. So you will have to balance that against what I say."

Angelico is right. His history in the Roman Curia was stormy by any standards, and is certainly well known.

"I agree," Angelico is saying now, "with the substance of both *Supplementary Reports*. There can be little doubt that one group—call it the Rhine Group, the Conciliarist Group, the Northerner Group, whatever you like— one group did take over in the Council. They put through statements of Church doctrine with a deliberate—I say deliberate—ambiguity useful for its originators. They wished to make it easy for non-Catholic Christians and, indeed, non-Christians to draw closer to the Church. Their intention was good, I think, on the whole. But it is this very ambiguity that has in large part brought us to our present crisis. For it has left us with little protection against a clever minority that wants now to hijack the Church itself."

"But there must have been people at the Council who could see the danger," Bamleke objects. "Why did the majority of the Council Bishops accept all that?"

"*Because* of the very ambiguity! Pope John had spoken about opening windows. Well, here the windows were opened! Every sort of interpretation could blow through the house, could even lodge permanently in the house of the Lord! Did in fact do so! You must try to remember the atmosphere at the Council—the media, the young Bishops, the young theologians, the Jews, the Protestants. *Freedom*. That was the most used word. *Openness! Reconciliation! Frankness! Fraternity! Understanding!* And, behind it all, for the first time in a long time, *power over the Roman Curia!* It was all so heady, so very heady! And none of us could have expected then how all this would be used later on.

"It was not the Bishops, the only authorized teachers in Christ's Church, but the young *theologians* who, by skillful maneuvering, took control of all the post-Council Commissions that were invested with the power to *interpret* and *implement* the decision of the Council." Angelico looks sharply at his questioners. He wants to be sure they have understood what he has said. "Note well! By clever maneuvering the young theologians got from the Bishops the very power to *interpret* and *implement* the Council's already ambiguous decisions. The results should not surprise any of us. At least not in hindsight."

"We ourselves know how this ambiguity was exploited," Kotoko comments. "We suffer from that exploitation. For instance, it is important in our black African populations that priesthood and episcopacy be separate and apart from the lay people. Our peoples have a great sense of the sacred, of the hieratic, of reverence, and of religious awe. But if you ask most Western theologians—the ones who are writing the books and articles nowadays, and teaching in the major seminaries of Europe and America, where our young men must go to get their formation—they say there should be no distinction at all between clergy and laity. No distinction in anything—dress, functions, respect, occupations of daily life, marriage, sex, and so on. This is catastrophic."

The others agree.

"The ambiguity has gone very far," Angelico reflects.

Every document of the Council is marked with the subtle ambiguity of which Angelico and the black Cardinals are speaking. The Vatican Council document on the Church does not state that the Catholic Church is the Church of Jesus; it says that the Church of Jesus subsists in the Catholic church. A subtle difference, one that in the innocence of a decade ago would not have been questioned between men of the same faith. The document on Liturgy deliberately omits the key Roman Catholic word *transsubstantiation,* thus opening the door for other non-Catholic interpretation of the very heart of the Catholic Mass, and of Catholic belief. The Pope's teaching authority is spoken of in such a way that it can be taken in the traditional sense—the Pope's personal privilege as Pope—or as merely part of the general teaching authority of the Church, as merely the chairman of an international board where he has the deciding vote and an extra dollop of respect.

The purpose of marriage is described as primarily the exercise of marital relations, rather than the total Christian aim of love, children, family. Cardinal Thule was one of the prime supporters of this new view at the Council. Hence it has been concluded that all else—contraception, abortion, divorce, even sodomy between consenting couples—are licit in order to achieve that marital love.

A commonplace but telling example of the Council's ambiguity is provided by Paragraph 17 of the Council's *Decree on the Renewal of Religious Life:* The clothes worn by monks, nuns, priests should, the Decree proclaims, "meet the requirements of health and be suited to the circumstances of time and place as well as to the service required by those who wear them. Clothes of men and women which do not correspond to these norms are to be changed." These "norms" are so general that they have indeed permitted the *total abolition* in many cases of *all* distinctive religious clothing. That was not the intention of the Bishops. But the ambiguity of the language the new theologians proposed—and the Bishops accepted—has allowed the theologians to *interpret* and *implement* the Decree in ways far beyond what the Bishops intended or anticipated.

When one understands that this ambiguity was applied systematically to *all* the teachings of the Second Vatican Council—and therefore to many of the essential dogmas of the Church—there can be no surprise that throughout the Catholic Church today many intellectuals, theologians, philosophers, writers, together with some Cardinals, bishops, priests, nuns, and ordinary layfolk can no longer bring themselves to recite the traditional *Credo*. It is this result of the Council that disturbs the Africans. And Angelico understands.

"Now as regards Pope Paul himself," Angelico is going to the heart of the question the Africans have asked but, for a moment, he stops and stares at the floor. Then he starts slowly. "Forgive me, Your Eminences, if I speak with apparent harshness of a man to whom I personally owe so much . . ." lifting his eyes to the ceiling, lost for an instant in some memory or some thought, or some prayer of his own, "may Montini himself help me by his prayers and forgive me any unintended wrong or hurt I do him now. But," lowering his eyes level with Bamleke's, "I can only say what I think.

"Pope Paul was the least fitted to cope with this situation." Angelico speaks now without pause, but with apparent difficulty and strain. "His theology was inadequate. His philosophy of man and history was theologically erroneous—not heretical, mind you—but simply erroneous.

"At heart, Montini thought that the function of the Church was not so much any more to convert, or to missionize, or to engage in polemics, or to engage in any social or political commentary or activity, or to bear a standard before the eyes of all men and women, or even to act on its own initiative in the society of human beings.

"He seemed to think that the Church's mission was simply to exist. To exist as a leaven. As a light. To open itself out and allow all sorts of influences to moderate and adapt and change and color the Church's own behavior, so that the Church would take on the stance suitable for the surrounding world. In this way, he thought, events might integrate all of humanity's goodness and beauty and love of the eternal under the Church's umbrella.

"The danger seems obvious now: that the world might change the Church rather than the other way around. But, at heart, Montini thought that all men seek goodness, are basically good. And he thought that the Church should not enter the socio-political order at all. It should stay away from all that, saving, sanctifying, adapting, and drawing all men by love to seek unity in the democratic achievement of universal brotherhood. . . ." Angelico gives a little smile as the sentence trails off. Then: "Actually I am quoting from memory the favorite author of Montini—Maritain; Jacques Maritain."

"But Maritain rejected all that when he was much older and near death!" Bamleke blurts out in his deep basso voice.

"Yes! Yes, indeed! But Montini was no philosopher and no writer; he was Pope. He could not change course so easily. Not once but many times he had compromised himself and his Church. With the so-called new theologians. With the self-styled Conciliarists. With the Jesuits. With the Protestants and the Orthodox, and with the Soviets in Eastern Europe. He couldn't undo the damage. He did what he could, of course. But he could not undo the damage."

"In that case, Eminence," now it is Azande who speaks, "what My Lord Cardinal Thule and My Lord Cardinal Lynch and others are proposing is merely an extension and continuation of Montini's erroneous step?"

"No! No! Not quite!" Angelico is almost rude in his quick retort. "Forgive me, Eminence. What I mean is: not a continuation, rather a consummation, a crowning. Montini put his own two feet in the hole. When he understood what he had done he did what little was left to him to see the Church was not lost in his error. Their Eminences, whatever be their motives, or their understanding of affairs, would have us put the entire body of the Church in the same hole—in over everybody's ears."

"One last question, Eminence," Azande's voice has an added tone of seriousness. "Is there any contingency in which Your Eminence would consider having your name put in nomination?"

There is a sudden silence. Angelico rises quickly and crosses over to the window that looks on to the streets. From the City around the *Domus Mariae* comes that low, quiet, rumbling sound of distant traffic that never ceases in Rome.

The others wait. They are feeling, sensitive men, all alive to the emotion of such a moment and to the struggle taking place in this stocky little Italian with the broad husky shoulders and the sensitivity of a child.

After a few moments, Angelico turns around. His face is composed, the eyes smiling; but no one of the blacks is taken in by the appearance of things. "Why don't we all reflect a little more about that? There are ... er ... problems. . . ."

The blacks stand up; they each bow to Angelico, murmur some simple words of parting, and leave. The last out, the senior, Makonde turns around to close the door after him and, almost by the way, throws a quick glance back to Angelico. Angelico's face has lost the smiling conventional composure of a moment ago. They are both surprised at the quick meeting of eyes. Then Makonde says softly: "Pope Pius who consecrated me, Venerable Brother, once said that awe was from God but fear is of the Devil. Is that awe or fear in your eyes?"

Angelico laughs lightly. "Pray for me. Pray for us. All of us," he answers.

"I will, Eminence," Makonde says, still looking at him, now with an open smile. "I will. Be at peace. Jesus will regulate all of us."

On the floor above, in Thule's apartment, a strategy session is about to begin among six Cardinals: Thule himself, Franzus of Eastern Europe, the Anglo-Saxon Buff, Lynch of Latin America, Tsa-Toke of the Orient, and Motzu the Asiatic. They are expecting Cardinal Francis and the black Africans to arrive shortly.

The dominating figure here is Thule. He has called the meeting in order to forge an alliance. He knows, as everybody knows, that already Lynch and the Cardinals who stand with him have a working agreement with Franzus. Both Cardinals, in addition, have the adhesion of most of the French Cardinals. Buff has been invited because of his access to British Commonwealth Cardinals, his dislike of the Roman Curia, and his acceptability for Protestant Church leaders.

Tsa-Toke, an ally of Franzus and of Lynch, is an invaluable asset: he is Asiatic and has lived under one of the toughest Marxist regimes on earth, is covertly anti-U.S.A., and has no hesitation in saying that Roman Catholics can collaborate with Marxist-Leninist regimes.

The Oriental, Francis, is an open door for Thule to the black Africans. Without Thule realizing it, Francis is privy to the fact that the Africans cannot stomach the attitudes of Lynch and Thule. But Francis holds his own counsel to himself. Thule will learn this only the hard way.

But Lynch and Franzus are Thule's main targets. With Buff he already has *de facto* understanding: Both foresee a Church in which Catholic and non-Catholic Christian can mingle and exchange rites, concepts, beliefs, customs, and mutual approval. Lynch and Franzus have come to this Conclave content to sit it out and not quite persuaded that they could get their favorite candidate elected.

Thule's aim is to get them all to unite behind one compromise candidate. He would be willing to go along with Lynch on the candidacy of Yiu the Asiatic and to join with him in an early rush vote. For Thule fears that, if the Conclave is prolonged beyond a few days, a sense of alarm will run through the Electors. They could easily shy away from Thule's plank of complete "openness" of the Church to non-Catholic Christians, or from a positive acceptance by the Church of Marxist governmental systems, the main plank of Lynch and Franzus. A combination of both might be too much for too many! And, so, the occasion would be lost.

Thule and Buff had met for a few minutes first, to coordinate their ideas on how to present their plan of an alliance. The first to join them are Lynch, Franzus, Tsa-Toke, and Motzu. Motzu is smiling, jaunty. Tsa-Toke is quiet, almost demure, a man of few—if any—words.

Surprisingly, Franzus takes the first initiative. "I think that when we are finished here tonight," he starts off, "we should have a concerted plan. And I think that plan should be implemented as soon as possible. There's a summary danger in any waiting period. We can't afford a delay." Thule and Buff exchange glances.

"Just what we were thinking, Eminence," Thule says cheerfully.

"But," Franzus adds, "what about this damnable *General Policy* and the *General Policy* candidate? Haven't they already got a clear majority going for all that?"

"This is exactly where we can act," Thule breaks in. "Briefly, Buff and myself want to jolt the expected procedure of the First Session tomorrow morning forcing a vote of approval or disapproval of the *General Policy*. If we all unite, if our presentation speeches are well worked out, we can have that *General Policy*—and its candidate—wiped out of consideration. That leaves a vacuum, and into that vacuum we will jump as the only group with a viable alternative."

"In short," Buff summarizes, "we must all agree that the idea of an Italian, even of a non-Roman Italian, candidate is no longer valid."

"Not so difficult as all that, Your Eminence," Thule comments gently and gravely. "In fact, I feel that a formal rejection of a non-Roman Italian candidate *and* of the *General Policy* in one vote tomorrow will be just the dynamic we need to send Conclave feeling veering off in the right direction. It's worth the gamble. Besides, there's an extraordinary spirit of independence in this Conclave. I don't think as many as all that accepted what the Camerlengo said."

"Well, we need *something* to change the present trend in the Conclave," Franzus muses. "From my experience and from what I have been told in the last year, the present trend to an Italian candidate will be disastrous. Simply will be at odds with reality. That's all." Franzus' entire world is bounded by the military might of the U.S.S.R., and by the rising revolution in Latin America. This, for him, is the reality. Francis arrives at this moment. He takes a seat. "Somebody fill me in," he says genially.

"The general idea, Your Eminence, is as follows," Thule obliges immediately. "We all know from what the Camerlengo said today, that, within the so-called *General Policy Framework*, only one type of candidate really stands a chance of obtaining a majority—even a small majority. He is to be Italian. The *General Policy* will be one either of close identification with, or of closely following the policy projection of, the Western powers—and, to be frank, this means the policy of the United States. That American policy is predicated on a five-to-ten year projection according to which U.S.S.R. will be allowed limited aggrandisement—the famous, or rather infamous, LA. How I dislike that expression! Anyway, LA will be allowed within Western Europe and the Mediterranean. And all this is planned in view of yet another period of detente affecting Africa and Latin America and India. This is to say, a period during which any and every effort on the part of capitalists and Communists—short of direct super-power confrontation—is allowed, in order to see which way the wind of human affairs will blow. Since most of the financial and economic interests of the Holy See have been bound to the United States, the *General Policy* now proposed for the Holy See in choosing a candidate has been fashioned accordingly. It's money and imperialism dictating the choice of Pope."

"And that means," Francis draws the conclusion, "that the Church will discourage—even officially oppose—the popular movements in Latin America, in Asia, and in Africa."

"Yes," Thule replies, "exactly where the future of the Church lies, the defenders and formulators of the *General Policy* wish to hamper and hamstring the Church."

"So," Franzus adds, "we want to eviscerate the *General Policy* and its candidacy."

"And we want to work out an agreement on one candidate," Buff finishes up, "who will satisfy all of us and have a maximum appeal for other Electors."

Thule follows the remarks of each one. He judges that this is the moment he must make his bid for a unified front behind his general idea of a new Papal policy. He knows he has to tread warily. He looks down at his hands, meditating. The heavy lids close away his feelings for a few moments.

"My brothers," he says finally, as he lifts his head, his eyes full of import, "there is a still graver reason why we would propose our alternative." He looks at Motzu and Lynch, then at Buff. "There is a new spirit blowing across the face of humanity in our days. If we get the type of candidate outlined in the *General Policy Statement* and according to the supposed majority agreement of the Electors—personally, I doubt that all the Electors are aware of what is going on—then the Church will slip into a backwater from which it will not emerge easily for several generations. For, in the *General Policy* that candidate is supposed to be an Italian; and he is supposed to have a Papal policy that hews closely to United States interests and policies in Europe and the Third World. But nothing—especially the United States—can stem the revolution. The U.S.A. is over the hill. If we back them, and if the new Pope backs them, the Church is also over the hill."

Buff intervenes to smooth over the one difficulty that is apparent to all present. Just because Lynch and Franzus advocate Marxization of Third

World countries, and even of Western Europe, does not mean they approve of Thule's open Church. In actual belief, Lynch and Franzus are Traditionalist. "We know, of course, that we have agreement on the main point—a non-Italian Pope. It is also clear, however, to the Cardinal and to me that some of you have serious misgivings about the 'new spirit' of which Cardinal Thule has just spoken. And sometimes the representative voices of that new spirit are frightening. But I don't think that the two positions are irreconcilable...."

"Frankly, Your Eminence," Francis breaks in, addressing himself to Buff, "it is not with us—not so much anyway—as with our African brothers that you are going to have difficulty. Already they have found your new Liturgy an unmanageable and uninspiring mess. We of the older Rite don't mind"— Cardinal Francis heads the Catholics who have retained their ancient Liturgy untouched by the changes introduced by the Second Vatican Council in the 'sixties—"but the Africans can't take that new Roman Liturgy. Mainly because it lacks all depth and mystery. Believe me, they are going to slide back to the ancient modes of worship in any way they can.

"And what they can't take, either, are your new theologians and your new theology. No use in arguing about it with them. For them, people like Küng, like Schillebeeckx, Curran, Heusing, Dulles, Baum, Laurentin, people like that are already non-Catholics, if not non-Christians. *There's* your difficulty!"

"Yes," Motzu adds, "and even the Charismatic movement, and all that. Don't you realize that especially the Africans are very conscious of their dignity and power as Bishops, and the centrality of power in Rome? Now, the Charismatics everywhere are very much on their own, following their own inspiration. If anything, they are telling the Bishops and Pope what should be done, and what the Holy Spirit tells them should be done! You know—it's too much! Really!"

"And you have another difficulty," Franzus adds. "All right! So, if the *General Policy* of this Conclave is pro-U.S.A., pro-West, the U.S.S.R. won't like it. But don't you realize we have survived in the Eastern bloc only because we remain largely Traditionalist? I mean, Lefebvre would be most welcome by us. Can you make it worth our while to be allied with you? We can't take the new theologians; for us, they are devils. And, if we do march with you, how are you going to put your new theology, your 'new spirit,' in harmony with the populations in Hungary, Poland, Lithuania, Latvia, Estonia, Slovakia, and so on?"

"Our main strength," Thule argues, "is the *need*, the universally felt need for change. A need so great that we can formulate it in the shape of a row of threats that can be exercised against the Church, if the Church does not bend with the destructive wind blowing today.

"First, there is the condition of the Church in the Western countries, including the U.S.A. It is pretty bad already, as you know. But its intellectual leaders have been willing to wait for a new Pope in the hope that he will make the adaptation these intellectuals see as necessary. If they don't get that from the next Pope, you can expect a real split, a schism. That is one grave threat to be outlined.

"And that, my dear Franzus, is the answer to your own difficulty. You say these theologians are devils. I don't know. I don't think so. All I know is that they give voice to a deep change. Don't think your Iron Curtain Catholics are exempt from that change. Perhaps, indeed, you yourself should change. Perhaps not. But the point is, outside the Iron Curtain countries, there is this vast movement. We must follow with it. It is to our advantage, to the advantage of all of us."

Franzus receives all this affably, and makes no objection.

"Then," Thule continues, "there is the Church in Africa and Asia— comprising about one-third of all Catholic bishops, about one million nuns, and about 200,000 priests and brothers. Now, the winds of change are blowing there. But who would want winds of change to blow all that into loose disarray and disloyalty to Rome? So, Rome must go along with change. Even though their Cardinals dislike the change, they cannot prevent it.

"And there is a third threat," Thule goes on. "It is the threat of the total strangulation of the Church in most of Western Europe within the limits of the LA policy. If Soviet Russia really dominates in that region, in Western Europe and the Mediterranean, and if it is not conciliated, then we can expect Soviet attitudes to be the same as they are in the countries already under Soviet control."

"Unless," Lynch chimes in, "unless the Church officially and publicly throws its weight behind some form of democratic socialism both in Europe and Latin America, the Church will be a nonentity within a generation." He pauses a little. "Including and perhaps beginning with my own beloved country," he concludes mournfully. The others nod sympathetically.

"Well, when the Africans arrive, tackle them on this specific point." Francis says this in such a way that some there begin to doubt that he is whole-heartedly with them. But Francis adds, "You need their votes."

"I already have had two long talks with Azande," Thule answers. "He understands the future I see for the Church in Africa. I also went into the question of restructuring Church administration. Yes, we need his vote and other African votes. But the ground is well prepared.

"I take it then," Thule looks at each one, "that we all agree on the need for us to stay together and form one voting block?" The expression on each face is positive. Franzus, with a glance at Lynch, nods.

"You must realize that my intention in inviting the Africans here is double-barreled. We need their votes. And we need the votes they can win for us. I have no doubt, for instance, that Azande can garner quite a few of the Italians, perhaps one or two Americans. I think the Africans can influence many of the British Commonwealth Cardinals as well as Ni Kan, Nei Hao and Lang Che-Ning. With the blacks on our side, we can start a ground swell. We need them. Believe me. We need them."

"Before the Africans come," Buff introduces a new theme, "there are some things which our Eminent Brother should outline for us." He looks over at Lynch. He already has had a word with Lynch, telling him that he must make sure Francis understands. If Francis is with them, he will be most influential in convincing the Africans. But neither Buff nor Thule wish Lynch to explain too much of his mind to the blacks. He might disturb them at this still delicate point.

"I will try to sum it all up very briefly," Lynch begins. "According to what I know, there is a great readiness and disposition of soul among my clergy, and indeed in the clergy throughout the Third World, particularly in Latin America, precisely for this gigantic new step, this daring risk of brotherhood, fraternization, and collaboration with our Marxist compatriots at home and abroad. And—I stress this with you, it's important—the clergy's attitude is tailored to the conditions of body and mind of the ordinary people, the masses of the ordinary people.

"In spite of opposition from the Roman Curia, Latin America now has a whole theology to fit our outlook. Men like Gustavo Gutierrez of Peru, Juan Luis Segundo of Uruguay, Hugo Assman of Brazil, Miguel Bonino in the Argentine, Sergio Torres of Chile. All these have affected the universities, the seminaries, the colleges, and the ordinary people. You must add to this picture the vital work of the Capuchin Fathers in Nicaragua and of the Jesuits in several places, but especially in Honduras, where the Fathers are said to have directly created the three peasant organizations that are actually fighting the monopolist and fascist central government. Great gains throughout!

"Besides," Lynch continues, "outside Latin America, our outlook is very pervasive and there is effective coordination between the Americas—North and South—and the Europeans. All this or a good part of it is due to the work of Fr. Antonio Arroyo who directs the Hispanic Consultation of Theology in the Americas, and to Margaret Schuler, among others, who works in the *American Christians Toward Socialism* group. We have supporters in almost all the dioceses of North America—the U.S. Bishops themselves financed to the tune of $15,000 the 1975 Detroit *Theology in the Americas Conference* where all our Christian Leftists and Liberation theologians met.

"As for myself in all this, my Brothers, I can say in all good conscience, I am a Democratic Socialist. I am of the Left. Because that is where Jesus is and that is where Jesus' Church should be officially today and tomorrow in this world."

"In other words, you—like me—are in favor of going with this tide, even though it involves violence?" Buff asks with a grim look.

"Yes," Lynch says pleasantly enough but quite firmly. "The Kingdom of God is taken by violence and the violent bear it away, as Jesus himself said. And in my view, guerilla priests and lay people are only using counterviolence methods. Can you blame the Jesuits, for example in El Salvador, for carrying guns and calling on guerilla protection when the capitalist vigilante groups threaten their lives?

"The point I wish to make, and my contribution, is this: we must state our position boldly, and stand up for this alliance between the people and the Church. We must insist that the Church render this service of justice and peace to the people. For this Jesus founded the Church. Some will say we are mixing politics and religion. But this sort of politics is deeper than your normal politics. This is the question of the human survival of the Church. The time is past when we can temporize or wait."

"I think," Buff says, "our African Brothers are coming."

When the eight blacks do enter, there is a moment of awkward silence. Somehow or other, the very presence of those men in their Cardinalitial robes seems to pull the attention of all away from any theorizing, down to a very concrete level. No one of these black men, Cardinals all, is a third generation Christian. None is European. Something vaguely disturbing stands between the whites and the blacks. And even the gregarious and self-confident Lynch is affected.

It is Francis the Oriental, who breaks the awkwardness with almost Levantine smoothness and jollity: "I stand between you two, black and white, the only one who can possibly understand you both. Make me Pope!"

Everyone laughs a little—Thule perhaps less than the others; for Francis has hit upon the very reason Thule needs him. No fool, this man, Thule knows. But in the end, where will he stand?

Everyone finds a place, sitting or standing. Azande has apparently been chosen as spokesman for the blacks. He remains standing, and addresses Thule.

Everyone listening to the black Cardinal is struck by Azande's youthful face and the silvery clear tones of his voice with that subtle sibilance of his pronunciation. Formerly Archbishop of his home capital, Azande was called to Rome in 1970 and has already occupied many important posts in the Vatican. People speak of Azande as Pope Paul's future black Pope. And, indeed, Azande may one day be just that. Now Azande speaks, and it is with a great smoothness and gentleness.

"Eminence, we have come at your most gracious invitation to listen. But, with Your Eminence's permission, we would like to ask our Venerable Brother Lynch a few questions." Buff stays sitting, as does Lynch. Thule is standing.

"My Lord Cardinal," Azande looks straight at Cardinal Lynch as he begins. "Four Jesuit Fathers—two of them from the United States—recently published a book called *The New China: A Catholic Response.* Has Your Eminence read it?"

Lynch nods. He has read it.

"Does Your Eminence agree with the authors that Maoism is more akin to Christianity than is Buddhism or Hinduism, and that the Holy Spirit is using Maoism to lead the Chinese to Christ?"

"Well, I don't know if that is quite what the authors . . ." Lynch begins.

"Let me quote to you, Eminence." Azande is sure and intent. He takes a single folded sheet of paper from his pocket. " 'Communism is preparing the way for the Gospel. Mao's ideology can speak to the Christian need for personal development, for the evolution of the total Christian Community, and for more productive Christian thought and action.'

"I do not think," Azande looks up, "that the authors could speak their mind more clearly. And you, Eminence, what do you think?"

Francis opens his mouth to speak, then thinks better of it. Buff begins to clear his throat as if to say something, but Azande holds up his hand gently.

"It is Cardinal Lynch we wish to hear. After all, his standpoint is half the plank on which the group proposes to stand."

"Frankly, Your Eminence," Lynch answers slowly with a long look in Azande's direction, "these things are difficult to express in exact language. We are all groping. For words. For solutions. The Church herself is groping. We in Conclave are groping. . . ."

The senior among the black Cardinals, Makonde, now takes over. "Eminence, to bring it down to concrete terms, and to stop groping where we need not grope, and to speak concretely about a country which is not your own, could we have a few short answers to a few simple questions?"

This is not really a question, but a statement of what Makonde intends to do. He is famous for his Number One, Number Two, Number Three, Number Four method of interrogating.

"Number One: Did Your Eminence approve of the Government of Salvador Allende?"

"Like all other major responsible leaders, I support every legitimate government."

"I am not talking of the parliamentary agreement. I am talking of his suppression of the media, his silencing of opponents among the clergy. Did Your Eminence take measures to stifle all opposition to Allende?"

"Yes. I did. I thought that none of my clergy should intervene in politics."

"But this did not apply to the Monsignore whom you sent around to the various political factions. Nor to the seminarians you dismissed because they criticized Allende, and the others you did not dismiss who supported Allende. Nor to the priests you transferred to remote parishes from urban areas, for the same reason. Nor to yourself who engaged in purely political discussions with the Allende representatives and with Allende himself."

"We have to represent Church interests." Lynch is quite calm and confident.

"Number Two: Did you know of, and if you did, did you assent to Allende's prepared program of liquidation?" Allende's people had prepared, under his instructions, lists of intellectuals, businessmen and women, priests, social workers, writers, and others, who were to be eliminated at the crucial point in Allende's Marxist revolution.

"If such methods were necessary in their country so that social justice prevail, then . . ."

"But did Your Eminence know of such plans, and did Your Eminence assent to them?"

"We had information to that effect. We were never asked in our country to assent or dissent about matters in another country."

"Number Three: Has Your Eminence been in correspondence with Hortense Allende, the dead dictator's widow, and with Cuban authorities since Allende's death?"

"As part of my function as national leader of my Church, yes. Moreover, the relevant section of the Secretariat of State here in Rome knew and approved of these tractations."

"Number Four: Does Your Eminence agree with those who say that Christ was a kind of Palestinian Che Guevara, and that Chou en-Lai should one day be canonized as a saint by the Church?"

Lynch cannot very well deny any of this. He has made public statements to this effect, and has supported similar statements by other Latin American clergymen. He nods slowly but firmly.

"Number Five: Would Your Eminence exhort the faithful to rise in armed revolt in order to install a Marxist government in your own country, or in Chile, or elsewhere either in Latin America, in Africa, or in other parts of the world?"

Lynch has made remarks about this also. "If this is the only way—and mind you, it may not be . . ."

"Thank you, Venerable Brother. Number Six: Do you think that the next Pope should declare capitalism pernicious and irreconcilable with Christian ideals and openly commit the Church of Jesus to an alliance with Marxists not only in Latin America, but in North America, in Europe, in Africa, in Asia, and everywhere in fact?"

"If it comes to that, but ..."

"That is not my question, Eminence. Should the next Pope, whatever be the circumstances, should he take that step?"

Lynch looks quietly at Thule for just a second or two. Then there is an apparently interminable wait, while Lynch looks first at Makonde straight in the eye and for just an instant—and then away past the seven silent blacks standing quietly, waiting.

When he speaks finally, his tone is quiet enough, but it has the hint of a harsh edge. "I have lived and worked in the Church all my life. I know the Continent inside and out. I know more surely than I know most other things that nothing, but absolutely nothing, short of violent upheaval—bloodshed in fact—is going to put bread in children's mouths, cure their diseases ..." his voice is slowly rising in genuine passion, "take the sores off their little limbs, wash their bodies, remove the lice and cockroaches and horseflies from their hair and faces, fill their little bellies with good food, give their fathers dignity in work and their mothers a proper home to care for, and their aging grandfathers and grandmothers comfort in their old age."

Lynch's eyes are full of tears now. Some of the black Cardinals turn away, embarrassed. Lynch turns on Makonde but in a kind of gentle anger, as if to convey sorrow rather than enmity.

"Venerable Brother! You in Africa, you have seen what we have seen; what the industrial monopolies, the capitalist dynasties, the colonialist corporations, the secret government operations have done!"

"Yes, my Brother." It is Duala of East Africa who answers without any trace of rancor. "But nowhere, nowhere has a Marxist or a socialist government in Africa, or for that matter, in Asia, cleaned those scabs on little limbs, cared for our lepers in remote villages, saved our abandoned babies. Mother Teresa is not a Marxist. No Marxist has treated our prostitutes— beyond shooting them by the million, as Mao did—or paid an honest day's pay for an honest day's work. Or let people live in dignity, or preserved the family as a unit, or protected them from oppression, or guarded their liberties from the rapacity of socialist bureaucrats and Marxist dictators." He pauses, his eyes gleaming with expression. "Nowhere, Venerable Brother! Nowhere."

Lynch does not answer.

Thule appears very impatient to jump in, but Azande keeps the initiative, as leader and spokesman for the blacks: "We have learned all we came to learn, Venerable Brothers. My Lord Cardinal Thule has privately explained other points to us. We suggest that we leave things as they now are, and that we all meet tomorrow with our Brother Cardinals to consult with the Holy

Spirit in Conclave Session." The blacks bow to Buff, to Thule, to Francis, to Lynch, and one by one, gravely, they file out.

There is silence. Buff stands up.

"Let us all pray," Thule says quite calmly, "that the same Holy Spirit enlighten every heart. For, at the present moment, my Brothers, everything seems to be in jeopardy."

A knock at the door interrupts what Buff is about to say. It is the young Monsignore from the Camerlengo's Office. Could Cardinal Thule step over to the Camerlengo's quarters in order to have a short word with him before he turns in for the remaining hours of the night? When? Whenever it suits His Eminence. Very well, then. In five minutes.

"I sense movement," Buff remarks acidly. "Perhaps, like Kant, the Camerlengo has some accurate and clear ideas."

When Thule enters the Camerlengo's office, he finds the Camerlengo already engrossed with Cardinal Masaccio, Cardinal Eakins of the United States, and Cardinal Witz. As far as Thule knows, Masaccio is the Conservative candidate, Eakins and Witz are both Traditionalists. The handshakes and bows are polite and perfunctory. These men all know each other, have measured each other, know more or less each other's aims, and are all used to the smooth exchange, the strong but quietly delivered rebuff, and the heartlessness of power politics that sometimes divide them. The Camerlengo starts speaking at once to Thule.

"Eminence," he says, "I have just had a talk with Lohngren. His Eminence, as you know, enjoys tremendous popularity with the Europeans, with many Africans, and with the North Americans."

There is no revelatory expression on Thule's face. Eakins sits bolt upright in his chair. Masaccio and Witz are seated facing each other, but they avoid all eye contact. All are looking at the Camerlengo.

"We have in this Office, several documents—let's not waste time perusing them now—which suggest that Your Eminence intends to make an effort— indeed, has already made an effort—to seize the initiative in this Conclave process I speak"—here he glances at his desk, then at Masaccio's face, then back to Thule—"not only of your planned address tomorrow—yes, yes you are marked down on my schedule as one of the speakers . . . yes, that's it, last to speak—but of the correspondence and conversations reliably reported here and elsewhere." The Camerlengo pauses, looking at his papers. Nobody looks at Thule directly. But Cardinal Thule feels that the slightest trace of reaction on his face or the smallest physical movement would be noticed and noted morbidly out of the side of each pair of eyes.

"I trust Your Eminence realizes," Thule says calmly, "that in all our pre-Conclave activity, we are certain for our part that all the Canons of the Church and the laws of our Holy Father, Paul 6, have been observed."

"Tut! Tut! Your Eminence!" the Camerlengo answers a little testily in mock reproach. "We know that! We know that! To be sure! No implication of a reproach, I assure you. It is just that I and the others"—a glance indicating Eakins and Witz and Masaccio—"felt that you should be made aware that your whole move may well be counter-productive." He pauses, to let this much sink in. "Counter-productive," he repeats, "for all of us, for Your Eminence as well as for us." The fixed smile on the Camerlengo's lips never quite fades, but is never reflected in his own eyes.

"Let me explain," he goes on in a lecturing tone of voice. "I have just finished talking with Lohngren. I am empowered to say in his name that, while the Cardinal is willing to be put in nomination, he has laid down specific circumstances under which he would not be willing, and when he will deliberately support the nomination of my Lord Cardinal Angelico."

Masaccio stirs in his chair, as if disturbed by some unexpected thought. Thule stiffens, looks quickly at Masaccio, who has moved only his eyes to meet Thule's, then to Eakins who is still looking at the Camerlengo, and to Witz who is staring at him with a full glance of steely blue eyes. Thule knows that, were Angelico to be supported by the Camerlengo, Angelico could give anybody a narrow race for Pope. And Angelico for Pope! Thule looks back again to the Camerlengo.

"What specific circumstances?" Thule's question is eliptical, even stern.

"Two, really, two main ones: If any candidate at all is put forward on the ground of Your Eminence's arguments, or if you, Eminence, are the one who proposes any candidate at all. So!" The smile again. "And when I say a 'candidate put forward on Your Eminence's arguments,' I mean a candidate of the *Ostkardinalaat* and the Latin Americans, and a candidate bound by policy to open the Church to Marxism and the Third World. Clear?"

"The brute fact is, my Brother," Witz says with a metallic note in his voice, familiar to those who know him, "the two grounds on which you would propose a candidate are known—wholehearted opening to what is now called 'democratic socialism,' and a totally new de-Catholicizing—you yourself prefer the term de-Romanizing, but some of us think that they mean the same thing: I know you don't . . ." Witz has got all this out in one breath and knows that his grammar is in knots, "we know, I mean, the second ground is openness to all other religions."

"And, Eminence," the Camerlengo steps in to relieve Witz, "our assessment is that, if you do make such a proposal on such grounds, there will be an immediate swing over. . . ."

"Away from any Curial consideration, Brother," Masaccio finishes the thought mournfully.

"And into the backyard of any Radicals, actual or potential, grouped around Angelico and Domenico and their friends," the Camerlengo draws the practical, political conclusion.

The three Cardinals continue their confrontation of Thule, each bombarding him, in turn, surrounding him with pressure. The Camerlengo picks up the barrage. "Now, My Lord Lohngren made it clear he would head such a swing," he takes up. "And I appeal to Your Eminence: does any of us think that an Angelico-sponsored nomination—much less an Angelico election— would be in the best interests of the Church? I ask of you. Think! But that, My Lord Cardinal," the Camerlengo says, "is the idea that has evolved. Even My Lord Masaccio . . ." he glances over at the Cardinal who stares back glassily, "has seen fit to throw his weight behind a Lohngren nomination and vote, Eminence." That Masaccio would be willing to back Lohngren, a German and a rival, is an impressive piece of Conclave news.

The Camerlengo has another twist to his argument coming. He wishes to throw some line out to Thule. With a change of tone he says: "Note Eminence, that the nomination of a non-Italian with the blessing of Curial approval is already a big step in the direction of Your Eminence's will and mentality. Lohngren is non-Roman, non-Italian, northern European."

Thule is quiet. He has an alert look, but seems in no way dejected. They see him glance momentarily at Eakins. Eakins is the only one who has not spoken, and Thule has that look in his eye which says 'I know why you are silent.'

"Of course," Witz interjects with emphasis, "the post of Secretariat of State would be open for a non-Italian. Or, failing that—the political situation here in Italy might require an Italian Secretary of State—then one of the chief posts in the Secretariat—Eastern Europe, Africa, and the U.S.A.—would be amenable to some acceptable arrangement. And you can take it that the Congregation for the Propagation of the Faith, the Prefecture for Economic Affairs, and the Institute for Religious Works are included in such a proposed arrangement. I don't think that I am speaking out of measure . . ." with a glance at the Camerlengo.

The Camerlengo nods in assent.

Masaccio looks at the Camerlengo as if for prearranged permission to mention something further, then turns to Thule. "We would, of course, depend on Your Eminence to talk seriously with Lynch. Oh, by the way, Eminence, no black African votes will be coming your way. They have been already to see Angelico."

Thule clenches his mouth tight at this news. He reflects for some seconds, with eyes cast down. At last, just as Eakins starts to wriggle uncomfortably in his chair, Thule speaks: "It seems to me, Venerable Brethren"—no trace of sarcasm in his voice—"that His Eminence Cardinal Eakins should also have spoken. After all, he is very well acquainted with the *Ostkardinalaat*. And this is not the first time that the idea of a pan-European candidate has been put forward."

Nobody in the Office has known for sure if Thule has received information about the discussion between Eakins and Karewsky, or about those between Calder and the Cardinals in other Eastern European countries.

Thule pauses for effect. Then: "Now, as regards any of my activities which Your Eminence says have been reported to you, I know you have paralleled them with your reports about other Cardinalitial moves." Here he stops for a moment. To Eakin's relief, Thule gets up. "These are grave matters, my Venerable Brothers." Thule looks around at the four faces. "Have my sincere thanks, all of you, for the frankness and sincerity with which you have spoken to me." The others remain seated; but the Camerlengo, as host, stands up, too. "Be sure, Eminence," Thule says to him, "that in no way will I impede the orderly procedure of Conclave events. You have my word. However, there could be one situation, you know," Thule says quietly, pursing his lips, "one situation where any commitment I give here falls away." The four others look at him. "If a substantial body of Italians decide that they will not go along with the *General Policy* based on the LA principle—" the Camerlengo goes slightly ashen at this, "—then anything I do, I and my group, would be merely to flow with the ensuing movement . . ." he breaks off and looks around at them. His eyes are suddenly bright. "Because that would, in my opinion, be overwhelming evidence of the will of the Holy Spirit."

Witz stands up to his full 6-foot-1-inch height, his face relaxed. He moves closer to Thule. "Otto," he says, using the Cardinal's first name, "we have our differences. But you must realize the Italian Cardinals are off-limits to all but the Curia. Non-Italian Cardinals are not supposed to canvass them. It's the rule. Besides, none of us can afford to let this Conclave get out of hand. If we all attack each other, if there is no trust at all, and no observance of customs, only the Church suffers." He turns around to the Camerlengo: "I will leave with the Cardinal. Goodnight my Brothers." He holds the door open for Thule. The two depart.

Masaccio is galvanized. He jumps out of his chair and rushes over to the Camerlengo's desk. "Have you any information about the Eastern Europeans?" he asks him. "Do you think he knows about the American Initiative?" Then before the Camerlengo can answer, he adds another more vehement question: "He wouldn't dare tamper with the Italians, would be?"

"As for the Eastern Europeans," Eakins tells him, "right now, I think, My Lord Calder is over with some of them." Eakins appears terribly pale, uncommonly tired, even for such a strained situation. To the Camerlengo he says: "I think that I shall retire. Thanks very much." Then to the others: "Rest well!"

The Camerlengo and Masaccio are left alone. They are old acquaintances. The Camerlengo sinks back into his swivel chair and lights a cigarette. Masaccio walks up and down a few times, then stops: "Do you think the occasion has escaped us?"

His companion blows out a long steam of smoke, draws in his breath: "No. Not at all. Not yet, anyway. We just have to be careful that both sides don't play off against the middle where we stand. You don't want to be a cat's paw for Lynch or for Angelico or for Thule."

Masaccio shudders involuntarily. "To tell you the truth, my friend," he says, with a shrug of his shoulders, "I don't think Angelico has any ambitions. That's the difficulty with the man. People have a dreadful habit of attaching destiny to the man who apparently has no ambitions. So that when events move favorably for them, it seems events themselves and only events have brought them to the fore. These seem selfless."

"I don't think we have much to worry about, really," the Camerlengo says after a pause. "You see, whatever tendency may exist among the Italians— and I doubt any real independent tendency is there—the prospect of a German . . . well, let's wait and see." Actually, the most unlikely candidate in Conclave 82 is a German. A German would normally be totally unacceptable to the Italian people and to the citizens of the Pope's diocese—Rome. Further, a German coming from capitalist Germany would be anathema for both Communist and Socialist parties in Italy. But the Camerlengo feels that, with a worse threat facing them, the Conclave would take Lohngren, if only as the lesser of evils. . . .

"But that's just the difficulty, Eminence," Masaccio's riposte is almost impatient. He frowns, frustration in his voice. "We've waited. *Dio mio!* We've waited this long! And now—well—we are beginning to see. And frankly I don't like what I see."

The Camerlengo's pre-Conclave strategy as far as most people have noticed has been to wait, to calm fears, to solicit opinions. Behind scenes he has worked with Eakins and others to try and head off Franzus and Thule. And he has done much else. But Masaccio is not to know this.

"We can always see the will of the Lord in all this, y'know," the Camerlengo says jokingly, but with a hint of seriousness.

Masaccio looks at him a moment, then smiles. *"In fine finali,* that is the only reason why we can go to sleep at night in all this huggermugger and excitement and pressure, my Brother. There's always that!" He shakes his head and makes as if to leave, then stops, and says over his shoulder: "But one would like, now and then anyway, to give God's will a—what's this your own expression was once?—'a little gentle shove with the thumb.' Good night, Your Eminence!"

Angelico has gone over to his old friend, Cardinal Domenico. Domenico told Angelico to fetch him from the Chapel, if he needed him. As they both leave, they pass Walker still sitting stiffly on his throne.

"Does he see us?" Angelico whispers.

As if in answer, Walker opens his eyes, stares at them for an instant, then lifts his right hand and makes the sign of the Cross in mid-air. His eyes close again.

"It is probably his blessing," Domenico whispers softly.

"That would be news," Angelico answers without rancor, when they are in the corridor. "By the way, there is no specific purpose for this visit, beyond getting some personal advice." They reach Domenico's apartment and sit facing each other. Angelico speaks quietly.

"I have just been touched again by some sort of invisible, black hand, Father, and my spirit is still quivering for some unfathomable reason."

For years, Angelico has known Domenico as "Father." Domenico's Cardinalate conferred after Angelico's own—when Angelico was fifty-two and Domenico was sixty-four—did not alter anything between these two men. Now, Angelico wants to explain why he feels uneasy.

"We had a short conversation," Angelico goes on, "the Africans and I. And at the end, a suggestion—a mere suggestion, mind you, nothing more, and an honest suggestion at that, made by Azande—brought back all of my old fears. You remember?"

Domenico remembers. He knew those fears. Ever since Angelico had entered the Vatican at Paul 6's bidding and worked with the Pope, Domenico had been a regular recipient of Angelico's confidences—mostly about his fears Angelico had been a favorite of Paul's. For ten years, until Angelico became too vulnerable to continue on in the Vatican, he had served as a Vatican aide. Angelico, with no fear for what people thought of him had been used by Paul 6 to effect some of the most earthshaking changes ever seen within the highest echelons of Vatican bureaucracy. In the Vatican, when the enemies you have made are such well established one-man power-centers as the venerable Cardinal Ottaviani—men whose views are much felt even in this Conclave, in spite of the fact that they are "retired"—you do not sleep easily.

Angelico's Vatican days have not been happy ones, then. But in some respects, they have been very heady. Power is heady. And corrupting. Angelico has learned that great lesson, painfully.

"You don't think, do you," Domenico asks him, "that there is any possibility of your being co-opted into nomination? Do you?"

Angelico starts to shake his head, then stops. "Not exactly, Father." His eyebrows are knotted in puzzlement. "Unless Thule really sabotages the *General Policy* and a stampede to the right starts. In that case . . ." then breaking off his soliloquy and looking back at Domenico, "No, Father. It's not so much the danger of that." His face is now clear of the puzzlement, as if he had dismissed a disturbing problem. "I have been formed and trained to deal with such things. No. It is just the old specter. I never thought that it could chill me to that extent."

Angelico had undergone a deep personnel crisis during his first twelve months at the Vatican. It was a crisis which few of his confreres and none of his subordinates could guess at. The young Monsignore, as he was then, seemed so forceful, so sure of himself, so ruthless and downright when it came to concrete decisions about personal and policy implementation. But the sudden access to power, the daily familiarity with all the chief pieces on the huge chessboard across which the Vatican plays the game of nations with politics, finances, religion, personal dynasties, worldwide Church interests. All that, together with Angelico's own deep involvement in elaborating, expounding, organizing, and implementing several decisions of Pope Paul 6— it was this weight of responsibility that brought on his crisis.

Angelico could not reconcile that deep and weighty involvement with his previous attitudes. He could not easily return each night to his private devotions after having spent his day in the hammer-and-tongs interplay of personalities, power moves, world issues, petty jealousies, occasional corruption, and naked hostilities that his job entailed.

Domenico had helped him over that first crisis; but he knew Angelico's wounds were deeper than even Angelico suspected.

"What is it precisely that bothers you now—or do you know more or less?" Domenico asks after a pause.

"Father, it is just an extension of my old trouble. As far as I am concerned, my beliefs and personal devotion to Our Lord require me to believe that any of my actions can be or should be—not merely Christlike as the old books admonish us—but actually quite adoptable by Jesus himself as his own actions. You used to say: How else can Jesus be universal? Isn't it by means of our acting in that way? And by as many human beings as possible acting in that way? So that their actions are homogenized and assimilated to the actions and behavior of Jesus, so much so that *his* grace can make all their actions his, in the real order of moral effect and supernatural grace? This is building up the mystical body of Christ to its full dimension, you used to say.

"Well, the mere mentioning of the *central power* of Christ's Church in direct relation to me—and even in that short conversation with the blacks—

that made me shudder! How can a Supreme Pontiff save his soul? Be Christlike, I mean? And that goes as well for those who work near him, as I have had to do, and shall again probably have to do. Even in lovely Turin or Florence or Venice, I find it difficult, moré difficult every day." Angelico has come directly to grips with the central problem of the "Church of Constantine"—the melding of worldly power with the Church, and of Churchly power with worldly affairs.

"Power does not taste good to you?"

"No, Father. It doesn't. I thought it would. It doesn't. At all."

"All right. Let's call a spade a spade. We would not be sincere, if we did not admit that power here in our Rome is quite like power in, say, Washington, in Moscow, in Peking, in Zurich. As in Washington, power here rests on an ethical code, a reasoned faith, expressed in dogmas of this worldly success. As in Moscow and Peking, our power vibrates with a passion of the heart, a spontaneous and emotional motivation giving us as many reasons for living as for dying. And, of course, this power in our Rome, the power of the bureaucracy, subjects all individuals to a heartless, impersonal, at times even baleful mechanism."

"Yes! Yes!" Angelico picks up the other man's thought. "Precisely! It is these forces I find almost demonic. They are too blind for any pity, too gargantuan to be controlled by something as puny as personal ambition, too fascinating to be forsaken for the prosaic fate of mere survival. Almost demonic! Because these forces make no distinction between right and wrong, discard all weak things, have no time for feeling, refer the brain continually to the bottom line of the yearly audit, dictate policy decisions according to the unrelenting question *'cui bono?'* (who is going to profit by this measure?), take death as failure, and grind out the long, shining avenues of their successes over the puny, piecemeal careers and personalities of all individuals who may be momentarily lifted up in their surge, but are inevitably buried in their wake."

Angelico rises and begins to walk to and fro. "Let me put you a question, Father. You may not wish to answer it. But it is on my mind." He stops pacing and looks at the floor. "How many of the College of Cardinals escape damage to their spirit from all this?"

"I know," Domenico breaks in a little wearily. "I've made the calculation myself from time to time. Man by man. I suppose you could safely say that a minimum of forty percent of the Electors are firm and genuine believers in the Christian faith. They believe that there is one God, that the Son of God was and is Jesus of Nazareth; that Jesus died for all men's sins and rose again alive, after being truly dead; that all who believe in Jesus will live immortally with God after their own death, and that only through Jesus can any human being attain that happiness; that Jesus, before he disappeared from human sight, established an ecclesial presence among men to last as long as the human universe lasts; and that this ecclesial presence is centered around the Bishop of Rome who is and will always be the only official and personal Vicar of Jesus among men.

"Another group of the Electors, roughly one-third of the total, do not really believe any of this. They profess loyalty to these beliefs. But this is a matter merely of words, though they regard this exterior conformity as necessary and valuable. After all, it has enabled them to flourish as personalities and as powers to be reckoned with. For them, their rank as Cardinals and their functions as Papal Electors have the value of gilt-edged membership cards in a highly privileged club with its own mystique. And, at that high level of power, a mystique is most useful to drown the scruples of conscience or to avoid the boredom of power.

"In between these two groups there is a minimum of, say, about twenty-five percent who hedge their bets. They are never in a hurry to change, but never so hidebound as to champion a perpetual status quo. In theology, conservative. In politics, open to gradual development. In morality, cautious. In heroism, of temperate enthusiasm. These are the ones who do not really _know_"—Domenico emphasizes the word—"so they are the gentle ones, because prudent agnostics, who hope that the teachings of their faith are correct. They would probably choose to die rather than deny those teachings. But they would prefer to go on living as long as they can, because perhaps after all the teachings may not mean quite what they seem to say."

Angelico is stockstill, staring at Domenico, a look of the same puzzlement on his face as before. But there is a trace of some relief dawning there too. "So many have the same crisis in their belief?" he murmurs.

"And some do not keep their belief. You have. Be satisfied. Now I think that you had better get back to your rooms. You will have visitors coming. If you have any time to spare later, call me on the telephone. If I don't answer, you know where to find me." Domenico has more prayers to say. He will be in the Chapel.

"Meanwhile," Domenico stands up, "take this with you as a thought: whoever is elected Pope, whoever he be, you and I and he and all the others know the sad but simple fact. The new Pope can do very little more than oversee developments which he neither initiates nor directs, and which he rarely sees to their end. The thing is too big for any one mortal span." They move slowly toward the door of Domenico's apartment. "Very few Popes— and you know this as well as the next man—have made any real difference to the substance of the Church. The Church gets such a Pope once or twice every five hundred years or so. And even then!"

Domenico opens the door and looks down the corridor as if gazing at some imaginary hall filled with present and past Papal candidates. "The best candidates usually never run for election. The worst have seldom won an election. The holiest are rarely elected. The satisfactory ones were no more than good stewards. We've had some really shameful ones, the 'black Popes.' But really they wrought petty ills to the Church's property and good name, grandiose harm to innumerable spirits, and the saddest evil to their own souls. The wisest—not always the holiest, by the way," Domenico throws a look at Angelico "—could at most and at their best moments, watch carefully. As a fisherman might watch for a slight moving shift in the winds, they wait for a message from the Spirit that moves the community of believers. And then they laboriously edge the rudder of state a few notches this way or that in order to comply with the new direction."

Domenico, the wise spiritual father, adviser to many great men, has spoken the kind of simple truth that gathers all the complexities and all the noisy issues, and allows them to rest in silence for just an instant. Then he looks at Angelico again. "Hurry! You'll be late. Stay in touch!"

"Whoever heard of a Bolognese who was a good sailor—or a good fisherman?" Angelico smiles gaily at his own joke on himself, and walks away toward his quarters.

Domenico smiles at Angelico's resilience, and steps back over his own threshhold.

In spirit they have both stepped back into the realities of Conclave.

For a few moments Domenico stands there. Then he moves over to the night table by his bed, glances at the numbers directory, takes up the phone and dials. A voice answers: "Uccello here."

"Eminence! Domenico! Would you have a few moments to spare before retiring?"

"Momentito, Eminence!" Domenico can hear him talking to someone; then, "Immediately, Eminence! Immediately!" Domenico hangs up, stands a moment thinking, then sits down.

A few minutes later, Uccello arrives.

"Well now, Eminence, what is on your mind?"

Uccello is sixty-four years old, formerly Bishop of Maleto, a Cardinal since 1974, and now posted to a big metropolis. The job of doing something about its 4,106 clergymen, its two million Catholics, its churches and convents, has given Uccello a deep knowledge of the social problems facing the Vatican in modern urban life. His city is a microcosm of every other big city that holds a Catholic population. A moderate Traditionalist in his theology, Uccello nevertheless has long been convinced that some changes must be made. But his transfer to a city from the calm of Maleto has given him a much more urgent idea of the dimensions of the Church's problem.

"Paolo," Domenico begins familiarly, "I must be frank with you. Angelico has just left me."

"Ah!" Uccello quietly exclaims, as if hearing the answer to a puzzle. "*Appunto!* Now I understand."

"Believe me, son, I don't think you do, or that you could quite understand. Angelico has no ambitions, at least not of the kind that interests us all in these days. But he may be facing too great a crisis. I say that much as his spiritual advisor.

"Paolo, tell me about the *Secret Reports.*" Uccello catches his breath suddenly, taken off guard.

"Now, in asking about the *Reports,*" Domenico continues, "I am not speaking only or even mainly as spiritual advisor to anyone. But I think that I should know. At this stage of things, it is very late and very dangerous for a majority of us to be taken by surprise. You know, I suppose, that more than one surprise is possible tomorrow?" The hesitation continues on Uccello's face.

"Believe me, I think that I should be brought up to date," Domenico presses on.

Uccello expels the air from his lungs as if in surrender. There is no deal here. Trust is rare in these circumstances, but Domenico is a rare man; and Uccello judges that he does urgently need to know what he is asking to be told.

Domenico's phone interrupts. He lifts the receiver.

"*Pronto!* Yes, Your Eminence.... No! No. Not yet. As a matter of fact, Eminence, I am here with a mutual friend.... What is that? ... Well, frankly, that is precisely what we are discussing now.... On the contrary, I think Your Eminence should.... Well, bring him along too.... Yes! Yes! Now.... Not at all, Eminence."

Domenico hangs up and turns to Uccello. "Ni Kan and Yiu are coming over—do not worry! They know about these *Reports*. They will help."

In a minute or two a light knock at the door announces the arrival of Ni Kan and Yiu.

"Take a seat, Eminences. You all know each other, I think. And, tonight, I am the ignorant one. I am silent but full of questions."

One of Domenico's great gifts is his ability to put people at their ease and evoke an atmosphere of trust and calm. He quickly brings Ni Kan and Yiu up to date, and then turns again to Uccello.

"Frankly," Uccello says with a deprecating gesture of his hands, "I don't know what the Camerlengo is going to say or do. I know he doesn't want the

Reports or any news about them circulated. But, for what it's worth, here's what I know.

"Since June 1977, the Secretariat has had these *Reports*—four to be exact. One about the Soviets, one about Latin America, one about the Italian Communists, and one about financial conditions and projections."

"We know of these," Ni Kan nods at him almost apologetically. "But we also know of a Report drawn up for the Camerlengo on his own orders."

Uccello is obviously surprised, as he whirls around to face Ni Kan: "And you know its subject matter?"

"His Eminence Cardinal Thule and the theologians," Ni Kan says unblinkingly.

"I have seen a copy," Yiu adds. "I think it's very relevant."

"So let's begin with that last-named *Report*, Eminence," Domenico says. Uccello has not seen it. They all fix their eyes on Yiu.

The *Report*, Yiu tells them, is a summary of a strategy proposal drawn up on the basis of contributions made by several European and American theologians, some of the so-called "new theologians." These contributions had been in the form of theological notes and had started in 1972, the year the thirty-four such "new theologians"—among them the most vocal ones for the last decade, Hans Küng and John Baptist Metz from Germany, Dutchman Edward Schillebeeckx, Charles Curran and John L. McKenzie of the United States, Gregory Baum from Canada, among others—issued a Declaration about what they called "stagnations" in the Church. In that Declaration, they outlined five ways to get rid of that stagnation. Briefly, as Yiu understood it, those theologians were advising all Roman Catholics to organize themselves in such a way as to burrow within the Church and force the Pope, his Roman Curia, and the Cardinals to introduce basic changes.

The tactic was to be able to confront the authorities with the fait accompli that could not be undone. This was to be done in so many areas of faith, morals, and religious practice that they would totally revolutionize the Church before most clergy and lay people understood what had happened. If, for instance, some Catholic Bishops could be induced to ordain women as priests and allow them to function as priests, then this fait accompli would, in their view, call for a rethinking of the Vatican's attitudes.

This strategy and tactic were to be applied to the most basic elements of Roman Catholic faith and practice, affecting the Sacraments themselves, and leaving no element untouched. They were to be applied to priestly celibacy as a test case; and then, after successfully abolishing clerical celibacy as a universal law, to all other issues—Papal Infallibility, abortion, homosexuality, intercommunion with other Christians, and so on. And, departing from the substance of the *Report* for a moment, Yiu adds, "We know that in Holland

and in France and elsewhere, priests have already married and, in violation of Church law, still remain at their posts in parishes where the parishioners will accept them in their married status."

After the success of the test case on priestly celibacy, the strategy called for the formulation of a sort of pact of union with Protestant churches. This could be brought about point by point: leave in abeyance all defined dogmas concerning the Virgin Mary (Assumption and Immaculate Conception); relegate the question of Papal Infallibility to later discussions and not require anybody to profess it now as an article of faith; declare that Christians can "believe" in the Bible while they deny that the Bible tells them anything of real past history; throw open for renewed interpretation the whole question of the Real Presence of Jesus in the Sacrament of the Eucharist; allow divorce, contraception, masturbation, and homosexuality under certain conditions, declare vasectomy and hysterectomy legitimate as contraceptives, premarital sex permissible under certain conditions; declare that capitalism is irreconcilable with Christianity.

Within the Church there would be a call for the dismantling of the Roman Curia, transferring to individual bishops in their own dioceses all the decisions that affect their own localities. Major decisions affecting many dioceses and the whole Church would be decided by an international synod of bishops over which the Pope would preside. There would be a complete restructuring of the Papacy, from the way the Pope is elected to a total denial of the Pope's primary function as Vicar of Jesus and Bishop of Rome, in favor of something like the function of a chairman of the board, but no longer as personally endowed with authority and infallibility.

Yiu rounds off his account by ticking off the agenda for achieving this vast change:

1. Gain control over affairs parish by parish, diocese by diocese, so that finally a majority of priests and bishops would be in agreement with the aims of the program.
2. Gain the maximum possible number of adherents among Seminary teachers and university professors, among publishers and editors, reporters and writers for magazines and diocesan papers.
3. Conferences of Bishops, national, international, and regional were to be the objects of special attention. The more the members attending such conferences from all parts of a country and, in some cases, from many parts of the world, were affected, the faster their influence would spread.
4. Organize meetings, first on the national level, then on the international level and regional level, at which growing numbers of priests and bishops would attend together with laymen. At these meetings, the elements of the formulation about the new format for the Church would be

expounded and discussed. Gatherings of Charismatic Catholics and other Christians, General Congregations of Religious Orders, these and other such occasions should be attended by "observers" intent on the program.

5. At certain meetings on the national and international level, only priests and bishops would attend. The idea was to "snowball" this tactic until one day they could hold an international meeting equivalent in its attendance by bishops—and at least some Cardinals—to the composition of a General Council of the Church. Only in this case, it would not be the Roman Curia and the Pope who would call such a Council. This was the most grandiose variation of the fait accompli tactic. For, faced with such an extensive insurrection, what could Rome do? Excommunicate everyone? Ridiculous!

As Yiu finished up his account, Ni Kan adds his own remarks. "What has struck us—myself and His Eminence Yiu and our friends—is the frequency and importance with which the name of My Lord Cardinal Thule, My Lord Cardinal Lynch, My Lord Cardinal Buff, and My Lord Cardinal Antonello turn up again and again in the pages of this *Report*. I am not surprised—neither would you be, I'm sure—to find Arceo of Cuernavacca, Helder y Camera of Recife, Gerety of New Jersey in the United States, Hurley of South Africa, Enrico Bartocelli of Lucca, John Zoa of Cameroon, and bishops of that sort." These men are all known as "liberal-minded" bishops. But what surprised Ni Kan was to find Cardinals mentioned as involved. He adds that anyone acquainted with and aware of the tactics used by Mao's government in China to detach the Chinese clergy from Rome, and to destroy Rome's influence with the people, would not be taken in by the falsity and the ultimate intent of this program and strategy.

"Well, now, we all know what Thule has in mind," Domenico remarks in a tone so sharp that the other three heads swing around sharply in disbelief; Domenico rarely uses a deprecatory tone about anyone, much less about dignitaries of the Church.

"Do you really think they are trying to force a Council on the Pope and the Curia?" Uccello's question is directed at them all.

"Look, Paolo," Domenico is calm and serious. "It's been tried plenty of times before. There was a man called Marsilius of Padua who died in 1343. He held that a Council of the Church was superior to the Pope. And after him, John Gerson, the all-powerful chancellor of Paris University, who died in 1429, had the same idea. And then we had those Gallicans in the seventeenth, eighteenth and nineteenth centuries, all trying to propagate the same thing. Do you know that in the year 1682, no less than seven archbishops, twenty-six bishops, and thirty-eight theologians, all Frenchmen, declared the Pope to be at the beck and call—and recall—of a General

Council? And they said the Pope's authority and infallibility were only the authority and infallibility of the bishops in the Church when you put them all together. Pope Alexander 8 condemned the lot of them. And now all those men are forgotten; and those who ignore all that history are at it all over again. If you read history you will find a whole gaggle of theologians—Theodoric of Niem, Theodoric of Vrie, Herman of Langestein, and many, many others—who are all as dead and as forgotten now as the Currans and the Baums and the Küngs and the Metzes and the Schillebeeckx will be in a hundred years' time.

"What bothers me is the presence of His Eminence Cardinal Thule and the other Cardinals on that side of the fence. This has gone much further than I thought." There is a short silence among the Cardinals.

"When I add all this information to what I know or hear about other *Secret Reports,*" Uccello finally says, breaking the silence, "I really don't think the Camerlengo knows what he is doing! Or he is being too clever for his pants."

"Accurate and clear ideas, eh?" It is Yiu with a glint of humor.

"Seriously, my Brothers!" Uccello exclaims quietly, "seriously! You two"—looking at Ni Kan and Yiu—"apparently have read the *Reports.* Your Eminence"—speaking to Domenico—"has not. They create quite a problem when put together with what we've just heard from my Lord Cardinal Ni Kan."

The *Report on the Soviets,* in effect, contains a substantial and sweeping offer to the Vatican by the Soviets, coming both indirectly through their puppets in Czechoslovakia and Hungary, and directly from Moscow. Peace pact, alliance, agreement on mutual disengagement—it can be called anything pleasing.

The Soviets would promise greater freedom for churchmen, dismantling of all anti-Catholic organizations, the cessation of all antireligious propaganda. In return for this, the Soviets want the Vatican to allow and, in one way or another, to bless the efforts of Christian Marxists, and—at the very least—to see that Roman Catholics in their satellite countries will no longer have the impression that Marxist ideas are any more irreconcilable with Catholicism than is capitalism. They want *at the minimum* a moratorium on all open opposition and criticism from the Vatican.

"What do you think they have now?" Ni Kan asks archly and with a bitterness born of experience.

"Well, whatever." Uccello goes on. "The *Report on the Italian Communists* is along the same lines, only it concerns particularly the Italian and, to a lesser degree, also the French Communists. It is an appeal by Marxists for collaboration in unifying the people for a wholesale economic reform and refurbishment of these two countries industrially and socially. It is distinctly anti-U.S., but offers a nonalignment position with the U.S.S.R. In return, they promise that good Communists can be good Catholics. And vice versa."

"Now, I think I know the *Latin American Report* better than anyone else here," Yiu interrupts. "Cardinals Franzus and Thule have been—are—working on me. I don't know the sources of that *Report,* but someone has put together a collection of statements by Latin American priests, bishops, and some four or five Cardinals. All the statements are reactions to and comments on the contexts of the *Reports on the Soviets* and on the *Italian Communists.*"

"Who communicated these *Reports*—or their contents—to the Latin Americans?" Uccello asks.

"No." Domenico answers as if he had just heard somebody's suggestion. "No. It's not Giacomo." Archbishop Giacomo Belli, Papal Nuncio in the area, could have been everyone's most logical suspect because of his physical location.

"Actually, it was no Latin American," Yiu goes on. "The *Reports* came through the Missionaries—priests and nuns—of El Salvador."

"What were the reactions and statements like?" Domenico asks.

"Mostly favorable. On certain conditions, the Latin American clergy would agree to the same general proposals of Marxism."

"What conditions?"

"Simply two: that our Brother Cardinals from Eastern Europe agreed; and that such an acceptance by the Vatican of an open-door alliance would not disrupt the Church's economic position immediately. They all stress the *immediate* part of the condition."

"Do you think that Franzus and Thule have seen these *Reports?*" Domenico is insisting now.

"I can answer that, I think," Yiu intervenes. "Because I know that copies were in Manila on their way to Peking. And if that is so, you can be sure that copies are in Moscow. And if in Moscow, you can be sure that Franzus saw them. And if Franzus saw them, Thule saw them."

Domenico has not yet established the connection he is seeking to clarify. Two parts puzzle him. Or rather he lacks answers to two questions. First, is the Thule group banking on the effect of these *Reports* to force the Conclave outcome over and beyond the agreed *General Policy?* That's a grave thought. Second, why is the Camerlengo not communicating any of this information to the Electors?

Uccello knows the Camerlengo and his character better than most. "The Camerlengo is absolutely confident—at least he was this morning—that most probably a *General Policy* candidate can be elected without much trouble. Or, failing that, some good pan-European like Lohngren or Garcia or even Witz can be proposed and elected."

"I must thank Your Eminences very, very much. I think we must presume that any alliance between Thule and Franzus will seek to profit from these

Reports." Domenico rises. "You have all been extremely frank; you know I will not betray the confidentiality of my sources. Why don't we all get some rest now?"

Yiu and Ni Kan are already on their feet and moving toward the door. Uccello is the last to leave. The two Asians are already gone when he turns to look at Domenico.

"Tell me, Father, can you envisage circumstances when you would have to make use, public use I mean, of this information?"

Domenico's eyes are grave. "Only if the most foolish of things were to take place."

"I see. Do you envisage that possibility now? In this Conclave? Tomorrow, for instance?"

Domenico moves over to a small table where his Breviary and Crucifix lie. "We are living in the most extraordinary of times, Paolo. A strange spirit is loose and roaming freely in the Church, not only in the streets of the city but in the chancery, in the sacristy, in the bishop's palace, in the Pope's household, even in the Sanctuary itself." He pauses. "The smoke Pope Paul spoke about, you know ..." he breaks off and looks at Uccello. Paul 6 had spoken about the "smoke and darkness of Satan entering the Church." "High Churchmen, Bishops, and Cardinals, seem to go off at a tangent without any forewarning." Then, looking away. "Each one of us must do what he must do. You. I. Thule. All of us. To Jesus we all answer only as individuals."

Uccello senses the regret and the determination behind the older man's thought. He turns to leave. At the door he finds Domenico behind him.

"I think I will go and say some prayers, Paolo."

Back in Kand's apartment, Karewsky and Garcia continue to brief him on the essentials of the *Reports.*

"We come now to the economic conditions of the Church," Karewsky says to Kand.

This part of the *Report* deals with the Vatican's *Prefecture of Economic Affairs*—the PECA—and with the *Institute for Religious Works*—the IRW.

"Is it competent and complete?" asks Kand.

"If the people in charge there know anything, it is money," answers Garcia with a slow smile that turns to stone. "Now, if you ask about their recommendations and the recommendations of the Camerlengo which are put together with the others, they're something else!"

"And as for their faith," Karewsky slips the words in subtly, "that's something else again. Later, you can read the parts in the *General Framework* that deal with the change over in investments. Let me give you a summary. You can read the details later."

In the late sixties, Paul 6 decided to transfer the major portion of Vatican investments into American stocks and real estate. Heading the operations was an Italian financier, Michele Sindona. While he was in charge, the Vatican reportedly suffered losses of over one billion dollars. "This however," Karewsky waves his hand in a gesture of dismissal, "is not the point. All those years, including this year, Vatican investments continued to pour into the United States. The point is that, whatever be the future policy of the next Pope—whether he opens Europe and Latin America to Marxism or not—Vatican financial sinews will be in the only place left on this earth where they can survive healthily.

"But this means that the economic life of the Vatican, of its Church, is tied to the economic policies of the United States. And economic policies of the United States determine the foreign policy of the United States."

"And that must mean," Kand interjects, "that Vatican policy has to, but *has* to conform to United States foreign policy—at least along general lines."

"You know what you must do with eggs," Karewsky throws his hands into the air, "if you wish to make an omelette, my friend!"

It is clear from the information contained in the *Financial Report* that the administration of Paul 6 has tied the hands of the next Vatican administration. And this becomes clear when Kand and the other two cover the next parts of the *General Framework*. Garcia summarizes for Kand.

"The economic policy of the Vatican hinges on certain contingencies, and on certain assumptions about those contingencies. A prime contingency is United States policy. That policy," explains Garcia, "is currently called 'trilateralism'; a three-sided complex. Usually, the three sides are taken to be the United States, Europe, and Japan. The United States would wish it that way. But that is not how things are seen working out.

"As things stand now, the three sides of that economic complex are the United States, Saudi Arabia, and Japan.

"According to the *Position Paper*, for the United States (and for the Vatican, therefore) Western Europe is seen as ceasing, in the coming five years, to be economically and politically autonomous. Its democracies, legitimate and illegitimate, will cease to be. Despite any attempt by the United States and Japan and others to head it off, Russian hegemony will run from Vladivostock to Cornwall, from Kirunna in the Arctic Circle to the warm Mediterranean waters lapping the shores of Sicily.

"The only 'accident' of history that could foreseeably prevent that hegemony would be either a nuclear war, or revolution in the U.S.S.R. But by revolution is meant not any mere change of Politburo Chairman, not any party purge, but a genuine revolution: bloody, universal, destructive, upheaving and shattering the entire Soviet system. A revolution of the many 'have-nots' against the few despotic 'haves.' But such a revolution is considered to be as unlikely as surrender by the Israelis to the PLO. And nuclear war is not envisaged quite yet.

"The projection runs on: Having acquired the technology and business know-how, the Soviets could float a convertible ruble based on their access to major gold supplies in the Soviet Union and in South Africa, thus challenging the dollar, swamping the West German mark and the Swiss franc, absorbing all the soft currencies, according as inflation and economic depression spread all over Europe. In the next five years, there will be very little likelihood that military force, the unthinkable 'midwife of history' as Karl Marx termed it, will enter the picture either as World War III, or even as something lesser.

"But, as bleak as the picture is painted in the *General Framework*, it would not seem to be the end of the world for the Vatican mind when Russian tanks rumble unopposed over West Germany and down over the Plain of Lombardy, and when Russian Soviet commissars are resident in Bonn, Paris, Rome, Geneva, Madrid, Stockholm, Athens, and Ankara. All major Swiss banks have been restructuring their facilities so as to be able to service their clients overseas, say in one or both of the Americas, in Japan, and in Hong Kong.

"Money supply is reckoned in the *General Framework* to be the pincers that would inexorably hold Western Europe firmly down on the unyielding anvil of economics, while Marxism will flatten out old Europe's petty differences in political systems and social practice and class distinctions, fashioning its nationalisms into a controlled delta of subservient populations. The opinion of some Vatican officials is cited according to which there is a 'conspiracy of silence' among Western government leaders who are well aware of where their nations are heading. But they keep up appearances and indulge in the shadow-play of local politics."

Before his companions can go on to give Kand the main conclusions of the *General Framework*, he gives his own down-to-earth summary. "The jig is up," Kand says quietly, looking at Garcia and Karewsky. *"Finita la commedia.* That's what they are telling us, isn't it?"

"That, I presume, is a statement of fact, not a question, my Brother," Garcia remarks with a slightly wan air. "In the *General Framework Paper*," he goes on to summarize, "the United States is pictured as settling on a deal with the Soviets; a tacit deal for a while, then quite explicitly. Now," he concludes, "the Vatican has tied its fortune economically and financially and politically to the United States."

"A few other subjects," Kand interrupts Garcia, "before we finish up. Israel for instance?"

"Already that is a secondary subject," Karewsky responds. "Doomed, at least according to the *Paper*. But not doomed to extinction, mind you. They might prefer that, our Israeli friends, Samson-like or Masada-like. But doomed to become a tenth-rate Levantine power swamped by the financial flood, economic power, and demographic spread of Islamic nations, notably the Saudis. The Israelis will not be able to compete. In the value-world of money and firepower where they have placed their destiny, they are doomed to lose out and sink to their due level. Christians, especially Americans, will not go on feeling guilty or responsible for all time for things they never did, or for a country which is not their own. So the flow will stop. And, in any case, the United States will not be able to afford to keep its Near East mistress."

"In short, my Eminent Brothers," Kand sits back in his chair, "in short, the final meaning for this Conclave of the *General Framework* and the other *Papers* is that the next Pope will preside over an entirely different world."

"Except that he won't be exactly presiding. He'll probably be pilgrimming."

"Pilgrimming? What does that mean?" Kand leans forward. "A pilgrim? The Pope? To where? For what? As a prisoner? What do you mean?" The other two laugh good-naturedly at the rush of questions from Kand.

"Well, for openers," Karewsky begins, "where will Christianity be centered? In the U.S.A.? Just think!—by the way, you can read this in *Position Paper 6*—under the title of *'The U.S.A. religiously considered and the American way of life,'* as they call it." He gives a summary of the *Paper*. The United States as a socio-political entity was set up more or less as a vast grille or iron network of laws, rights, obligations, checks, and balances. Anything that did not dissolve and melt into or could not be soldered onto that grille was doomed from the beginning of the American experience to fall through the holes into the kitchen midden of history.

"*Position Paper 6* states that with the passage of American history, formal religion, then any kind of religious morality, has shown that it can not be melted into the grille or soldered onto it. And so, one by one, any moral or religious principles in the public life of the nation had to drop out of sight and mind into the nothingness of that rubbish heap of past things, until all that remains today is a practically unworkable system of legal methods, laws, and constitutional balances, imposed on 220 million people, most of whom are still believers in some religious morality.

"So the whole thing must come apart at the seams finally. Or rather that grille will become too oppressive for the mass of the people. They will revolt and not know where to turn without destroying that grille—the American system and way of life. So the United States could not be the center of Roman Catholicism."

"And in all honesty, do you think that the center could be in Europe, in Italy, in Rome?" Garcia takes up. "Hardly. The majority of European Catholics do not go to Mass or Sacraments. Great sections of France, Italy, Holland, Germany, Austria are de-Christianized—many people in those sections are not even baptized. Catholicism, according to the *Position Paper* is undergoing a maximum period of disorientation. Already in the early seventies, it was clear that many Cardinals, bishops, priests, intellectuals, besides lay people, believed no longer in the fundamentals—the Resurrection of Jesus, his divinity, the historic reality of his sacrifice on Calvary, the human soul, the Eucharist and other Sacraments."

Based on its own accurate, up-to-date statistics and very frank reports about the decline in religious observance, in priestly and religious vocations, and in personal morals, the Vatican mind has arrived at the same conclusions as it draws from its consideration of Western Europe's fate.

Over all, throughout Western Europe and in the old Catholic countries, there is no rational probability of a religious revival. Religion in the West is banished to the realm of personal belief and family life:

"Religion has no socially regulative functions any longer, no societal identity, no political legitimacy. This has come about, because all social control, socialization, and societal identity are rationally coordinated in the impersonal and anonymous environment, inevitable in industrial and post-industrial societies. More acutely, the realms of family and personal belief are recessive areas: constantly invaded and diminished by their environment. And any cold-blooded assessment tells us that, barring an impossible and mythical return to the Stone Age, this process cannot be reversed. It can only keep going on its one-way trend."

Religious observance, therefore, as a sign of inner religious belief, will go on being diminished. The authors and cosigners of the *Position Papers* are as impressed by the enthusiasm of, say, Catholic Charismatics in Kansas City, Missouri, or Dublin, Ireland, as they are by the Kimbangyist Movement in Zaire, Scientology in Britain, or the Human Potential Movement, the Children of God, and Hare Krishna in the United States. All such movements with their claims to esoteric knowledge, their proposals to liberate the powers of the self, the real self, and the salvation they claim can be obtained only within their sacred community, such movements are seen as weak gestures of despair against an irremovable technology and all-enveloping impersonality and isolation of modern society.

"And we know," Garcia concludes a little grimly, "that neither in Africa nor Asia is there any sign of vast expansion for Christianity or Roman Catholicism."

Kand is silent. He reads a few paragraphs from *Position Papers* open on his desk, where Garcia has marked particular places. There is no more coldly analytic mind, he reflects, than the mind of the Roman Catholic assessing the situation of his own Church and his own belief.

"In the coming period, this widening disbelief, already an accomplished fact, will become a live issue splitting the Church, depriving it of many good minds and many trained specialists as well as of many of the rank-and-file. There no longer will be the old sense of a discrepancy between what is spoken and what is known. Furthermore, the position of the Holy Father will necessarily undergo a severe overhauling: Church organization and the descending hierarchy of authority and discipline will become more diversified—in order to survive in some form or other. Large bodies of non-Catholic Christians will draw nearer and attempt association or amalgamation with Catholics, thus necessitating adaptations in the Papal role. De-Romanization of Roman Catholicism, which is a fact ever since the invention of the telegraph, will be hastened toward completion. The Church of Constantine is on the way out of human affairs."

Kand looks up. There is silence among the three men for a few moments. Then Kand says incredulously, almost angrily: "But, in the name of God, what were Masaccio and Vasari speaking about then at the meeting? They have read all this material. They cosigned it all, didn't they?"

"What do you think Thule and Lynch and Franzus are speaking about right now, my friend?" Garcia says with a narrow look at him. "The first two really don't know what to do and want to stand pat. Hold the fort sort of thing. Keep the best face in public. Whatever you like. Just ignorant good will with a dosage of personal ambition. The others think they know what we should do. They are running after the fashions of the times. Frankly, I don't know which attitude is more stupid."

"Well, Eminences," Karewsky looks at his watch, "it is almost a quarter to eleven. Cardinal Kand may have forgotten, but he and I have a meeting to attend." The Eastern European Cardinals are due to caucus at eleven o'clock.

"As do I," Garcia says affably.

When Thule returns to his apartment, he finds Buff, Franzus, and Francis still seated. On his way back from the Camerlengo, Thule has formed a decision. He sits down. The others are silent. "I have been thinking of the mood at this evening's Preliminary Session," Thule begins, "and it seems to me that in view of our recent conversation with Azande and the others, we should decide on a very bold move."

"It seems to me, for my part," Franzus says, "if we do not move quickly, we will lose a certain momentum already built up. Moreover, I do not quite trust the simplicity and geniality of Domenico. Angelico I know—we all know—is predictable. But Domenico! Now there's a man who could lead us down the garden path all smiles, all concessions, all simplicity and scholarly detachment. And then when we're about to praise the garden, suddenly we'd probably find ourselves outside the gate and Domenico laughing through the grille at us."

"Not laughing, friend," Buff adds somberly. "Not laughing. Worse than that. Offering a prayer of thanks to the Virgin!"

"Well, anyway, things will not come to that." Thule is full of tense self-confidence. It is infectious. The others relax.

"All right," Buff becomes practical. "What's on our agenda?"

"First," says Thule, "I want His Eminence here," indicating Franzus, "to tell us what was or is the final outcome of the Latin American and *Ostkardinalaat* maneuvering in which Eakins and Tobey and the others were involved. A lot depends on that." What Thule is after is an update on the effort to forge an alliance between Latin American Cardinals and Cardinals from Eastern Europe.

"It's simple. It's clear," Franzus says, "that you know what Eakins and Tobey tried to arrange. I think, really, that Bronzino, Braun and the Camerlengo were behind it. . . ."

"In fact, we know they were, Brothers," Buff's remark is made with the faintest trace of cynicism.

"Anyway," Franzus goes on, "they thought it was all arranged. That, indeed, the Eastern European Cardinals would stand with the Latin Americans—and vice versa—behind a *General Framework Policy* candidate, provided he was a sort of . . . what shall I call it . . . ? oh, a kind of hybrid, a Conservative who was Progressivist and a Progressivist who was Conservative." He breaks off and looks around among the others a moment. "It's probably all in those *Reports,* of course. Not that I've seen them. All of them, anyway. . . ."

"You don't need to see them," Thule says hastily. "A mishmash. But go on. What about Kand?"

"Oh, he was out of it. I was told to leave him out."

"Why did the Camerlengo and company want him out of it?"

"Not he," Franzus swallows. "You see, all this time I was talking with our own people . . ." he pauses, looks at Thule, "and er . . . er. . . ."

"Quite clear, Eminence!"

"So!" Franzus gives a Germanic zed sound to the 's' sound. It speaks volumes to the others. "In the meantime, by a separate route, I got to the Latin Americans." He turns to Thule. "We must remember the kind offices of

Menendez Arceo in this matter. Afterward, you know?" Bishop of Cuernavaca in Mexico, Menendez Arceo is one of the most outspoken propagators of the movement for a democratic socialism. "I am a social revolutionary," the Bishop is supposed to have stated openly. And he was reported as saying that Chou en-Lai should be canonized as a saint of the Church.

"And?" Thule pursues the question.

"They agreed to make a break from the *General Policy*, if a viable road were opened for them. Question is, can we open such a road?"

"I think so." Thule is definitive. "Here's what I propose. First I go to Lowe and explain to him that what we need now is *not* the pan-European papal style. That, as you know, was thought up as a transition between an Italianate Papacy, such as we have had up to this, and a truly international Papacy, a Papacy that would be non-nationalistic, non-denominational non-classbound, non-ethnically closed, non-geographically determined. And it was a good idea. But we have a new momentum now. Phew! What a chance, once and for all, to rid the Church of 'Constantine's Church' . . . if I can speak in that fashion, paradoxically . . . ?"

"We understand, Brother. Believe me! We understand." Franzus is suddenly pervfervid and emphatic. "We understand only too well!"

Thule goes on animatedly. "We get Lowe to acquiesce in not being put forward. No! No! Believe me! Lowe will be the first to understand." He responds to the disbelieving look on Franzus' face.

"All right," Franzus goes on. "But what about Yiu?"

Thule nods silently. "Yiu, Eminence! Yiu as the candidate put forward by Progressivists like myself *and* by those who favor a wide and complete *apertura* to the 'East'!" Thule is referring to the pro-Marxist-alliance group. "Yiu will be our *coalition* candidate!"

"Of course." Buff is pleased. "Yiu would be perfect. He will draw many European and Italian votes. His stock stands high with the Africans. So that, in spite of the fracas with Azande, they can with easy conscience vote with us."

"And don't forget," Thule adds, "Yiu is by nature Conservative. Only, all have noticed, when push comes to shove, he can be as quick to act with the Left wing as any of us." Yiu's history in his home country has indeed been of this kind. When the government cracked down on dissidents, Yiu loyally supported the nuns and priests who were arrested or attacked by the government.

"Besides, Yiu represents one great advantage. Automatically, he will get Ni Kan's vote and Koi-Lo-Po's and Lang-Che-Ning's and the Indians' votes, and God knows what else in virtue of all of those—oh, I forgot Nei Hao's vote, he'll get that too."

Buff looks at Thule. "I think this about does it." He straightens up and becomes serious. "You had better get to Lowe before the First Session tomorrow!"

"Don't worry! Don't worry! It will be taken care of." Thule reflects a while, then adds: "On second thought, I think I will ask Lowe to hold himself ready as a possible stand-in for seconding the vote proposal. Angelico ... well, you never know, do you, really?" He looks at Buff.

"No, I suppose not," the Anglo-Saxon says slowly. "And now that you say so, what about having a stand-in for yourself as proposer of the vote?"

"Like who?"

"Like me!"

Thule looks at Buff for a moment. "Yes. I suppose so. You never know. Some maneuver may truss me up. You? All right. You can do it, I know."

"Surely! Nothing to worry about." Buff is sure.

"If all is wisely arranged then," Franzus stands up, "I will be off. You propose the nomination. Angelico is supposed to second it—or, if necessary, Lowe. Is that it?"

Thule's voice rises in warning. "Eminence, be careful: that's not the way to handle it. Angelico ... well he may want out. There's always Lowe, as we have just agreed. Fine. But be careful. I am not going to propose a nomination first thing. No, Eminence! Oh no! We have to eviscerate the *General Policy.* What I shall propose is another *policy.* We vote on *that.* If we cannot kill the *General Policy,* we cannot kill the *General Policy* nominations! First things first! It's issues, not names, that decide Conclaves! Issues! This time: the issue of Conservativism enshrined in the *General Policy* over against the issue of 'opening,' of *apertura,* of the new and open Church, of open Christianity and open Papacy and open salvation, as enshrined in the Coalition Policy! Got it?"

"Aha! I understand. Better! Much better thought out than I had imagined! More long-range in thought. That way we don't burn our bridges before it's time!"

"Right!"

"By the way," Buff is about to leave when the thought strikes him, "you did hand in our names with the Camerlengo so that our speaking order is secure for tomorrow?"

"Oh, yes. All in order. And remember, we each deal with one aspect or point. My Lord Lynch has his own idea. I shall propose the broad lines. My Lord Franzus here will speak of how Christians and Marxists can live together—he should know something about that, and who can gainsay him? You, My Lord Buff, you will have to use your speaking position in order to demolish whatever some opposition speakers will have said ... And I thought My Lord Francis could adduce the evidence from. . . ."

Francis protests gently but firmly, as he stands up. "My Lord Thule, I had better wait, hadn't I? You've handed in my name for a speaking position. But when I was over with the Camerlengo this evening on another matter, the poor man was so hard-pressed to find space for all the major speakers that I conceded my priority. Besides, I felt it would have been too suspicious a move on my part, if I held on to it. He did press me to renounce it. 'You can have a back-up speech later' the Camerlengo said to me. And I know he was speaking as if the *General Policy* was still viable. I couldn't press the point, I felt, without. . . ."

"Excellent!" Buff decides for all. Thule smiles, acquiescing in the idea. Only Franzus reacts momentarily in a different fashion. A shadow of doubt flits across his eyes. But Francis sees it. "My Brother!" he says, "don't worry! We Orientals have been having the last word for the last five thousand years! I'll do my best!" Then he breaks into a smile. He nods.

Franzus hesitates a moment. Then he too breaks into a smile. He nods. Sometimes, Francis reminds him of those canny farmers in his native land whom nobody ever got to do anything they did not want to do. Always a laugh. Always a pleasant joke. But a will like granite.

As he passes out the door, there are little beads of perspiration around Francis' upper lip. That was a close shave. This is his thought. In his rooms, he closes the door, lifts the phone and calls Domenico.

Buff, Franzus, and the others depart for some rest in their own rooms. Thule calls Lowe and speaks on the phone with him for about twenty minutes. Then he rises and makes his way to Cardinal Yiu's apartment.

While Thule and his colleagues have been formulating a working plan, Karewsky has been with Terebelski in his apartment. There also Bonkowski has come, together with Eakins and Tobey. Eakins and Tobey are still endeavoring to break the working agreement between the Latin Americans and the East Europeans. And the first big question on their minds is Franzus. The second problem is presented by the Latin Americans.

"Well, when we spoke to Franzus in September," Tobey tells Terebelski, "Franzus was just as much with us as you were when my colleague, Eakins, saw you in August. It was fine. He was with us. For the *General Policy,* I mean. I don't think we have to worry."

"I shall worry until it's all over," Karewsky says gently. "We are Slavs. They are not. That's all. And My Lord Thule is very intelligent. You know that!"

"But, Eminence," Eakins breaks in. "There's too much riding on this. Remember, what we propose is neither what I suspect friend Thule wants, nor what friend Franzus wants. It's really an alignment of Conservative religious policy with what we know, or think we know is, or will be, United States Governmental policy. Now, that is an awful lot to risk. Agreed?"

"Yes! But there's no risk really," Tobey assures him. "I have known these people all my life. They're all the same. Mystical. Vague. Great Catholics, though. And tough as nails really."

"Well, if you say so." Eakins murmurs, still doubtful.

"So be it, Eminence," Karewsky says with a slightly satiric expression on his brow and along his round cheekbones and mouth.

"In fact, what I am more concerned about is the Latin American issue," Tobey goes on. "What about Lynch? Will *he* go along with the *General Policy?*"

"The word there is clear," Eakins rejoins. "I have it through our friends in Panama and Cuernavaca—besides what Lynch said to the Brazilians. Lynch will go as Franzus goes."

"So it all hangs on Franzus, eh?" Karewsky remarks.

At this point Kand arrives. "I came only to greet you all, and to ask a question," he says to Terebelski. "From the last words I heard My Lord Karewsky saying, I believe I have arrived at just the right moment. I had intended to ask: Is Franzus secured?"

The usually taciturn Bonkowski breaks in: "I detect a certain note of doubt in your voice, Eminence. . . ."

"Well, to be frank, we received some disturbing reports shortly before coming down to Rome."

"What reports. Tell us!" Eakins is alarmed. Kand glances at Karewsky and catches the warning signal in his eyes.

"Oh, really nothing," Kand says lamely. "Just something about—er— Franzus having difficulty with the Government, and about Franzus' fears."

"Oh, that," Tobey says. "Sure! Franzus has his fears. In fact we all have."

"Well, where do we stand with Franzus?" Kand asks again.

"We have secured Franzus' adhesion," Tobey answers quickly.

"I know that. But that was over six months ago. What about now? Tonight? Tomorrow?" Kand is insistent. Eakins and Tobey look at each other. Then Terebelski takes over.

"Look, Brothers. Our information is that Franzus is going to go for a pan-European policy; that Thule will tag along because he cannot do otherwise; that the Camerlengo can assure us of the Italians. It's a break with tradition for them. But they've seen the light, we think." Terebelski's face is relaxed, semi-smiling, reassuring. He stands up as if to bring the meeting to an end, and turns so that only Karewsky sees his face. On it, Karewsky reads a different message. Terebelski has that cold, hard, granite-like expression that Karewsky and others have seen him wear again and again during his clashes with his home governments and with their Russian masters. Wordlessly,

Terebelski is telling Karewsky now: "No more. Say no more. The whole thing is too subtle for them to understand. Too cunning for them to accept." So Karewsky rises too.

"Eminence! I think that all is set. Let's all get a good night's sleep."

The two Americans move into the corridor. "All the same," Tobey is saying, "I would like a short word with Lynch and Marquez and the others." Eakins is shaking his head.

Karewsky stops at the door and looks back at Terebelski. "Well it should come out all right, Eminence? What do you think?"

"It should be all right," the other says hesitantly. "It should work out. Be sure and have a word with Domenico in the morning." Karewsky departs.

When Terebelski and Kand are alone, Kand takes out a sheaf of papers from his pocket.

"There are no copies, Brother," he says softly to Terebelski. "I must take them away with me again." The other nods and starts to read, Kand passing over page after page as Terebelski hands back each page he has read. It takes them less than a quarter of an hour. Kand folds the papers and puts them back in his pocket.

Terebelski is already on the phone to Domenico. "Yes, Eminence, I have seen the lists. . . . Not so many as I thought . . . even in the United States . . . about, oh, about. . . ." He breaks off and looks at Kand who signals with one hand. "About five bishops. Sixty to eighty priests, some nuns. . . . Rome? Do you mean, oh, the Vatican. Well, mainly laymen. . . . Yes. Mainly among the lay personnel, but there are two or three auxilliary bishops and about four monsignori in the Secretariat and—guess what?—about three to six in the Commission. Yes!" Terebelski listens for a while, then cups his hand over the speaker, and turns to Kand. "How recent, up-to-date I mean, are the lists?"

"They came from Moscow ten days ago," Kand answers shortly.

Terebelski gets back on the phone to Domenico: "Most recent." He listens a while; then, "and we can deal with the individuals later? After the Conclave! Good! I've got it." He says good night, and hangs up. He stands biting his lip for a moment, then turns to Kand.

"Domenico thinks we should hold the lists in reserve. To be used—if and when! Understand?"

"But couldn't they serve a useful purpose now?"

"Yes, they could, in fact, a devastating effect. But, to be used most effectively, both Franzus and Lynch would have to be present. About Lynch I don't care. But there's this one thing about Franzus." He breaks off.

"Well?" Kand asks.

Terebelski answers finally, taking a deep breath, "Let's say this. You have your sources. Would you like to see those compromised?"

Kand goes white and withdraws into his chair, as if he had been struck. "Oh, no! For the love of the Good Jesus, no, not that!"

"Well, then, if they are read out in Franzus presence, we are not sure that your sources will not be compromised."

"But there will be time to alert them. When I return home. . . ."

"Eminence," Terebelski interrupts with a grim voice, "that evening, the evening of the day we read them out here in Conclave, that evening, perhaps even sooner . . ." he breaks off, staring at Kand.

"But how?" Kand stops, realization flooding his eyes. "Oh, no . . . I see! Oh my God! To that extent? My God!"

"Yes," Terebelski grinds the word from between his teeth. "To that extent, Eminence."

There is silence between them. Kand speaks as if he were talking to himself: "So all these turncoat clerics go on living double lives, burrowing away, gnawing at our faith, corroding and betraying."

"No," Terebelski comments. "We'll catch them. Lop them off, one by one, always for obvious reasons. And, forever after, they are marked men."

After a while Kand rises, stands meditating a while, then: "Should Domenico see them—the lists I mean?"

"No." The other man shakes his head. "Not necessary. He knows a bit already. . . . There are other sources." Kand looks around with curiosity in his eyes.

"Arnaud?"

"Well. All right. Let us say that the good Jesuit Father had a very pleasant trip to Moscow last year. Not that Arnaud knows." Terebelski says this with a little grin. "A good mailman, that's our Father for you!"

"That at least," Kand says. They both laugh a little. Then Kand departs.

As Thule enters, Yiu rises quickly. His movements are all very quick but not impetuous, and not so much lithe as subtle. Thule notes this as something he has seen in Orientals. Yiu takes both of Thule's hands in his and bows his head, his body bending slightly at the waist.

"My Eminent Lord Yiu, I am sorry to break in on you at this late hour. We have a busy day ahead of us tomorrow. . . ." Yiu bows a little further, and shows his well-known boyish grin. Even his motioning Thule to an armchair has that tentative quality which amounts to an offering, not an indication of his will.

Thule sits down. There does not seem to be any need for words from him. Then Yiu sits down easily, blinking slowly, still smiling, his head bowed over his desk. He closes the notebook in front of him, and turns his body fully around to face Thule. Cardinal Thule notes the smile still on Yiu's mouth and in the crowsfeet around the Asiatic's eyes—but not within the eyes. They are blinking, watching, blinking.

"Eminence," Thule begins, "I have just been in consultation with some of my like-minded colleagues. We have formed a coalition. For, both to myself, as a leader of one group formed mainly of Europeans, and to my brother Franzus from the East, it does seem vital that we compromise in order to facilitate the work of the Holy Spirit. . . ."

At the mention of the Holy Spirit, Yiu gives a little nod of his head, smiles more broadly, and gestures with his right hand. As if in assent. Though it might be something else that he meant, Thule notes. But he continues.

"We wish as a group to put your Eminence's name in nomination tomorrow." Yiu is unsmiling now but still blinking. "Of course, not until the Second Session. We all have to decide on policy in the First Session." Yiu is smiling again. "Policy is so important, Your Eminence! It decides all other issues, including the candidate-elect for Pope!"

His last statement is more of a question. And Yiu again broadens his smile, but says nothing. By now, *any* change in his facial expression is something voluble.

"I take it then that Your Eminence has no objection to being put in nomination—eventually—as candidate for the coalition?" Then, as Yiu still says nothing, Thule goes on. "You see, Eminence, as proposed candidate we all have to ask you to answer certain questions, so that the generality know your mind . . ." he breaks off, looking questioningly at Yiu.

Yiu looks away, still smiling gently. His eyes are on the desk in front of him, but he is obviously thinking. "It is a great honor . . ." he pronounces the 'honor' in a thick, emphatic manner, and he looks up, still smiling that impersonal smile, and finds Thule's eyes, "to be chosen, even considered, Your Eminence." Silence. Then he continues. "I esteem Your Eminence and the Cardinals from Europe and our Third World and North and South America. But," he looks down again at his desk, "my age and my lack of knowledge." He pauses. Then he turns around again, as if he had made up his mind. "Should our Brother Cardinal Angelico participate, it would be reassuring."

Thule livens up. "Precisely, Eminence! Precisely! As a matter of fact, I have—we, I should say—have this in mind." He waits for another reaction. Yiu smiles broadly at him again. This must be enough for Thule. He has an assent. Propriety requires him to leave his point alone.

"However," Thule hastens to reassure Yiu on another point, "what I wish Your Eminence to understand is that, should Your Eminence wish, we can put off the final voting until the Third or even Fourth Sessions. It will mean another day or so of Conclave, but no matter!" Then as an afterthought:

"There are arrangements we have to make, you understand ... and, oh, of course, you also, Eminence, your own arrangements, too." No *papabile* enters the final balloting without having agreed with friend and opponent on certain conditions affecting both general lines of policy and details.

Now there is a gentle silence. Thule rises, leisurely. Yiu does likewise. They bow to each other, each smiling in his own way. Thule is almost at the door and Yiu's hand is on the knob opening it, when the Asiatic says, as if it were part of a sustained conversation still going on between the two of them: "And the Americans. . . ." Not a question. Not an objection. Not even a simple statement. A piece of a thought. Thule is careful to keep within the flow. "Almighty God walks with us and with them." This seems to be the most appropriately innocuous thing to say at that moment.

Outside in the corridor, a sudden thought enters Thule's head. "The Americans"? The Americans? Did he mean the Cardinals? Or the Government? Or the Latin Americans? Or what? He looks back at Yiu's closed door and shakes his head slightly, then goes on to his apartment. He is not finally sure that he has understood correctly where the Asiatic stands or what he will do.

Domenico was right. As Angelico moves down the corridor at his usual semi-trot, he sees seven figures standing beneath the ceiling light outside the door of his apartment. Riccioni is there with the Iberians, Cortez, Balboa, Rodriguez, and Da Gomez. Behind them, Azande. Angelico is profuse in his apologies for being late, as he shows them in.

From the beginning it is Riccioni who takes over.

"Eminence, I represent a majority of Italian Cardinals. And our four Iberian colleagues speak for various other groups. We decided to come and see you in order to get some advice from you. Frankly, as we see the situation, there seems little hope that our—I allude to the Italians I represent—that our preferred candidate, My Lord Vasari, will make even a good first showing. However, compromise is always possible and bearable.

"In the light of this we have some questions to put to you, because we think that you were perfectly acquainted with the policy of Pope Paul, and with the mind of the Camerlengo as he worked in Paul's Pontificate. You speak, therefore, from hard-nosed experience. I think you share our beliefs and concepts about the Church and the office of Pope—all in line with the Councils and the defined dogmas of the Church, and the believing instincts of the faithful Catholic people everywhere."

Angelico nods to all this. He still does not know in what direction Riccioni's questions lie.

"The questions we have concern what the Church should do. You see, all of us agree that influence and power in the temporal order of politics, earthly rules and governments, all this can no longer be part of the Papacy. It should never have been—at least to the degree that it was. Anyway, that is the way we see things today.

"What then is to be the attitude and policy of the Church, the action of the Church? We have a rather clear idea of what My Lord Thule would propose. I know what my group would propose. But is there any alternative?"

Angelico's answer is negative. "Eminence, I do not know. If there is, I haven't got it today. Frankly, I am as much at a loss as Your Eminences. I suppose it all depends on what is decided the Vatican and the Papacy should become."

"In other words," Azande is speaking now, "there must be a change of some kind or other?"

"Yes! Yes! Of course! Isn't it already changing, the whole thing?"

"Change there is," Riccioni answers. "But we do not know what that change is. No one does. But we are talking of willed change, of deliberate policy change, not the changes imposed willy-nilly on the Church by Providence in the shape of events and unavoidable happenings. What, in your opinion, Eminence, are the options, given the state of things in which His Holiness, Pope Paul 6, has left things?" There is just a note of bitterness in those last words. "Let me, first of all, categorize two obvious alternatives.

"The Vatican can go on more or less as it is going: essentially a clerical bureaucracy located within a sovereign state of its own; holding extensive power and control through its various ministries over every aspect of Church life throughout the world; exercising at least an influence of presence with governments, and international organizations through its diplomatic corps, its corporate financing, and such things. It can stay strictly hierarchic, appointive, and not elective in its various offices—save the Papacy—deriving its power from the Pope. From the Pope as head of the Church, from the Pope as endowed with infallibility and a general teaching authority, and from the Pope as gifted with the prestige of Peter's successor.

"This is, as you see, the ancient and well-established constitutional monarchic oligarchy of the Church that evolved from what Constantine did for Pope Sylvester and for the Church of the fourth century. So long ago! And it has survived every sort of calamity, inner weakness, and external enemy. Traditionalists and Conservatives share this view. The only difference between them is that Conservatives would allow slow, minor changes, whereas Traditionalists will allow little if any change."

"Couldn't the Church, therefore, strengthen itself in this posture? Liquidate by excommunication all those who are attempting to destroy this constitution? Tighten its ranks, in other words. Ride out the storm. Let all these pygmies perish while it rides out the storm, and wait for a later day when conditions turn for the better?" Rodriguez has always preferred the Traditionalist position, but remains a Conservative.

"It could," Angelico answers. "It could try that. But that means it leaves all the work to Providence. This is what you call the Church of Constantine, of Gregory the Great, of Leo 3. It has survived, done great things, and survived."

"Well?"

"The difficulty does not lie there. The difficulty is to find out if this is what Jesus wants from us right now. After all, none of us here thinks the Lord wanted Pius 7 to reclaim all the Papal States at the Council of Vienna in 1815. Pius did, though. And he got them. We think he should not have. But, anyway, the Church survived."

"I suppose the other obvious alternative is the Thule proposal?" Riccioni's question.

"Yes, more or less. And, let me say, it has its merits. The proposal is simple: Let's sail out trustfully and boldly into the human ocean, removing as many barriers as possible, reexamining many—even all—of our cherished positions. This means, practically speaking, that the Vatican ceases to be the Vatican. Oh, I know," this said in quick response to the look on Riccioni's face, "it looks unacceptable. For in such a proposal, the position of the Pope would be totally changed and the official policy of the Church would be totally aligned with what nowadays is reckoned to be the Third World and with the Marxist-Socialist side of international politics and economics. Yes. Yes. I know it would be different."

"But can Your Eminence see what the successor of Peter would become if Thule's proposal were accepted?"

"Well, let's outline it. He would, in effect, be the permanently presiding chairman of an international board of Christians, and the accepted father figure on a still wider international board of, let us say, 'religionists.' No?

"For the proposal of Thule and company is that we should cast aside all fear, that we should trust in the Holy Spirit and, for a time anyway, let all practices and shades of Christian belief mingle, cohabit, combine, blend, coexist, modify each other, eliminate one or the other. A holy confusion, something like a new Pentecost—as Cardinal Thule understands Pentecost, of course!

"In that case, the College of Cardinals becomes an anachronism. For there would no longer be a hierarchic Vatican. The Pope, as Bishop of Rome and honored head of Christianity, would organize his bureaucracy much as the Reverend Mr. Potter organizes his bureaucracy at the World Council of Churches. And, really, much to the same effect. The Pope would cease to have an international stature diplomatically and financially, or to possess an independent State of the Vatican City. And, see how easy union—I can hear Thule say it!—with Eastern Orthodoxy and Protestants would immediately become. But to assume that this would remove the Church from worldly politics is absurd. One look at the World Council of Churches will tell you that!

"Now," Angelico's voice is becoming trenchant, "we all know here that this would be an attempt at suicide. Any admission of all other Christian sects as equals. Any placing of Peter's successor as a first among equals—with an Anglican equal, with a Russian Orthodox equal, with a Lutheran equal, with an Armenian Orthodox equal, with an Episcopalian equal; with all the possible equals—and I am thinking of them all, from the Latter Day Saints over to the Bahai and the Jews for Jesus and the Jehovah Witnesses and anything like that, all the others—all that for me spells death and damnation and the end of us all and of Jesus' Church.

"And there's worse. The state of belief and doctrine is bad enough now. What do you think it would be like the day Thule's proposal were implemented, or on the morrow?"

"Has Your Eminence any other alternative to these two?" Riccioni asks.

"No, Eminence. I have not. No. I have not. I don't think—and I think that you don't think—that the Conservative, middle of the road, change-slowly position of a Masaccio is worth a tinker's curse. And I pray God that He grant us all light, because we have to agree on the policy to be followed by the next Pope, whoever he is. And may God have mercy on him and on us. Something has to be done!"

Riccioni has a disappointed and sad air: He came expecting some enlightenment. Azande seems impassive. The three Iberians have remained serious-faced making no more comments.

"Can we take it then, Eminence," Riccioni asks Angelico, "that your mind about candidates falls more or less on the Right or toward the Center with a bias towards the Right?" This is a regular question and can cause no resentment or surprise. Angelico is looking down at his own hands as they rest on his desk.

The impassive Azande, who has stood up by this time, takes a step forward. "I think His Eminence has answered fairly clearly all our questions."

Riccioni looks from Azande's angular face to Angelico's big eyes. He senses a certain relief in Angelico and a plea in Azande. No more will be learned tonight, he realizes, "Yes, I suppose so, Eminence! I bid you good night, Eminences!"

When Riccioni is gone, Angelico stands, goes around the desk, and stops for a moment with the others.

"Events may push you out of your present position, my friends."

"Eminence," Rodriguez raises his voice, "we have to return to Garcia's apartment for a meeting. We just want to tell you of our group's decision. We have decided to go with a Lohngren nomination, if the case arises. We cannot in conscience back my Lord Riccioni's candidate, My Lord Cardinal Vasari. Masaccio and Ferro are both, we think, on the wrong track. Nor can we see our way to supporting a Thule nominee. Now, unless you have an alternative—and we think you are one of the few capable of producing an alternative—then you leave us with *no* alternative."

Angelico throws his hands in the air. Those present notice the beads of perspiration on his forehead. Angelico is shrugging off any suggestion that he offer himself as a candidate. But another, deeper struggle is wracking him silently and—except for those beads of perspiration—invisibly.

Azande, the sensitive one, is the first to start moving out. "Eminences! We must all get to bed. My Lord Cardinal Angelico has talked long enough."

When he is alone, Angelico starts unbuttoning his cassock. Before he kneels to pray, he hears the footsteps of the last few Cardinals on their way back to their rooms, returning from long consultations. Once in bed he lies there sleepless. Running through his mind are echoes of the conversation just ended, intertwined with a swarm of questions without answers, and his own reactions. *"Unless you have an alternative." Why me? "Is there any other viable alternative?" Is there? Is there? I don't know. . . . I don't know. . . . "If you don't know, Eminence, who knows. . . ." I don't know. . . . I still don't know . . . is there? "What other alternative?" None? Then, it's Lohngren—at best; Thule's candidate—at the worst. Or perhaps there's worse still. "Can there be worse?" I don't know. . . . Why me? How could the Pope's position be worse than in the Thule plan?*

The Camerlengo has been able to calm the fears of the British Commonwealth and Oceanic Cardinals. Their fears were simple: that the central managers of the Vatican would go along too easily with an attempt to oppose a Thule-Franzus proposal. As Desai put it: "For all we know, Eminence, the choice of a Third World candidate may be just the solution of our problems." And as Nei Hao of Oceania said: "All we need is, a few years hence, for Third World Cardinals—some in Latin America and some in Africa—to find out that they cannot in conscience even agree with the precepts and recommendations of a European Pope and his Roman Ministries. Your Eminence knows what that would mean."

Oh, yes. The Camerlengo knows. Total schism. A splitting up of the Church. And he took just five seconds and three words to tell the Cardinal that, in his dry way: "Kaput, Eminence, Kaput!" In the end, he had sent them away with at least a hope that great care would be exercised.

In the three-quarters of an hour before his bedtime, the Camerlengo received the Cardinals from the East. They threw him off balance. They had come led by Terebelski. The Camerlengo has never got on with Terebelski whom he once nicknamed, in a fit of anger, "Our Holy Father of Central Europe" because of the man's pontifical manner. But it has taken such a Cardinal as Terebelski to keep two Communist regimes at bay and hew out a sizable area of influence for his Church in a Stalinist and post-Stalinist regime.

"*Eminenz,*" Terebelski had announced with the Germanic touch to his accent that also irritated the Camerlengo, "we have talked with Cardinal Calder who spoke for at least three of his Western colleagues, Sargent, Artel, and Buonarroti, and for some Europeans and Latin Americans."

"Yes, *Eminence,*" the Camerlengo had responded giving the French nasal sound to the title. "I too. . . ."

"*Eminenz,*" Terebelski had continued imperturbably, as if he had not heard the interruption, "we—our group—have decided to withdraw our adhesion to the *General Policy* as agreed upon according to the *Position Papers.* We will wait until the First Session tomorrow, in order to declare our decision." In telling him this, Terebelski was observing Conclave convention. Having once promised to follow the Camerlengo's policy, he must reveal any change in decision.

Then, they had briefly discussed the leanings of the Latin Americans. It was all inconclusive. Terebelski and his companions had adopted a stand-off wait-and-see attitude.

Now, the Camerlengo is tidying up his table and giving last instructions to the young Monsignore, while he still mulls over the situation. A thought strikes him. He picks up the telephone and calls Angelico.

"I think Your Eminence had better chat with Cardinal Domenico," is Angelico's comment when the Camerlengo quickly explains the crumbling wall of support for the *General Policy Framework.* "He is probably still in the Chapel. Goodnight, Eminence."

As the Camerlengo approaches the Chapel, Domenico is coming out, slowly, deep in thought. For the second time this evening, the Camerlengo does not get in what he wants to say. He barely starts. Domenico gives him one shrewd glance, then says somewhat brusquely: "I know well our trouble, Eminence. I know. But unless my Brother Cardinals become aware of all the facts, they are going to dissent en masse from the *General Policy.*"

"What do you counsel, Father?"

"Beyond recommending openness about all relevant facts, just prayer, Eminence! Pray! Goodnight, Eminence."

The young Monsignore is the last to leave the Secretary's Office. He turns out the lights, closes and locks the door of the outer office which gives on to the corridor. For the duration of the Conclave, besides helping the Camerlengo in his office, the Monsignore will organize the priest-confessors so that they are available for Cardinals' confessions, make sure that material supplies are maintained, and see to the general order of the timetable. He must awaken the confessors at 5 A.M. each day.

Now it is almost 1 A.M. The City outside is asleep. On Vatican Hill a special quiet seems to flow in, as activity trails off into silence. It is the quiet after one more evening's events in the long history of Rome. The same quiet that settled on the same hill after Nero's banquet when Peter died, and the Church of the morrow was unknown to those he left to carry on the message of Jesus' love and Jesus' salvation to all nations.

The First Day

One of those yellow-gold Roman mornings. A cloudless blue sky filled with that luminosity seen only here in the provinces of Latio and in the Cyclades. The sun giving that sheen of old burnished gold to the earth browns and the ochre facades of Rome's palazzi. Everything is still green up on the Pincio and in the Villa Borghese. Over in the Trastevere, the people are hanging out the bedsheets from the windows and calling down to the cafes and the itinerant coffee-vendors for their morning *capocinos*. The sharp east wind that blows from the sea drops as the sun rises.

The night guards on duty at the *Domus Mariae* have just been relieved by the dawn shift. The day's supply of vegetables and meat is already being unloaded. *"Eh beh!"* the carter murmurs with quiet irreverence, *"che mangiano bene, i nostri illustrissimi principi! Andiamo!"* (Well, may they eat well, our most illustrious princes. Let's go) *"Mu andem!"* (Let's go!) his companion rejoins, as he swings into the driver's seat.

The three Cardinals whose rooms are on ground level with the Courtyard are awakened by the departing truck. Two of them turn over to sleep again. The third, Yiu, sits up and glances at his watch, decides to get up.

Inside the Conclave area, very little else is stirring. The young Monsignore's alarm clock rouses him at 5 o'clock sharp. He immediately telephones the priest-confessors. Then he gets ready for the day's work. By 6 o'clock he has said Mass, had some breakfast, and heads for the Camerlengo's office.

As he opens the door from the main corridor, he hears the sound of voices from the Camerlengo's study. In a momentary decision, he knocks and enters: "Good morning, Eminence! May I bring you some coffee?"

The Camerlengo must have been up for at least two hours. Shaved and fully dressed, he is seated at his desk. Seated across from him are Cardinals Braun and Bronzino. The three glance up from their papers at the Monsignore's youthful face. On their laps, on the Camerlengo's desk, and on the side tables are scattered papers and documents and lists of figures. "The financial assessments" is the Monsignore's thought.

"We could all do with some coffee, Monsignore," the Camerlengo answers cheerily. Bronzino and Braun nod.

After he has delivered the coffee to the three Cardinals, the Monsignore receives some lists for typing. "By the way, Monsignore, we will be having some visitors. The names are on your desk. Admit them. But keep all others away for about one half hour . . ." a knock interrupts him. The door of the outer office opens. They hear some light, irregular footsteps, and the young Cardinal with the stutter appears smiling and fresh-faced in the doorway of the study.

"Aha! Good morning, Eminence!" the Camerlengo beams at him. The others present greet the young Cardinal cordially but with some obvious curiosity. "I have invited our young friend as an *amicus curiae*—which he has been, and is, in both senses of the term. You know, he's done a lot of private and confidential work for us over the years." Then to the Cardinal. "Come, come, Eminence! Have a seat. We were just starting." The other Cardinals sit down again, and the meeting resumes.

"Before our other friends arrive, let's get the picture straight." The Camerlengo unlocks one drawer in the desk, takes out a sheaf of typewritten papers, and places them at his right hand. "Here's how we'll do it. I have here unique copies of the financials for 1977–78 and the projected 1979 budget. The perspective of this report, as you will see, is very advantageous for us. The material is presented over against the economic, social, and political background of the United States and Europe. I think, in this respect, the projections and analysis are excellent." Still talking, he passes the top sheet of his documents to Bronzino. "You will get the general picture anyway. All this material is *entre nous* for the moment.

"We start with the state of investments as of Fall 1977." All wait for the quick-eyed Bronzino to scan it. Bronzino is just checking it—he knows more about the subject than any Cardinal in the Conclave. He then passes it to Braun, who knows only some of the contents, and then receives the second page from the Camerlengo. In a few minutes the process is in full swing. Each time a sheet has passed through four pairs of hands, the last man puts it face down on the desk at the Camerlengo's left hand.

When this reading is over, he opens the desk drawer, places the documents inside, closes and locks the drawer, then leans his elbows on the desk and looks downward at his writing pad. All present now realize that the financial health of the Vatican depends on the health of the United States.

"Your Eminences, no doubt, can now appreciate the difficulty—and my attitudes."

"I can see more than a mere doctrinal danger in the Progressivist move," Bronzino comments.

"I thought," the Camerlengo goes on, "that I could explain all this to him—to Thule, I mean—and thus cut off the movement at the pass."

"And?" Braun's query.

"Oh! He seemed to see the hand of God or something like that in all of it." A pause. "The hand of God, if you please."

"Now, how much of all this do we explain shortly to our friends?"

"All of it, but in general terms. Enough so they understand the gravity of any cutting away from the *General Policy Framework,* and/or from close identification with Washington." He looks up earnestly: "We present it always as a temporary measure, of course! Temporary." The others nod. The office door opens. The young Monsignore appears.

"Our friends are here?" the Camerlengo enquires, his voice carrying to the outer office. "Yes, come in, Eminences! Come in!" The Asiatic is the first. "My Lord Yiu, how good of you! Good morning, Pietro!" Masaccio is obviously in his well-known, smiling, morning good humor. He greets Lowe, Lohngren, and Vasari with equal warmth. "You all know each other." The Monsignore brings in some folding chairs, opens them, and all sit down.

"Now my friends, this is, as you know, the usual pre-Session briefing for presumed candidates. And I thought our colleagues here ..." looking at Braun and Bronzino and Lohngren and the young Cardinal, "would be able to help us to get rapidly and thoroughly through it all." He very correctly reminds the small group that the purpose of this briefing, which has been a Conclave practice since early in this century, is not so much to prepare the *papabili* to step, possibly, into the previous Pope's shoes, as it is to give them an idea of the economic and financial factors that govern the Church's actions in various parts of the world—religious, diplomatic, and political as well as ecclesiastical actions. He looks at the Monsignore. "Monsignore will distribute some work sheets to you all which summarize our position and the facts as this Office sees them." The Camerlengo always refers to himself as "the Office," or "this Office." The papers are distributed to the four *papabili* and to the others.

The Camerlengo looks at his copy. "I think everything is clear here."

There is a silence for a couple of minutes, as the Cardinals run through the materials. Cardinal Braun is complimented on the year's contributions from the Catholics in his home diocese. Lowe wants to know how much the Sindona affair cost the Vatican. But Bronzino and the Camerlengo "fudge" on this point. The documents reflect the huge transfer of stocks and property investments from Europe to the United States which the Vatican undertook in the late sixties.

"Then, my Brothers, this is the situation," Yiu says as he lays down his papers. "Any sharp veering away from political and diplomatic alignment with the Atlantic side will endanger our acceptability there; and there, precisely, we have sunk our major interests. Is that the conclusion?"

"More or less. There are nuances, of course." Bronzino is careful. "But that can be taken as a good summary."

"It seems to me, if that is fixed policy," now it is the young Cardinal who speaks, "then anything outside an Italian pro-Curial candidate—or a pan-European candidate acceptable to the Curia—anything outside those two possibilities is ruled out unless we wish to court high danger. And who would want to do that?"

The Camerlengo flings down his pencil in an emotional outburst. "Exactly! That is why, Eminences! That is clearly why some form of the *General Policy* is advisable. I have been saying this to everyone." Instinctively all turn and look at Yiu. No one of them speaks. Yiu looks up, and grimaces as he talks. He is the one *papabile* here who, in the Camerlengo's terms, is unacceptable.

"As if that were the only reason against my candidacy, Brothers! Let's be frank and realistic! There is also my age, you know that. And my skin-color. Oh, yes! It matters; and don't act as if it didn't. Can you imagine what the Italian Communists and Latin American dynasties would say if the Pope were a little yellow man? And my country's regime! Isn't it a factor too? But don't worry. I will not ever be put in nomination successfully. Don't worry!"

"But we have to worry, Eminence," the Camerlengo chides him paternally. "We have to be realistic. And . . ." glancing around, "we all know what Eastern fury can accomplish!" The reference to Thule causes no amusement.

"Understood!" Yiu says cryptically. "Understood! Don't worry!"

"Well then," the Camerlengo rises, his aim obviously accomplished with Yiu's assurance, "if we have finished I am sure we all have things to do before 9 o'clock Mass. I want to thank you all, Eminences! Thanks very, very much. My mind is relieved."

As they troop out, the Camerlengo signals to the young Cardinal to stay. In the confidential work the young Cardinal has done for him and the Vatican, he has shown real promise, this young man. The Camerlengo knows what an important experience this Conclave could be for him. If he can give him a bit of guidance, he will—and happily.

"My friend," he confides, "we do of course, have an alternative plan—should an anti-U.S. Pope be elected and it become imperative to cut the Atlantic knot. But I wasn't going to talk about that now, nor were Bronzino or Braun. They are au courant, of course. Lohngren knows nothing. We would only take such a recourse and follow that alternate plan if it is decided to ride down to the bottom of the trough—I mean really go poor with the Third World."

"But who would decide that the whole machine should, as you say, ride to the bottom of the trough?"

The young Cardinal's question is natural enough, perhaps. But in its attempt to draw him out, the Camerlengo finds it out of character for the younger man. His eyes narrow for one tiny moment. Then his face clears and he smiles indulgently. "You, young man, are too young to hear all these dreadful secrets! Go on! Let me get back to my work. I will never finish it in time. Peace!"

The Cardinal goes out through the outer office, bows his head to the young Monsignore and passes on out into the corridor. The Monsignore rises and goes in to see the Camerlengo. "If I didn't know better, Eminence," he says in that irreverent tone that a trusted servant uses with a master, "I would say the Cardinal didn't find out and is still puzzling about something vital."

The Camerlengo, who is writing busily, does not raise his head. The Monsignore knows his manner, and he waits. A small wry smile appears at the corner of the older man's mouth. Still bowed over his writing pad, he stops writing, glances up under his eyebrows at the Monsignore. The gleam in his eyes is a telltale sign of his inner self. He looks down again at the line of writing where he has stopped, says very curtly: "The old dog for the long road, and the pup for the puddle, as they used to say in Beham." And he starts writing again. The reference to his native town strikes the Monsignore as peculiar. The Camerlengo never refers to it or to any personal matter when talking with his subordinates. Retirement?—the Monsignore asks himself as he leaves his boss. And then another question to himself: Do any of us every really grow up? Or ever cease to be little boys from such and such a little place where our hearts remain always?

By 6 o'clock, Domenico, too, has said his Mass and had some coffee. He is back in his apartment when Yiu appears at the door. He has come directly from the meeting at the Camerlengo's office. Domenico waves his hand airily when Yiu apologizes for the early hour. "It is not early for me, Eminence, I assure you. Not early at all!" He looks at Yiu's stony face. "I guess one thing: You have been approached." Yiu nods.

"Thule?" Yiu nods.

"Nomination or . . ." Yiu nods.

"Before or after the Policy vote?"

"After." Yiu barely opens his mouth. His eyes are narrow slits.

"Did you consent explicitly to be put in nomination?"

"His Eminence took it that such was the case."

Domenico smiles slightly at this answer of Yiu's. He can just imagine the scene. Two kinds of Westerners talk or try to talk with Orientals, Domenico thinks briefly. Those who think they know what Oriental silences and brevity mean. And those who know they do not know.

"Very well, Eminence. Here's what's going to happen. You will be nominated by Thule—probably in the Second Session. He will have to put forth a policy for his candidate first of all. He must do that in the First Session and get it passed. Then he will nominate you in the Second Session. Angelico has been asked to second the proposal. He will rise to speak . . . but he will not second. . . ."

"Won't?" Yiu's eyebrows rise.

"No. Then when Thule and his supporters realize their failure to carry Angelico's support, there will probably be an attempt to rush your renomination and the seconding. It's an old Conclave trick, by the way, and Thule will know it is his best chance. Sit tight. Never refuse directly and explicitly. Above all, don't speak unless you have to. No matter what the temptation to do so. Or the irritation! Make difficulties. But don't get mixed up in the melee."

Yiu looks at Domenico, then rises. "Ni Kan should be told." Yiu and Ni Kan are close friends.

"Ni Kan knows."

At 6:45 a.m., Angelico telephones Domenico. Thule has spent ten minutes with Angelico before going on to say his private Mass. Angelico is worried, and cannot wait to tell Domenico.

"His Eminence, Thule, was with me just now," he says, the moment that Domenico answers.

"And?"

"He asked me to second Yiu's nomination, and to unite the Radicals with his group. And I said yes."

"You agreed! Why?"

"To gain time. Wishing to gain time."

"But if you said 'no,' he'd be stymied for another hour or two and into the morning Session."

"I don't think so. There are others. Or, at least one other."

"Marquez?"

"Yes. He would be one. So my saying 'yes' now at least holds him up from seeking out someone else surer than me." There is silence between them, as Domenico turns over the various alternatives.

Angelico is the first to break the silence. "Can we risk letting it go to a policy vote in the First Session?" His fear is that Thule will be successful in getting the Conclave to approve of his policy. Once that happens the *papabile* elected would be sworn to implement that policy.

"It'll be a near thing," Domenico comments.

"How near?"

"Too near for peace of mind! But not disastrously near—at least that's what I think. I think I can always break it."

"Even a rush?"

"Yes. I think so. Yes, yes. It's always a gamble. But, otherwise, we will never scotch the 'Thule movement.' It can go on and on even after the Conclave."

"Well then. . . ."

"No. We'll let it go. As we said."

"And then?"

"Register to speak at the beginning of the Second Session," Domenico tells Angelico. "Depending on what happens in the First Session, we'll decide what to do later in the Second."

"But, Father, supposing it all goes fast in the First Session, and I am called upon to second a rush nomination?"

"It won't come to that. I have checked. There are at least six scheduled speakers, main speakers. Thule is last. Don't worry. We'll only get to the *Policy* vote."

"You yourself are not speaking, Father?"

"No."

"Why?"

"I want that rope to be as long as it possibly can be. We have some heavy bodies to hang on it. The longer, the surer, the cockier, the more detailed in their explanations they become, the longer and stronger that rope will be."

"What about the Camerlengo?"

"Until he sees, finally, that his *General Policy* is in ruins, he won't even begin to come around." As Angelico is about to reply, Domenico interrupts. Someone is knocking at his door. "Eminence, go and say your Mass. And pray well. We will talk later."

Domenico's visitors are Eakins and Lohngren.

"Eminences! Come in!"

"We have celebrated Mass already, Eminence, as you did yourself." Lohngren knows Domenico's habits.

"May we have a moment of your time?" Now it is Eakins who speaks, smiling.

"Hah! Your American politeness. Remember it was I who phoned you at the ungodly hour of 5:30 this morning!" The three sit down. Domenico wastes no time. "Eminences, the brute fact is that the pan-European proposal is stillborn." He pauses. Eakins' face has dropped. Lohngren closes his mouth tight, then asks an important question.

"How?"

"Simple. You North Americans are divided," he says to Eakins. "Sargent will go with Vasari and the Traditionalists, as will Braun. You know that. They didn't really change.

"But Calder and. . . ."

"Calder went along on condition that Terebelski assured them of Karewski, Bonkowsky, Kand, Franzus, and some others; and as long as you, Eminence," he means Lohngren, "could bring the other Germans—and now you cannot be sure of them, can you? And as long as your friend, Marsellais could deliver you the French." Marsellais again, Bishop of Louon President of the European Bishops' Conference, the all-powerful Pope-maker in non-Italian Europe. His name figures in every strategy vote count. "Now, Marsellais cannot deliver, will not or does not deliver. I don't know which. Anyway, he's changed."

"In what direction?"

"Thule et al."

"And the Spaniards?"

"In the middle. In the middle, Eminences!"

"But in a first balloting, we can still make a strong showing and follow that up later with. . . ."

"I doubt it—your strong showing. But even if you did, the tide is turning. You see, the linchpin is this: If the *General Policy* is dead—and I think that there can be no doubt it is, by the way—" the others nod glumly, "then your solution is next: i.e., let's have a non-Italian, a European candidate. And, then, a later Conclave can proceed to a non-European. Now that's a lovely idea. But what on earth indicates to you that the Africans want a European? Why should they? And the Latin Americans? Why should they accept anything from capitalist Europe?

"Oh no Eminences! If from the beginning you openly discountenanced the *General Policy* by suggesting your pan-European solution, you have cancelled the need for the whole first half of Thule's argument before he says a word. You open the door wide and you fall right into the hands of Thule and the Progressivists! For you have no candidate or policy they will accept once you open that door. And they have both, ready and willing and easy, or so they think."

Eakins looks at Lohngren, then back to Domenico. "Why has Terebelski changed? After all, there were commitments."

"And still are, Eminence!" Domenico answers realistically. "But when the conditions under which commitments are made have changed, the commitments fall to pieces—you know that!" Eakins still has something on his mind. Domenico knows how to wait.

Lohngren looks at him then at Eakins: "I think, Eminence, you had better explain a little about the pan-European proposal." Eakins waits a while, then turns around to Domenico.

"Eminence, the plan was a little more complicated than would appear at first sight. The entire exercise of forming a pan-European bloc was not really meant to get a non-Italian elected. It was conceived originally to freeze a bloc of votes so that they would go neither to My Lord Angelico nor to My Lord Thule's side. Neither to the Radicals nor the Progressivists. The plan was meant to sow so much divisiveness in these two groups, that the Conservatives would be the strongest alternative."

"The delayed action, eh?" Domenico understands the old political game. "Having beaten down any Thule putsch and skeletized any support for Angelico, then the pan-European candidate on being nominated would refuse categorically and throw his support behind . . ." Domenico thrusts his head forward like a hawk seeking prey, "behind whom, Eminence?"

There is an awkward silence. Domenico remains tense for a few more seconds, then relaxes and looks at the lists of Electors that lie on his desk. A half minute passes before he speaks. His tone is sepulchral and quiet.

"I see a very dark hand, a very long and dark hand, stretching out of the labyrinthine folds, all velvet, all silent, all smooth, reaching out and getting a stranglehold on whatever initiative there is for renewal, for good, for fresh hope. And I am speaking of God's people, in that last phrase, Eminences." He looks up and smiles a little grimly at the other two, then looks down again. He lifts a sheet of paper off his desk, reads a little then drops it. "Such plotting and planning is sad, Eminences. Very sad.

"And I will tell you how sad. It's sad because, first of all, it has failed before it could even spring. It failed. The plan is bankrupt. Thule has you surrounded.

"It's sad, secondly, because as you know better than I do, those bishops outside who know of your plot have had their hopes raised—they expect huge liberalizations, huge changes. But bearable changes. But they are not so clever at maneuvering as you. They believe in your alternative. Not as a plot, but for its own sake. Now, can you imagine their chagrin when you are beaten, so to speak? When you, Eminence, shoo in somebody like Vasari or Ferro, who is anathema to those bishops? Can you imagine what is going to happen? And what damage do you think Thule and his Progressivist theologians are going to do after, the Conclave? Can you imagine? Have you foreseen all that? No! You didn't stop to think!"

"Then what alternatives are there?" Eakins' question.

"Alternatives! Alternatives! Alternatives! I hear nothing but that word and question from those who have gone around for a couple of years blithely forging their own very private and miserable alternatives! Alternatives?" Domenico is almost laughing in a sardonic way, but his innate kindness stops him short of it.

Lohngren takes up. "And so, Eminence? Now? Right now"—looking at his watch—"in approximately three hours, what?"

"This, simply this. Let Thule run, as far, as fast, as explicit, as outrageous, as presumptuous as he can and as he wishes."

"But that will mean certain death for the *General Policy,* and *then?*"

"No." Domenico is almost reproving in his response. "Come, come! We can have no false hopes. We must serve Jesus better. We all know that the *General Policy* is dead already. That's a fact. It only remains to put that fact on display."

"So what do we do?"

"Pray, Eminence, pray! And when the time comes, use your heads. The Second Session will be crucial."

Eakins looks at him. "Eminence, whatever happens, we will not support any move in Angelico's direction. For Angelico means a whole host of things we have fought against."

"I know. I know." Domenico looks at him. "I know, Eminence. But why did you set yourself up as the executioner of Capovero and the others? And why tag along with the anti-Paul group?" Dom Dino Capovero, one of Pope Paul 6's personal assistants, had been, with his close associates, in constant clash with Eakins and his supporters. A whole army of powerful Vatican officials wanted Angelico's head. For Angelico was hated for much.

"But," Domenico concludes, "this is not a time for vendettas, or for mutual backscratching. The times are critical."

But Eakins is not satisfied. He starts again to ask Domenico if another way cannot be found to make a genuine pan-European candidacy viable. Eakins still fears an Angelico movement.

Domenico looks at him for a moment, his eyes narrowing, then he uses a cold, lofty tone of voice. "Eminence! Look at it like this. Your home city is a very big, very rich, very fast, very powerful city and diocese. It is a very big political center. You have ample there to occupy you. When you come here, remember that you can in no way introduce any interests other than Rome's—even if those other interests coincide with Rome's. None of us finally can be messenger boys for anyone. Just messengers of Jesus, our Lord." There is no word from Eakins. But his face has no pleasantry in its look.

Lohngren stands up. Eakins follows suit. "I suppose it will be the Second or even the Third Session?" Lohngren asks.

"The vote on a candidate? Yes. One of the two. The policy vote will probably be in the First Session. Let's pray and work. Good morning, Eminences!"

When Eakins and Lohngren leave Domenico, he crosses to his desk and telephones. "Eminence?" He is speaking to Riccioni now. "Have you got a few moments . . . ? At 7:30? Very Well. Here? Fine! Thanks!" He hangs up.

When Riccioni arrives, it is obvious that he has had a bad night. And a short night's sleep. He is very pale. And his expression is one of profound distress.

"I don't know what to tell you, Eminence," he begins to Domenico once they are seated together. "Everything seems to be crumbling around us. What are we to do? Go into schism? It's as bad as that, at times it really seems so. Last night, it was obvious that Thule was digging his feet in. This morning, I was over with the Americans—Braun and Bronzino were there, too—and it is obvious that any collapse of the *General Policy* is going to mean a danger to our long-range investment plans. I wouldn't mind that so much, if it didn't also entail honeymooning with non-Catholics and Marxists."

"Eminence," Domenico says gently, "the *General Policy* is as dead as the dodo. Start from there."

"But where do we go from *there*, Brother? To cap it all, it seems that Lombardi is heading a fission among the Italians. Incredible! Incredible!"

Lombardi is a foreign-born Italian. At fifty-seven years old, he has climbed rapidly from simple priest to Bishop to Cardinal and Prefect of a Roman Congregation. Lombardi is suspected by many to be too liberal—and certainly too young for any responsibility.

"Not incredible at all! We already know they are split!" Domenico rejoins.

"So we are faced with a huge, yawning chasm of heterodoxy, Protestantism, secularization of the Liturgy—as if we hadn't gone far enough already. And politization of the Church in the name of the proletarian revolution! *Dio!* It's too much. We've got to do *something*." Riccioni is looking into the middle distance and speaking, as it were, to the ceiling.

"Eminence," Domenico still speaks gently, "I share all your distress. But the solution does not lie in our losing our presence of mind or going hog-wild." Riccioni's temper is well-known. Demenico needs to be certain that he himself will retain control of events in the crucial Sessions coming up.

"I know. I'm inclined to go hog-wild. I see red. *Dio!* I see red in another sense!" exclaims Riccioni.

"Now, Eminence, we are not there yet. And you know that as well as I do."

"But, Domenico, have you seen or heard of the plan—I mean Thule's plan for a new International Council of Theologians who would function with the Pope and the *Congregation for the Faith* and with the Bishops' *Synod*, and which would not be merely consultative but could lay down doctrinal regulations? Have you seen that plan?"

"Yes," Domenico says quietly. "I've seen it. It stinks." One of Thule's pet projects has been the creation of a permanent body of theologians meeting every year for a couple of months in Rome. The members would be appointed by the bishops around the world. There would be 12 permanent members drawn from Protestant churches who would not be mere observers: They would participate in the proceedings. The Council would be a legislative body: The Pope would be obliged ex officio to follow its majority rulings.

"Can you imagine what Küng, what Dulles, what Schillebeeckx and all the others would do in that Council?" Riccioni asks in horror. "And the permanent Protestant members?"

"Eminence, look!" Domenico remonstrates and soothes the old Cardinal. "We all know that Küng and Dulles and Curran and Schillebeeckx and the others are more Protestant than Catholic. They and many others are close to heresy in matters such as the Incarnation, the Trinity, priestly celibacy, sexual morality, and so on. But we can deal with them, Eminence. We can manage them. We can salvage what is good. We can reject and expel the rest. Do not worry on that score. . . ."

"But beyond all that, what about the Marxization of the Church? I always said Montini's *Ostpolitik* was crazy. I told Roncalli (Pope John 23) that *he* was wrong. I've been saying so for years to Montini and Casaroli and Silvestrini and all the other intellectual greyhounds at the Secretariat."

"We have moral imperatives," Domenico says reprovingly, "to seek justice and peace in the world." His voice has hardened ever so slightly. "We cannot and should not stop talking to each and every government, be they non-Catholic or Communist or what-not. Do you want us to retire from the world? Of course not, Eminence! What's bothering you is bothering me. It is the *way* in which all this is being done. . . ."

"Precisely!" Riccioni is on fire again. "Precisely, Eminence. The way in which we do it. Have we no alternative?"

"Oh no! Not that again!" Domenico says in mock horror flinging up his hands in protest. "Every one of you comes in through that door crying about alternatives. What have you been doing all this time, Eminence? Why haven't you developed an alternative?"

"We have! We have!" Riccioni is off again. "The age old doctrine. A return to. . . ."

"No, Eminence." Domenico is calm again. "No! What you must get into your head is that there is no going back. You cannot. We cannot. The Church cannot. No going back."

"Then we'll fight. Every inch of the way. Every minute of every hour of every day. For months, if necessary!"

"And how long would you really last, Riccioni?" Domenico becomes harsh in tone. "Tell me, how many of you are there? Have you anyone you can really rely upon? In the Conclave, I mean. And today? This morning? How many?"

"Well, there's myself. There's Dowd, Nolasco, Braun, Maderno, Pozzo, Duccio, Vasari, Lamennais, Carracci, Walker, Houdon, Bronzino"—Riccioni falters—"and that's only the beginning."

"You name twelve. I'm not sure even of all of them. But, for argument's sake, let's go on. How many more? Ten more? Twenty more?" Riccioni's response is silence. He unfolds his arms and looks at Domenico for a long moment. When he speaks, he is subdued in tone. Even in all his fury and temperament, he does see.

"What do you counsel, Domenico?"

"First of all, we must not panic. For this reason I want to ask you a favor, Riccioni. Please! Do not make a major speech. Harass them all you want. Interrupt them. Council against them in private. Heckle them. But in public session do not, I repeat, do not, make any major speech."

"Why not, Domenico? Why should . . ."

"Because, when you start, you are like a red rag to a bull. You simply rub most of them the wrong way. And they immediately want to oppose you. Pardon me, Eminence! But that is the fact, is it not?"

Riccioni nods mournfully, but says nothing.

"So," Domenico repeats. "Harass them! Harangue them with one-liners. Applaud at the right time! Yawn. Do what you can. But no major speeches."

Riccioni is quiet again, for a little while. Then he speaks in a very resigned tone. "Very well, Domenico. But you know what galls me and what I cannot understand? Well, the Camerlengo and company here have been flirting with Masaccio for almost two years now. And *you* know, if Masaccio got the election, the Camerlengo and his friends would be the first to go. Between Masaccio and myself there is more than a small difference. Yet, they cannot see that they are safer with us, with me, with the Traditionalist bloc. We won't boot them out!"

"Masaccio and the Conservatives have almost as small a chance as your Eminence—I mean your Eminence's ideas—of prevailing. Look! These things are not predictions; it's just what is *going* to happen. The fact is that a vast change has taken place *out there* in the Church. In the *people* of the Church, I mean. That is the Church, you know! Neither the Conservative nor Traditionalist plan will correspond with the reality of that change. Now, here comes Thule and Franzus and Buff and Lombardi and Marquez and all the others, the young Turks!—with a different plan. And screaming the house down that they know what is going on!"

"Do they?" Riccioni asks incredulously. Domenico pauses and looks away. He thinks.

"Yes and no," he says finally. "Yes and no. They certainly see what causes our problems—the big change. I don't think they understand that change. And I find their solution is social and political rubbish and—in terms of what Jesus' Church should be—dangerous stupidity. But they do see the change."

"May the good Lord Jesus, Lord of all, save our Church!" Riccioni says as he rises. His short prayer is sincere and fervent. He stands for a moment looking at the floor. Then: "I will do as you suggest. But, how long must we so temporize?"

"As long as is necessary to create a strong hanging-halter." Domenico's lifeless tone emphasizes his meaning.

Riccioni shoots a quick glance at him. "Should I speak to Masaccio?" he asks Domenico.

"No, I've been on the phone with him. He's all right. He understands. He's better now than he was last night. He's all right, Eminence!" Domenico glances at his watch. "In five minutes the bell is going to ring for the Mass of the Holy Spirit. A crucial day begins." Riccioni understands that Domenico is still asking if he can rely on Riccioni's staying under control.

"Domenico!" Riccioni has regained his peace and some measure of confidence. "Let's go and give a good account of ourselves."

"Right, Eminence!" Domenico rejoins warmly. "Right!" He smiles. "Haven't you Venetian fishermen a phrase that covers a dark dawn that will be followed by a brilliant day?"

Riccioni's old good humor rises. "No dark day in Venice is followed by brilliance of sunshine. If we start off bad, we are bad to the end!"

"Let's go, Riccioni! God Bless!"

It is 8:45 A.M., and the bell is ringing for the Mass of the Holy Spirit in the House Chapel. This morning, it is the Camerlengo who will be the celebrant. All the Cardinals are supposed to attend, unless their health forbids it.

Across in the other wing of the Conclave area, the caucus of the Latin American Cardinals is just breaking up. It has been held in the apartment of Teofilo. Present there also were Zubaran, Hildebrandt, Ribera, Gris, and the young Cardinal with the stutter.

At the bell, they disperse quickly. Some return to their rooms on their way to the Chapel. Others go straight to the Chapel.

The young Cardinal goes back to his room, ostensibly to pick up his prayer book and some notes. He automatically fingers the ruby on his pectoral cross. This seems a habitual and frequent gesture of his. He reflects. This is not the best of mornings for the Cardinal. He had a dream this morning just before awakening—or so it seems to him now. One of those repetitive nagging dreams. He cannot remember its sequence—if it had any. All he can recall now is a skewed perspective in which something delicate and beautiful—a butterfly, a moth—flowing in many colors landed on his hand or near him in some intimate way. He has a lingering sensation in his memory of fire and crumpling wings, melting colors. It is all he can remember. But the sense of loss is deep. He hurries down to the Chapel.

Inside, except for Patti and Morris—both feeling unwell this morning—all the Cardinal Electors are kneeling. The Camerlengo has begun celebrating the Mass. An air of tranquility and unison pervades the Chapel. As the young Cardinal slips into the nearest pew, he finds himself beside Reynolds of Oceania. Some emotion, unbidden, and uncontrolled but not violent, wells up in him. And right through the Mass, it stays present with him, like the voice of a gentle visitor asking to be admitted.

As the other Electors recite the Mass prayers, he joins in sporadically. Each time he says any of those words out loud, he feels that the great granite millstone time has been for him up to this moment is now melting. The arched Chapel itself becomes like a flimsy kite flying skyward into the unknown. And all its occupants are become in some disturbing way unknown and alien to him. And the sanctuary with the Camerlengo celebrating at the Altar is a vault of dreams burned by the fire from the Altar candles and the two flickering red sanctuary lamps permanently lit on either side. He fingers that ruby on his pectoral cross and remembers again the Embassy reception three months ago where he was feted and congratulated, then introduced into the Ambassador's private quarters. There they presented him with the heavily bejewelled pectoral cross. "It is special," the Ambassador had said. "Later we will explain about it." They had explained. Dim snatches from his memory of this early morning's dream float down his consciousness and mingle with a new sense of regret for what was done by him, and by what he is bound to do.

Only when the Camerlengo turns around at the end of Mass, only then does the Cardinal return to himself fully. It is 9:40 A.M. As he rises and genuflects, he takes in the Altar and the pews and the wall frescoes and the Cardinals around him shuffling out. Again that feeling of the alien, the being not-at-home any longer. Once, all such things and people used to be near him, intimately near as a veil of holy air, as the intangible joy of holy fire. Now he sees them as far off or, maybe, it is he himself who is far off. He turns his back and with the others makes his way to the main door and the busses.

THE FIRST SESSION

In his temporary office off the Upper Room, the Camerlengo waits until the young Monsignore comes for him. Outside, most of the Electors are chatting while they wait for the warning bell announcing the First Session. There is an air of anticipation and camaraderie. But many are exchanging little confidences, passing words of advice, assessing the numbers of Electors in favor of this or that issue, and probing each other on those issues.

Promptly at 9:45 A.M. the warning bell rings. Already, little knots of Cardinals have gathered inside the main door.

The young Monsignore is sitting at his table just outside, taking notes, receiving messages and commissions, giving out messages. At three minutes to ten, the young Monsignore stands up, goes to the Camerlengo and announces: "Just two minutes more, Eminence!"

"In a moment." The Camerlengo's voice comes as a cracking whip. When he emerges, his face is white and his look worried. "Good! Let's go!"

Within minutes, he enters the Conclave. The young Monsignore closes and locks the doors from the outside. He sits down at his table, takes out his watch, winds it, places it on the table, opens his diary, and starts writing.

Inside, all proceeds according to rule and convention. The Camerlengo briskly announces the first order of the day to be the election of this First Session's three presiding Cardinals, its Presidents. This, the Camerlengo proposes, can be done in a simple way. Each of the three main political groups in the Conclave will nominate a representative. These three Cardinals will then agree on the identity of the three Presidents of this Session. A general voice and hand vote will confirm or reject their choices. Still using the same method they will then elect three Scrutineers who will count the ballots, and three Revisers who will check the ballot count performed by the Scrutineers. Lastly, the Cardinals will appoint three *Infirmarii* who will carry ballots that must be filled by any Cardinal who is confined to bed or to his room during a voting session.

These elections do not take long, as all are agreed on getting the Conclave off to a quick start. Within twenty minutes, Koi-Lo-Po of Oceania is named the First President, to be flanked by Tobey of the United States and Lamy of France as co-Presidents.

The Scrutineers are Thule, Bronzino, and Kiel. Uccello of the Roman Curia, Constable of India, and Lang-Che-Ning of Oceania become the Revisers. The *Infirmarii* are Ni Kan, Franzus, and Chaega.

The Scrutineers, the Revisers, and the *Infirmarii* remain seated in their places. The three Presidents move up to the Long Table. The Camerlengo shakes each one's hand. There is some amiable applause. Then he goes to his own place. Everybody settles back.

Koi-Lo-Po puts on his reading glasses, glances at the schedule in front of him, takes off his glasses, and holds a short low-voiced conversation with his co-Presidents.

The he addresses the Conclave. "My Brother Cardinals, My Most Eminent Lords Tobey and Lamy join with me in thanking your Eminences for the confidence bestowed on us by this appointment. We will endeavor to fulfill our duties as efficiently as we can." He stops. Tobey is shoving a typewritten notice toward him along the table. Koi-Lo-Po puts on his reading glasses again. It takes him a few seconds to read what Tobey has passed to him. Looking over the top of his glasses he goes on addressing the Cardinals.

"It is suggested by the Camerlengo—who, I am sure, has sounded out all shades of opinion amongst you—that we hold a first and preliminary balloting about the status of the *General Policy*." Tobey looks over at the Camerlengo who has closed his eyes and sunk his head on his chest.

"In order to expedite matters, I suggest—and this is the idea of my fellow-Presidents also—that we have a voice-and-hand vote as to whether we should proceed to the balloting on the *General Policy*." He pauses. There are no objections. "So, will all those Reverend Cardinals in favor of a first balloting on the status of the *General Policy*, please raise their hands and declare themselves clearly by saying '*Ita*.' "

Ni Kan's hand is the first to go up, followed by Yiu's, Thule's, Franzus', Marquez's, and then a whole forest of hands; all this is accompanied by a chorus of "*Ita!*" in over a hundred different tones and accents. Koi-Lo-Po scans the assembly, compares notes with his co-Presidents.

"Will all those against a first balloting on this issue now signify their dissent by raising their hands and declaring their intention by saying '*Non*' out loud." Three voices say '*Non!*'—Vasari, Pincio, and Bronzino. Their hands follow; then about ten other Cardinals join them in saying '*Non*' and raising their hands.

"Clearly, Most Eminent Brothers, the majority is in favor of a balloting. So let us proceed with it. Your ballot, to be valid, must carry three elements: your name; a symbol or a verse of Scripture that will be a means of verifying your ballot without uncovering your name in case of any doubt; and then your actual vote itself. You first write your name. Then make a fold along the dotted line so that your name is covered. Then inscribe your choice of symbol or Scripture verse. Then make another fold along the second dotted line, and on the outside of the ballot write *placet* (it pleases) if you approve of the *General Policy* and wish it to be the framework of our discussions. If you disapprove, you write the words *non placet* (it does not please).

"My co-Presidents will now distribute the special ballot papers. I suggest that the Scrutineers and Revisers get their ballots marked as soon as possible, and then take their places at the side tables. In order to hurry things, I am going to ask the three Scrutineers, the three Revisers, and the three *Infirmarii* to help in the distribution of the ballot papers. Please let all Electors wait until this distribution is complete before filling out their ballot."

Already Tobey and Lamy have stood up. Koi-Lo-Po hands them each a packet of ten ballot papers. Franzus, Ni Kan, and Chaega are at his side receiving similar packets of ten ballot papers. After them, Thule, Bronzino, and Kiel arrive for their packets. Within minutes, Lamy is back. But Koi-Lo-Po makes him wait until all the others have finished.

"How many, Reverend Brothers, have as yet no ballot papers?" he asks. Eight hands are lifted. Koi-Lo-Po counts out eight more ballots. Lamy distributes them. Then the Revisers, Scrutineers and *Infirmarii* regain their seats. Koi-Lo-Po rings the silver bell of the President. The Cardinals start marking the ballots.

Koi-Lo-Po, having marked his ballot, looks up and waits, watching until finally each Cardinal Elector has stopped writing and is sitting back on his throne. He has whispered words with his co-Presidents.

"Eminences, seeing that we are not balloting about a Papal candidate but on the issue of a policy, my co-Presidents and I feel that it would be quickest and most desirable if some of our younger officials—My Lords Chaega, let us say, and Kiel—went around and collected the ballots."

But there is an immediate outcry at this. No one wants that. Too much chance of deception. There is a chorus of *"Non!" "Non placet!" "Non!"* The majority wishes that everyone place his ballot, publicly, alone in full view of all, into the chalice provided for ballots. The chalice is on the Altar.

"So let it be, Eminent Brothers!" Koi-Lo-Po shrugs. "So let it be. We will proceed according to rule."

The three Scrutineers take up places by the Altar on which the chalice stands. Then the Camerlengo as senior Cardinal stands up, proceeds quickly to the Altar, genuflects and swears out loud: "I swear by this Holy Altar that I have chosen as best as God has given me to see," rises, drops his ballot into the Chalice, and returns to his place. Already, Pincio and Ferro, as the next two in seniority, are waiting to do likewise. The process really goes faster than most had anticipated. All are concentrating with the Scrutineers on each hand as it is raised, and as it drops the cream-colored ballot paper into the Chalice.

Within twenty minutes, the balloting is over. The scrutiny starts. The three Scrutineers take the chalice to their own table. Seated there, Thule, as the senior Scrutineer, takes out one ballot, notes the vote on a sheet of paper provided with two columns, and passes the vote to the next senior Scrutineer,

Bronzino, who does likewise and gives the ballot to Kiel who reads the vote out loud—*"Placet"* he reads in a loud firm voice from the first ballot. Then he drops the ballot into another chalice. While Thule is extracting the next ballot Kiel is marking that first *placet* on his own sheet of paper. And throughout the assembly of Cardinals, each one is keeping his own tally.

The atmosphere of the Conclave changes palpably according as this process continues. After a burst of 17 *non-placets* following on the heels of that first *placet*, there then comes a series of 28 *placets*. As the number of these positive votes mounts past 25, there is a visible relaxing on certain faces. Vasari and Pincio smile at each other. The Camerlengo begins to perk up and look his usual businesslike self. "Just ten more, please God! Ten more! And we have the start we need!" Masaccio whispers half out loud to his neighbors. One third is 39. Only two-thirds plus one are needed for victory.

But then, the *non-placets* start again. The Camerlengo, sedulously marking his tallysheet, sees the number rising ... 54, 55, 56 ... in the *non-placet* column. When the number reaches 71 and is still rising, he lays his pencil down calmly and sits back. Opposite him, he finds Angelico's eyes glued on his. "It's all over with your *General Policy*, my friend," is Angelico's silent message. "I know, my friend. I know. You were right," says the Camerlengo's silent answering stare.

The twenty or so minutes which the Scrutiny has taken have passed like three minutes. The three Scrutineers compare their columns, find that they tally, then Thule takes his own tally-sheet, Bronzino and Kiel initial it. Thule walks up to the President's table and hands it to Koi-Lo-Po. Koi-Lo-Po glances at his columns: 82 *non-placets*, 35 *placets*. The *General Policy* is finished.

"Eminences! The Scrutiny is as follows: *Placet*, 35; *Non-placet*, 82." The Camerlengo's face is inscrutable. Lohngren glances at him and then at Angelico. Angelico is watching everyone, but seems neither elated nor depressed. Domenico has his arms folded, his eyes cast down looking at his writing table. On the faces of the older Cardinals—Pincio, Vasari, Riccioni, and others—there is a mixture of consternation and steely determination. Ni Kan is doodling. Buff is seen nodding wisely to Franzus. Thule is very calm and grave.

"Eminences!" Koi-Lo-Po goes on, "properly speaking we should ask the Revisers to review the results of the Scrutineers. But seeing, again, that this is a vote on issues and not on persons, would it please Your Eminences to dispense with the Revision, and to proceed with our business?" There are a few silent moments. People look around at each other. No one has any objection. For a moment, it looks as if Azande is going to say something, but Angelico cranes around and gives him a stare.

"Well, then, Eminences, it looks as if we must declare the will of this

Conclave to be that the *General Policy* is dropped." He looks at the Camerlengo and feels a great compassion. For the Camerlengo is suffering deeply and bravely. "So, the Holy Spirit has spoken." It is meant for that man's consolation. What the Camerlengo has worked at for at least three years has come crumbling down within one half hour.

Koi-Lo-Po continues: "At this juncture, my Brothers, would it be outlandish of me to make a suggestion—which is purely of my own initiative and a deviation from the agenda? We need an orientation now, in order to find a fresh path—and quickly. I propose we ask some Brother Cardinal whom we all venerate to give us his mind on the matter. And offhand, it seems to me that My Lord Domenico is that venerable person." Koi-Lo-Po looks around searching the faces. "For all of us! What do you think, Eminences!"

There is a general murmur of assent, some light applause, and cries of *"Bravo! a Domenico la parola!"* (Let Domenico speak). Koi-Lo-Po looks over at Domenico and nods his head smilingly. Domenico still seated, looks at Koi-Lo-Po, then glances around at his fellow-electors. He smiles indulgently and pleasurably, then starts to rise from his seat.

"Most Eminent President, beloved Colleagues!" It is the voice of Cardinal Buff. The Anglo-Saxon has an amiable but wary look on his face which says that he wants to be friendly but please don't interfere with him, that he hates being interfered with. "I am as lost in admiration of our Brother, My Lord Domenico as any one of us here." Buff smiles sunnily at all and sundry. "I would like"—he emphasizes that 'would'—"to point out, however, that for our own sakes we should proceed constitutionally—especially in a crisis of this nature." His look becomes paternal and solicitous. "We cannot act too circumspectly."

Thule has a solemn look on his face at this moment. The Camerlengo is taking notes. Franzus is signalling Lynch in order to alert him: "You're the first to speak!"

"Now," Buff goes on in a brisk, let's-get-it-over-with tone, "we have already a list of speakers, all registered duly and lawfully and *comme il faut* with the Camerlengo last evening, if I'm not mistaken. They really have priority, you know, over all of us, even over our most venerable Lord Cardinal Domenico." Buff gives his most unctuous beam of a smile toward Domenico. "You," he looks again at Domenico, "Your Eminence would be the first to agree. Yes?" Domenico nods quietly. Buff looks then at Koi-Lo-Po and sits down.

There is an uneasy feeling in the assembly. The President has already conferred with his two confreres. Koi-Lo-Po wants a fight with no one. Not now.

"My Lord Cardinal Buff is to be thanked," Koi-Lo-Po announces in a formal tone. "Time, as well as good orderly procedure, requires us to hasten along arranged paths. I call therefore on His Eminence, My Most Reverend Lord Cardinal Lynch!"

Lynch stands up, walks quietly to the Altar, kneels a moment, rises, and turns to speak. There is no hurry in his manner, only dispatch: He has something important to say, and it must be said now.

"Venerable Brothers. I stand before you at this moment to make a solemn announcement. I announce what, it seems to me, is the essential fact dominating our choice of a new Pope. I beg you to listen to me with all the wisdom and love of Christ's Church. For, whether we realize it or not, today in this Conclave, we are deciding for or against the life of that Church such as we have always known her.

"The Church as the body of Jesus' salvation will live for always, of course. But we are busy with the institutional Church. That is our 'job'." The Cardinal's tones are soft, his words limpid; and through his voice there runs that charming sense of gentleness that his country generates in its children.

"The announcement is simple: The Christian world is dead and gone. Not merely the Christian heartland in southern Europe. But the Christian world. The entire complex of culture, thought, feeling, art, morality, folkways, public decorum, international mores—all that Christian world is no more.

"We live in a still cemetery today, and the tombstones of this cemetery record the occupants of each sad grave." No one among Lynch's listeners has any doubts that an intense sadness and regret fills him as he pours out these words. Tears are present in more than one pair of eyes. He would have said these things even had the *General Policy* vote been different. But by their vote they have said, in effect, that they know an era has ended. They must find a new way.

"Tombstones, I said. . . . The Family. The Human Person. The Parish. The Diocese. The Catholic School. The Catholic Political Party. The Catholic Newspaper. Magazine. Printing-Press. Chivalric Honor. The Love Poem. Church Music. The Latin Liturgy. The Dogmatic Voice. The Dignity of Priesthood. The Inviolability of the Sex Act. The Uniqueness of Heterosexuality. . . . Need I go on listing all the names on those silent tombstones? We are surrounded by them, Eminent Brothers." He pauses.

"We all know them. Some of us still act as if they were living and breathing with us. But, in our heart of hearts, we know that we are living with ghosts, walking with memories of the dead. That whole Christian world is dead. And we had better put the memory behind us. And . . ." he catches himself as if he had forgotten elements of prime importance, "the Privilege of all-male Priesthood. The Petrine Privilege. The Privilege of Money. The Privilege of the Elite. All the Privileges, my Most Eminent Brothers, all gone."

At this stage, some of the Cardinals are murmuring. Vasari is saying something over the heads of the Cardinals near him to Borromini who is seated down from him. Thule is gesturing to Franzus. The Camerlengo is a study in languor. He cannot stand the Hispanic manner, even in the best of circumstances.

"*Vivit Christus!*" (Christ lives) Vasari exclaims suddenly from his place.

"*Vivit et vivet semper!*" (He lives and will always live) Riccioni cries out perfervidly, with a sharp glance of congratulations to Vasari.

The Cardinal President rings his bell. Lynch smiles indulgently. "Indeed Christ is alive. Christ will always live. Amen!" About forty Cardinals add their Amens to this. Lynch goes on, a shining look on his face. "But am I saying anything else but restating clearly the conclusions in the *General Framework Paper,* over which we all have pondered, asking ourselves how we have come to such straits?" At this, there are some rumbles of commentary from the ranks. Lynch takes it up immediately. "Those who would object— and I understand their objections, believe me—are merely afraid.

"Fear, my Venerable Brethren. Just plain fear. But we serve a Lord who said: 'Fear not! It is I.' So let us not fear." Lynch looks around calmly, smiling gently.

"But, Brothers, far more telling for us than craven fear or misunderstandings is the judgment we should pass on this already dead Christian world. ..." Again there is an exclamation of "*Vivit Christus! Ecclesia Christi Vivit!*" (Christ is alive! The Church of Christ is alive!) Lynch holds up his hand in a small gesture of annoyance at being stalled.

"I said 'the Christian world is dead,' not 'the Christian religion is dead' or that 'the Christian Church is dead.' Your very confusion of that Christian world with the Church of Christ may be the greatest danger the Church faces. They are not one and the same thing, you know, Venerable Lord Vasari. And I am speaking of the Christian world, the world created by Christians." There is silence now from Vasari's corner.

"And the judgment which we should not be afraid to pronounce, my Most Eminent Brothers, is that this Christian world had to die. It failed in its task. So it had to die.

"Christians set out on a temporal task: to create a socio-political framework for all men, in which the truths of the Gospel of Jesus would be realized. That was the dream of Gregory the Great, of the early Fathers who spoke of Heaven upon earth, of an earthly paradise.

"And after one thousand years of predominance, what was the world like? What sort of a paradise on earth had Christians produced?

"They produced a world in which everything—temporal politics, economics, culture, marriage, family, work, country—everything was supposed to be subject to the sacral role of clergymen, the Bishop of Rome and his clerical bureaucracy in Rome and elsewhere. Yes, it had a unity. The unity of a holy empire. It imposed an intellectual unity and a political unity, within predetermined intellectual structures and predetermined political structures.

"And most poignantly, it made everything temporal an instrument of the spiritual: the spiritual role of priest and pope, the supernatural teachings of theologians, the guided thinking of philosophers. More to the point, everything temporal, social and political was used to further the spiritual. Physical means (war, torture, punishment) and psychological means (exile, excommunication, censorship and the like).

"Everything on earth was supposed to serve for the establishment of a social and political structure dedicated to the cause of Christ.

"And what did happen? What actually did take place, my Brothers? What sort of a world did Christians spawn?

"A society in which the elite dominated and the masses were kept beneath, because that society connived at cruelty, it condoned slavery, it controlled the poverty of millions. It stifled intellectual initiative.

"It made clerical privileges a means of fomenting personal ambitions and family fortunes. It produced a humanism—at its height in the Renaissance—which was anthropocentric, and *selfishly* anthropocentric. It evolved the capitalist society, the corporation society, a society dedicated to money, to paper, to machines, to wealth, to economics, to mechanical evolution, to the meaning of the laboring masses, to a massification of finance in the manipulative hands of the privileged few. The bourgeois intellectual. The bourgeois priest. The bourgeois Pope. The bourgeois Church. The bourgeois capitalist system. A system, by the way, which cannibalized itself. It enthroned reason as the crown of faith. And then it made reason all-sufficient, and the individual the sole reason for all living and being. The bourgeois world. The Christian world.

"But there was one more and deeper mistake. It shut up divine truth in a cloaked tabernacle of privileged infallibility. It made divine worship and religious practice rubber-stamp formulas. It laid happiness away in Heaven—as the Americans say, pie-in-the-sky-when-you-die. It outlawed and exiled all other religious thinking and activity from the City of God.

"But, as many had predicted down the centuries, the City of Man revolted. And, as many never foresaw, the City of God, the *socio-political* City of God created by Christians, disintegrated. The working classes turned away from and rejected that City of God in the nineteenth and twentieth centuries. And the intellectuals broke out of their iron chains, shattering the mental hold the Christian world had upon them until then. There were giants in those days, to quote Scripture at this point. Darwin, Freud, Hegel, Comte, Marx. And they made war on the bourgeois gentleman and the bourgeois God and his bourgeois Church and the bourgeois salvation of that bourgeois Church.

"And now around us in the ruins of that Christian world, we see masses rising up in a war of desperation, intent on giving birth to a wholly new humanism, the humanism of collective man, no longer slave but master of all the machines.

"Thus the death of the Christian world, my Brothers!

"There can be only two reactions to this death. One, which doubtless My Lord Cardinal Riccioni and those of like mind will champion. It is reactionary. It says: Let us return to our pure beginnings, to primitive faith. Let us correct the deviations. Let us tighten our ranks, expel the deviants.

"But where in such a reaction, may I ask you, is the confidence in Christ's grace? Are we so dead with sin, so bound by Calvinistic pessimism, so inept, that we can only go back? Run back to the shelter of broken walls and shattered towers? Inhabit the graveyard of all our yesteryears?

"No! I trust Christ more than that. You all, Venerable Brothers, trust Christ more than that!"

There are now a few scattered *"Ita's"* flung at Lynch. Some Cardinals are impressed by the gentle force of this intense man, and by his obviously good intentions.

"And, just as importantly as all that, I trust men and women more than that. I trust they are good, that they desire the best in all things for all others, that they seek the truth, that they are willing to cooperate for the good and for truth's sake. I trust my fellow man. And, to quote Tertullian, I am human. Nothing human is alien to me." There is some hand-clapping at this.

"I ask of you, what sort of Churchmen would we be, if we were to hide the truth beneath the dead stones of our broken City of God—the City we built, the Christian world that is dead and gone? If we strike away the hands that are stretched out in willing cooperation?

"But if we do not adopt the reactions and attitudes of My Lord Riccioni we have only *one*, I repeat, *one*, alternative: progressivist. We cannot stand pat. We cannot wait and delay and procrastinate. We cannot adopt a policy of slow change, of gradual adaptation.

"It is an illusion to think we have a choice of *slow* change. With all respect for My Lords Masaccio and Ferro and their supporters, it is relatively easy— not too easy at all, really!—but relatively easier for them to counsel slow gradualness. But this in the wide world of Latin America and Africa and— yes!—in their beloved Europe and Italy and Rome itself, this is a counsel of acceptance, not of slow change at all, but of slow death by bleeding.

"And in this matter, those who call themselves radicals—My Lords Angelico, Lohngren, Wilz, Yiu and Domenico and all of them—I appeal to you: you and we are within touching distance of each other. Can we not join hands in a common effort?" He smiles at Angelico, then at Lohngren, his arms outstretched, his eyes speaking volumes of appeal and gentleness and forebearance.

Angelico looks stolidly at him in response, and blinks a wan smile. Lohngren does not look up. Domenico is seated with his arms folded against his chest as if protecting himself from any assault of the speaker's kindness.

"Today, this moment, in the sacred Assembly, there are some with us whose faces we cannot see, whose words we cannot hear, whose eyes we cannot read. These presences are nevertheless with us. They are the ones who came before us, who had offered to them a chance to correct the ancient errors, and who failed to take that opportunity.

"Not far from where I stand, Pope Leo 3 stood with Charlemagne in 800 A.D. on Christmas Day and decided that the Spirit of Christ needed the naked sword. He refused to rely on Christ alone, and chose to rely on the sword of men. And, you know, Jesus said it: 'They who live by the sword, shall perish by the sword.' And the world of Leo 3, the world he made possible by the Emperor's sword, has perished. Hasn't it?

"And not 400 yards from where we sit, in the Tower of San Angelo Pope Clement 7 had a choice: to renounce all temporal power, to return to the simplicity of the Gospel, to care for the masses. He refused.

"In the Apostolic Palace from which we have just come, in the Sistine Chapel where Conclaves were held for centuries before today, Pius 7 and Pius 9 walked and talked and planned. Either could have read the voice of history. Either could have opened up to the voices of millions. But, shame on us, on all of us, both fought to hold on to that ancient idea of the Christian world—even when it lay in ruins about them.

"Once again, my Brothers! Once again, the good Lord, the sweet Lord Jesus, offers us the same opportunity! What a patient and all-powerful Lord we serve, Eminent Brothers! Once again, we have a powerful opportunity. The voices cry to us. Humanity appeals to us. Shall we this one more time— the last time, perhaps—refuse to join all men and seek that common good which surely was the purpose of all Christ's labors and the aim of his Church as servant of mankind, and is the aim of its Pope, Christ's Vicar, Peter's successor, as the servant of the servants of God and of mankind?

"Let no one here be in any doubt. We in this Conclave are deciding on the life or the death of the institution of the Church of Jesus.

"I leave to my Brothers who will speak later the further elaboration of what the life of the Church should be, and what sort of a Church it should become, once we—as those through whom the Holy Spirit of Jesus channels his intentions and his grace for all men—once we have chosen a successor of Peter, and have afforded him the sum total of our opinions and our hopes.

"I thank you, my Eminent Brothers. May God bless us all in these vitally important days!"

As Lynch moves back to this place, there is a little buzz of conversation. But Koi-Lo-Po's voice breaks in, benign and insistently official: "My Most Reverend Lord, Cardinal Pericle Vasari!"

As Vasari speaks, his words exude appeal and faith. "My Venerable Brothers, if we act in such a way as to destroy this Rome, this ancient Papal chancellery, this grandeur, will we not be undoing God's own creation? Will we not be liquidating a manifestation of Christ's presence that all somehow or other feel, and which is one of the very signs of the Church's divinity? Think well, before you accept any opinion to the contrary." Vasari pauses and gazes with a meditative look at the Cardinals; when he speaks again, his voice trembles with feeling.

"In Rome, we have an abiding presence—not a mere memory of a past presence. We have a resident strength—not a mere hope for, or a remembered promise of strength. Outsiders sense the presence, and the strength. Beneath the hooded domes of our basilicas, flitting across the ancient ruins and weathered monuments of our Rome, high above the pillared altar roods, echoing in the triumphal trumpet notes of a High Mass in St. Peter's, brooding around the white robed figure of the Pope, there is, outsiders sense—and they are correct in their instinct—some dynamic presence, some covert strength. But there is no way for them to understand the substance of that presence—no way but by faith. It is an intra-Roman Catholic—it is our—possession. We Catholics!"

He turns and looks up to the ceiling for inspiration. His voice loses the tremulo and resounds with a strong note of confidence. "And this presence, my Brothers, this presence is Jesus—" he gestures upward as if to Heaven. "Not Jesus merely as the one who, as one modern writer put it, in his own person once afforded Western mankind the only completely convincing example it has ever had of the active love of goodness as the inspiring principle of all human actions—although that, Eminent Brothers, Jesus did certainly do for all mankind.

"But, limited to that view, Jesus and his actions are taken as irrevocably past. As just another historical model.

"The presence of Jesus with our Rome is of every today and for every tomorrow, just as it was during all Rome's yesterdays." His eyes are flowing as he lifts them to look over the Cardinals' heads. "No, Venerable Brothers! Think well before you lay a hand to dispel the sanctuary of that presence!

"And now, some among us want to dispel the house in which that presence exists! Think well!" He looks around appealingly. "Think well, my Venerable Brothers. Think well before you lay a hand to dispel the sanctuary of that presence!" He draws a hand across his eyes and is silent for a moment.

Then he brightens up. "And have you noticed? There is a growing feeling among non-Catholics that the Pope and his Vatican and all that he signifies represent something capital for Christianity in a way that no other Christian leader does. Have you noticed? When Pope Paul 6 traveled in that all-white plane to five Continents, more than one non-Catholic remarked, as he watched it winging its way through the skies, 'there goes the principal representative of Jesus on earth, even though I don't agree with his teachings and do not profess adhesion to his Church.' There is, simply, a growing affection and appreciation for what the Papacy signifies. What happens to and in Rome now matters to a majority of non-Catholics and non-Christians. Surely you are not going to lay a hand on the home of that presence!

"Of course, some of our Roman claims may leave outsiders cold,"—the tone is now matter-of-fact and with a small edge of semi-triumph—"but what they take as the very preposterousness of our claims rings a bell in their memory, the sound of some impossible dream centering around a fantastic idea: not that there is a simple chairman of the board, a viceroy of some absent ruler, or an emissary of a distant god. But that there is one whose ecclesial person ensures the presence of the great mystery of God and of Jesus—in sum, the man who is the personal representative of Jesus, of the only religious leader in human history who claimed to be God and whom his followers claim to be alive and personally represented here today in Rome.

"I can see My Lord Lynch and My Lord Buff bridling—just as I have seen many outsiders bridling." This is said humorously and with a gentle reproaching voice. No one can take offense. Buff squiggles on his seat and coughs to himself. Thule lifts his eyes to Heaven in a deprecating gesture, then gulps for air.

"But it is true. The mere proposition of such a dream arouses some primal emotion and passion that is not quite pinioned by the limits of thought or reason. Under the first impact of that passion, and before outsiders get a hold of themselves, they sense that nearby a window has been opened on to a beauty always hoped for, but never seen by mortal eyes; and that they are listening for a wisdom far beyond the brain and mind of man. The wisdom of peace and final rapture echoing softly in tones of the ineffable authority and in that irresistible lovingness that men have always dreamed belonged to God, and to God's unique triumph over time, and over death, and over pain, and over all finite things."

He turns to the Presidents: "I thank you, My Lord Cardinals, for the indulgence of your time, and I thank all of you, my Colleagues. You will forgive me if I say that it is with sorrow I acknowledge that the proposition of My Lord Lynch would eviscerate this Rome, this sacred home of Jesus' presence. And in the coming speeches I am sure you will hear a concept of Papacy which is in reality a sharp knife placed on the jugular vein of Christianity, as Peter knew it, as Pius 12 knew it, as beloved John 23 knew it.

"Let us not be failing in our charity for our Colleagues. But neither let us be deceived by the neo-intellectualism which masks all that many progressive-minded Cardinal Electors propose. For with such words and concepts, the grace of our Lord Jesus does not reside."

With this clenched-fist blow placed firmly and quietly on Lynch's jaw and Thule's jaw, Vasari bows, smiles around sunnily, and goes to his place. There are several seconds of hand-clapping and a few cries of "Bravo!"

Kai-Lo-Po waits for a while, for quiet, then clears his throat: "My Most Reverend Lord Buff!"

Buff takes his time for the customary prayer at the Altar, and when he turns to face the Cardinals, his expression is a trifle stiff perhaps, but apparently confident. Like all Anglo-Saxons speaking in public, he gives a first impression of reciting a lesson. But as he warms to his subject, he becomes more relaxed.

"There is a point in the life of an institution as in the life of an individual, when its past is so much with it—and so grievously with it—that nothing will soothe the deep ache, nothing will ease that dreadful destructive boredom of this 'being-too-much-for-oneself,' as Goethe once remarked, nothing will give relief but a total break with all that it has become." Buff pauses and looks around in order to create a special silence for what follows. Then: "For Rome that moment is now here." There is some hand-clapping. "In fact, many would say that it has been here for quite a long time."

More applause. But now some Cardinals are making remarks out loud. "We don't need to be told all this." "Solutions, please." "Solutions!" "No carping, please!" Buff remains calm, testing the atmosphere as he looks around.

"I say again, the point for total break is now! To admit this is to admit the truth. It is to face up to a brute fact. This bureaucracy which is the Vatican. This pomp that is Papal. Even this august assembly—we, all of us here—we are here, not as servants of God, not as humble imitators of Jesus washing the feet of the lowliest disciples, but as grand hierarchs, Princes if you please, Princes of a Church professedly the Church of Nazareth's Carpenter and of Calvary's bleeding victim, the most despised and condemned of men!"

Objections now are coming from all quarters, drowning the applause, the *"Ita's."* Riccioni is on his feet. "This ancient and venerable College of Cardinals has been an object of awe and genuine reverence for our direst enemies even. . . ."

"Our direst enemies, eh?" Buff cuts Riccioni off before he can finish the sentence. Riccioni is not accustomed to being interrupted. Before he can take up again, Buff goes on. "I remember reading in a life of John Milton, the

British poet, that during his stay in Rome he used to attend the theatrical productions of the Barberini Pope in the Barberini Palace—as all the Romans did and all the Cardinals did in their finery and with their retinues and servants and hangers-on. And it was the sight of all those Roman Cardinals— their glorious ermine and scarlet robes, their pride, their lordliness, their contemptuous glances, their behavior as a caste of people above all other mortals, the whole gathering of their presence, all that gave Milton the imagery for that part of his poem *Paradise Lost* in which he describes the meeting of Pandemonium—the Conclave of all the Demons and Devils and False Gods. Remember? Remember, My Lord Tobey?"

Tobey is delighted. He half rises and nods vigorously as if to reinforce everything Milton implied about the Roman Cardinals and their Conclave. Tobey is in full sympathy with everything that the Cardinal is saying—but for reasons very different from those of the Cardinal.

"How in the name of sweet Jesus"—Buff is almost pleading now—"how did we come to that point of apparent ungodliness? We have to ask how!"

"I wish, Most Eminent President, and my Reverend Colleagues," Vasari is on his feet quietly but swiftly, his face tense with what some take as anger, others as embarrassment, "I wish to protest with as firm and charitable a voice as possible the slur being cast on the venerable and sacred office of Cardinal. Not because I, unworthy one, have been chosen by God for it. But because it does in no way help our deliberations. I protest, My Lord Cardinal." He sits down, glaring at Buff.

Buff continues with barely a pause or change of tone. But Vasari is too powerful to ignore, and Buff's words show that. "Nor do I wish to cast any slur on any living person or on this sacred office. I, too, am unworthy of it." He meets Vasari's angry stare. "The point I am making, or trying to make, as clearly as I can, is simply this: The mentality of our non-Catholic brethren has been conditioned by what Cardinals have been and what Cardinals have done—not by what Cardinals thought and think about themselves and their sacred office." Applause and objections threaten to drown Buff out altogether.

"Hear me out, Reverend Colleagues! Hear me out! For we will never decide wisely how to approach our separated brethren, unless *we* remember things *they* remember. . . ."

"Don't they remember Cardinal Mindzenty, Cardinal Stephinac, Cardinal Slipyi? Why do you say they only remember the ill and not the good?" It is Vasari again, anger and annoyance undisguised now.

"Of course. But that is the way with humans. One of the best and most famous of poets, and a truly wise man, said it better than I could ever put it: 'The evil men do lives after them.' And so it is with the idea of Roman Cardinal."

Vasari, still standing, interrupts again, but Riccioni drowns out both of them as he rises in explosive impatience. "I think, My Lord Cardinal Buff, that you suffer from a strange fantasy that all non-Catholics spend all their time gloating over our past mistakes. Couldn't Your Eminence discuss what our Protestant brethren know rather than what Your Eminence knows so well?"

"Aye, Most Eminent Cardinal! Indeed I can." Buff bulldozes through the opening Riccioni has mistakenly given him. "Our separated brethren know about Cardinal Richelieu—his cruel statecraft, his indifference to human pain. They know about Cardinal Caesar Borgia—the incest, his murder of his father's favorite on his father's very lap. They know about Cardinal Robert of Geneva, a famous pikeman in his own right, massacring the whole town of Cesena—six thousand men, women, and children—at the head of his Breton pikeman brigade.

"Surely," Buff continues, "many Popes were busy about the Lord's work. But others—the ones the world remembers—led armies, commanded fleets, rode into battle, hoarded money for their families, used the power of office to arrange their nieces' marriages and their nephews' careers. They died holily. And they died unholily. In other words, my Venerable Brothers, this holy office of Vicar of Jesus, and this sacred order of Cardinal bureaucrats and clergy *has* merited *real* reproaches. Neither the occupant of Peter's chair nor my Lord Cardinals—to which group I belong and am proud to belong—can look at the world, at our separated brethren in particular, as if we had no heritage of guilt.

"We scandalized them all. We persecuted many. We plotted against their lives and their political liberties. We massacred their populations. We supervised their torturing. We pillaged their countries and cities. We punished like any devil of a dictator or any godless Roman pagan. It is this I want to bring out—not for its own sake, but as an explanation of what our non-Catholic brothers think of us, and—this is crucial—as a conditioner of our behavior in turning to them and sincerely seeking union with them in Christ Jesus."

"Your Eminence would have us apologize, I suppose!" Riccioni pursues the duel.

"Yes, I would! We owe an apology. Not an explanation, but a grieving expression of our regret. . . ."

"Churchmen," Riccioni interrupts, "have certainly been guilty. All of us are sorry for. . . ."

"Yes. Also for some of our Popes. Our separated brothers cannot really accept us unless we acknowledge how far away from the behavior of Jesus' representatives many of our Popes were. . . ."

Riccioni and Vasari and a dozen Cardinals rise, all objecting. And the words of some can be understood in the din of voices.

At this point the President intervenes. "My Lord Cardinals! There is no one of us who does not regret past mistakes. Now, if Your Eminences will allow the Most Eminent Cardinal to continue, His Eminence will move on to his next point."

"I thank you, My Lord Cardinal President. What we need to remind ourselves of is that, if we are in disrepute, if men do not accept our message, if they suspect us of double-dealing, if they consider us to be instruments of evil, if they refuse to admit our claim to be the collaborators of the Vicar of Jesus, the successor of Peter, if they deride our Conclave, and its change of Pope—whoever he be—know that they have good reason to be fearful and suspicious, and even derogatory."

"What about the Popes and Cardinals who were saints and martyrs? Why don't you mention them?" Vasari is on his feet again.

"Surely, there were saints among them. And martyrs. But there were also debauchees and cruel men and avaricious men. Some directed their actions by astrology. Some bought their way into the Papacy. Others killed for it."

Bronzino rises to a point of order. "I would remind His Eminence that the Borgias are no longer with us. What practical issue is His Eminence discussing?"

"So practical an issue, my dear Brother, that Pope Paul 6 in his new rules of 1976 had to lay down a rule that, even if someone bought his way into the Papacy, he had to be accepted as Pope—once the election was valid. Think on what would make a Pope in the late twentieth century lay down such a rule! Think! Venerable Brother!"

Cardinal Walker has caught the President's eye. He rises to speak. "Your Eminences. For fear that anyone here does not balance the picture, I wish to remind you all that those we opposed in the past were, a lot of them, disgraceful in their lives. Luther himself was a debauchee. Even in his last published work, he displayed a filthy mind."

"Oh, yes, I know. I know that Martin Luther was a debauchee," Buff breaks in, "and I have read his last pamphlet. The language is utterly disgraceful, and the mind he shows is that of a very lecherous, vulgar, anally and genitally preoccupied man, whose own bodily functions seem to dominate his fundamental ideas of God, of man, of moral behavior. I pray for Luther every day of my life because, although he did wrong, I think that from the very start he was a very sick, *very* sick individual. . . ."

"And you wish to speak of this syphilitic apostate in the same breath with Popes and Cardinals of the Holy Roman Church?" Walker is contemptuously calm in his question.

Buff looks at Walker, purses his lips, then says icily. "And about the one man in the whole history of the written word to whom a book on syphilis was dedicated by its author because, as the author wrote in the book, that man displayed in his august person the hope of cure from that awful disease. That person was a Cardinal of the Holy Roman Catholic, and Apostolic Church. Did my Eminent Brother know that?"

Now Domenico has stood up. "Will His Eminence please tell us why he has singled out us Cardinals for this abuse?" He sits down; a reproach from Domenico is a bad mark. Buff is chastened.

"My Brothers, please understand me. If I seem to reproach you—and myself. If I seem to cast ugly aspersion on our grade and on our sacred office of Cardinal. It is not from contempt. Only concern that we see ourselves as many, very many, of our adversaries and, also, very many men and women of good will who are otherwise attracted to the Church see us."

Now there is quiet attention among the Cardinals. Buff presses his point home. "How many of us see ourselves, see the entire Papacy and Vatican as those men and women see us? Think for a moment of a devout Anglican worshipper in Durham Cathedral, an enthusiastic Baptist singing in his chapel in Atlanta, Georgia, a pious Lutheran in Stuttgart, Germany. Believe me, my Venerable Brothers, believe me full of love and fidelity when I tell you that on their lips you will find the words that their first ancestors hurled at Rome. You remember Hütten's words to the army of German Lands-knechts, Imperial Spanish troops, and rebellious Italian Papal serfs, as they all surrounded the Rome of Clement 7 in 1527: 'Rise up! Reclaim the rights of the German Empire. End the temporal power of priesthood!'

"And when they sacked Rome and entered the Castle of San Angelo where Clement and his Cardinals had taken refuge, what did they find? They found the Cardinals and Clement weeping for the loss of their wealth and their power! It was Bishop Stafileo who gave the true reason for the sack and destruction of Rome and the sacrileges that the Spaniards and Germans committed there. He said at the reassembled Roman Rota on May 3, 1528 . . ." Buff is reading from his notes: " 'What destroyed Rome? It was because all flesh has become corrupt. Because we are not citizens of the Holy City of Rome, but of Babylon, the city of corruption, full of sodomy, simony, idolatry, hypocrisy, pride, fraud.' My Brothers, the present-day Cardinal Prefect of that Sacred Rota will testify to the accuracy of these statements. And the point is, my Colleagues, we have a past that should determine to some degree our judgment on our separated brothers today. Is not that just and moderate as a judgment?"

"There is no point in allowing the Church to be diminished in her strength for the sake of the individual and the mistakes of the individual. Our faith demands all sacrifices for the sake of the Church's good standing!" Vasari is angry.

"Sometimes, listening to remarks of this kind," Buff says patiently, "I am reminded of what Savanarola said about the Church of Rome in his day: 'If the Roman Church were to lose 10,000 ducats of her revenues, excommunications would be hurled, swords drawn, and all Christians called upon for aid. If 100,000 souls are brought to ruin, the Chief Shepherd merely listens to the counsels of those intent on destroying Catholicity.' But they burnt Savanarola. So I will desist from quoting the fiery monk any more." Buff smiles, and there is some scattered applause.

"Come now, Brother, your purpose is not to make us laugh at ourselves— nice and all though that may be." It is Thule now trying to help Buff get back on the rails and make his main point.

"No, my Venerable Brother! But it does enable me to reach the conclusion which is the overall attitude I think we should have in this matter of ecumenism. We must make no mistake about it: The higher echelons and inner circles of our Roman bureaucracy carry, as an unmistakable trait, a certain mystery that shrouds them in awesomeness.

"For the lay mind, as for many clerical ones, there is something frightening about a group of men like us: Celibates all; obedient as one man to invisible voices; men of inviolable dignity even when others find us ridiculous; coordinated in group reverence; accoutered as for sacrosanct worship; driven by interests as wide as our world is and as diverse as foreign exchange deals involving rubles, dollars, yen or the size of Communion wafers to be used in Ruanda, or the collateral to be raised on a Watergate apartment house; versed in cold rationality, yet undeniably exercising what others consider an irrational hold on the hearts and lives of literally millions.

"We appear occasionally in public amid the ermine and magenta and cloth-of-gold of ceremonies performed gravely according to milleniar rules and cozened in the stately and soaring folds of Gregorian Chant. Yet all the while we are guarded from the curiosity of outside prying eyes by the most rigid rule of secrecy—a rule that is bolstered within our ranks by the direst spiritual penalties, and on the outside with punitive capabilities that no man in his right mind will incur.

"Now tell me, has the simplicity of Jesus come to this? In us, his claimant representatives? No doubt about it, my Venerable Brothers. Think back— each one of you—think back to the time when we were each one, simple priests, as yet quite outside and far below this hierarchic body, this inner sanctum of Roman power. Think! And remember! For I remember clearly my first impression of the 'higher-ups,' the local hierarchy and the Roman authorities. What mystery! What fearfulness! What dire overtones even a passing contact with them produced in me—and I am sure in each one of you. Wasn't it that which attracted us—in part, anyhow?

"For their conversation always seemed to echo a background and mentality more mysterious and Macchiavellian than I had ever known or would easily probe. And, even if I discovered, or thought to discover, the diabolic smile behind the patient smile of a Cardinal, or if I sensed a confident cunning beneath the velvet smoothness of Vatican diplomatic language and relaxed address, or if I experienced a certain lack of mercy, a ruthlessness in Roman Ministries—with no human touch—even all this did not dispel my sense of their secret power.

"What was transacted within those privileged circles of Cardinals and Vatican Ministries and Papal Officials sometimes seemed to be the human reflection of the superhuman, yes, the cosmic struggle between the fallen Archangel, Lucifer, and Jesus. It almost seemed, in other words, to be the Christian verson of Semitic Job's drama, in which Jesus turns directly on the Archangel Lucifer as one he knows personally and full well, and Lucifer speaks back to God as a working part of God's own universe."

Suddenly Buff is interrupted. The Camerlengo has risen.

"What on earth is His Eminence trying to do or say or ask?" he protests, exaggerated weariness in his voice. There is a stir of surprise at this open-handed slap at Buff.

"My question, Your Eminence, is one we are *all* asking in some way: How has the Church come to this point? And we are all asking further: If it has come to this point, is it not time for that break we are thinking of but will not mention here? Isn't the dead burden of that Rome of the Caesar Popes far too much for the Popes of Jesus to bear?

"And I do not intend to answer these poignant questions, my Brothers. I do not intend to. Because everyone of us here knows the answer.

"What I do ask you is this—and it is the central question confronting us in this Conclave. Are we going willingly and deliberately to break with this load of our past? Break with it in such a way that no American Baptist can again speak of the Pope as 'that foreign Ruler,' no German Lutheran can think of Rome as 'the Red Lady of the Mediterranean,' no pious Protestant can find the mysteries of demonic power intertwined with the mysteries of Jesus in our Roman basilicas and our Vatican offices, no Marxist can conclude that in championing the Sacrifice of Jesus and the exclusive right to dispense his love, we are marketing something that will maintain the level of our portfolio returns and guarantee us the necessary collateral for new investments in real estate.

"Are we? Are we going to do that?"

Ending on the tip of that sharp question, Buff gives a look of gratitude to the President's table and goes to his place. In his own way, Buff has thrown a disturbing thought at his colleagues: Has the Papacy indeed amassed such a reputation that it is now itself a real obstacle to faith in the Church? Is Lynch correct? And is the Papacy dead with that old Christian world?

Already, as Buff reaches his place, Koi-Lo-Po is calling out—evidently with some personal pleasure, for he has a large smile as he speaks: "My Most Reverend Lord, Cardinal Henry Walker!"

Adlai Stevenson, who once had accepted a Coca Cola from Walker, told one of his aides later that "even the bottle seemed to mean something special when he gave it to you." Walker has a way of investing the littlest action with ponderous significance. So now as he ambles painfully to the Altar, some papers in his hand, and then turns around to speak, all seems fraught with meaning. Earlier in his life this man was the best educated Roman Catholic Bishop in his own country to have come on the scene in the past hundred years, and probably the finest public speaker of his generation. Fluent in three European languages, deeply read in theology and literature, a formidable antagonist in an argument, Walker was almost bound to end up in Rome. He was of the stuff whereof men of power are made. At a certain moment his reputation as a gourmet was excessively commented upon and other traits were falsely ascribed to him.

"Most Eminent President, I have been delegated to speak for a large group of most Reverend Cardinal Electors and in addition for many Cardinals who are not present here, and for many learned and pious bishops throughout the Church. And what I have to say will tell you much about those who have new things to propose to us. About the men who have stood here and offered to us their flowery plans that they compare with the thorns of our past deeds." A glaze of anger burns in Walker's eyes. "Our message to the Electors of this august Conclave is sharp and clear: The will of the majority of Bishops who participated in the Ecumenical Council during the 'sixties has been twisted. Their good faith has been betrayed." There is a general muttering among the Cardinals. Walker appears to be out for blood with guns loaded.

"The assent of the Council of Bishops has been used—I should say prostituted—for purposes that contradict their original intention. . . ."

Walker is stopped by a cry from among the Cardinals—nobody seems to know whose voice it is—"No lectures in moral behavior, please, Reverend!"

Walker returns the barb. "Oh, don't worry, my Most Eminent Fathers and friends. I know to what you refer. I know what I am guilty of. I know, better than any of you. But, I believe in the grace of our Lord Jesus. I believe that it cleanses, that it makes the soul come alive again, that it quickens the spirit.

And I believe that the Lord Jesus listens to the penitent, and that He punishes those who decry the sins already repented. . . ."

Another interruption. "Shame! Shame!"

"Imitate Your Eminence's Heavenly Father!" Walker shoots back, glaring in the general direction of the cry.

The Cardinal President intervenes, reminding the Electors of the decorum and mutual respect they must observe.

"I thank you, Most Eminent Cardinal President, I thank you." Walker then turns back to the Electors. "I would not have you in any doubt as to what has happened, my Brothers, with the will of our Ecumenical Council—especially in view of the speeches we have listened to this morning.

"I can speak firsthand because I participated in the Council. True, my own ambitions were then closely identified with the stances I took. I think, under God, that the accumulation of years and the bodily miseries the Lord has sent me since then, together with the years I have spent in this sacred City and my functions near the Holy Father—all this has sharply defined in my own memory all that happened." He glances toward the place from where those derogatory cries came a little time ago. "Anyway, Brothers, be sure of one thing. I have no personal axe to grind in this Conclave.

"It would be ridiculous and ineffectual of me to review the entire Council here and now. But let me give you one typical example, in order to substantiate my statement that there has been trickery and treachery and—worse than all that—betrayal of our duty to preserve and hand on the sacred traditions of the Church Apostolic." Walker is already breathing heavily. He wipes his face with a large white handkerchief.

"Everyone here is familiar with the document known as the CSL, the *Constitution of the Sacred Liturgy*. Let me take a few small points about that CSL." He replaces his handkerchief in his left sleeve. "Anyone who participated in the Council as I did—every session of it—as Terebelski did, as Riccioni did, as we all did, we old-timers!" Murmurs of *"Ita!"* come from about a dozen throats. "All of us knew—the 1,922 Bishops participating in the vote—that the Canon of the Mass (the central portion of the Roman Catholic Mass) was, according to the will of the vast majority of those 1,922 Bishops, *always* to be said and to remain in Latin—" He breaks off with an incredulous look, to emphasize his words. The drama of the pause brings full attention. He has chosen a point that has caused pain and strife and near schism.

His own voice breaks the silence. "Knew it? Did I say 'the Bishops knew it'? Let me be precise Brothers. The Bishops did more. They *stated* so! They *legislated* so! Let me quote to you: In Article 36 of that CSL, they said,

'A particular law remains in force: the use of the Latin language is to be preserved in the Latin Rites.'

"These were our very words," and he brandishes a paper in his hand as though offering it to all present to read it for themselves. "Note that we Bishops *commanded* it. We used the imperative form: *servetur*. We did *not* advise. We did *not* recommend. We did *not* make a bland statement. We *commanded!* This was our will. The will of the Council. The Ecumenical Council. *The Cannon of the Mass was never to be said in any language but in Latin.*

"Now, you all know that we Bishops of the Council made a distinction between the *presidential* parts of the Mass—those that concern the priest as priest, as surrogate for Jesus—and the *popular* parts—those parts of the Mass which directly involve the people, such as the Gospel, the Epistle, the prayers for public well-being, and so on. And we laid down in that same Article 36, paragraph 3 of the CSL, that the competent authorities were to decide whether—note the word 'whether'—the vernacular language was to be used even in the *popular* parts. In other words, as far as we Bishops were concerned, the vernacular *need never* be used in the popular parts and *must never* be used in the *presidential* parts.

"I repeat yet again, we were 1,922 Bishops who voted on those very words. It could not have been more clear.

"Now, what actually happened to our Mass? To our Latin Canon? And, I might add, to Mass attendance?" Walker's face reflects pure disgust. "Well, today, there are at least nine different vernacular Canons. There is *no* official Latin Canon of the Mass at all! That's what happened.

"But how? How could something so completely opposed to the will of the Council come about—and above all how could it come about in the name of the Council?

"I remember in 1965 just after the Council was finished, that monster which was created by trickery and plot—I refer to the post-Council Commission set up to implement our will, the will of the Bishops—that monster of a Commission was asked by about fifteen different national hierarchies and bishops from Europe, Asia, Africa, and America, about the Canon, the *Latin* Canon. What answer do you think the Commission gave them? Think a moment. I should leave it to your imagination, Reverend Fathers." Walker grins wryly. "But if I did, it would probably be twisted by the enemies of the Mass. The answer that the Commission consistently gave was: 'Permission for dropping Latin and translating the Canon into the various vernacular languages will never be given.' This, if you please, was what we were told. So we all went home satisfied."

Cardinal Thule is on his feet on a point of order. "Can the Eminent Cardinal substantiate these statements?" Thule's agitation is obvious.

"I have it here in a letter embossed with the Commission's coat of arms and Roman address; it is dated December 22, 1965. . . ."

"The Electors cannot see the letter, Reverend Brother...."

"I have it in my hand!" Walker booms, peevishly waving a sheet of paper, "and you and the others may have twenty copies at my expense, if you wish...."

"Yes, but who signed that letter, Eminent Brother? Perhaps it came from some lower echelon office of the Commission who...."

"It is signed," Walker rasps, "by the Archbishop then at the head of the Commission." He looks up and gazes at the Electors with an expression of disgust. The silence among the Cardinals is deathly. That Archbishop was the man whom Paul was forced to fire from the Commission on the Liturgy. The reasons were very grave. "And more about the Archbishop shortly."

Walker tackles his main subject again. "How did it happen then, my Brothers, that the express will of the majority of Bishops was directly contradicted and contravened?"

Thule is on his feet again. "I think it is quite clear that the members of the Commission consulted the Bishops after the Council was finished, and that they merely formulated a general wish of...."

"It happened, my dear and Venerable Brother," Walker's booming voice drowns out Thule's, "because it was decided *in camera* between half a dozen individual Bishops, three Cardinals—of whom my Venerable Brother was one, by the way—and a select group of theologians, the *periti*. Do you all remember the *periti* at the Council? Do you?" Walker is looking around at them all now, like an old lion, shaking his head and glaring at every pair of eyes. "Do you?"

Buff is on his feet: "I would like to remind my Colleagues that the *periti* were picked by individual Bishops for their skill in tradition and in theological knowledge. And besides...."

"We have no need for a lesson from His Eminence on the meaning of the word '*periti*.'" Walker's sarcasm is as commanding as his anger. "*Periti.*" He mouths the word as if it had a strange sound and a still stranger meaning. "Of course! One versed in something or other. In this case, in theology. We Council Bishops all had our *periti*. But the *periti* at this *in camera* meeting were more than mere advisors on theology. By the way, I should say meetings—but there was one particularly fateful meeting about which my Eminent Brother knows more than any of us." He looks again at Thule.

Thule had held a special meeting with the most progressive *periti* at the Council; and between them it was decided that they should seek to plant doctrinal "time bombs" within the text of the Council's documents which the Bishop would approve. A time bomb in this sense was a sentence susceptible of more than one interpretation. For the Bishops, such a sentence would have one meaning. But later, as happened actually, the Commission would give another and sometimes totally different meaning to the seemingly innocuous phrase.

Walker has caused consternation in the Conclave. At least four or five Cardinals, mainly from Latin America, are on their feet trying to get permission to intervene. One, Marquez, succeeds. "Our Brother, Cardinal Walker, will have to be sure to have proof of this grave accusation."

"It's all here, my Most Eminent Brother, it's all here." Walker holds up still another sheaf of papers. He is smiling, but not pleasantly. "These cost me much work. Let me see now," he flicks over a few pages. "Ah yes!" A pause as he reads the names of the most controversial and modernist of the Vatican Council *periti.*

"Is our Eminent Brother saying," Marquez insists on pushing Walker all the way, "that there was a sort of agreement between these men and others yet unnamed?"

"Yes. I am!" Even though everyone present had by now understood the meaning of what Walker was saying, his final affirmation that there had been nothing less than a plot to suborn the will of the Council is still a bombshell. The President cannot bring the Cardinals to order. Walker has nearly to shout in order to be heard. "I am saying precisely that, Reverend Brother. There was a cohesive, predetermined plan established by a small handful of Bishops and *periti*, a plan which we know now in detail, a plan which has been followed meticulously."

"We must know, Eminent Brothers," Thule is glaring defiance, "we must know, what are the details of this—plot, this plan."

"Very well! First: Place the time bombs, those ambiguous statements, in Council documents. In our official CSL, for example, a statement as in Article 21 which says: 'The Liturgy is made of unchangeable elements divinely instituted, and elements subject to change,' Or, in Article 33: 'Although the sacred Liturgy is above all else the worship of the Divine Majesty, it likewise contains abundant instruction for the faithful.' Or, in Article 38: 'The revision of liturgical books should allow for legitimate variations and adaptations to different groups, regions, and peoples, especially in mission lands.'

"Now, Fathers, all such statements were understood by us Bishops in one sense, a conservative, traditionalist sense. Step number one was to get such statements into the official documents.

"Second step: Pack the post-Council Commission, set up for the implementation of our decisions, with people who would explode the time bombs. The general secretary of the post-Council Commission was Bugnini, Hannibal Bugnini.

"Step three: In the name of the Council—now disbanded and scattered to the four winds—send out a series of decrees, ordering changes. And coordinate these new and revolutionary decrees with the unofficial and unilateral changes started by complaisant and plotting Bishops and *periti* and priests in various dioceses of the Church. . . ."

"I say again, I hope the Eminent Cardinal can substantiate all this by documents, proven and authenticated." It is Thule. And he is clearly agitated.

"Your Eminence has a copy of every document I hold in my hands, and of every letter between His Eminence and the *periti* and the Archbishop in charge of the Commission and. . . ." Cardinal Thule rises to interrupt Walker again, but this time the President intervenes: "Please allow the Cardinal to continue." Walker glares around and then goes on.

"Step Four: Translate the Canon of the Mass into the vernacular everywhere. And forbid, I repeat, forbid the Latin everywhere. And translate all liturgical books into the vernacular.

"Step Five: Adapt the Liturgy of the Mass to each and every region and locality and language, so that there is no longer any uniformity throughout the world. And adapt it so that everywhere it is not regarded as a participation in the Sacrifice of Jesus on Calvary. Instead, it is thought of as a communal meal of fellowship with emphasis on the Bible, particularly on the Old Testament, and on social problems. And let the laity, not the priest, have the principal functions. The priest should be merely a master of ceremonies."

"What on earth has all this to do with the grave decision we have in hand?" It is Thule now taking a different tack to derail Walker's argument.

"My Brothers," Walker appeals almost with a groan, "why indeed do I tell you all this? Merely and simply to tell you that the will of the Council has been prostituted—and with it the entire act of your Catholic Faith, the Sacrifice of the Holy Mass. And to tell you that we should not, at this most crucial time, put our trust in the propositions of those who were implicated in such monumental deceit and corruption."

"But how can the Cardinal neglect to mention the renewal which has followed the Council?"

Thule is not ready for the storm that breaks around his head. *"Renewal?"* Walker shouts the word. *"Renewal?"* He rounds on Thule with a thunder of words. "Let me tell you what your *renewal* has meant. Let's take a few, cold, hard facts." He looks quickly through some of the papers on his table.

"Renewal should mean, principally, a greater zeal for the Mass, eh? A greater attendance at the Mass, eh? And more interest in the Sacraments, eh? And an increasingly influential function of the priest, eh? Greater, or at least, sustained conversions to the Church, eh? After all, these are the *signs* of renewal. How else can you speak of renewal if not in such terms?

"Well, look at the facts since 1965, when this cursed renewal, this so-called liturgical reform was initiated by our friends. Mass attendance since 1965 has declined. Enormously! England and Wales by 16 percent. France by 66 percent. Italy by 50 percent. U.S.A. by 30 percent. Renewal eh?

"And priestly vocations. Again, decline. England and Wales by 25 percent, France by 47 percent, Holland by 97 percent. Holland! The showcase Church—where all seminaries have been closed since 1970! Italy by 45 percent. U.S.A. by 64 percent. Renewal!

"And Baptisms. Again decline! England and Wales by 59 percent, U.S.A. by 49 percent.

"Nuns? A decline of 24.6 percent throughout the Church. Since 1965, 35,000 nuns have left the convent. And 14,000 priests abandoned their priesthood.

"Renewal? Need I go on? And these are just random readings. Any of my Eminent Colleagues can have a copy of these documents." He throws the papers on the President's table.

Then he turns to look at Thule and Buff. "And do you know, there is a funny twist to it all. And I am not talking about pop Masses, marijuana Masses, Masses with crackers and whiskey instead of bread and wine, teenage Masses with Coca-Cola and hot-cross buns—all part of your renewal, My Eminent Brothers! Do you realize that the Latin Mass is the only version of the Mass *not* generally allowed? Only allowed with special permission? How do you figure that? You can have the Mass in any language EXCEPT!!!"—he roars the word—"in Latin! And Archbishop Lefebvre and his Traditionalists are trounced for objecting while the plotters—yes, plotters—aren't even scolded." Walker sees both Buff and Marquez ready to jump to their feet, but he holds up his hand. "I will have finished in a little while. Please let me finish, Eminent Brothers.

"As to the other changes in the Mass, all surprises! Every one!" Walker is referring to the scores of small changes in the words and ritual of Catholic worship and in the laws of the Church that have been forced on Roman Catholics for the last dozen years. "We Bishops never decreed Communion in the hand, for example. We never decreed that the priest should face the people. We never decreed that a table—again that idea of a meal and not a holy Sacrifice—should be used instead of an altar. We talked over these things at the Council, and decided against every one of them! Why were we not asked again? Who decided otherwise? I will tell you: That small group of *periti*, supported by a few Bishops and some Cardinals."

Buff does finally intervene: "Say what you will, Your Eminence, I do not believe it is prudent to insist that these changes were the results of a deliberate plan. . . ."

"Now why, Eminent Brother, do you persevere in saying things like that? Why? Are you afraid? And can any one of my Eminent Brothers still think that all this was not deliberate?"

"But to suggest that there was some sort of nefarious plan. . . ."

"I do, I do think that, Eminent Brother. Yes. I do. I do more than that. I point the finger at those Bishops and those Cardinals who have acquired memberships—profitable memberships, by the way—in anti-Catholic anti-Christian organizations, clubs, and the like."

Thule is on his feet. "I think that in such a grave case, not only is documentary proof needed, but His Eminence should have alerted the authorities long ago."

"Well as a matter of fact," Walker answers, almost smacking his lips, "as a matter of fact, I have the documentary proof here in my hands—you may have it if you want. And as a matter of fact, the Camerlengo has had that documentary proof for well over three years." Then, to the whole group, "Why didn't you know about it? Well . . ." he glances over at the Camerlango. "Reasons of State, perhaps. . . .

"My Lord Cardinal Buff asked us moments ago, how has the Church come to this point? He did not, I realize, intend the question to be answered in quite this way, but I believe I have given you *one* example of how we have come to this point. And let me answer his next question: Yes, it is time we broke with the past. Not as His Eminence meant, perhaps. But in this sense: That we all operate in complete frankness for the duration of this Conclave." He looks around, over all the faces. "For, let everyone be put on notice: We *have* a sacred duty: to elect a successor to Peter and a Vicar for the Lord Jesus. I am deliberately restraining myself from all further comment for the moment. But, I say again, let everyone be put on notice: We will fight against any attempt on anybody's part—anybody that is to say, outside the Conclave—to exercise even a minimum influence on the election of that successor and that Vicar. So help me, God!"

This last statement, its violence and the implication of collusion between some Cardinals and outside powers, brings a wave of murmurs and remarks. Someone from the back cries out: "Vetos on the election? Are you implying that someone is breaking the law of the Conclave by bringing in a veto amongst us?" In the past history of Conclaves various governments were given the right by Popes to veto an undesirable *papabile*; and Cardinals would come bearing a command from their King or Emperor to the effect that such-and-such a Cardinal could not be elected Pope.

"Vetos? Vetos? Who's speaking of vetos? And what finally is a veto? Haven't you all brought some sort of veto? The best of us!

"Do you think that my Most Eminent Brother, My Lord Cardinal Artel is going to sanction or lobby for a candidate whom he knows is unacceptable to the Carter Administration? Or that Cardinal Delacoste is going to support someone unacceptable to the people sitting in the Elysée Palace? Or

Cardinal Franzus support someone unacceptable to Moscow? Candor, Brothers! We must proceed with candor.

"Now, of course, these most Eminent and Reverend Cardinals only *know* that someone is unacceptable. They have not been *instructed* by their governments to take any kind of action. No government official has told them to veto a particular candidate. But let's not be naive!"

"I demand, Reverend Lord Cardinal President," Marquez is angry as he intervenes, "that the Eminent Cardinal clarify the situation and his words. Does he mean that the Freemasons have a finger in our Conclave, or that some of the super powers have influence behind closed doors here today?"

"No. I am not referring to the Freemasons primarily, or even secondarily, although, my Eminent Brother, which of us would deny that the Grand Orient does not pull some puppeteer strings here inside our Conclave?

"No. It is something far more sinister. There is abroad in the world of man, in the society of men and women, whether it be in the U.S.A, in Switzerland, in the U.S.S.R., among the nations of Africa and Latin America, there is abroad a more comprehensive, more subtle, more far-reaching organization of particular men who give loyalty to no particular countries but to very particular principles, according to which they have in mind a very particular destiny for, among other institutions, this Holy Roman Catholic and Apostolic Church. For them, Freemasons are puppets. And Marxists are puppets besides being temporary impediments to the working out of their will and intention." Walker stops. His lips are moving, his eyes for the moment raised to the ceiling of the Conclave Hall. As he remains silent, a silence falls, too, on the Cardinals, who are fascinated and stunned.

After a lapse of some seconds, Walker speaks very quietly. "May Christ have mercy on us all, so that we make the correct decisions in this Conclave. For on us and on no one else depends the life and the death of millions. And the peace or the agony of this Church. And the perseverance of many Christians. May God have mercy on us and give us light."

He bows to the Presidents.

One Cardinal comments to his neighbor, "To think that Hank Walker would be fighting for the old colors! Who would have thought it?" He is not the only one with the same thought. But this Conclave is surprising in many ways.

Out of the corner of his eye, as Walker returns to his place, he catches the chocolate-brown blur of Cardinal Coutinho's face. Coutinho is an old friend. On the faces of Thule, Franzus, Buff, and Marquez, one can read a mixture of anger and determination. The majority of the Electors have not absorbed all that Walker has told them. But, even so, there is a fresh sensation among them. For the first time since the Conclave began, each Cardinal has begun to feel the real tug and push of a Papal Conclave. Big issues now occupy the forefront of their minds.

When Koi-Lo-Po calls out Franzus' name in the customary official manner, there is a change of mood. Almost a curiosity shared. Very few of the Cardinals know Franzus personally. Even those who have met him on the rare occasions when he has traveled outside his own country, or when they have gone to see him, always confessed later that they had not really got to know him. There is about Franzus some inscrutable element. There can be no doubt, however, about his eloquence. Words come easily to him.

"Venerable Brothers, if anybody had told me twenty years ago that I would be standing here proposing what I propose, it would have filled me with disbelief. Nevertheless, these are the strange ways of Providence. And, today, I want to propose we all adopt a fresh look at Marxism. You see we all, individually and collectively, must do what we have to do. To my Brothers from the East, especially from the Eastern democracies, as well as to my Brothers from Africa, I have something to communicate that is difficult to put into words. Nevertheless, it is in my opinion the truth.

"Let me be simple about this, and let me use a simple image to convey my meaning.

"Last summer, I had occasion to visit some friends of mine who live near the shores of our beautiful Lake Placid at the foot of the Hollow Hills. Our destination—six of us were traveling together by car—was the hilly peninsula of Tarnton. But, as we approached the lake in a southwesterly direction from the city, we passed fields of poppies on either side of the road. So great was the glory of those flowers that we stopped the car, got out, all six of us, and walked for five or ten minutes in the fields, all the while discussing our mutual interests.

"Suddenly, in the middle of what seemed an endless plain of poppies, one of us stopped and said: 'Look! Look! Look! Look at your skin, your eyes, your hair, your teeth, even your black clothes. Look! Look at them! They are on fire. We are walking inside the sun! And we are not consumed! A miracle of God! Look, I ask you!'

"And, indeed, it was as he said. That glory and irridescence of scarlet reflected from the scores of thousands of poppies was coloring everything we were. And even the air around us seemed to have been transfused with a scarlet haze.

"Inside the sun! And not consumed! That, by way of image is what I wish to convey to you, my Colleagues, about us who live within the Marxist-Leninist regimes of our country and the democratice republics of the East.

"Yes, surely, we are within the fierce sunburst of the Red star. It colors all we can see, and all you can see of us and of our lives. Yet, as Christians, we are not consumed. We do not perish. We have done more than merely survive. We flourish. Think on it, my Brothers, we flourish! Inside the sun, we flourish!

"Oh, I know you have questions to put to me. I know that you have one question in particular to ask us—to ask me, as spokesman for those Christians I am living with. It is a question I have answered one thousand times, if once, as it came from my priests, my fellow bishops, my ordinary believers. *Can Christians accept Marxism? Is Leninist Communism compatible with the Gospels?* And I know what past Popes have written. And I say to you: None of them lived under a Marxist regime; and none of them have had a working alliance forced on them with sincere Marxists. Theoretically and in abstract dogma, any such alliance can be shown to be impossible. But, believe me, in real life it works out differently.

"Let me give you in simple terms the answer I have given to all those priests and bishops and layfolk who asked me the same question as you surely wish to.

"The answer is that, in the concrete circumstances of our day, in this year, at this time, given the unbridgeable chasm between the haves and the have-nots, between our Christian ideal and the opposing conditions that are the hard realities for the overwhelming majority of mankind—and given that failure, as My Lord Lynch pointed out, of the classical Christian world to be simply Christian—given all that, a passage through Marxism seems to be the necessary condition for ending the spiritual alienation of the overwhelming majority of mankind.

"For in truth, Brothers, Communism's value, its identity even, is not—as many Westerners think—merely as an economic solution. We know! We know how many flaws there are in Communism as an economic theory. But the real value of Communism, its very identity, lies in the fact that it is an absolute historical exigency; it is the only way. . . ."

Riccioni is on his feet signaling to the President for permission to intervene. At the President's direction Franzus sits down in a chair at the President's table, smiling quietly to himself.

"My Lord Cardinals," Riccioni begins in a distressed fashion, "if My Lord Cardinal Franzus needs any refurbishing of his grasp of Church teaching, the dogmatic statements of the Popes, and what Christian piety demands, as well as the holiness which Christ demands of his Church. . . ."

"Yes," it is Franzus, still seated, smiling still. "Of course. Of course! My Lord Cardinal Riccioni has all the time in the world to read books and attend conferences. But as Marx said, it is easy to be a saint when you have no wish to be human. Now," glancing at the First President, "if I may continue. . . ."

"Because Christ became human," Riccioni is trying to continue, "was incarnated, the Church has to sanctify all; and Marxism will not allow the Church. . . ."

"Our problem is precisely that, My Lord Cardinal," Franzus retorts. "Christ became human. This is a human Church. A human world, by the way. We will not abandon it. We want to remain part of it all. . . ."

"You were about to speak of the only way," the emotional Riccioni is practically shouting, and his voice has become hoarse, "well, my Brother, be on notice, the only way to achieve holiness, for the Church, is for the Church to remain separate from error."

The Cardinal President makes a sign to Riccioni: Franzus has precedence, and he must be allowed to finish his address. Riccioni slumps down.

Franzus stands again, ready to go much further still. "To continue, my Brothers. Not only is Communism a historical necessity; the atheism of Marxists is a necessary condition for Christians to pass through in order to achieve redemption from alienation—the alienation which that ancient Christian world imposed on them and on all men." All during Franzus' remarks and the Riccioni intervention, tempers had been heating up. Now, Franzus' words are like a fire; tempers explode. Cries of "Treachery!" "Treason!", "Evil!", "Compromise with Satan!" are met with counter-cries of "Hear him out!", "Let the Holy Spirit speak through the least of us!", "We all have something to contribute!" The silver bell of the Cardinal President tinkles impotently through it all. Franzus is no longer smiling. But Thule nods to him; and Buff joins his palms above his head and gives Franzus the sign of congratulations.

Vasari manages to obtain permission to speak. The clamor dies down except for isolated conversations and an odd cry of disgust or support. Vasari is flushed deep red in the face. His right fist is closed on the palm of his left hand.

"My Lord Cardinals, we have the right, I think—and I think that a majority of you stand with me in this—to know what in the name of true reason and true faith our Most Eminent Brother," this last said with a touch of sarcasm and suspicion, as if Vasari was naming something malodorous, "can possibly mean by 'a necessary atheism.' Let him tell us!"

Cries of "Bravo Vasari!" (Good, Vasari.) "Bene detto! Vasari!" (Well said, Vasari.) Vasari turns to Franzus and motions to him that he has the floor.

"Somebody said to me before this Session that I speak as if atheism was a mere consequence of Marxism. Atheism they said is the principle, the fount and origin of Marxism. To be sure! If by 'atheism' you mean a rejection of an intellectual system tied to a bourgeois system of government. To be sure! If by 'atheism' you mean rejection of an economic development based on elitism and monopolism and dynasticism—dynasty of corporation, of families, of class. To be sure! But again," he seeks out Vasari with his eyes, and his look is flint-hard, uncompromising, "that atheism is a necessary passage of purification! And this is the only step that will enable a total requisitioning of human energies to solve mankind's problems." Even in his intense concentration, Franzus becomes aware of the restlessness and rising tempers.

He continues with even greater insistence. "When that is done, when fundamentals are taken care of, I am convinced the realities of human existence will be laid bare; and then that initial atheism will be eliminated. By that time, new structures of human life—for the individual, for the family, for the city, for the state, for the nation, for all the nations—will have arisen. And these will properly house the spirit of religion in man. Listen to me! None of you, my Brothers, is so foolish as to imagine that all men and women have to be converted to the true faith and to the highest virtue before we transform the political and social regimes which oppress them. Or do you?"

There is an angry challenge from the back of the Conclave assembly: "What would Cardinal Stephinac or Mindzenty say to you today, Franzus? What would he say, tell us?"

Franzus looks in the direction of the voice. "Well, which of us adhered to the policy of Pope Paul 6? He received Premier Kadar in the Vatican you know! He eliminated your Mindzenty! Don't you think my attitude is like that of Paul 6?"

Vasari is on his feet thundering, "Nobody here has approved of the *Ostpolitik* of the preceding Holy Father." And Riccioni is joining Vasari by hissing between his teeth—an ancient Conclave habit for indicating disapproval.

"Be that as it may, my Brother. I assure you, I do not disparage Cardinals Mindzenty and Stephinac. Let me tell those Venerable Brothers whose voices are strident with pain, I too know all about Communist prisons, all about Communist oppression, interrogations and information-getting methods. All about it." Franzus' voice is so vibrant and so deep that there is an instant silence. They see tears on his cheeks now. The man is really weeping. "And, if any of my Venerable Brothers have the stomach for it, and the rules of modesty allow, I will show them in private some living reminders of a Communist lash and a Communist pincers. The lash, they will notice, is one-half-inch wide. The pincers open to a space of two inches." He pauses. He has everybody's attention. He looks up again with reddened eyes at the Cardinals. "As I say, we know what suffering is. We know! Your catalogue of Communism's tortures and punishments is vastly incomplete, compared to ours." In this oblique way, Franzus is trying to tell Vasari and all the others that they cannot understand Stephinac or Mindzenty, and they cannot understand his motives. "Yet, I wonder, in passing, what sort of a comparison a historian could make. Yes, surely, the Marxist states have amassed an agonizing corpus of imprisonment, assassination, massacres, calumny, isolation, torture, slavery of the mind, the penalty of living death—all of which we know to be true. I wonder if we should perhaps compare all that Gulag of agony with the earlier Gulag of agony imposed by the Church, and by Christians in the name of the Church. On Muslims. On Jews. On heretics. In the so-called witchhunts. In the religious wars. In Charlemagne's Christianizing of Europe by killing thousands of people at a time because they refused to convert. In the slavery of African blacks, of Latin American Indians—and some of this in the recent past, mind you . . ." Franzus' voice rings out, now.

"And how Christians ate *each other* in their mutual hatred! The massacres of the Thirty Years War. The cannibalism in Pomerania during the same war. The starvation of the Irish Catholic peasants. There's no need to go on. But did any official Christian theologians condemn Christianity on account of all that? Those that tried—a Savanarola, a Huss, others—you know what happened to *them!* And remember too, the gentle scholars we did away with merely because they were searching for the truth—a Giordano Bruno, for example, whom we burned alive because he said the earth was round. No, let us not compare Gulags!

"Let us rather talk of what Marxism is out to destroy. In a word, the bourgeois man—his society, his capitalism, his prostitution of religion to profit, his elitism, his neglect of his fellow men; and let us be quite clear what we mean by bourgeois man and see his innate tendency to profound blasphemy."

Uccello, red in the face, his arms waving, cannot remain quiet. "You talk about blasphemy, Eminence! You talk about blasphemy!" And over opposite him, it is Cardinal Tucci, his voice quavering: "Are we to go on like this, Eminences, hearing all that is truly lovely degraded by one of our number, about whose true intentions we—some of us—have doubts? Are we?"

"My Brothers, I told you a moment ago that behind the simple answer I have given to so many who ask if Christians can accept Marxism, behind the simple answer, there lies a frank analysis of the past, and just as frank an appraisal of the present and the future of the world, and of Jesus' Church. I ask you now: Will you let me share it with you, Brothers?" Some cries of *"Ita"* greet the question. And Franzus goes on, now; he has won the chance to make his case.

"Let's look then, at the bourgeois man that disturbed my Lord Uccello so much a moment ago. For, like it or not, the question that faces us is precisely bourgeois man, bourgeois Christian man. The essential note of that man is that everything about him is geared to exploitation of nature, the furtherance of technology, and the use of all forces in our world in order to multiply money for the bourgeois man's use and enjoyment.

"Don't tell me this is a Christian outlook! Or even a humanist, a properly humanist outlook! Yet this is precisely the type of human being and the type of civilization that Christianity produced. In the concepts of theologians and the reasoning of philosphers from Aquinas to Rousseau and down to Karl

Marx, the supernatural was used for the exploitation of nature and of our fellow man.

"And that use, that exploitation, was carried to such a point that the very institutional Church itself, and the very civilization it fostered and created and maintained, was impregnated with the idea of alienating man from his world. Of subjecting him to the cruel exigencies of material things—to the loss or lack of such things, or to the slavery to such things—for the sake of the profits of a few. And the leadership of Christ's Church was placed in the hands of, or at least at the disposal of, those bourgeois few—the kings, the princes, the *noblesse,* and *ancien régime,* the dictators, the Bourbons, the Hohenzollerns, and all the rest. And, today, it is at the disposal of dictators and international corporations and financial monopolies.

"Make no mistake about it. That old Christian world, the *ancien régime* with its triple-tiered society—clergy, nobility and working classes—served a purpose. It was, once upon a time, organically suitable for all the world. For all were bound together by bonds of loyalty, fealty, service, faith, authenticity. All old, beautiful values. And highly personalized.

"But, as Marx saw, naked historical forces disrupted it. Notably, one: The rise of the mercantile and industrial class of the 1800s and the 1900s. And then that huge mass of workers produced for the few. And the clergy, the Church, was aligned with the few. And between those few and the working class there was now no loyalty or fealty, nothing personal—but only the wage contract. In place of the Medieval economy, there now was the capitalist regime: interest, lending, capital investment, profit-margins, exploitation of natural resources, and the slavery of the factory and the production-line system. We went along with all that, you know, Brothers! Nothing personalistic. And Christianity accepted this situation!

"And, finally, the masses—those inert, obedient, suffering masses—began to move. By an irresistible, historical necessity, they began to move. So, the imminent dynamism of Communism started. It was given voice by a Marx, by an Engels, by a Lenin. And note well—for this is brute historical fact, whether we like it or not: Whatever leadership of the Spirit of Christ once lay between the jeweled hands and upon the crowned heads of Princes, that leadership has passed to the proletariat. Whatever Messianic character the ruling classes have borne for so long, that Messianic character has ceased to be theirs. It has passed, if anywhere, to the proletariat.

"Of course, it is frightening. For us. Myopic as we are! For we can see no transcendent, nothing of what we call Spirit. We only see historical reality, separate from any transcendent. But that is because we never incarnated the Spirit of Jesus in all of life.

"And now there has been and is this frightening descent back into the primordial and concrete substrata of human life, into the materialism of policy, the materialism of values, the materialism of politics, of sociology, of art, of music. Why? *Because, there is no other way of liberation!"*

While Franzus is plunging on, a little drama is being played out among his listeners. Each sentence of Franzus' has seemed to provoke more and more irritation among some Cardinals. Now some are whispering, passing notes, gesturing to each other. Domenico, who had sat impassively from the beginning, becomes aware of the increasing activity. Partly with calming gestures, partly by word of mouth, now and again by writing short notes, he succeeds in preventing any interruption. For Domenico wants Franzus to have his full say. Once and for all, the Electors as a body must hear with their own ears as full an expression as is possible of an opinion and a policy that has already gained great vogue among Roman Catholics, lay and clerical.

Franzus appears unaware of any disruption and, completely caught up with the drama of his vision, proceeds without interruption. "And now the proletariat is the bearer of the new mission, the mother of a new liberation, the Messianic victim and newsbearer. As the majority occupying the lowest rung in the ladder, the proletariat everywhere is on the move. And Marxism has become the necessary spark to fire its activity. This is the historical reality of our day.

"No doubt about it, Venerable Brothers—that proletariat will in its movement lead to a resurrection from our dead past and from our materialism. Through it we will see a total deliverance from our bourgeois Gulag. We will see human time cut in two, and the Calvary of Jesus ending in a genuine resurrection for all men and women. And Marx shall meet with Jesus at the final Omega point when the human spirit rises out of the primordial mud and slime of our materialism.

"Do not, my Brothers, do not lightly—or through fear—throw away the movement of two-thirds of humanity. That would be a new Manicheanism on your part. For then, with our Christian bourgeois God we would confront another irreconcilable and opposing deity, the masses.

"What good is there in Marxism, you ask? I answer: What good is there in your Christianity. For Marxism shares much with true Christianity. And if one be good, the other must be good.

"Communism seeks the integration of individuals with the group, with humanity. So do genuine Christians.

"Communism holds that the economic system of production and distribution of goods and services has an essential importance for the life of the group, its culture, its humanism, its beliefs. So do genuine Christians.

"Communism says that it was bourgeois capitalism, blessed and fomented by the Church, which developed the usurious character of capitalism from which all the ills of our world have flowed—poverty, malnutrition, wars, colonialism, slaveries, drug traffic, fascism, dictatorial regimes. So do genuine Christians.

"Communism says that Christian capitalism, and only this system in the 12,000 years of recorded culture, has given rise to class warfare—all sanctioned by the Church in the recent past. So do genuine Christians.

"Communism says that in the transformation of the family, man and woman will be economically equal. The Communist hope of a paradise of joy and freedom is based on that equality. The genuine Christian wants the same thing. The genuine Christian rejects the chauvinism, the hypocrisy and the cruelty of the bourgeois marriage.

"Bourgeois man with his oppression, his godliness, his anarchy, is hateful to Communists. He is also hateful to genuine Christians."

Ignoring Domenico's gestures to stay calm, Riccioni has gone over for a whispered consultation with Domenico. Riccioni's face is a picture of indignation. After a few minutes he returns to his place, folds his arms on his chest, closes his eyes, and waits. But then there is a shout from Franzus' left. "What was that? What did my Reverend Brother say?"

Tucci is standing. "What will be the end of all this movement through materialism and atheism that you are endeavoring to sanctify?"

"The ultimate object, the ultimate end of it all? In a word, my Eminent Brother and Cardinal, it is this: transfigurations. Men and women, knowing that the grace of Jesus has changed them, will work together to realize and effect universal change. . . ."

"An example, Your Eminence," Tucci interrupts testily, ill concealing his anger, "a concrete example, please, of this strange atheist miracle!"

"You want an example? For well over 500 years, the Church has been teaching us about the dignity of man and his divine vocation to a noble destiny. Well, suppose we stop talking about it. Suppose instead we insist that all men and women *have* dignity, and *can* follow such a high vocation? How to do this? We must be sure every person has food and drink, clothes, a place to live, work to do, medical care, and so on. That is a concrete example for Your Eminence!"

"The Church has been insisting on this and telling . . ." it is the Camerlengo who rises, interrupting without warning, obviously intending to lacerate Franzus. But Franzus interrupts him in turn.

"Nobody in the barrios of Brazil, the shanty towns around Lima, Caracas, Algiers, nobody in Harlem, New York, in the slums of Barcelona, in the Sahel, in Calcutta, in Bombay, believes what you say, Eminence. Oh, not that you are not sincere. In word, that is. But the actions you sanction belie your words! And, as I say, they don't believe you out there among the suffering masses of people. They simply don't believe you at all. They know otherwise.

You can believe all you say, if that makes you happy, Eminence. But that is all it is—*you* making *yourself* happy."

Nobody had ever addressed the Camerlengo in this fashion and with such brutal personal reference. He sits down. Franzus now faces Antonello who has permission to speak.

"We have all seen again and again the first thing the Communists do is tear the Cross down, Reverend Brother!"

Franzus says nothing for a moment. Then he speaks mildly to Antonello. "Reverend Cardinal, if they don't tear it down, we should. We! We should! How dare we, professedly servants of the Poor Carpenter, how dare we wear one jewel in our pectoral crosses, or in our rings! How dare we use gold or silver for our chalices and crosses and mitres and croziers, when one baby— one, I say—" his voice rises to a bellow of protest, "one baby is dying with a swollen belly and skeletal limbs on a garbage dump in Karachi! How dare we!" Antonello sits down, his head bowed. He cannot cope with this type of discussion.

"To return to my main theme, and to end. I realize, Eminent Brothers, I realize all your fears. Believe me. But we need to walk with this movement of the masses, and to walk without fear. Compromise is no longer possible for the Church of Christ. We must have no more to do with capitalist idolatry of wealth. Our first Christian ancestors could not compromise with Roman idolatry. Nor can we, their Roman descendants, compromise with this idolatry. We have to abandon the whole élan of appetites which drives us to hoard, to appropriate, to accumulate. We have to leave behind the entire framework of values about the primacy of money and the necessity of gain which has been bequeathed to us by our late Christian world and its dead creators.

"No man sews a patch of new cloth on an old garment, Jesus said. And no one pours new wine into old wineskins. Our civilization and all our structures of state and city are nothing more than an old, worn garment. Our structures of Church and family are old wineskins. That old garment only shows our shame. The wineskins can turn the wine; and the wine of fine and human feeling has drained out of them. We need to seek new wineskins for our new wine, a wholly new garment to clothe the nakedness and misery of humanity. For surely this is the primary meaning of the salvation of Jesus."

Franzus' closing works, the generally deft way in which he handled any heckling, and the tone of pleading interlaced with what nobody doubts is his piety—all this has apparently produced a profound effect amongst the Electors. There is no outcry. But every Cardinal seems to be talking to his neighbor. On Franzus' closing words even Koi-Lo-Po starts a small conversation of his own with his two co-Presidents.

Suddenly there is silence, and Koi-Lo-Po realizes that the Electors are waiting for him to announce the next speaker. In an extra loud voice, as if to compensate for his mistake, he announces: "My Most Reverend Lord Cardinal Thule!"

Thule has waited quietly for the announcement, not budging from his place until it is fully made and a little applause has greeted the announcement of his name. After a deliberate walk and a slow prayer at the Altar, he faces the Electors, open-faced, grave-eyed, solemn-toned. There is a certain majesty in Thule's whole performance. It impresses everybody. The majesty of it. And the sincerity.

"It falls to me, Venerable Brothers, to explain to you as briefly and as clearly as I can, the essential lines, the dominant features, as it were, of the Church and of the Papacy, as we see them. By 'we' I mean those of us who feel it necessary to oppose the *General Policy* candidates list—and who feel above all that we must oppose the grounds and presumptions stated in the *General Policy* as the basis upon which any valid *General Policy* candidate would be obliged, *ex officio,* to work and to govern the Church of Jesus.

"I think the frank if disturbing words of my Most Eminent Cardinals Lynch and Franzus have made it abundantly clear that we, as heirs of the Church of the Middle Ages, of the Renaissance, and of the Enlightenment, have a debt to all Christians. We owe them an act of apology. We owe them a frank recognition of our past failures. And we owe them a faithful service in the future. We owe this to humanity in the name of Christ!"

Thule pauses. Some of the Cardinals seem to see tears brimming in his eyes. Certainly, when he takes up again his voice has a deep quaver to it, as if while speaking he is barely holding the lid on some powerful feeling. "My Brothers, you will forgive me, if I ill control the passion and the certainty that has been gnawing at me all these years."

There is now that sort of silence among the Electors that falls on people who expect something embarrassing to happen in their midst. But Thule goes on evenly enough, though still with that throb of inner emotion.

"When I think of the concepts of the holy, of the sacred, of the profane, of the secular, of God, of man that have been current coin in the Christian world, and when I think of the evils perpetrated on humanity, on men, on women, on children—in the name of those concepts—Yes! I weep for that. But my tears and emotion are also the beginning of a deep joy." He looks around at the faces, studying the expressions on each one. "For among us, in our hands, through our minds and our voices there is a gentle light breaking, a hope of salvation."

"The world will always be evil and profane. We are the keepers of the sacred and of the holy, in the middle of this evil." Tucci is very angry at Thule.

"But that is not Christian," Thule answers. He forms each syllable clearly and cuttingly now, like the strokes of an axe. "The holy is not pure, and the profane just impure. That is not true Christian teaching or theology. That is Judaism. That is paganism. Whatever you like. But not Christianity! That is a denial of the Incarnation. For Jesus became a man, became part of this universe; and all of it is holy, all of it is sacred. He interiorized every-thing. . . ."

"To judge from your remarks," Tucci is speaking again, "you would reduce Jesus to the status of proto-man! The spirit is never confused with matter. The two are completely separate. The All-Holy lives in this evil world."

"And you, my Brother, would reduce Christianity to a Judaic formalism of clean and unclean. You would make piety a physical thing, and worship a social thing, like the Greek and Roman pagans." Thule remains firm.

"We, like Jesus and Paul, cannot be of this world ever. We are on a pilgrimage in this world!" Tucci is angry.

"*Christians!* We are *Christians!* And we believe that Christ has renovated all things; we believe that God's goodness is *here* with the sons of men. . . ."

"And My Lord Cardinal makes no distinction between the temporal and the spiritual therefore?" now it is Bronzino, not famous either for interven-tions or verbal fights. Thule turns and stares at Bronzino.

"If anybody can tell us the distinction between the temporal and the spiritual, between the physical and the metaphysical," Thule says softly, "it is My Lord Sergio Bronzino. After all, he has had that experience in Washington, he and his family." A dull silence. The reference was lost on no one. Bronzino's face is flushed in anger. He appeals to Koi-Lo-Po.

"The Eminent Cardinal Thule will please avoid remarks that injure charity and fraternal union," the President chides Thule.

"An admonition that applies to all of us, all of us," Thule grates the words out. "Now, of course, I agree there is a distinction between the temporal and the spiritual. Each is a different activity. Both are tending to the Kingdom of God. . . ."

"And the Prince of this World!" Riccioni stands, speaking calmly with the air of a master swordsman presenting the tip of his blade to an adversary's throat. "Has he been converted, this Prince of the World whom Jesus condemned so violently? Or has he too been divinized, Eminence?" It has been a contention of Riccioni and the Traditionalists that Thule and the "new theologians" act as if the Devil, the "Prince of this World," had become good and no longer tempts human beings.

Thule crosses himself, with a chastened look, but goes on courageously. "Venerable Brothers, I would not have you mistake my meaning or hear me in fear. The Church is holy. The world is not. Granted. The world is holy insofar as it is more than the world, in other words insofar as it is assumed into the incarnation of Christ. And what Christ began we must achieve. It would be a gross treachery to our race and to our world if we were not to see that the values of the Gospel penetrate all of human existence, that those values are reproduced in the socio-political and cultural and personal orders of human society."

Now there is another interruption. Coutinho of Asia, known ally of Ferro, one of the Conservative *papabili*, has secured permission to speak. "What then is our Eminent Brother proposing that is new or different or enlightening? Would his Eminence please tell us what is the Kingdom of God according to his mind? And what is the framework of thought about that Kingdom with which we should elect the 264th successor to Peter the Apostle?"

Thule answers unhesitatingly. "I will tell My Lord Cardinal Coutinho and all of you, Brothers. The Kingdom of God is the kingdom to come. It is not to be confused with this world, this material universe with its human society and its Prince. The Kingdom of God is to come. And we, here on this earth, are to build toward it. But we are not to—we cannot, it would be blasphemous to say that we must—we are not to strive to make this world itself the Kingdom of God.

"What we must do, we can do: work at transforming the social regime of the world, the political regime of the world, thus making the world a place of a truly and fully human life."

"I think," Riccioni breaks in, "if His Eminence will allow me a word. We should remind ourselves that the Church's task is to save souls. We have over and over again learned from our own history that socio-political activity corrupts the spiritual aims of the Church. Why, if My Lord Franzus' painful rehearsal of some of the dark times of our history means *anything*, it means that!"

"No, Eminent Brother! No!" Thule is sure in his emphatic refusal of what the Cardinal is saying. "That entire Medieval world, that old Christianity, that Christian world, as my Eminent Colleagues pointed out, is at an end. The aim *then* was to create a sacred empire of God and of Christ over all things—men, women, families, money, nations, politics, social structures, art—everything. And, for over 1600 years, the Church was bent on bringing the supernatural down and making it part and parcel of this world and making every temporal thing—water and wine, the sword and the cross, politics and rule of government—making all these things minister to a sacred empire, making them instruments of that holy empire.

"You know the result as well as I do, my Eminent Brother. You know that thus we Christians tied up the office of Peter with that of dictator, the office of shepherd with that of soldier, the office of priest with that of executioner, the office of dispenser of grace with that of financier and broker. . . ."

"That is exactly what I am saying, Eminence," Riccioni breaks in glacially. "We thus corrupted our philosophy. All you are proposing is a change of cast. . . ."

"We did worse. We spawned a rationalism that scorned man so much that it removed God from man. And we gave birth to a revolution that so divinized man that it removed God from all creation. We are the true father of Descartes and his agnosticism! Of Marx and his atheism! Of all the rationalists! Saint Bonaventure said it well when he told your Aquinas that he was father to all the heretics!"

"It would be well," objects Vasari heavily, "if our Eminent Brethren did not confuse our Aquinas with the rationalists and heretics."

The President coughs discreetly. "Let us all leave the name of Saint Thomas in blessing."

"I thank My Most Eminent Lord President." Thule bows graciously to the long table. "What we now must see coming and work mightily for is a new Christendom. In it, the temporal is not subordinated to the spiritual. The Church remains detached from all responsibility of administering and dealing on temporal terms with that world. But each Christian is in conscience bound to work for a new temporal order."

"What new order, Eminence?" Uccello chimes in.

"It is here already. Inchoate, but here."

"If so," Nobili objects, "is it one and the same as the Church?"

"Christians will no longer seek to establish a unity of belief and thought, a unity of intellectual and political structures. Nor will they use any temporal means to coerce men into a unity of Spirit. Nor will they strive to establish social and juridical structures devoted to spreading the redemption of Christ."

Tucci is again on his feet; Thule yields the floor. "Your Eminences may be as confused as I am at this point. We know the Christian world which the Church created over a period of a thousand years. Must we decry that world now? Must we condemn it?"

"Yes!" Now Uccello is standing. "And must we then yield to a world where, we are told, the welfare of everyone will be somehow taken care of, even though apparently there will be no moral guidance for everyday life, if I understand our Venerable Brother Cardinal correctly."

"In that world you love so much, in that Kingdom of Christ, the Kingdom you long so much after," Thule is in complete control of his thought, "in that world in order to evaluate anything—person, thing, place, action—everything was, as I said a moment ago, referred to some measure outside of men and women, exterior to the human beings. In that world, we were good at figuring out laws of material production, rates and methods of technological progress, norms for utilizing the raw materials of nature in order to create wealth, to increase wealth. And so there was and is wealth for some and merely suffering and penury for the majority. And over this world, the Pope and his Curia presided. And if you call *that* Christian, if *that* is your Kingdom of Christ, then your Kingdom is not of Heaven, and your concept of Christian life has nothing to do with the Gospel of Christ! Once upon a time, in the Christian world, all authority in that Kingdom on earth was centered in the Papacy."

"I do not see," Bronzino takes up the argument from his place, "how Christendom can change its age-old belief of submission to the *central* authority of the Pope." He sits down.

"Then try to see, Brother! In the new Christendom, in the world toward which we and the future Pontiff with his whole Church must labor, we Christians will no longer seek to develop, much less impose, a common doctrine and unity of belief. We will not even insist on a theoretical doctrinal minimum. For what we will share with this world is a work of transforming the socio-political regime. So that you can say we have in common with all men a hard-headed problem, not a Christian problem, but a socio-political problem to be solved by Christians in conjunction with all other men of good will—and the vast majority of men are of good will!"

"Are we then to become just social workers and political scientists?" Riccioni's blood is rising again. "Hasn't the Church got the answer already in its Papal teaching, in its principles? If we renounce that, are we not a nation-state without a nation? Are we not merely a social agency?"

"No, Eminent Brother, I am not saying that. That would be naive. We would be naive to accept that today. Naive with the dogmatism of Medieval times. We must be realists. We must see the human work to be accomplished. True, divine grace and divine love *will* pass through us, and through the mortal fabric of our world. Divine grace will transpenetrate our instincts, our work, our days, our lives, our whole universe."

"A Christian's task is to cultivate holiness!" Tucci objection.

"But that is because you make a false separation. You would satisfy yourselves that you are being good Christians if you practice the works of piety, celebrate the feast days of Christ, the Virgin, the Saints, the Martyrs, defend the material possessions of the Church. You then think that you have acquitted yourselves of all duties to the City of Man and to the temporal order of things in this world of ours.

"But you haven't! You have merely packaged the Church neatly and laid it in one corner, and left the world in another corner. And thus, you leave the world go to the Prince of this world and to his Hell. And you have sinned. Surely against God. But primarily against your brothers and your sisters, men and women who are good, who deserve what is good, who need liberty and blessings of material welfare in order to seek the Kingdom of which you speak so much and so glowingly!

⤙ "To separate the City of God and the City of Man is moral Pharisaism. You sacrifice the human to the divine. No wonder we gave birth to the cynical Machiavelli, who sacrified all morality; and to warrior Popes and papal warriors who sacrified the human for the divine in us—if even they had *that* good a motive! And no wonder we gave birth to so many heretics."

"Then tell us, Eminence," Domenico is asking in his usual mild way, "what socio-political order you have in mind?"

"What socio-political order? One in which there is no disparity of social classes, for one thing. One which is to be made up of totally new social structures that will permit a massive diversity. One that encourages and works for the administrative and political autonomy of regional units. And this in such a way that politics, the sociology of family and of city and of state, would foment a thoroughly personalist conception of life. . . ."

"A race of egotists? Is that it? Or a race of human ants? Is that it?" Tucci is contemptuous.

"No! But certainly a personalist socialism that will be democratic!"

"Will it also be sanctified by religion?" Tucci is obviously baiting Thule. "And what do you mean by that almost vulgar term 'personalist' which doesn't mean personal—or does it?"

"We believe that any creature of God is holy—precisely because Christ did die for all. Now as regards the terms 'personalist' and 'personalistic.' I learned them from the writings of Pope Pius 12. And for your information, the Pope used these terms to mean everything that safeguarded the dignity of the human person."

"But," interjects Riccioni, "as you know, the Communists used this term with their own meaning. All that nonsense again!"

Domenico comes in now with a mild but dangerous question: "And what economic base do you envisage for your new socialism?"

"The economic basis? An economic system founded on a few simple but far-reaching principles:

"One: that we make a complete break, a violent rupture with the bourgeois capitalist system of Western democracy. That worn system is founded on the elitist and on the monopolistic policies of the Industrial Revolution. It is a residue of the past. And it stands or falls by its exploitative economy, where money, and profit-making are primary—are everything.

"The proletarian hitherto has had to consent to hand over his labor for a wage—thus depriving him of a value-basis for his dignity. As we see the future, he will no longer be saddled with this condition which diminishes the accumulation of his value and the building of his dignity. Without the fertility of money at the expense of the proletarian's labor, capitalism will wither away.

"Two: The new socio-political regime will overturn the basic dictum of capitalism that says: You will get nothing for nothing. And which says: To get something, you must have something. To overturn this, I say we should make it astoundingly true that all men and women *have* something for nothing! Have as many things as *possible* for nothing! Have, at *least*, a sufficiency of good things, of necessary things!"

"And where then is the Biblical command to work, to gain our livelihood by the sweat of our brows?" Domenico is still in pursuit.

"Such social morality seems to be just a grab bag of useful things, suitable things, advantageous things, prosperous things, all tied together with the string of practical motives. But we advocate a spiritual realism based on a regime of spiritual unity."

"And what sort of a Church are you going to allow us?" Nobili asks. "The Church: What's to become of it?"

"The Church? What sort of Church? In what relationship with non-Catholics, with non-Christians? Here is the nub of it all my Eminent Brothers: The very core of it all! We must work and strive so that all, believers and unbelievers, non-Catholics, non-Christians, atheists, all inhabit—I should say cohabit—the City of Man with us. Nay, we must go further, and be the first to defend their right to so live, and to be left at peace and alone in their liberty, without being harassed by 'evangelists' or bothered by 'missionaries. . . .' "

"Christ said: 'Go forth, teach all nations.' Are we to stop all our vast missionary effort?" Domenico takes up again, still boring away quietly at Thule.

"The Reverend Cardinal knows as well as I do that the missionary effort is largely token today, and that it succeeded insofar as the missionaires traveled beneath a colonialist or imperialist flag. Those days are over now. Over forever! We are no longer a little fire of light and warmth, the beleaguered empire of the sacred, surrounded by the darkness of unbelief. We live in a world of the creature who is endowed with a holy freedom and who will rise in expectation of the Kingdom of God, if freedom but be allowed to that creature—man, woman, nations, all!"

"If we are to have no more missionaries, no more evangelists, as you say, how then does any movement start that will convert the world?" Domenico is reasoning calmly with Thule. "How, Eminence, are we to start?"

"How do we begin to realize all this in concrete fact? Really only one starting point: As many Christians as possible must be aware, and must truly understand, that a new Christianity must be inaugurated—and that they must take whatever means necessary in order to bring about the necessary changes. And we say that there is no more palpable, more public, more electrifying way of putting the maximum number of Christians on notice than by the election of a Pope and a Papal policy that correspond to the exigencies of this new Christendom!"

Domenico continues to draw out Thule's line of reasoning. "I take it you are therefore not against violence—say, the violence of the poor rising in Latin America?"

"I think that it was our Lord Jesus who said that the Kingdom of Heaven is taken by violence, and that the violent bear it away as their prize. If violence erupts, if violence is imposed, if violence is the only alternative to a continuation of the present bourgeois capitalist regime in international finance and commerce and industry, if only violence will feed the two-thirds of humanity who go to bed hungry every night of every year of their short and miserable lives, then I say, *yes!* All of our theologians have said *yes!* Conscience itself says *yes!* Yes! Yes! Yes! Violence as counter-violence. Yes! Violence. And I see Christ with a homemade whip in his hands overturning the money-changers in the Temple, destroying their tables, scattering their money. Violence? Yes! Counter-violence? Yes!"

"But," Domenico puts in quietly, "doesn't love perish in violence? And isn't truth lost when blood is shed, when anger reigns?"

"I think that my Eminent Brother forgets the nature of love, and love of truth, as well as of truth itself. Whatever happens, we must be living witnesses to the basic truth of our Christian belief, namely: All that is not love, that does not spring from love, that does not end in love, all that will perish. And this too we must remember—and the Eminent Cardinal should know it better than most of us—namely, that love is tender, but it can also be a brute force—as brutal and as cutting as truth. If, on its path, love discovers locked doors—especially in the person or persons it loves—then love can give birth to murderous horror, even to hatred. Remember, the Great God himself hates sin and all irrevocably identified with sin. What do you think Hell is, Eminent Brothers?"

"Do we then stop spreading the Gospel, Eminent Brother?" Domenico's quiet questioning again, drawing Thule out more and more explicitly.

"No. I do not advocate that we cease preaching the Gospel. But I think my Eminent Colleagues should stop deceiving themselves. We must conform to reality—the historical reality today, a reality that apparently is feared by such men as My Lord Cardinal Walker in his love of uniformity and conformity above all else." Thule's blow at Walker is a calculated risk. Walker remains impassive.

"The reality to be faced today is that, because of our own Church's sins, we are condemned to a new Christianity. It will not be a homogeneous Christianity, united and concentrated around an acknowledged head and coagulated by unity in doctrine and practice. That is the old idea, the old Christianity that did not work; and it is dead.

"Rather, Christianity will be a leaven spread over a network of like-minded communities all over our beloved earth. And the successor to Peter will become once more the pilgrim he is supposed to be, as Christ was, as Peter the Apostle was.

"The new Christianity will—as it does already, to a large degree—consist of a series of small centers differing one from the other in practice, in language, in understanding of beliefs, and sometimes in doctrine. But it will be united in one practical task: the overall organization of a new socio-political regime."

The President is signaling Thule to pause. He has granted Riccioni permission to speak. "Eminences, I think we all realize that what our Colleague is proposing would turn our minds and energies into sociology and politics and economics." Riccioni pauses, then raises his voice passionately. "With all our faults, let us never forsake our quest for holiness. Holiness! My Brethren!"

"Holiness?" Thule intervenes. "Oh yes, the Church will still pursue holiness and urge its children to do so also. But a new category of holiness. For instance, we should cease talking of religious monks and nuns as being in a state of perfection, and all layfolk as being in an imperfect state. What hypocrisy! Again, that widespread doctrine is based on the old idea of the separation of the Church and the world, of Christian and non-Christian and of Catholic and non-Catholic, of the pure and the impure, of the elect and the rejected."

"What on earth then, are we supposed to become?" Riccioni is on the attack. "Are we to marry all non-Catholic religions and cohabit with all the erroneous sects the Church has already condemned! Are we to care nothing for the pursuit of Christian holiness and perfection, whether by monks or nuns or blue-collar workers or anybody?"

"Of course, not! Of course not, my dearest Brother. I am not advocating we cohabit with Protestantism, with Marxism, with atheism, with any 'ism' at all whatever!" Thule looks around with a denunciatory look in his eyes, as if he were dealing with the childishness of men. "Anybody who speaks like that is caught up in a despicable Platonist system of thought that sees ideas as large as hippoptami and collective nouns as giant clouds." Planting his feet apart and folding his arms over his chest, he adopts a dogmatic and declaratory tone.

"There is no such thing as Protestantism, or Marxism. Or Judaism. Or atheism. True, there are Protestants in the United States and elsewhere, Marxists in the U.S.S.R. and elsewhere, and atheists in France and elsewhere, and Catholics all over the place. And if we turn around and consort with, say Marxists or Protestants, and with non-Christians, or with atheists, we are consorting with human beings. And, over and above the Marxism or the atheism or the Protestantism or whatever they profess, these groups of people are loaded with a long-lived heritage, and full of contingencies, of fatalities, of destinies, all of which go beyond their professions of Marxism, of Protestantism, of atheism. And that load of history and of dynamisms urges them willy-nilly on the road to one great event—the liberation of all flesh, of all men and women, from any form of slavery. We wish to be involved with them and all humanity. But we do this, not as Christians—if you simply put it like that—but as Christian members of our temporal world. It is a grave distinction."

"But," Domenico insists, "aren't there countries—the U.S.S.R., Cambodia, Czechoslovakia—where we know there is no present hope for us?"

"I don't think it is part of genuine Christianity to look at individual countries like that. It is the same as taking airy-fairy ideas and Platonic concepts as though they were real flesh. The U.S.S.R. is not Marxism. The U.S.A. is not Protestantism or capitalism. Neither France nor Sweden are atheism. And no country on earth is Catholicism. Marxism, Protestantism, atheism, these are all abstracts. . . ."

"The doctrine of Saint Thomas is quite firm and clear on this point," Nobili says, trying to break in.

"You, Reverend Brother, can live with your abstract essences, if you will. But Thomas Aquinas, whom you claim, would deride your notion of reality."

"And you, Eminence, the terms you use for reality sound awfully nebulous," Domenico again with a brief comment.

"I said 'fatalities and contingencies of destiny' and. . . ."

"Too vague! Too vague!" The cries come from all sides at Thule. Riccioni shouts out over the cries: "You would have us trust a nebulous hope! Give us an example of your contingencies and fatalities! Give us one!" And he looks at his sympathisers as if to say: 'Let's see how he fields *that one!*'

Thule, however, is imperturbable. He has thought it all out. His answer comes easily. Yet all that Thule is saying today has a very confusing effect on his hearers. They sense that he is near the truth, but they fear he is sufficiently short of the truth to make all he proposes dangerous and seductive. At the same time, over and above the appearance of truth, there is Thule's obvious sincerity. Nobody doubts that he believes in what he says.

"Well, take the Soviet Union, for example." Thule rounds on Riccioni. "For you, for most people in the West, the U.S.S.R. is a static monolith. They —and you—are not permitted the information you need to understand that a demographic time bomb is ticking away in the U.S.S.R.

"Now, many of you may not know that the Soviet Union includes fifteen nationalities, each with its own homeland, customs, language, dress, folk customs and so on. Russia, actual Russia, is in the middle of those homelands. Six of them are European and lie to the west of 'Russia'—the Ukrainian homeland, the Byelorussian, the Moldavian, the Lithuanian, the Latvian, the Estonian. That is 65 million people! Then there are eight Asiatic homelands to the east of 'Russia,' in Central Asia and the Caucasus—the Kirghize, Turkmen, Uzbek, Tadzhik, Azerbaijani, Kazakj, and so on. About another 65 million people.

"By the year 2000, these Eastern nationalities will be in a majority. Do you think they are going to leave the power in the hands of the 'Russians' and Western Soviet peoples? And what new democracy will they have culturally, religiously, politically, economically? You can see the 'fatalities' and 'contingencies' present in this complex situation. And it is precisely that situation we are facing."

"And, if your assessment is correct and your proposals apt, what can we do?" Domenico's question seems calm.

"Do? Our primary task? To work so that ethical elements dominate all those socio-political facts. That is it."

"How can we do that, if we stop actively promoting our faith?"

"How? By effecting the establishiment of social and political structures that facilitate the rise of faith, of intelligence, of love—all from the depths of human souls, so that we may all go on together to the discovery of the spiritual realities that really dominate human existence."

"What can his Eminence mean by these woolly terms?" Riccioni is sarcastic but not unkind. He is too mystified for that. "What, in sum, does it mean we have to do?"

"It will mean a total recasting of our human structure—cultural, political, social, intellectual, familial, personal. A total recasting."

"Western democracy is therefore out?" Walker suddenly booms the question.

"The best that can be said about Western democracies—I realize it isn't much—is that they were founded on the principle that the world, and all that is in it, is the territory of man alone with nature, and that neither man *nor* nature have *any* real inner relationship to a transcendent and exigent God. Nor even to the sacred. Nor even to a devil. And if you think that such a political and economic system can lead of itself to a renewal of Christianity, then our differences are very much more profound than either of us even realized. . . ."

"But," says Domenico with a deceptive mildness, "are we then talking about an end to our civilization?"

"Yes. But not just an end. I am talking of a new civilization, a fresh distillation of culture. And, no, I am not talking of a specifically Christian civilization and culture. Just human civilization and culture which bear the imprint of the Christian way of life, and are animated by Christian forms."

"Why does His Eminence seem to be so much in sympathy with all this destruction and innovation?" Domenico, still at Thule.

"Because, my Brother, this corresponds to the historical epoch in which we are—the epoch which faces the Church for the next five hundred years. We must prepare for that. That is the job of Conclave!"

"Our function here, it seems to me," Vasari objects, "is to choose Peter's successor. What have we to do with social movements—I mean as a Conclave?"

"We *have* to be concerned! Because before our very eyes, there has already begun a vast and steadily moving process toward the kind of world I have described. And, unless we ally ourselves with it, we shall perish. All over, whether in China, in Russia, in Europe, in Latin America, in Africa, or in North America—but there less than elsewhere since it is the citadel of bourgeois capitalism—wherever you turn, you find intimate traces of a new birth of wisdom, a turning away from rigid rationalism and from the cold abstractions of Roman scholasticism. You can trace out the general lines of a new vital synthesis outlook in theology and religion—the Charismatic movement; the rising self-consciousness of ethnic minorities; the sudden appearance of spiritual lights in a shower all over the world; the voice of layfolk in Church matters; the new sense of the invisible; the decline of leaders and powerful heads, as if the mass of people were stronger, too strong to be led by one individual; the amazing generosity and freemindedness of the younger generation; a greater mercy and compassion for the criminal, for the imprisoned; a loosening of the grip of scientists on the masses and on the intellectuals—as if people sensed finally what deformities and damage this science of the capitalist world has wrought! And, at last, there is a general horror of war; and, specifically among Christians, there is a fresh consciousness of the social regimen—an element that was completely lacking in the former Christian world and that today still lacks woefully to the capitalist bourgeois mind."

"And is not this to reduce all our ecclesial character to a crass economism? Is our theology to be infected with the changing times of commercial trends and our piety to be an exercise in bourgeois financial policy?" Bronzino has not risen to ask this question.

"No. We do not advocate making Catholicism into a mere pawn of economics. The very point at stake! In our late Christian world human progress was measured by that rule. And, no! We do not advocate that Catholicism be identified with any political system; but in that old Christian world, political facts and social facts were regarded in the same way as physical facts—they were to be measured, treated, and judged in the very same way as physical facts, without regard for the people and the lives involved. And that, of course, was amoral—an amorality, by the way, with which Churchmen easily cohabited when it was a question of investments, collateral, banking procedures, profit-margins, and such like." He looks around with an all-knowing, all-embracing look. "Ah, yes! My Brothers and Eminent Colleagues!"

"Let me remind His Eminence," Cardinal Braun of the United States is standing, "that only because we are powerfully independent financially have we been able to act independently."

"My Venerable and Most Eminent Colleagues, we have not been able to act at all! You know the world no longer listens to us Christians. It has been like that for a very long time. But now another day is here when men will stop and listen just one more time to what we have to say; and they will look momentarily at what we are about. A little part of their attention—that's all we are getting. By the grace of God they will stop and wait for us to speak our mind. For they have a query! By this election of a Pope, and by the agendum we place in his hands officially as our spiritual leader and as Peter's successor, we answer men and women of today. That will be our answer to them.

"You know: These men and women of our day have vast problems and agonizing questions, basic questions. 'How do we feed each other? How do we avoid killing each other? How can we like each other? How do we create beauty in city, home, family, nation? How do we change the criminal's mind and the twisted mind of the insane?'

"If we answer, 'Our attitude to your problems, men and women of this century, is a Catholic attitude,' then we have lost their attention. One by one, and finally in large masses, they will turn away from us, face the long road ahead of them, and go on trudging the human pilgrimage toward a sunrise that keeps evading their arrival but always dances on their furthest horizon. The rainbow of their dreams!

"If our answer is, 'We too are human. We belong with you. We are Christians, we are Catholics. Of course, our human reactions and passions are colored by our faith. But we are with you as fellow-humans, colaborers in our human task'; then they will smile at us and with us. And, together with them we can all trudge as human pilgrims on that road of human destiny."

"What good will that do?" Vasari is outraged. "What about the authoritative message we are supposed to announce to human beings! Where is the Primacy of Peter?"

"These men and women will realize that we do, indeed, have our faith and our spiritual life, even as they have their temporal and worldly problems to solve, and—this is the nodal point of agreement—it will be apparent that our faith and our spiritual life unites us with them. When we labor with them, all the shining values of Christ's Gospel will be reflected and enmeshed in the common work we undertake with our fellow humans. For our work will be to fill human life, all human lives, with love and to ensure that all alive on the face of this beloved planet live their temporal lives better and happily and according to the light God gives them."

Thule has little more to add. His tone is quieter. "My Lord Cardinals, this is the general framework of the Papal Policy and Church policy that we think the next Pope should follow and foment among Roman Catholics. If you, My Lord Vasari, feel outraged, and if you, My Lord Riccioni, feel I have erred, you will have ample time to say so. But first, feel the pulse of our Brother Cardinals. For they," Thule breaks off and looks around, "they have listened attentively to all I have had to say."

Thule gives a little bow in three directions so as to take in the entire assembly, then goes to his place as deliberately as he left it.

Buzzes of conversation have started already. But Thule is barely in his place when Bronzino has obtained permission to speak.

"I think, Most Reverend Eminences, my Brother Cardinals, while we can all appreciate His Eminence's sentiments, the fact of the matter is that he presents us with no alternative to our dilemma—if indeed, dilemma we have.

"I, for one, and His Eminence Cardinal Braun, and all the other Eminent Cardinals and Reverend Bishops who work with us have set down what we perceive to be the condition of the Church financially and economically. Dilemma, obviously we have *not!* Difficulties due to worldwide inflation we have certainly. But *dilemma?*" He pauses. A twinkle of humor flashes across his eyes. "Well, yes; perhaps the Cardinal is in a dilemma . . ." he gives Thule a full-eyed stare. Thule's response is silence.

"Now as regards the wide world. It makes me feel slightly sick to hear people talking about the proletariat. The proletariat rising, and all that sort of talk.

"What we have, today, is quite simple. There are few countries where some sort of democracy—republican democracy—exists. Personalistic democracy does not exist and has not existed since the time of Pericles—if even then. And don't be fooled by any protestations from the Swiss. Their democracy is neither personalistic nor republican. No country is so much in the grip of a financial oligarchy as Switzerland.

"Anyway. By republican democracy I mean a political system in which the people govern through freely elected representatives. The old individual regime of princes never attained this. Well, in the United States, in the United Kingdom, France, Italy, Germany, Switzerland, Spain, Portugal, Canada, Australia, New Zealand, South Africa, and in a few more places the semblance of such democracy exists. Republican democracy, I mean. Mind you: I know that democracy is greatly attenuated. Actually, it is big financial monopolies, enormous parliamentary lobbies, and well entrenched political parties—usually, all together, representing not more that 5 percent of each population—that really run each so-called democracy, just as it—the 5 percent—wishes.

"No one, I suppose, is going to try and tell us that the satellites of the U.S.S.R. are democracies—even My Lord Thule or My Lord Franzus.... Above *all* My Lord Franzus!

"There is, of course, the Scandinavian model of so-called socialist democracies. But, again, we know they are more vulnerable to inflation and economic breakdown than a democracy along American lines. In fact, socialism of the Scandinavian kind has never worked anywhere at any time. It just pretends to work for a while, then breaks down, and they call in the capitalists to mend the old machine.

"Elsewhere, in what are called—depending on one's mind, or on the time of day—socialist, Social Democratic, or Democratic Socialist systems, we find strong-arm governments. They are generally either dictatorships of one man; or dictatorships of oligarchies; or dictatorships of particular tribes." Bronzino pauses; then suddenly he turns full blast on Thule. "What in the name of Jesus Christ can democratic socialism then be? A Marxist Communist state? An outright dictatorship? What is it?"

"If I may be allowed to intervene?" Buff appeals to the President and receives a nod of approval. The Anglo-Saxon turns around and looks at Braun and Bronzino, then at Uccello.

"It was Pope Paul himself in 1971 who set our minds along this way, the Progressivist way, of thinking," he speaks in the tones of the schoolmaster beginning a lesson to particularly ignorant children. "Let me remind His Eminence and all our Italian Brothers—in fact all of you, who, like them, are still back in the Cold War period of his Holiness Pope Pius 12—let me remind you of Pope Paul's words." He looks down at his notes. "I quote:

'It is necessary to invent forms of modern democracy.... We must have a pluralism of options for social change ... the same Christian faith may lead to different commitments....'

"And most importantly," Buff says, looking at Domenico, "most importantly, the following:

'False philosophical teachings cannot be identified with historical move- ments that have economic, social, cultural, and political ends.'

"I put it to you," the Anglo-Saxon concludes, "that the whole *philosophical* thing of Marxism is a farrago of bad theories. But economic, social, cultural, and political Marxism is a *concrete movement of the masses today*—and the *only* one that promises liberation and elevation of the majority of humans. It is this that My Lords Thule and Franzus are saying. Believe me, my Beloved Colleagues, and I know what I am saying." Buff is almost smirking with surety. "My Eminent Brothers Thule and Franzus believe all the truths of our faith as well and as deeply and as feelingly as My Lords Braun and Bronzino."

"In other words," Cardinal Sargent is speaking from his place, "you do not sanction our American democracy as the most suitable form of government today, as an ideal in fact, in our present world?"

"That is correct, Eminences!" Thule booms out the words from his place.

Domenico is on his feet. He sees where Sargent is going to drag the argument, and he knows that he will lose the argument in the process, and that the whole thing will become a red herring.

"My Eminent Lord President, if I can have a word . . ." Domenico signals to the President. "My Lord Cardinal Sargent, My Lord Thule, please permit me a word between yours." He looks around at the assembly. "My Most Eminent Cardinals, whether we like it or not, the fact is that the idea of a democracy in the American sense of the word arose directly from the idea of power that was developed by the Church of Rome in its infancy." His tone is a serious and calm one. He is lecturing now. And when Domenico lectures, Cardinals listen.

"For the first time in history, I think, it was the early Christian community in Rome who believed that all power—political as well—came from God. And they said that this power came directly to the Pope, so that he had unlimited supremacy. Very shortly later the Christian wrinkle on this matter was that power came to the Pope through the voice of the people. For as you know, the early Popes were chosen by the voice of the people, the *vox populi*. But only the *choice* came from the people, the *indication* of whom *God* wanted as leader. *Not* the power of that God!

"It is not a Christian idea to say that the people is the *source* of the power, that power resides in the people as in its source. Christians *should* say that the people is a channel of *choice—not* of power. And those early Christians held that all power, political included, came to princes and to governments through the Pope. This is basic Christian teaching.

"Insofar as American democracy makes the people the *source* of power, American democracy is not Christian.

"Now, I know that the idea of a sacerdotal regime—supreme over all other authority—was rejected by the rational independence of the eighteenth century and subsequent. . . ."

"It is not rejected today by true believers!" Vasari shouts at Domenico angrily.

"No. I suppose that your true believers like Archbishop Lefebvre," Thule retorts immediately, "together with your *Opus Dei* people, the Phalanx for the Faith, the Knights of Queen Mary, the Defense of Family, Fatherland and Property Organization, the Knights of Columbus, that all these true believers don't reject that idea. But, believe me, Eminence, the rest of the world does!" Thule's tones are brutal and his facts so overwhelmingly to the point that Vasari remains with his mouth open.

Domenico goes on. "This is the secular element in society! It is there, whether we like it or not. We have to deal with it. But let no one here propose American democracy as the ideal. It isn't. It is basically a completely secular system that was, until fairly recently, infused with the Christianity of some of its founders and of the majority of its people. I repeat—until fairly recently. I say that because any Christian influence there is slowly draining out of the American system. So, in this sense, My Lords Thule, Franzus and Buff are correct. American democracy offers no viable substitute for democratic socialism or for Marxism—though I suspect the two are the same thing—eh, Lord Franzus? Don't answer yet!"

Domenico stands silent and looks around. Then: "No doubt about it, my Brothers, every one of us, whether we realize it or not, uses Marxism as a scientific method, as a rigorous method of examining social and political reality. We test the value of history today, balancing between our theories and our proposals to revolutionize human society. That's *basic* Marxism." Again a pause.

"And that, my Brothers, you may be surprised to know, is a quotation from His Holiness Pope Paul 6."

Domenico sits down. There is a general silence. Some, especially the Americans and British Commonwealth Cardinals seem stunned. Domenico appears to be on Thule's side. The Italians are whispering among themselves.

"All the same," Cardinal Lippi objects, as he rises, "I must protest in the name of that Christian country and people that is the United States of America."

"*Bravo! Bravo! Lippi! Bravo!*" It is Buonarroti applauding Lippi. Lippi waves to him.

"As for our Eminent Brother, he surely agrees with the Coalition Policy. After all, he himself said at Fatima in Portugal this year that he wholeheartedly supports the sincere efforts of the people and the Government of Portugal toward building a new society—more just, more human, and more full. Democratic socialism in other words!" Thule is quoting Buonarroti's own words—just one more indication to the listeners that Thule has done his homework.

The Cardinal President breaks in: "I think we have heard enough so that everyone understands. Let us not wrangle over petty points. We have graver issues to decide. I think that we should propose to take a preliminary vote on the *Policy* change, Eminent Brothers, that is to say if none of you. . . ."

"We have a question for our Eminent Brother, Cardinal Thule." It is Uccello speaking for the non-Roman Italian Cardinals. He rises. With the President's assent, Uccello turns to Thule. "Eminence, we all thank you for your address. We wish to ask you about the position of the Holy Father. And be concrete in your answers, please, for our sakes. How do you see the function of the Pope in relation to the greater non-Catholic communions, say the Anglican, the Coptic, the Orthodox?"

"We can take the word of the former Archbishop of Canterbury on that," Thule answers as he stands to reply. "You will remember that Lord Michael Ramsey proposed recently that the Pope could be accepted as the presiding Bishop of the Anglican Church." Thule is speaking suavely. "What we have to remember is that we cannot hope to achieve universal Church authority by *absorbing* non-Catholic bodies. They simply will not be absorbed. We Roman Catholics have to broaden ourselves ecumenically. After all, already both Protestants and Orthodox concede to the Pope a primacy of honor. We start there, then!"

"And what about unity of belief?" Azande's question.

"Belief?" Thule answers. "We all know there is a growing convergence on fundamentals about social justice, and political equality and human dignity. And, as Catholic Bishop Lessard of Savannah, Georgia, said, there is an explicit acceptance of compatibility in a *common* faith, with a *pluralism* of expression."

"You would, therefore, eliminate unity of belief in expression, under Roman authority?" This time it is Sargent who tackles Thule.

"My Eminent Brother, the Roman mentality with its authoritarianism, is like the Chinese Mandarin mentality which lasted all of 1300 years until 1905: a self-indoctrinating, self-perpetuating, labyrinthine system of examinations and norms and formulas and expressions of self-acceptance. It collapsed. And so is our Roman mentality collapsing. *Collapsing!*" He accompanies the repetition with a quick closing of his fingers to a clenched fist. "What we need, we have! Believers."

"And Papal infallibility?" It is Vasari fuming, and still after Thule, trying to trip him up.

"Look, Eminence. The First Vatican Council defined Papal infallibility as a dogma to be believed by all the faithful. And it may be true that the Pope has such authority. . . ."

There are some cries of "shame!" "Shut up!" "Silence him!" "Retract!"

Thule is not at all put out. He continues serenely, like a heavy barge shoving its bulk through a school of minnows. "In our time, all teaching has to have some kind of verisimilitude. Now, if a Pope were to exercise infallibility today, it would probably have no verisimilitude. After all, our aim today is to return to some of our early Christian simplicity in prayer, in devotion, in work, and in love of all men."

"I seem to hear in the Cardinal's words," Kiel is speaking without rising from his chair, "echoes of what many theologians, Progressivist theologians, are saying today. People like Dulles in the United States, Küng in Germany, Schillebeeckx in Holland, Laurentin in France. And all I want to add here is that, while theologians have a duty to study, they have *no* privilege to teach the faith! That is for us Bishops, the Cardinal included, *provided* he stays in union with his fellow Bishops. That function of teaching belongs to Bishops." Kiel, one of Paul 6's most recent Cardinals, is known to be a Radical.

"Eminent Brother," Thule retorts, "I have no intention of infringing on the authority of Bishops. I merely. . . ."

"No, Eminence?" Kiel asks tendentiously. "But isn't it a fact you gave support to the 1972 statement of thirty-four theologians—people like McKenzie and Curran in the United States, Küng and Lohfink in Germany, Schillebeeckx of Holland—who told priests and people alike to *bypass the Bishops* and choose their own ways of doing things? Isn't that so?" The declaration of the thirty-four theologians had exhorted Roman Catholics to seek ways of changing their Bishops by forcing their hands.

There is now a feeling of sudden stop in the assembly. This may be the downfall of Thule. And that would not fit in with the plans of Angelico and Domenico. Domenico realizes that the only way to get this Conclave to make a *real* change—a change that is not a mere political sop—is to offer it two extremes: The Progressivist extreme of Thule, or the Radical extreme he and others champion. He also fears that any suppression of Thule before the Conclave has had a chance to vote on Thule's proposals will not solve the growing problem in the Church. For one thing, many Christians share Thule's views. Those views are flourishing, as they burrow from within as a kind of guerilla underground of ideas. At all costs, according to Domenico's plan, Thule must be allowed to hang himself completely. For another thing, Thule is useful for making sure that there is no return to the *General Policy* system. All temporary opposition must be headed off. If the risk is that the Conclave will go with Thule, that risk must be taken.

Domenico signals to Angelico, who rises: "I think we should let the Cardinal's expression pass—whether we like it or not. He is trying to explain a very difficult situation." Thule bows in Angelico's direction.

But Lohngren bridles. He has lost his temper. He stands and, eyes blazing, addresses Thule. "Does His Eminence think that we are going to reject the institutional Church of centuries? What is this ideal Church he is talking about? Where on earth has he got the idea that we can return to the early days of Christianity? And, are we all to dabble in politics now?"

But Thule has a word for him, too. "My Most Eminent Brother, you and the other Bishops of Germany issued a 1,400-word document on June 29, 1977, and its main theme was a plea for the political and economic unity of Europe. What do you call that? Is that not politicking? Is that not dabbling in Europolitics? And is that allowed you but not to anyone else? Didn't your people say that the obstacles to European unity can only be overcome if Christians play their part and take what you called a calculated risk? Why may you do that and not others?"

Lohngren is ready to answer; he looks over at Angelico who makes a subsiding motion with his hand. "Let it go," Angelico is telling him.

The last to pressure Thule is Tobey. The American rises in a leisurely fashion and with the assent of the President.

"Eminence," he begins, "I guess it is the self-consoling habit of non-Americans to blame the United States for all the ills of the world." This is as far as Tobey gets. Buff interrupts.

"Really, Eminence, we don't blame you Americans for anything you haven't done. We blame you for supplying one-third of all Idi Amin's gold each year—99 percent of it to buy coffee from him. And for exporting $6 million in goods to Idi Amin's Uganda, including $1 million in aircraft, $500,000 in strategically important power-generating equipment, and another half million dollars in engines for armored carriers." Tobey looks slightly off balance.

"And we blame you for the U.S. drug companies who finance birth control campaigns in my country," Cardinal Iago Motzu of Oceania adds in.

"And for supporting the regime which has arrested 60,000 people since 1972," adds another Oceanian, Cardinal Obata.

"In other words, Eminent Brothers," Thule ends the chorus, "fair is fair. The whole world is grateful to the good old generous U.S.A. Between 1946 and 1976 you gave away $192 billion to foreign governments all over the globe. Many thanks. But what is the result? Poverty, want, inflation, starvation, terrorism, revolution.

"Very well, we say. Now it is time for a solution not based on naive policies, but a solution born of the Spirit. And that is the *Coalition Policy*—a solution born of the Spirit." And with that Thule takes his seat, obviously satisfied that he has scored very well indeed.

The President now confers with his two colleagues on either side of him at the long table. Then he announces: "If no other Eminent Cardinal wishes to speak, or if there is no further point on which an Eminent Cardinal has a question for the *Coalition Policy* speakers ..." he looks around and sees Franzus on his feet. He nods to him.

"Eminent Brothers, I must remind you—from stray remarks passed in the heat of the past twenty minutes, some of you may have a wrong impression.

Let me make it clear. We are not proposing that we forsake Christianity and embrace Marxism and atheism." He shudders visibly. "I do not know how to reassure you of my own attachment to Christ and to Christ's Church and of the burning loyalty of all our bishops and priests and layfolk." He straightens, and the expression on his face becomes clear and happy, as if a fresh conviction had taken over in him.

"Why do you think His Holiness Pope Paul received the First Secretary of the Hungarian Communist Party, Janos Kadar, in the Vatican? And didn't Kadar praise Pope Paul's tenacity and sincerity? And didn't Kadar, on his return to Hungary, tell a press conference that Hungary's socialist society knows how to live together with believers? And didn't Pope Paul, while greeting Kadar and his party, openly refer to the difficulties between the Church and the regime in Hungary? And isn't all this very healthy?"

"The Vatican is always ready," Witz quietly interrupts, rearing his 6-foot frame unmistakably into view of all, "to speak to anyone, the Devil included, if it makes life easier for believers to practise their religion. But is Your Eminence trying to tell us that an alliance between Marxists and Catholics had the past Pope's *blessing,* and *should* have the blessing of this Conclave and of the Pope it elects?"

"No, Eminence." Franzus is quick to answer. "No. But the decisions about such matters should now be left to the local diocesan and parish authorities."

"And the central authority of Rome?" Riccioni almost screams at Franzus. The Electors are electrified by his shrill tones. Franzus says nothing.

Buff, however, rises, and is at his most cutting and sardonic. "It really appears that His Eminence Riccioni believes that the Roman bureaucracy can deal in a straight manner with a Marxist government. And, really, this is the limit of credulity! My Brothers, is there even one of us here who does not know the self-serving machinations of that tight little Mafia ... " there is an audible hiss, as many Electors draw in a breath of sharp surprise. The blood drains out of the Camerlengo's face. Vasari slumps forward, his face in his hands. Riccioni's eyes have turned to stone as he stares at Buff. Buff has drawn the long knife of calculated insult against the power of the "inner club" that develops around every Pope. Angelico and Domenico both make calming motions with their hands to various Electors.

The Anglo-Saxon, meanwhile, is just warming to his subject. "When you think of that little secretive group!" Buff now enunciates every syllable slowly, bitingly, in a dry clipped tone; and each word emerges from his lips as though it had been leading a distinct and private life of its own. There appears to be nothing sly, nothing arcane about his thin, sparse figure. But, his listeners realize, there are subtle and elemental forces at work inside Buff, as if his Christianity were separate from his mind, as if his Cardinalitial dignity was merely a cloak but not a constituent element of his life. Lohngren leans forward and whispers to Kiel: "Perhaps he will throw off his clothes and appear as Satan!"

"This little band of acquaintances." Buff prolongs the sibilant ending of the last word as if it were a code of introduction to deep and dark secrets. "Around Pope Paul 6. All friends! Old friends!" He smiles around connivingly at the Cardinals, looking like a man who wishes to share something with them. "The managers!" Now the Electors are looking at each other in stupefaction. No one has ever opened fire as frankly and devastatingly as this on the inner club. Clearly Buff is going to name names.

"Villot! Benelli! The Secretariat of State! And now, Caprio in Benelli's place! One of the friends, of course. One of the old friends! Don Pasquale Macchi, personal assistant to Pope Paul! How well he helped Pope Paul to wield Papal influence! And that special privileged part of the Secretariat: the *Ostpolitik*-makers! Casaroli and Silvestrini. And Dino Monduzzi in charge of all the Pope's private audiences, with his carefully kept books and his little notations. Vagnozzi and Marčinkus in economic and financial affairs—religious works! If you please, Eminences! Religious works! Do you imagine the religiosity of transferring $40 million from Zurich to New York? Imagine! And then the chain of command via old friends abroad. A Pio Laghi in the Argentine to watchdog the vital area, for instance. And all the other friends located in the Holy Office, in the Congregation for the Propagation of the Faith, and the other key ministries. All friends!" Buff pauses and looks around. He has obtained the effect he sought. All have known the "Mafia." Many have chafed at its cronyism, its immunity, its autonomy.

"What binds them all together in spite of their constant bickering and their perpetual jockeying for more power at somebody else's expense? That most of them come from Faenza or thereabouts? That 'they all can make spaghetti,' as the saying goes? Perhaps. But the real bond is power. These, my Brothers, are the power brokers of Christ's Church. And the crux of the question before us today, as we prepare to vote on policy is the question of power: Are we going to allow the destiny of this Church to be decided by their internal petty power politics?" His voice rises in querulousness. Then it sinks back to a chatty tone.

"I read a book last year by one of the real holy men of our time, Bede Griffiths. The book was *Return to the Center*. And he points out there that no traditional forms are sacrosanct. For nothing in the present Church which was built on the original Jewish bases, nothing of its dogma, its sacraments, formulas, its hierarchical organization, nothing is exempt from change. How much longer"—the querulous combative tone is there again—"shall this inner club, this little society of mutual friends and allies at the heart of the institutional Church impose outmoded ideas on us all?

"They have calmness and stability and relaxed certainty written on their faces, haven't they? You know, as I do, that they lead lives in a world of their own, enjoyable, confident, in luscious power, beautiful with monuments and relics, far—too far—removed from social reality, consumed in the superb extravagance, and in waste of resources on petty politics, with a ritualized using up of time, and a cultivated grace of dress and behavior that gives their lives a dream-like quality.

"As for us in the provinces, what have we to do with all this? What, I ask you, Eminences?" He waits for a moment, then finishes abruptly: "Let me hear no more of that 'central authority of Rome.' Let the *Church* speak! The universal Church!" He sits down solemnly.

Almost immediately, Riccioni is on his feet protesting, without waiting for permission from the President. Scorn and rage are his weapons.

"I don't think any Cardinal here, except perhaps My Lord Buff, is going to trek all the way to Bede Griffiths' ashram, his Shantivanam, his Forest of Peace, in order to get advice on the problems of Christ's Church. . . ." Cries of *"Bravo Riccioni! Bravo!"* are sent up by a number of Italians.

"But let's forget that part of it," Riccioni continues. "And let's forget the scurrilous attack on Vatican personnel also. Of course, Anglo-Saxons have been excluded from the government of the Church for so long they have forgotten the art of ecclesiastical affairs—if they ever knew it. It is as distressing to me as it is to you, I am sure, Eminences, to hear all that biting contempt from His Eminence. It is as distressing as the sacrilege perpetrated by Communist gangsters who smashed the Thirteenth century windows of the Church of Santa Croce in Florence last year! Just sacrilege one more time in the life of the Church!

"Of course, here in Rome we see that we are being outclassed and shunted aside by the dominating presence of the new Marxist culture—besides being defeated politically. Still, I don't care how many times Pope Paul met with Rome's Communist Mayor Giulio Argan. It is immaterial. The Christian community in Rome has been removed from power. And our Christian traditions are no longer paid any heed at City Hall. *No Matter!* So, too, no matter that some foreigners do not understand how the central bureaucracy of the Church functions—with *all* its faults.

"But I do wish to say, in the name of my Brothers, that we will never consent to an alliance, or even a working plan of collaboration, with Marxists. *Never!* And we will, if necessary, stay in this Conclave, and keep you all here with us, until this time next year, if this is the price we must pay and you must pay!" Flushed, red and shaking, Riccioni sits down.

Already, Marquez has permission to speak. His tone is mild and conciliatory. "Really, my Eminent Brothers, it is facts that count here"—glancing at Riccioni—"and not fears.

"Take São Paulo, for instance. It has twelve million people, 1,100 restaurants, a nightlife that never stops, a flourishing homosexual trade in bars, hotels, clothes shops. A bottle of Scotch whisky costs $100. A Mercedes costs $50,000 and the streets are clogged with them. The latest discotheque cost over $1 million to build. The beautiful people get up every evening for the nightlife which begins at midnight in places like the Mur D'Hera. And, oh, I forgot to tell you, the beautiful people are just under 5 percent of the population. The others? Hidden from view, living in squalor, in dirt, in hunger, in prostitution, in servitude to ill-paid jobs. Now, how long can the Church back this sort of regime? How long, I ask you? How long can it last?" There is a dead silence. "But what, you may ask, has the Church to do with all this? Well, we don't condemn it. And we do enjoy it, at least at the fringes, and sometimes in the center of it.

"As a human settlement, São Paulo has too much iron, too much cement, too much money, too much misery, and too much slavery." He stops and thinks. "You know," he continues as if reflecting out loud, "there does exist really a form of slavery as bad as any slavery in the old colonial days. And, just as the Church really did nothing official to condemn and eradicate slavery in colonial days, so today. Neither in Latin America, nor in countries like Equatorial Africa or the Cameroons or Morocco do we as a Church do anything against the existent slavery."

Marquez has more. "Oh, yes. My Lord Franzus has his wounds, his stripes, his sufferings. And they are terrible. But do you forget that in Latin America there are prisons with their tortures and master-torturers? And death-squads? And the dead bodies found every day in the shanty parts of the cities? And the people who disappear and are never found again—perhaps they grumbled against the regime or tried to redress some injustice, say a rape or a robbery?

"How long, I ask you, how long is all this going to continue and how long are we going to be identified with it, because we do not wage war on it?" There are some indistinct calls to Marquez from the rows of Cardinals, but no one pays attention to them.

Marquez' tone gets calmer now. "What is the matter really? Isn't it the same thing that ails the whole of the capitalist system? The big corporations employ a small number of people, use huge amounts of capital and much raw material, to manufacture sophisticated goods for an elite market, producing exuberant rates of economic growth. And in doing all this, those companies and interest groups prolong the inequalities of the colonial period, they rigidify social classes. They increase poverty and suffering. And the end result? The money and plenty and pleasure stay within the small privileged groups—the 5 percent in Brazil, the 11 percent in the U.S.A., and so on.

"But the people of God in their millions are bypassed by this vicious circle of the privileged, of the beautiful, of the feckless people. And isn't democratic socialism or some form of it the only way to break that dreadful circle of horror? That, Eminences, is all we are trying to say to you all."

"And I wish to add this!" Lynch is on his feet as Marquez sits. The President at the long table throws his eyes to Heaven in a despairing gesture.

"Let no one have any doubts as to the intentions of the United States capitalists in my beloved country," Lynch says animatedly as he looks around. "No matter what talk there is about human rights, the United States Government pursues the same selfish purposes. Unscrupulously! You all have heard by now how, for instance, the major portion of the AID program, over $397 and a half million, was used merely to bolster the former Frei regime of Chile against the politics of Salvador Allende. It's been pretty much the same in my country. And, you have heard, as well, that the attempt to audit the misuse of such funds was quashed from Washington. This is just an example of the obstacles we are up against in our fight for liberation."

Then he adopts a pleading attitude. "My Brothers! There are now eighty-six non-aligned nations, all poor, all endeavoring to create some sort of socialist regime, all laboring to liberate men and women and children from poverty, starvation and misery. The Coalition's principle in this Conclave is this: Let us align ourselves with the downtrodden majority. And let us effect the basic liberation of our fellow human beings! The future of the Church lies with the masses of humanity!"

It is now a few minutes past 1:30 P.M. This First Session should have ended at noon. But there is no question of ending now. The discussions, the arguments, the fire of anger, the revelations have indeed begun to forge a new feeling among the Electors. They have been affected by something of what Franzus said, some of the compassion and feeling of Marquez, and something of Buff's disgust for the bureaucracy.

The Conclave President, sensitive to the mood of the assembly, is the first to note the new attitude. The mass of the Electors is looking at him as if to say: "Yes, you are right. It is time. Let us get on with the preliminary voting on the question of what *General Policy* we will adopt. We have heard enough. We have suffered enough. Let's get on with it!" It is as if the President felt a real majority of the Electors beginning to move and to get restless because they have made up their minds and would like to express themselves out loud and as one body.

"If I am not mistaken, Eminent Brothers, we are ready for a vote," the President expresses the mood of the Conclave. A chorus of voices greets this remark. *"Ita!" "Bravo" "Procedamus!" "Bene!"*

At this moment, Marquez rises to make the formal proposal. Thule sent over a long note a few moments ago. Practically everyone in Conclave is aware of this. For now, everyone in Conclave is alive to any and all maneuvers and moves. Marquez is very quick in his delivery and very sure of himself. "Eminent Lord Presidents, my Eminent Brothers! In place of the now abandoned *General Policy*, we have a newly proposed policy. May I call it the *Policy of Flexible Openness*. For, in truth, what My Lord Thule and his sympathisers propose is, genuinely, a Church policy that would make the Church of Rome a reasonably elastic church, not wholly unyielding, not wholly resistant.

"We need today a Church that will proceed on a situationist view of things: The view that dogmas are culturally conditioned expressions of revelation; that membership in Christ's Church is primarily, and in certain cases need only be, by community in spirit, but not by conformity of mind on behavior or concepts; that morals be interpreted for each time and each place—always depending on the teaching of approved theologians.

"And we must have a Church which teaches that authority is compatible with pluralism and—what is just as important—with human dignity and freedom. Finally, overall Church policy must hew faithfully and closely and supremely to the agonizing economical and political reality—a new regimen for human society which is long overdue. In a word, a *Policy of Flexible Openness*."

Marquez drops his voice. "Frankly, my Brothers, only by such a *Policy* will we, in my opinion—and will the next Pontiff—demonstrate the all-encompassing love of God, our Creator." As Marquez finishes, several conversations have started among the Electors.

Hildebrandt is the first to say *"Ita!"* loudly. He is followed by several dozen others. Marquez looks at Koi-Lo-Po: "Eminent President, I think you know the will of the majority." He turns around and finds several pairs of eyes on him, approving, content, smiling. Lynch, Franzus, Lombardi, Lowe, Zubaran. When he sits down, there is some brief and hearty applause.

Koi-Lo-Po takes off his spectacles: "I take it there is no substantial dissent." When no dissenting voice is raised: "I suggest that this time the Revisers sit on the opposite side of the table from the Scrutineers. According as the Scrutineers perform their work, ballot by ballot, the Revisers will take up theirs. In this way, we can hasten the vote. The Camerlengo was asked about this earlier today, and he takes this as a perfectly valid adaptation of our Conclave Rules."

Koi-Lo-Po gives one last look around to make sure that no one wishes to speak, and then makes a sign to the elected Conclave officials. They come and receive the ballot papers as before. Within ten minutes, all the ballots have been distributed. The balloting begins. Each Elector goes through the personal ritual of depositing his ballot in the Chalice, having first pronounced the ritual oath.

This time the scrutiny and the revision procedure take place in a wholly different atmosphere. The voting is again *placet* (for the new policy) and *non placet* (against it). The voice of the third Scrutineer announcing the *placet* or *non placet* is the accompaniment to a peculiar mixture of elation or depression felt by each of the electors. The *placet* column each Elector is keeping informally grows and grows in length, while the *non placet* column remains short and sparse and discouraging. And, according as the approving votes are read out and noted, it is obvious that a big majority—perhaps the needed overall majority of two-thirds plus one—is in formation in favor of the new *Policy*. Each extra *placet* announced seems to swell some volume of elation. And, in contrast, throughout the rows of Electors, certain Cardinals seem to flatten further and further back in their places as if an invisible depression lay on them increasingly.

Shortly before 2 P.M., every ballot paper has been handled by the Scrutineers and Revisers. When Koi-Lo-Po receives the official tally, everyone present already knows the results. "Eminences! *Placet*—77 votes. *Non placet*—41 votes. I have the honor to tell Your Eminences officially that the new *Policy* has missed the needed two-thirds plus one by three votes only." A sound like a half-suppressed sigh is heard from various parts of the assembly.

Koi-Lo-Po goes on. "It is now past our mealtime. I suggest we break off. Dinner will be served ten minutes after our arrival home. Optional, of course, as all the meals. Siesta hour will be just that—one hour, from 2:45 to 3:45 P.M. The warning bell will ring promptly at 3:40. The Second Session will begin punctually at 4 P.M." He gives his silver bell a small perfunctory ring and stands up. Within twenty minutes, all have returned to the *Domus Mariae*.

AFTERNOON: 2:00 P.M.—4:00 P.M.

Domenico is one of the first out of the dining room. Back in his room, he has a pile of reading material, sheaves of documents and reports to get through. By a quarter to three, the Conclave area is quiet; all have retired to sleep or to confer or to read.

A decisive conversation is being held in Buff's apartment. Franzus is there, as is Thule, Lowe, Marquez, Lombardi, Francis, Manuel.

"The question is now: Do we nominate?" Thule puts the decision to his peers.

"I don't fancy this balloting too much. Not right now, anyway." Buff's comment. "For one thing, it is tricky. We have no experience in it at all. The votes could swing upward and downward and sideways and around the place. I've seen it happen in other assemblies. I've heard of it."

"Yes," Lynch agrees. Thule nods.

"Well then," Thule's jaw tightens, "our alternative is to nominate and then force a rush vote by acclamation instead of by balloting."

"That I like," Marquez breaks in. "We are, right now, just three votes short of an overall majority. Surely we can garner a mere three votes ... and it is better to rush it now before any other group that is mapping strategy can get a chance to grasp the initiative and sway the Conclave."

By 3:20 P.M., Angelico telephones Domenico. "You know what you have to do, Angelico?" Dominico asks him. "Give me another ten minutes or so. Then pass along here, and we can chat until the bell rings."

When the warning bell rings at 3:45, Domenico has finished laying his plans with Angelico. As they both walk toward the Assembly Hall, they are joined by the young Cardinal with the stutter.

"Eminence!" Angelico greets him. "How goes it with you?"

"Fine! Fine!" the young Cardinal answers quietly, falling into step with the two of them. "I was chatting with Marquez and Manuel just now. I suppose we are going to have what the Camerlengo would call a denoument?" There is a gap in the conversation; then the young Cardinal goes on. "Tell me, Eminence," turning his head in Domenico's direction, "why do they say you are against the new *Policy?*"

Angelico, knowing Domenico, senses the older man freezing up. He decides to keep up the facade of camaraderie. "Oh, Cardinal Domenico here is best at home in Medieval times, Eminence!" It is a gauche remark, but Angelico has no real idea how to be humorous.

"Yes," Domenico says, with no smile, "that's it, Medieval times." They enter the bus together.

At the door of the Assembly Hall, the young Cardinal leaves them and goes over to chat with two of his compatriots. "I don't know why," Domenico remarks to Angelico, "but I cannot warm to our young Colleague. I cannot. I try. I cannot." The old man shakes his head.

THE SECOND SESSION

The first business in this Second Session is the election of new Presidents. Witz is chosen as President, flanked by Hildebrandt and Uccello as Assistant Presidents. The Scrutineers are Ferro, Makonde, and Buff. The Revisers are all black: Bamleke, Saleke, and Azande. The *Infirmarii* are Kiel, Hartley, and Francis. Towering over the long table even when he sits down, Witz glances at the schedule. Then in clipped Germanic tones, he announces:

"My Most Eminent Lord Cardinal Thule to the podium!"

Of Thule it can never be said that he enters a scene trailing clouds of ambiguity. His physique—face and body—is definitive, stamped with character as obtrusive as one of the stone bridges in Norway. He has no veil over his eyes. They are unclouded. They take you in wholly, and their concentration is emphasized by the controlled movement of a massive head turning hither and thither like an armored turret.

Thule's once bulky frame is now bordering on the gaunt, but the large bone structure remains as mute monument to its flower of years ago and as guarantee of many more winters he shall outlive. Few among his listeners know the rolling plains of his native land. But those who are acquainted with the land of Otto Thule recall and savor the resident strength wafting over those fields, dales, and woodlands, where gray skies and rain and uneventful landscapes always seem to be cloaked in some intangible mystique. The cynics would say it was because that land has been the cockpit of Europe since the days of Julius Caesar, and armies and generals and tribes hurtled over it leaving traces of the greatness and the madnesses that drove them on. The sympathetic would surmise that, after all, an obscure Nordic tribe carried and still carries some ancient primeval dignity that neither time nor haughty overlords nor Nazi invaders have quenched.

In Thule's voice which already has the oncoming echoes of the old man's cavernous timbre, there is that indefinable note—sometimes reminiscent of group-chant, sometimes of brusque command—which compels attention but does not attract affection. Nordic also is the texture of his mind as it issues in words.

And, as paradox to all this, as in every true Northerner, there is a purple thread of mysticism running through the most hard-headed of his words. To confuse that mystic trait with emotionalism would be an error. Emotionalism can be cool, can be broken. But mysticism is a dark fire that feeds on sources unreachable by the waters of reason and impervious to the bite of comment or the lash of indignity.

Thule obviously has his own private vision of divinity. And his gifts of personality and public performance enable him to cast visions of power, dreams and fears over audiences. This audience of Cardinal Electors, no less than the audiences of 25,000 and more he has addressed all over the world, is pliable to his sentiments. He dominates them. Naturally. This afternoon it is a deft and masterful performance on Thule's part.

His introductory words are, each one of them, rounded and well-aimed. As he must, he first proposes a new policy. Once it has been approved, he can go on and nominate Yiu. "Eminent Lord Cardinal Presidents! Beloved Brothers and Colleagues! Our problem is, as we have said, a simple one: how best do we go forward to meet the men and women of our day as they move irrevocably across the borders from the desert of a world that has ceased to exist, into the new world of tomorrow." Thule moves slowly toward his right. "Can we take that step?" A short pause. "No doubt in Heaven or on earth. We can!" He looks around. "We can!"

He glances at Domenico and then at the Cardinals at the end of the assembly. "We will refuse, Eminent Brothers, to be left behind like old men, by ourselves, lonely, deceitful, grieving, and soon to be dead." A momentary sense of horror runs through most of the Electors. One or two of them look around at the bald or balding heads and sagging features of some Cardinals. Thule has used a near-at-heart image to convey his meaning.

He follows with a thumbnail sketch of the "new" Church he envisions. The tone is businesslike, and zestful. And, this time, he is not interrupted with questions or challenges. His whole being is intent now on holding the lead gained in the morning session, and on building upon it with every tool at his command.

"Open, my Brothers! Open to God's skies. A Church of that sort is what we need. No longer guided by fear. No longer resting on long memories. No longer in a state of siege. But open! All of us, bearing our message and commingling with the sons and daughters of God our common Father. For if we are open, we will receive God's spirit anew!" He concludes his introductory words with a trenchant statement: "It is in this spirit and with this outlook that we think our nominated candidate should be considered as the best—as symbol and as operative—in the Kingdom of God on earth."

He deals next with the principal objection to the *Coalition Policy*. "Some will object through fear of loss." He looks around in silence to let the words sink in. "Our supernatural values are so precious. How could we expose them to adulteration by Protestant, by Jew, by Muslim, by non-believers, by contamination with those immersed completely in the tangible?" His voice takes on a hammer-blow note. "I answer: Our supernatural values are, to be sure, intangibles. But, these crucial intangibles are not, repeat, not, abstractions. The Incarnation of our Lord Jesus *has* taken place! And the supernatural is now *embedded* in this human universe!" His voice becomes somber and grave now, and slowly rises to a crescendo. "God our Father has placed his *shekinah*, his tabernacle, his dwelling place, among the sons and daughters of men all over this globe. We cannot sit down alone in the murky passivity of an ecclesiastical clam bed, and let the ocean waters of human evolution roll over us again and again!

"Some others will object: This *Policy* move implies a lack of analysis. It asks us to move into a vast uncharted area, and not to consider even the socio-political and psychological analyses of our contemporaries." Thule is now trying to win over the scholastic mentality and the formalism of the Traditionalist Cardinals.

"I answer firmly: Reality is never geometric and symmetrical, never clean-cut, clearly defined, tidy, harmonious sounding. Reality, as one philosopher remarked, is a great big, fuzzy, irregular, pulsating thing, full of booming and movement here and there and everywhere, lit by flashes of growth. I answer too: For hundreds of years, men in the West who were taught by us Churchmen have been busy trying to take reality apart, piece by piece, as if it were nothing more than a machine—a rationally planned, complex machine.

"What we need is a new *integration!* There is, indeed, such an integration already born. We have to go with it. It is of God, of spirit, of humanity."

After a pause, Thule turns to the last and final objection—the objection to the political activist role that the *Coalition Policy* implies or, rather, demands. His audience is ready for his analysis. They are enjoying his words, they like the strength of his personality. All seems clear-cut, sure, prescient, guidance-full. Thule is at his best. They know it. And so does he.

"Can we be indifferent to the brute fact that our Earth will not tolerate endless exponential growth in material consumption? Can we? As Christians can we hide our head in the sand of piety and incense, and say that this is not our concern? Life and death *are* our concern! *Waste* is our concern! I say: We cannot hide brute facts beneath spiritual protestations.

"Can we ignore the brute fact that our growth is limited to the tolerance ceiling of the ecosphere for heat-absorption? I say: We cannot, since we aid mightily in the spiraling of man's race to that ceiling.

"I say the Church lives, whether we like it or not, the life of our time. We have to groan and labor with all of creation, as Saint Paul says. We believe the life we lead here on earth is not our final experience. But, if we stand aside from the economic and political dilemma of our fellow-men, this may be our last political and economic experience."

Thule feels by the attention he is getting that the minds of the Electors have opened out to him, accepting his meanings. He decides to sum up and to open the gate for the rush.

"I have no illusions. Nor do you, I am sure. We are distrusted as Churchmen. We are in a dangerous era of transition, our present situation a razor's edge, and our future problematic—at best. We are blamed for a past we did not create. We only have the future to make.

"Our institutional Church is for many an abomination of Pharisees—you, I, our clergy, and all. For many others, it is a hotbed of entrenched aristocrats—business dynasties, industrial monopolies, banking families, investment clubs, financial cartels, real estate proprietors—our allies one and all! For many, this Church has been anathema during long centuries.

"For many others, the faithful, she has become like an old wife: They can hardly speak to her—except to grumble and complain that their dinner is cold

and dry. So, having fallen out of love with Church and civilization, they tend
to be destroyed mainly by self-disgust. And, in our Church's structure, there
is a withering and stifling of parish, of diocese, of convent, of episcopal
palace, of Papal authority."

He looks around slowly in the silence he has created; then, deliberately and
dignifiedly: "This day, Venerable Brothers, this day, the Holy Spirit can
renew our faith and our minds, so that we go forward and achieve what our
incarnated Lord Jesus began. Let us make our choice wisely, my Colleagues,
and bravely! God is with us! I thank you all!"

He bows to the President and without again looking at his audience, Thule
walks slowly to his place.

Witz, an old hand at public meetings, coughs long and loudly. It creates the
necessary diversion. And he cuts in immediately: "My Most Reverend Lord
Cardinal Angelico."

Angelico's rotund face is drawn and white. No longer smiling, nor even his
old bustling self, the Cardinal Archbishop, former Vatican aide, gives the
impression of deep concentration. He stands in front of his little writing
table, bows to the Cardinal President, looks over at the Electors opposite
him, then turns around so as to take in the rows of Electors and those seated
at the far end of the assembly. The sky outside is murky and clouded,
although some light falls on the ceiling and walls.

"My Eminent Lord Cardinals, it is not my intent to say yea or nay to the
forcefully expressed proposal of My Lord Cardinal Thule." Angelico's voice
falters; he seems to have lost the end of his thought or some phrase
memorized for the occasion. He is supposed to second Thule's proposal both
of *Coalition Policy* and of Yiu—this is the thought of all listening to him. Why
doesn't he? Or how is he going to get around to it now?

Marquez turns around to smile reassuringly at Lynch. Thule clears his
throat. He will not be at ease until that seconding speech is over and done
with. He begins a mental check of the votes.

Walker, as far as Azande can see, has his eyes closed and a funny
expression on his face like a man who is waiting for the dentist to get on with
it. Ni Kan is doodling a vertical row of Chinese characters. As Angelico stops,
Ni Kan's hand stops. Everybody is waiting.

"In agreeing to second the proposal, Venerable Brothers, I am mindful of
my duty as Elector and as Cardinal of his Holy Roman Catholic and
Apostolic Church. My Most Eminent Lord Thule has stated that a vote for
the Coalition is the only viable alternative in our dilemma."

Ni Kan is doodling again. The Camerlengo throws a look at Angelico, then looks away as if averting his eyes from a painful sight or the agony of another man whom he cannot or will not help. If only all Italians had a little rational logic, he thinks.

"Why is the Traditionalist position not also viable?" Angelico's rhetorical question has no sting of contempt in it. "Because, Brothers, it leaves us with no intitiative. In such a policy, we choose to dig our feet in hard at a point about 500 years ago. From that stance, we could try, but would only fail more and more dismally to reach the millions of this age and of the next 50 years, and the next 500 years. Indeed ...," his voice increases in vibrancy, "to choose a Traditionalist policy, and, accordingly a new Traditionalist Pope, would be to accept what is imposed on us, namely a state of siege."

Riccioni, hunched over, looking at his hands on his lap, raises his eyebrows slightly, but shows no other sign of emotion. Vasari wets his lips. He is folding and unfolding a sheet of paper. He fold it down to its smallest compass, then undoes all the folds and starts all over again, folding and folding and folding.

"But then, is the Conservative stand not viable? After all, we have a Conservative Church now, by and large, and Heaven knows there is change and some reaching out, no?" Angelico looks across at Massaccio and smiles a little as if to say: *Hear me out, Pietro. Hear me out completely, before you jump down my throat!* Masaccio has a deadpan expression.

"But no, it won't work. And do you know why? I'll tell you why. Because," Angelico answers his own question, "the heart of that position consists in allowing ourselves to be slowly but surely 'maneuvered' into change. Oh, of course with dignity. But certainly not of our own deliberate exclusive, responsible will. We would make change after change. Again, it would allow us no initiative—unless you think that cooperating with some *fait accompli* is initiative on our part.

"We agree today, let us say by way of example, that we must allow women priests, because it is imposed by circumstances. Theological circumstances? Hardly! Just social pressure closing in on us. And then, the day after tomorrow, we find that such a change implies something totally unacceptable.

"In other words, the Conservative and the Traditionalist positions have the same problem: paralysis and stagnation. It's just that the Conservative position gives the *illusion* of movement and progress, an illusion that disguises what is *really* destruction and regression. As events overtook us, we would be increasingly helpless to do anything about them, but could only suffer their consequences. We would, in a matter of short years, suffer a rain of blows that could break us to pieces—us and our Church.

"The Church today is in the middle of an active world, changing profoundly and swiftly—more profoundly and more completely perhaps than at any earlier time. And, at the same time, both the Traditionalist and the

Conservative positions are open to outside initiatives—but have none of their own. Both are merely and only reactions. Like hanging beads, they might tinkle a pleasant tune when pushed by the winds of events. But the sound of Salvation is not a tinkle tune, nor the Church of Salvation a row of helpless beads."

Angelico turns now from the Cardinals and faces the Presidents at the long table. All three are looking at him, waiting for his seconding proposal.

Down at the end of the assembly, Cardinals Bamleke and Garcia are whispering in conversation. Walker is stiff, motionless. His pained expression has somewhat eased as if the worst were here and the tension of anticipation over. But his eyes remain closed. From the gestures of Bamleke and Garcia, it is clear that one of them is thinking of intervening. Ni Kan starts a third column of doodles. Thule is sitting quite still, his lips moving silently in prayer. Domenico is sitting demurely, his arms folded, his eyes on Angelico's face. Domenico, the trusted realist!

"My Eminent and Venerable Cardinal Presidents," Angelico's voice has taken on a sudden high pitch.

"My Lord Thule has proposed that we proceed at once to the election both of the policy he has proposed and of My Lord Yiu as Supreme Pontiff—the candidate who, as My Lord Thule points out, is favored by two strong groups among us; a 'fusion candidate' if you will. Backed by those whom we all (and they themselves) call Progressivists—the completely open Church is their slogan. And backed as well by the democratic socialist minded group—those who say salvation is in the peoples of the earth, er, I should say, in the proletariat."

Lynch nods. The description seems accurate enough: and the Coalition is strong. Irresistible. Thule waits. The Camerlengo has a weary expression.

"My Lord President, it is an agreed-upon convention in Conclave that no Eminent Lord Cardinal will be acclaimed and thus elected unless he has been asked to give prior sign that he has no fundamental objection—indeed he may object right up to the moment prior to acclamation. I am well aware that, even over his objection, he can be nominated and elected. But he must be given the chance to register his reaction. Is this not so, My Lord President?" The question ends on an upbeat note. Angelico's mouth remains open, his eyes on the Cardinal President at the long table. The Cardinal looks right and left at his two colleagues, receiving their nodded agreement, then, in turn, nods in assent to Angelico's question. Neither Thule nor any of his supporters show any alarm. They like this step-by-step method of Angelico's. They take it as Angelico's way of making sure that all points of Conclave procedure are observed. In that way there can be no challenges later.

"Well, then," Angelico resumes, but the small diminutive figure of Yiu is already standing as Angelico's eyes seek him out.

"My Most Eminent and Venerable Lord Cardinal Presidents, my Beloved Brothers and Colleagues, I will wait until My Lord Cardinal Angelico has finished before assenting to be put in nomination." He sits down.

Angelico looks at Yiu, then slowly his eyes survey the rows of faces. Thule is leaning forward, his eyes wide and staring. Walker's eyes are closed still, the pained expression is back. Buff is gesturing to Lynch. And on the majority of faces Angelico reads a certain tension—some have a better-you-than-me expression, others a look of disbelief, and still others sheer puzzlement. Ni Kan has stopped doodling, pencil still in hand, his eyes inscrutable, examing Yiu's face. "My God, much ado about nothing," The Camerlengo mutters half out loud to himself, and studies his notes.

Angelico's face takes on a look of hard granite. "We must state categorically that both the Progressivist and the democratic socialist position are totally unacceptable!" The words come out like hammer blows literally flattening some Cardinals against the backs of their chairs, stunned but not doubting what they have heard. Those words resound with that old stridency that Vatican hands had known well enough during Angelico's tough years in authority there. How many in the Vatican and particularly in the Secretariat of State know that signal of his displeasure! Walker's eyes open wide and he stares at one or two Cardinals nearby, then up at Angelico. The silence is electric.

Angelico's pause is dramatic but short enough to preclude any letdown of attention from the Electors. "The Progressivist view puts us completely in the hands of volatile and non-ecclesiastical and non-Catholic and non-Christian forces. The democratic socialists would have us prostitute—" He stops a moment, then, "yes, prostitute ourselves, our tradition, our grace, our hopes to the one force in our present world that surely carries the mark of Satan's cloven hoof." He catches a glimpse of Lynch and Thule, livid and pale and, by turns, signaling to each other.

"Oh, of course! Of course! Cardinal Thule bids us trust. And Cardinal Lynch bids us suffer. And Cardinal Buff bids us be big-minded."

Now Angelico's sarcasm is heavy and pointed. He is looking straight at Thule, unblinking, no soft lines around the eyes, his mouth curling around each syllable.

"Whatever happens, whatever aberration in doctrine, whatever departure from tradition takes place, Cardinal Thule asserts he can see beyond it. He sees beyond the welter of events. And he tells us: All is well. But His Eminence can't go on forever and ever understanding and perceiving and seeing through. He says he and his friends have analyzed the situation, and he knows what's going on, and we need not worry about what is on the other side of the opaque position that he would have the Church take up.

"But, I say," he looks away from Thule now and at Yiu, "I say: If you can penetrate the opaqueness of that position; if you know what's on the other side; if you know what will happen when we march to the sound of the Cardinal's drum, then tell us! Yet when we ask him, what will happen to dogma, he doesn't know—except that it will be all right, he assures us. What will happen to devotion to the Virgin? He doesn't know—except that it will be all right, he assures us. What will happen to Papal Infallibility? He doesn't know—except that it will be all right, he assures us." Angelico looks around. His anger and disgust are clear.

"He doesn't know! My Eminent Brother from the East! He does *not* know! And do you know why? Because if you go on seeing through everything, penetrating everything, seeing beyond everything. If the social problem is a window you see through. And the political problem is a window you see through. And the question of Anglican orders is a window you see through. And Papal Infallibility is a window you see through. And atheistic Marxism is a window you see through. And human sexuality and religious vows and private property and the historicity of the Gospels, and the divinity of Jesus and the resurrection of Jesus and the existence of an afterlife and the life of the fetus and war and peace and creation and God's very existence—if all are windows you can see through, so that there is not really anything that stops your sight; if there is no place where you take up a position, *do you know what you end up seeing?* Do you *know?*" Angelico glances around, his voice held at that high pitch of a combative and contemptuous question.

"Nothing! Nothing! You see *Nothing!* You've *never* seen anything. And you're going to see nothing *ever.* You'll see nothing at all. And everything worth seeing, and worth stopping at, you've seen through, penetrated, understood—with His Eminence—and passed on to the next transparent, volatile, insubstantial window, and so on and so on and so on ... to infinity. And this, my Venerable Brethren, this is not the stuff of which faith and true belief is made." Angelico's voice is the only sound. When he pauses, the silence is immense.

There is a sense of some sickening, some deep revulsion in Thule and Buff. Lynch has his head on his hands sobbing quietly. Walker's eyes are open, filled with that old gleam he used to have about fourteen years ago when he came to Rome for the Second Vatican Council, and those around him said to each other, "that one is intelligent! He will go far in the Eternal City!"

When Angelico takes up again, his voice is deep and calm and slow. He moves his head and eyes and body from side to side, in order to take everybody into his flow of thought. "The fact is, Eminent Brothers, the Progressivists and the Democratic Socialists would have all our theology turned into a science of social welfare. They would turn our moral theology into a political restructuring of human society. They would turn our traditional piety and devotion into a science of life defined and studied according to a sexuality, an anthropology, and a psychology that are not of God—and which are bankrupt, anyway, in our world. No! I say again: No! They will not do!

"And they will not do, my Eminent Brothers—apart from their inherent surrender of all our values—because, like Traditionalists and Conservatives, these Democratic Socialists would leave the initiative to non-Christians. They place us at the disposal of our enemies." He stops a moment, then repeats: "Our *enemies!* At the disposal of our enemies." As he repeats and dins home the thought, he turns to face every part of the assembly. "With no initiative of our own. No initiative, but imitation of our enemies. Our enemies." Finally, as he ends, he has turned around and is looking at Franzus.

"So," Angelico turns again quickly, as though collecting himself, and addresses the long table, "so, My Lord Cardinal Presidents, there will be no seconding of My Lord Thule's policy proposal. Nor will there be any nomination of My Lord Yiu . . ." he breaks off and looks down at the Asiatic. Yiu shows a mouthful of teeth, and blinks behind his glasses. Otherwise he does not stir. "But there will be one question. There is one question we must answer. All hinges on that question and on the answer to it." He bites his lip while thinking. Those who have known Angelico in the past recognize that habit. It usually precedes some deeply felt expression of his ideas.

"Having eliminated the Traditionalist, the Conservative, and the Democratic Socialist stances as being no viable alternatives, as being merely capitulations—means of saying formally: 'Let's go along with events, and let events decide our fate'—permit me to ask you this question. You answer it yourselves, my Eminent Cardinals! It is this: have we any further alternative? *Is* there one? Or have we run out of solutions? And are we boxed into a *cul-de-sac?* Because if there is no other alternative, let us prepare for slow and sure disintegration." Angelico pauses before bowing to the Cardinal Presidents as a signal he has finished, then adds most sincerely: "For any hurt, for any offense—unintentional I assure you—in my words or gestures, I ask Your Eminences' forgiveness." With that, Angelico makes his way to his place. He is perspiring.

During the last few minutes of Angelico's speech, Thule and Buff have been communicating by notes. Clearly they cannot let their chance go without a fight. Thule's proposals must be seconded. And, clearly, Yiu is their man. They cannot switch candidates in mid-Session.

Buff catches the eye of the President, and he rises to repair the damage done by Angelico. The Anglo-Saxon now resorts to a recognized Conclave maneuver: A renomination and seconding of their Policy and candidate.

Buff, at this moment, is a spare and rumpled patrician taken aback by the rough-and-tumble of Conclave dispute. "In spite of what seems a most unintelligible change of heart on the part of His Eminence Angelico," Buff gives Angelico an icy glare, "I wish, Most Eminent President and Most Beloved and Esteemed Colleagues, to take refuge beneath the ancient and established custom of renomination. Not only that, I wish also to point out that, all and any practice to the contrary, there is nothing in the Constitution of the Conclave that forbids us to nominate, second and even elect an unwilling candidate." He turns around and gazes full-eyed at Yiu. "Unwilling candidates have often made the best of Popes in the past!"

"*Bravo!* Buff! *Bravo!* Yiu! Yiu! *Bravo!*" The cries echo and echo around. Buff waits until they die down, trying to estimate how much strength they represent. "I therefore propose the *Coalition Policy* for adoption by the Conclave; and I propose the name of my good and Eminent Lord Cardinal Yiu, to be put in ballot as Pope." Again, there are cries of approval and a few isolated hand-claps. Buff sits down. He is not sure. Perhaps Angelico has not cut into their chances.

Lowe quickly obtains permission to speak. "In the name of many Cardinals of Europe and abroad, I wish Most Eminent Cardinal President to second the proposal of our Most Eminent Cardinal Buff: for the *Coalition Policy* and for the nomination of our Most Eminent Lord Cardinal Yiu." There is silence. Most of the Electors cannot forget that, just the previous evening, Lowe's name had been put in nomination. Some of them still regard Lowe as most *papabile.*

Domenico seizes the moment of indecision, before any enthusiasm can start in reaction to the new nomination and seconding, or to Lowe personally and as a *papabile.* Domenico catches the eye of the President. He turns then to face Marquez. "The Cardinal says that this is not a Church designed for maintaining the bourgeois *status quo.* And, as we all know, he organizes people's Masses in his diocese that conclude, not with the *Salve Regina,* not with any prayer, in fact, but with a song to human rights. And all this is fine— as long as his freedom lasts. But I must assume that with all his awareness of what is happening in the world, His Eminence has no illusions that a Marxist regime is going to allow him his freedom! The type of situation in Russia, in any of the satellite countries—does His Eminence really want that same situation in Latin America? Or the situation in Maoist China? Or the situation in Castro's Cuba?

"Remember that it is not only the family and culture that is being stamped out there in these places. It is the human mind itself. Does he really want that situation throughout the length and the breadth of Latin America? Surely his own capital is bad. But does he want it to resemble Peking—a murdered city, a disfigured cadaver of what was one of the most beautiful cities in the Orient? Does he really want that? Or another Pnom-Penh?"

Domenico turns to other speakers. "I respect, of course, His Eminence Cardinal Lowe, as do you all. But we all know also that the Cardinal's tongue is less wise than his mind. And his seconding of this nomination is one more example of his indiscretion in speaking out of turn. . . ." Cries of "Shame! Retract! Stand down! *Bravo!* Nonsense!" come at Domenico from many sides. Thule and the others are impatient for the vote. But Domenico does not yield. .

"After all, Cardinal Lowe actually said in public that he would like to propose a toast to the profoundly religious morality of King Henry of England and the holy self-sacrifice with which he sought the message of the Gospel! King Henry! And this about a man who brazenly declared that all brothels, all the rapes, murders, thefts, and adulteries of mankind have wrought less abomination than the Popish Mass! How could you, Eminence, sincerely propose a toast to a sacriligeous blasphemer of that kind? Yet the Cardinal did that—and much more. I think mainly because he is afflicted with ecumenomania. Non-Catholics must be pleased at any cost! Of course, if your intention is to curry favor with the Lutherans . . ." he looks at Lowe.

Lowe's well-known stolidity serves him in good stead now. He does not budge or speak. The blood has mounted to his face. But he knows better than to take on Domenico. For, if Domenico is scattering all these stinging pebbles of criticism, he surmises, they must be the harbingers of some mighty sledgehammer blows he is planning. This has always been Domenico's tactic.

But his tactic now is more subtle. Domenico bows to the President and sits down. Thule looks a little surprised. He is about to ask permission to speak when, again unexpectedly, the reedlike tones of Cardinal Tsa-Toke are heard.

He is brief, but his words are powerful in their very matter-of-factness. "My Brothers, before you proceed, take my testimony. It is simple. Unadorned. For what it is. Marxism has two faces. One it wears before it gets power. The other, after it gets power. We know. In my country. In my Asia. Our country is in the grip of terror. One vast concentration camp. One ant hill. Do you know what it is to live with daily terror in your street, at your corner, in your bedroom, in the school, in the factory, in the Church—when a Church is open? *You* don't. *We* do. Don't have anything to do with it.

"Please! We are full of hunger and slavery. Re-education courses. Prisons. Slave gangs. Torture. Executions. Total misery is our lot. Our children are reared to distrust us. To hate us. To report on us. In neighboring countries also there is hell. Over 2.5 million have been put to death. The cities emptied. The villages devastated. No food. Only work. Work for all. Young girls. Old women. Aged men. Little children of six and seven. Churches, pagodas, schools, libraries, ancient temples, all are gone. Think well before you accept what some foolish ones are calling a working relationship with that. If you have to live under Marxism, pray your faith can outlive it. Thank you."

There is a reverential silence after this. Tsa-Toke appears to be a living symbol of suffering, of silent pain. Thule does not know how to deal with such a man. As he hesitates before rising to propose that the assembly proceed to voting, still another voice breaks in.

It is Yiu. "My refusal to be put in nomination, Eminent Brothers, I know, would not invalidate the nomination. So you may go ahead as you will. I have, however, one quick question for My Eminent Lord Thule and the members of his Coalition group." Yiu appears quite animated and his voice is at a high pitch.

"Do I correctly understand the Eminent Cardinal's mind and that of his Colleagues in the Coalition that, while Marxism as an ideology is opposed irreducibly to Christianity, a working arrangement can be established, a sort of hands-off-each-other collaboration, all and only for changing the social regimen and the political structure of nations?"

Thule looks quickly to Buff and Franzus. Franzus rises: "That, Eminence, is our understanding, always remembering that, in such a process, Marxism itself will necessarily undergo some changes, of course!"

"One other question." Yiu is being brief and to the point. "Has any arrangement been already worked out?" A silence follows this question. Most of the Electors are stumped by the question. Yiu remains standing and looking at Franzus.

Buff rises hastily. "I do not see what sense the Eminent Cardinal's question can make, since the *Coalition Policy* is not yet official—we hope it will be— how could any arrangement have been made?"

"Very well," Yiu answers tranquilly. "I will put my question in another way, to His Eminence Cardinal Franzus." He turns again to face the Cardinal. "Your Eminence, before you left your home town to come here, did you hold conversations with members of the Government?"

"Any contact with the Government is performed through the relevant office of my chancery. I can say positively that I had no conversation with any Government official or officials on the eve of my departure for the Conclave."

"Let me put it this way, Eminence." Yiu's tone belies his tenacity. "Did you have conversations with anyone who spoke for the Government or who speaks with the Government?"

"I am not quite sure what you mean, Eminence." Franzus answers with a show of puzzlement. "Many who pass through my doors at home talk, I am sure, with members of the Government. Many of them, for all I can know, are members of the Government. I don't quite know what to answer you."

"But, specifically, do you know of anyone with whom you spoke about Conclave matters and who speaks with Government officials?"

"As I said, Eminence, there are many. . . ."

"No, no, Eminence. I am referring to one conversation in particular. Let me be more specific. Do you know a man named Roan Kale?" Franzus' face flushes. He answers stonily.

"I think that among my acquaintances there must be a man by that name. Roan and Kale are both very common names, like Rodriguez in Spain and Smith in England, you know what I mean." A pause, while he mutters "Roan Kale, Roan Kale . . . Roan Kale. . . ."

"Did Your Eminence not have a conversation with a Roan Kale just one day before leaving for Rome?" Franzus knits his eyebrows and gazes at the ceiling. He shifts from one foot to the other. Yiu stares at him steadily. Finally Franzus lowers his eyes, looks at him, then averts his eyes.

"Yes, now—vaguely, you understand, I remember, yes, I did have a conversation with a Roan Kale. Yes, I did, Eminence."

"Did the question of the Conclave come up?"

"Oh, I'm sure my forthcoming trip came up as an item of conversation. In fact, all our layfolk who visited me in those days preceding my departure came, as you will understand, to wish me well and bring little gifts. It's our national custom, you know, Eminence."

"But was specific mention of the Conclave made?"

"Other than my trip to Rome for the Conclave, you mean, Eminence? Oh, I suppose that like all the others, he was interested in the affairs of the Pope and of the Church. Yes, I suppose it did come up."

"I mean, in particular, Eminence, specifically . . . " Yiu keeps on using that word, and it strikes the listening Electors both as strange and as significant, "had Roan Kale anything to state about the attitude of the Government?"

"I really cannot recall exactly all the details. . . ."

"Eminence, it was two and a half days ago. . . ."

"Roan Kale could not really talk about our Government's attitude since he is not, as far as I remember, a member of the Government at all. No, as a matter of fact, he is in the travel business, as far as I can recall. . . ."

"I did not say 'your Government,' Eminence," is Yiu's reply, and he pauses.

"Well, Eminence, what other governm . . . " Franzus breaks off and glances quickly around at Thule and Buff, then back to Yiu. Thule nods and gets to his feet.

"Eminent Lord Cardinal President, I really cannot see where this line of discussion—interrogation would be an apter term—leads us. Besides the time is. . . ."

"If His Eminence will permit," it is Domenico, "all of us would like to know what especially My Lord Cardinal Yiu wishes to know. I think his Eminence Franzus should answer My Lord Yiu."

For three or four seconds, Thule stares at Domenico full in the eyes, measuring his strength of will and trying to fathom what Domenico knows, how far he will go. Then his gaze wavers, and he sits down again.

All look at Yiu and then at Franzus.

"What I wish to know, Eminence, is precisely this," Yiu continues. "In Your Eminence's conversation with Roan Kale, was there a discussion of the attitude of the Soviet Government to the two or three possible outcomes of the Conclave? And, more specifically, did Roan Kale transmit to Your Eminence any notice of what action the Government of the Soviet Union might undertake depending on the outcome of the Conclave?" As Franzus' eyebrows knit further and further in bleak knots, Yiu goes on. "More specifically still, was it mentioned between you—from him to you, that is to say—that if a Pope emerged from this Conclave who declared open season on collaboration with Communist parties and Marxist colleagues in Europe and Latin America—particularly in Latin America—the Soviet Government would undertake certain actions?"

Now all eyes are on Franzus. His face is as stone, so lacking is it at this moment in any expression. After a short nervous wait: "How could His Eminence think that Roan Kale could speak on behalf of the Soviet Government?" The maneuver was a mistake on Franzus' part. He should have guessed.

"Because," Yiu replies with the characteristic nasal sound to his words, but evenly and without changing the tranquil look on his face, "because Roan Kale is an employee of Russian State Security, of the KGB, in fact."

By this time, a ripple of consternation is running through the Electors. They sense they have, until this moment, been left out of some essential part of the Conclave drama, and now all are being drawn into it. All eyes are on Franzus again. Thule signals to the Presidents, but they have already given the Camerlengo the nod.

The Camerlengo is in a distraught condition of mind, if one reads the expression on his face. He rises and speaks in his usual laconic accent; but no one listening to him misses the tone of anxiety and worry in his voice. As Camerlengo he has lost control of his first—probably his last—Conclave.

"Personally, His Eminence Franzus has always given the Secretariat—as he should—an account of all his discussions with officials. I think this entire matter is a red herring. We should call cloture on it all and proceed with our main business." As he finishes, his eyes are full of appeal to the Presidents. He even casts a mournful look of appeal over at Domenico and Angelico. He glares at Yiu and Ni Kan as if they and all Asiatics were the cause of all his trouble, but remains standing as if expecting a challenge.

He is clearly frightened by something; and each Elector is vividly conscious of his fright. They have never seen the Camerlengo in this condition. He actually knows that the conversation Yiu is trying to pin down did take place. But he wishes no news of it or of its contents to be broadcast, not merely because the details would be disturbing to many Electors on whose votes he had counted for the now defunct *General Policy*, but also because any information about that conversation will inevitably entail notice of other *Secret Reports*. Neither the Camerlengo nor Thule want those *Secret Reports* to become official documents of the Conclave. Strange bedfellows.

"Very well!" It is Domenico who breaks in. "The Camerlengo makes a lot of sense, Eminences! Why waste our time on one small issue—or one small part of the main issue?" The Camerlengo's face softens in genuine gratitude and relief. Franzus relaxes visibly. Thule and Buff are more at ease.

"In fact," Domenico continues in a loud voice, "I think we should get on to the big issue." He looks around, waiting to throw the bombshell he holds in his hand until some of the previous excitement has died down, and the Electors have stopped whispering among themselves. Domenico has calculated that he has just one chance of stopping the *Coalition* bloc. He must take that chance now. There is finally silence.

"I propose," Domenico raises his voice and looks around, repeating his words, "I propose that the Camerlengo help solve our difficulties." He looks at the Camerlengo. "By immediately putting into the hands of the Electors— all the Electors—copies of the *Secret Reports* which his Office has received during the past fourteen months."

For one moment, there is that short silence of incomprehension. Nobody expected Domenico to say what he has just said. The Camerlengo is stunned, incredulous. The generality know nothing of the *Secret Reports*. And for some seconds they sit there, every mind trying to understand what has just been said, or to refashion it into what each one expected him to say.

And then pandemonium breaks loose. They suddenly realize: "*Secret Reports*! We never saw any *Secret Reports*! . . . What *Secret Reports*?" The conventional cement of this Conclave Session has been liquified and melted. There are now 116 Cardinals thrown completely out of kilter. Several of them leave their places. Thule and Buff move over to Franzus. The Camerlengo has dashed up to the long table to talk with the Presidents. Marquez and Lynch have gathered a number of Latin Americans around them. Four Americans are speaking with Terebelski and Karewsky. Many Cardinals are still sitting on their thrones looking on the scene and talking to their neighbors. Domenico has sat down. Angelico is over with him talking volubly. Ni Kan is doodling on the pad in front of him. Yiu is talking at Ni Kan who does not look at him. Walker is sitting bolt upright on his throne, his arms folded as usual. He looks up at the President's table, over to the

Thule-Buff-Franzus group, then over to Yiu and Ni Kan, then back to the long table. He seems to be watching and taking mental notes. His study is interrupted by Riccioni and Vasari who come over to him in animated conversation. Only the blacks and Indians do not move from their places and do not engage in conversation. They look around, occasionally smiling at each other, and wait.

Finally, the Cardinal President rings his silver bell, once, twice, three times, then a fourth time more insistently and loudly. Slowly disentangling themselves from knots and groups of their colleagues, the Cardinals regain their seats. Calm returns. The Cardinal President looks around, then at the Camerlengo directly. The Camerlengo stands up. His tone is dry, succinct, cold, furious.

"Eminences, after consultations with our Cardinal Presidents, it seems advisable to suspend this Session's proceedings. Because of possible misrepresentations . . . " he gives Domenico a swift cutting glance, "I think that copies of the so-called *Secret Reports* should be placed in the hands of you all. I say 'so-called' *Secret Reports,* because in reality they are merely confidential memoranda drawn up by various people within and without the Church. If every confidential memo and letter is secret, then I suppose you can call these *Reports* secret. I have to tell you, however, that they have hitherto remained confidential—or, if you will—if some will—'secret'—because they had nothing directly to do with the originally agreed-upon *General Policy* of the Conclave. And, as you know, we have enough to do here in Conclave without overloading the agenda."

"But now, they have very much to do with our business and our Conclave issues." It is Domenico in a manner as calm and cold and succinct as the Camerlengo's own. The latter wilts. The strain on him is more than he can take.

"Of course, Eminence! Of course!" Then he takes his seat.

But some of the others do not want to give up as easily as the Camerlengo—they have none of his realism. And they do not know Domenico as well as the Camerlengo knows this stubborn man. Delacoste is the one who tries, out of loyalty to the Camerlengo, and in defense of the position of the Left, to head off the Domenico proposal.

"Most Reverend Eminences, let me appeal to you for one second of your time. I and my colleagues feel that no good use will be made of this sensitive material by the majority of us Electors who are not immersed in such matters of statecraft and the politics of the international world. After all, most of us are simple pastors of souls, you know."

But Domenico will not let the moment pass, as the Camerlengo knows he will not. "Tell me, My Lord Cardinal," he says easily, "do you agree with Bishop Henri Donze of Lourdes, that the apparitions of the Immaculate

Virgin at the shrine took place—I quote the Bishop—in order to show forth Lourdes as a sign of service of the Faith for a civilization of love? Is that the meaning of Lourdes?"

The question is unexpected and seems to some to be crazily unrelated to this crisis; but Delacoste understands it fully. Donze's speech, in which he had used this sort of language, had caused tremendous furore. Vatican officials and Pope Paul 6 had labeled his mode of speech "double-speak" and "crassly vague about the specially religious import of the Virgin's Shrine," and so on. Delacoste realizes all that; and he also realizes that Domenico has set a trap for him. Domenico must know the contents of at least one of the *Secret Reports*. For that type of "double-speak" is part of one recommendation, Delacoste knows, in one of the *Reports*, which treats of relations with Protestants who reject the Catholic attitude to the Virgin Mary.

Out of the corner of his eye, Delacoste sees Thule rising, and he is alarmed: Thule may provoke an explosion. But Domenico will not tolerate any interference or allow the new initiative to be taken out of his own hands.

"My Lord Thule," Domenico says, rounding on Thule and speaking in an excessively loud, crackling voice, "you may have spoken to thousands round the world . . ." he pauses for the little sound of laughter among the Cardinals, "as you will continue to do around the world. But that does not immediately qualify you to speak on Lourdes or to intervene at this moment between me and my Eminent Brother." Thule does not know how to take this. He half smiles, looks at the President, then decides to sit down again.

Delacoste meanwhile, has made up his mind. He looks at Domenico for one long moment, then smiles and says indulgently: "I will rely on the teaching authority of the Church to inform me as to the meaning of Lourdes. Now what My Lord Donze has said, is, as Your Eminence knows, quite another matter."

Domenico smiles back, the gentle smile of the fencer who knows that the challenge of his blade has been met with retreat.

At this stage Witz rings his silver bell. It is ten minutes to six. Delacoste looks at the President's table, then at Domenico, and sits down. Witz hastens to terminate this Second Session.

"With everybody's consent, will the Most Reverend Cardinal Electors please disperse. It will take about an hour for the copying service to supply all with the needed documentation." He pauses to read a handwritten note just handed to him. Then:

"I have been asked by the Most Reverend Camerlengo to announce that, in addition to the *Reports* already mentioned, he has the following at your disposal—on an individual basis, of course. The written records, such as they are, from the Secret Archives of all past Conclaves—as you know, such records are not complete. But such as they are.

"Secondly, the dossier of correspondence between the Holy See, on the one hand, and the U.S.S.R. and its satellite countries on the other hand, between the years 1950–1976. Lastly, a summary of the Holy See's intelligence activities and its results in Eastern Europe and the Far East between the years 1955–1975.

"Supper will be one half-hour later than usual. We will all convene tomorrow after the Mass of the Holy Spirit at 10 A.M. This Second Session is now at an end." He rises, as do the two co-Presidents.

The moment Witz gives the signal, the Cardinals rise to go. There is no sudden outburst of conversation. The majority are a little dazed by what has happened. There is no consternation except on the Camerlengo's face. Thule has a set and firm look. Franzus is obviously frightened and goes over to Buff who looks drained. Angelico is beetroot-red. Domenico looks at no one. His expression is unreadable.

Most of the Cardinals leave the Assembly Hall singly. A few groups of twos and threes form outside, but within minutes they have gone. The young Cardinal with the stutter is one of the first out, boards the bus, and is soon back in his room. He sits down at his desk, his finger on his pectoral cross and on that ruby.

Azande remains seated for quite a while, then stands up slowly and walks outside. He looks around, catches the young Monsignore's eye, smiles, murmurs "Experience! Monsignore! Experience!" and then is on his way.

The Monsignore puts his head inside the doors, gazes at the empty rows of seats. Then he closes the doors and hurries off. Within twenty minutes all the Cardinals are back in the *Domus Mariae.*

NIGHT: 6:00 P.M.–1:00 A.M.

Through the young Monsignore and his aides, the Camerlengo sets in motion the process of polycoping the *Reports.* At the request of Eakins and the Americans, he also shows them the dossier of the 1950–1976 correspondence between the Holy See and the U.S.S.R. Then the Camerlengo sits down for a moment at his desk to telephone Masaccio. As his hand reaches out for the telephone, Edouardo Ruzzo, chief of security, knocks and steps in without waiting for admission. This is a prearranged thing between the Camerlengo and himself in any time of critical decision.

"What is it, Ruzzo?"

"A totally new twist to our problem, Eminence." The Camerlengo's expression is one of alarm. He takes his hand from the telephone and stands up, with a question in his eye. Ruzzo goes on.

"It would seem that, as we determined, there is one who is a recorder-sender...."

"That we knew. And...?"

"It now seems that we have another—a sender who is not a receiver or a recorder."

The Camerlengo sits down heavily. "You're sure?"

"Sure. Yes."

"Have either been located yet?"

"No. But with any luck that ought not be long in coming."

"How long? We've very little time. And we have a crisis. A real crisis. Outside intervention is the last thing we want now."

"By midnight. By the way, Eminence, can you give us any shortcuts—I mean, can you indicate any quarter that would be more likely than others?" Ruzzo looks at the Cardinal with those soulful, innocent eyes of his. The Camerlengo stares at him blankly, then turns his head to look at two lists of names hanging on the side wall of his office. His eyes run quickly from name to name. He stops, scribbles one name on a scratch pad, then returns to the lists. Again, he stops. notes down another name, finishes reading off the lists. He tears off the sheet containing the two names and hands it to Ruzzo.

"That's the best I can do Ruzzo. The first is highly probable. The second is only a hunch."

As Ruzzo reaches for the sheet, he reads both names upside down and nods with a quiet smile. He gives an innocent look at the Cardinal. "The old and the young." Then briskly, "Very Good, Eminence!"

On his way out, Ruzzo stands aside for Thule who is about to knock on the door. The Camerlengo sees him framed in the doorway and bids him come in.

"I know I should be waiting in my room for those *Reports*," Thule says half-apologetically, "but something came up."

"It's all right. It's all right. Come in and sit down. Are all the Cardinals back in their rooms?"

"Mostly, as far as I can see. Waiting for the copies. Some are paying little short visits. I know there is a large contingent over in Lynch's place—Marquez, Lombardi, Perez, Manuel, and others."

"Buff and Franzus, I suppose?"

"Yes. And one or two more. I've just come from there."

Immediately after the end of the Second Session, Thule had gone to Buff's room with Franzus and Lombardi and the young Cardinal with the stutter. The only subject discussed was Angelico. Angelico was the danger. Were the afternoon's events and Domenico's interventions merely the opening gambit in an Angelico nomination move? Thule has come over, really, to consult the Camerlengo about it all.

"I frankly do not think so," the Camerlengo answers Thule. "There's no indication that this is the plan. Frankly, I do not know on earth or in Heaven what Domenico is after, or Angelico, for that matter. But I'm almost certain it's not an Angelico nomination."

As if to deepen their puzzlement further, the young Monsignore comes in at this point with a note from Domenico. Could he please have from the Camerlengo the Secret Archives records of past Conclaves? The Camerlengo reads the note to Thule and looks questioningly at him, but he is also in the dark; he then signs the note and indicates seven large manila envelopes lying on a side table. The Monsignore takes them and departs for Domenico's apartment. The Camerlengo and Thule look at each other silently for a moment, then they begin to laugh helplessly.

The Camerlengo picks up their earlier thought. "No, No. I really don't think there is a move toward Angelico's nomination, or Domenico's own nomination. I simply don't know. Any more than I understand why Domenico wants those records now. I don't know what's going on. I don't know what's going to happen."

"Well, from what you know of those *Reports*," Thule asks tentatively, "what damage will be done or what changes of mood and persuasion will be effected, when they become general Conclave property?"

"Enormous changes," his companion answers glumly. "As to damage. Well, for example, I think the pan-European candidacy is a dead duck—wait till they've read the financial report alone, not to speak of the other ones. I think your Third World proposal is as dead as a doornail—wait till you read the *U.S.S.R. Report*. And it is now a toss-up between a Conservative and a Traditionalist . . ." he bares his teeth in a sharp intake of breath, "with even odds either way." He looks away with an annoyed air. "Oh yes, damage there is."

Thule realizes that there is nothing more to be learned here now. He must wait until the Camerlengo has regained his peace of mind.

"Call me later on this evening," the Camerlengo says wearily. "And have a good read!"

Thule leaves the Camerlengo in the inner office and goes out. He finds the Monsignore chatting to the young Cardinal with the stutter.

"Well! Surprise! I thought you were going to wait for me over at Buff's!"

"Oh! Just a small change, Eminence," the young Cardinal smiles at him quietly. "I want to see the Camerlengo on a personal matter."

Inside, the Camerlengo hears the voices and calls out. The Young Cardinal appears at his door.

"May I come in, Eminence? For a moment?"

"Of course! Of course!" His mouth tightens.

"Eminence, may I have the *Intelligence Records* for 1955–1975 for an hour or so? I shall have them back by 9 o'clock."

Without an instant's hesitation, the Cammerlengo prevaricates. "It is already out, little Brother. But, be sure, you will have it the moment it is returned to this office."

"Perhaps, I could share them with whoever. . . ."

"Pardon, Eminence. You know our rule. We do not give out the names of those who have such sensitive documents in their possession."

"Oh yes. Of course. Pardon the lapse. Tell me, Eminence, can I help you in any way? You must have a lot of details to attend to."

The older man rises, smiling now. He is tired. Perhaps they can meet later or early tomorrow morning? He accompanies the young Cardinal to the outer door, shows him out, then turns and beckons to the young Monsignore. Inside, at his desk, he takes out three heavy files and hands them to his assistant.

"Take these over to Braun. Tell him to keep them under wraps for the next twelve hours, and not to show them to anyone. I will send for them."

As the Monsignore disappears with the files, the Camerlengo looks up and down the corridor. At one end he can see Edouardo Ruzzo standing with an aide. Both men are perfectly still and silent. The Camerlengo returns to his desk. Three quarters of an hour to supper. The copies should be ready in about fifteen minutes. The Monsignore will be back with his helpers shortly. He looks at the telephone for a moment, remembers the call to Masaccio that was interrupted by Ruzzo, and decides to delay it again. He starts to make notes. He expects to be inundated with vistors after supper—better now to get all essential work done.

Shortly after 6 o'clock, when Domenico reaches his apartment, Angelico joins him. As they start chatting, Canaletto knocks at the door and puts his head in. His face falls when he sees Angelico.

"Oh, pardon, Father! I will come back later."

"No. No," Domenico rejoins. "What is it?"

"A few of us would like to have a word with you, Father. . . ."

"I suggest you all wait until you get your reading done," Domenico says, not unpleasantly. "And, by the way, Canaletto—you won't mind my saying this, Angelico—neither I nor Angelico is a potential candidate! Carry the good word back! You know what I mean." Canaletto turns red, gives Angelico a glance, smiles nervously at Domenico and withdraws.

Angelico gives Domenico some stray bits of news. Apparently the British Commonwealth Cardinals are to get together with the Americans at about 9:15 P.M. The Asians are all gathering in Kinigoshi's room at about the same time. The Poles, Germans, Africans, French, and Spanish are all to caucus separately. One group of Italians is to meet in Riccioni's apartment, another in Masaccio's, a third in Canaletto's. Angelico would like to see Domenico and Azande after supper. But Domenico doesn't want this—it might give the wrong impression.

"For the last time, Eminence," Domenico says seriously to Angelico, "would you like to run for nomination?" Angelico's answer is emphatically negative.

They then talk for a while. His plan, Domenico explains, is to let things develop now. About 11 o'clock, the first news might be coming in about the reactions of the Electors to the *Reports.*

"Do you think much will have changed?" Angelico's question.

"Quite a lot. For one thing, it will be do-or-die, now-or-never for at least five of our beloved Colleagues."

"Franzus? Thule? Lynch?" Angelico looks at him.

"At least those. But also, I feel, for Masaccio and Ferro. I remember their names are on the readers' list of these *Reports.* So they knew about them. And now all the Electors will realize this."

"And the pan-European idea?"

"As far as Lohngren goes, it's dead. His name is also there as one of the readers."

"Has the Thule-Franzus thing any future now?"

"Quite! Of course! Still quite possible! We have to face that tomorrow."

As Angelico rises, Domenico hands him an envelope. "As you pass by the Camerlengo's place, hand in this note to the Monsignore. I need some documentation." When he is alone again, Domenico is able to work without interruption for only a few minutes before his phone rings. It is the young Cardinal. Would His Eminence by any chance have the Intelligence dossier?

"No, as a matter of fact, I haven't," Domenico answers. "Sorry." When the Cardinal rings off, Domenico calls the Camerlengo.

"Pieter," he says familiarly to the Camerlengo, "a young friend of yours was just looking for the Intelligence dossier."

"*Gott!*" the Cardinal Camerlengo swears. Then: "Don't worry."

"I am not worrying for my own sake, Pieter. . . ."

"Ruzzo is attending to that matter. It will be all right."

"I hope so," is Domenico's thought as he hangs up.

At about 7:15 P.M., the perspiring Monsignore enters on his 'delivery round' with copies of the reports for Domenico. The Monsignore places the copies on Domenico's desk. Then: "Eminence, may I ask a favor?" Without waiting for a reply, he goes on: "Tomorrow, when they announce the Pope-elect's name to the crowds on the Piazza, may I stand on the balcony?" Domenico stares at him, totally caught off his guard. Then, catching the gleam of deviltry in the Monsignore's eye, he bursts out laughing. "Out!" he says with mock imperiousness. "You shall be reported to Ruzzo!"

Domenico takes a good fifteen minutes to leaf through the *Reports* and get their general gist before the Supper bell.

There are only a few Cardinals present in the Dining Room. Eakins and Delacoste are sitting beside each other. Nei Hao is off in one corner by himself, as is Walker, in another corner. Yiu and Kotoko are together. At the end of one of the tables Domenico sees the young Cardinal with the stutter. He is lost in thought, his left hand, in that idle habitual gesture, fingering his pectoral cross.

Domenico sits down within voice-distance of Walker and starts eating. The silence between him and Walker is broken only once or twice.

"May we count on you to keep those jaws open, Eminence!" Domenico asks smilingly.

Walker nods, displaying his jowls. "By the way, the Camerlengo will not be in for supper. He is closeted with Ferro, Masaccio, and Calder." Domenico replies, "A panic session no doubt. Their panic. Not ours."

Halfway through the meal, about sixteen Electors come in, mostly Latin Americans, all with a very subdued look about them.

As Walker leaves, he passes by Domenico's chair and stops. "Can we presume that tomorrow there will be unanimity, Father?" he asks quietly.

"Tomorrow, let us all make it good, Henry! Let's make it a good Session. They won't forgive you for a long time—nor me, for that matter. But let's make it good, very, very good!"

Walker's smile is his only reply.

The gross effect of the reading of the *Reports* by the Electors is, strangely enough, not one of vast disillusionment or of anger at being duped as to actual situations obtaining in the Church. Every Elector, in his own way, has always been aware of the need for confidentiality and secrecy. The structural principle of Church government has, after all, always been marked by those two traits.

But there is surprise. For although every Elector knows, for instance, that the Vatican deals in large investment sums, the reading of detailed accounts concerning the month-to-month transactions performed by Vatican representatives brings home to the Electors the hard truth that the possession and management of so much money necessarily leads those entrusted with it into areas of activity, ways of thought, and centers of interest that often are irreconcilable with Gospel values. And many times the possession and management of so much money foments that pride and ruthlessness that the laws of religion and ethics forbid the Chistian—above all the Christian official.

The *Reports* have, as primary effect, an enlightening of the general body of Electors as to the why and the wherefore of certain moves, both within the Conclave and in the years immediately preceding the Conclave. One such pre-Conclave move was the socio-political and psychologizing vogue that appeared in that period. For the last five years, there has been noticeable throughout the Church a constantly reappearing emphasis on problems that, once upon a time, Churchmen held to be exclusively the domain of politicians, social engineers, psychologists, civil rights workers, community leaders, ethnic enthusiasts, and government agencies.

From the beginning of the seventies, priests, nuns, religious brothers, and bishops seemed to have gone all out in an effort, not merely to 'belong' in all the civil and political movements of their region—as well as to be au courant in whatever psychology fad happened to be in fashion—but to substitute such activity for any expert preaching of Christian doctrine and for any professional teaching of Christian spirituality. It is neither unusual nor unexpected, for example, to come across priests using graphology instead of theology in premarriage instruction. Nor is there any surprise about the American Bishops organizing national meetings on such questions as ethnic origin or the possession of land; or even about bishops who identify themselves explicitly and openly with revolutionary factions.

But, unusual or not, unexpected or not, the whole vogue has been mystifying for the majority of Cardinals—except for those few who have entered the vogue enthusiastically themselves. The nub of the mystification has been at the preponderantly left-wing tendency that has marked this purely secular behavior of Christian Churchmen. There has been hardly one visible and recognized alliance between right-wing causes and the officials of the Church.

Now it is clear to every Elector from the two *Reports*—the *Russian Initiative* and the *Liberation*—that the whole development was by no means accidental. It was not, as Lynch keeps insisting, a happenstance and· the movement of the Holy Spirit, but a well orchestrated plan.

By discreet and effectively coordinated actions, in Europe and in the Americas, large numbers of Catholic clergy and intellectuals, together with many nuns and brothers and lay activists, had been brought to see "temporary" alliance with Marxism as advisable, and a certain degree of Marxization as an inevitable step in the road of "Christian liberation." There can be no doubt about the coordinated character of this development.

The substance of the *Russian Initiative Report* is a suggested agreement or working plan between the Vatican, on the one hand, and the U.S.S.R. as the operating center of Western European Marxism and the preponderant influence in Latin American left-wing politics, on the other hand. The U.S.S.R. desires that the Vatican make certain undertakings: To ease, in a slow and gradual manner, any explicit and formal anti-Marxist statements in official documents and pronouncements. To avoid any formal condemnation of liberation theology or of membership in the Communist parties of any European country (Pius 12 had issued just such a condemnation in the forties). To increase the number of open diplomatic contacts between the Vatican, on the one hand, and the U.S.S.R. and its Eastern satellites on the other hand, by just such means as the visits to the Pope in 1977 by Janos Kadar of Hungary and Hruska of Czechoslovakia and corresponding visits by Vatican diplomats to Communist countries.

Without envisaging an immediate (but certainly future) opening of formal diplomatic relations between the Vatican and Moscow, contacts are to be multiplied, and relationships developed *pari passu* with the diplomatic relationship between the Vatican and the United States, which only maintains a personal representative of the American President at the Vatican, but not an ambassador.

At the same time the Vatican is to decrease any official Roman Catholic backing for right-wing regimes, especially in Latin America. It is to discourage right-wing pressures (say, from right-wing organizations such as the *Opus Dei* and the Knights of Columbus) in Spain and Ireland.

Finally, the Vatican is to sanction the Marxist-Christian dialogues started in several countries, and thus nourish a certain sympathy between justice-loving Christians and political renewal-loving Marxists.

In return for these concessions, the U.S.S.R. would sanction the restoration of the Catholic hierarcy in the Baltic countries, in Czechoslovakia, and in other satellite countries. It would ease up on antireligious laws throughout the satellite countries, laws which have kept Roman Catholics out of public office, government jobs, and academic life. It promises to effect a special form of submission by the Russian Orthodox Patriarchate of Moscow and the Patriarchate of Constantinople to the Pope as to the head of the Church, and to the Vatican, as to the central governing body of the Church. In the event that the Russian sphere of influence extends westward beyond its 1977 borders, special consideration would be given to the property of the Holy See, and special privileges of worship would be allowed it.

The *Liberation Report*, when taken with the Russian Initiative, provides the accompanying panel to what many see as a diptych of Russian Communist plans for easing into a takeover of the West, as well as of the place envisaged by present Vatican planners for the Roman Catholic Church within that new area of Russian influence and domination.

The *Liberation Report* concerns mainly the spread of the theology of "liberation," starting in Latin America and spreading out northward into the United States and across to Europe. The essential teaching of this new theology, first formulated by Latin American theologians, is that the first and essential step in Christ's salvation of the human race is the liberation of all men and women from the yoke of capitalism—chiefly and evilly represented by the United States. The Church, according to this theology, should be the servant of the human race and of its history. And the Church should not only allow, it should sanction and foment, any revolutionary violence (called justifiable counter-violence) in order to unseat and eradicate the centers of capitalism.

The *Report, Christians for Socialism,* describes two organizations—Priests for Latin America and the Intercultural Committee for Dialogue and Action in Latin America—as fronts for Russian Communist penetration. It cites names of such theologians as Fathers Gustavo Gutierrez, Giuleo Gerardi, Pablo Richard, and Gonzalez Arroyo, and indicates the various steps by which the principles of this theology of "liberation" are to be spread. It is to be taught in seminaries and universities. It is to be the subject of Bishops' Conferences, of theologians' congresses and conventions, of pastoral letters written each year by the Bishops to their dioceses, and of books, pamphlets and handbooks. Priests and nuns and others engaged directly in the ministry are to identify with guerilla and revolutionary movements. Left-wing supportive cadres are to be formed in each parish and each diocese—always under the guise of Catholic action and the Church's apostolate among the faithful. Politics and religion are thus to be identified and confused.

At the same time there is to be continual incitement of right-wing resentments that will obviously develop, provoking them into violent, repressive measures. The religious orders such as the Dominicans, Jesuits, and Maryknoll Fathers and Sisters are to be used to champion the rights of the people against such repressive regimes. At Bishops' conferences and at various regional and international congresses, care would be taken to adopt official language sufficiently ambiguous to satisfy the requirements of believers *and* to justify violence and revolutionary methods of takeover. All nationalistic issues (such as the Panama Canal, for example) are to be used; and local prelates are to be led into identifying themselves with these causes.

At the same time there is to be a continuing effort to leaven the American Bishops, the clergy, and laity of the United States into a feeling of guilt about American capitalism's sins and excesses in Latin America, as well as approval of the practical principles of the theology of liberation.

The thrust of this plan is to be localized first in Latin America and generalized later. In Latin America the idea is to prepare for the day when it will be possible to form the first nucleus of the U.S.S.L.M., the United Socialist States of Latin America. It cannot be started unless the collaboration of the clergy is assured.

Both in Latin America and in Europe, the "liberation" motif is to be inculcated. For instance, the principal popular piety of Latin America is devotion to Our Lady of Guadalupe, as the Shrine of Lourdes is in France, where the Virgin is also venerated. The apparitions of the Virgin in both places, the much-venerated picture of the Virgin in Guadalupe, and the miracles performed at Lourdes are to be described as "acts in the service of a civilization of love from which the cruelty of capitalism and the oppression of bourgeois society is to be excluded."

With these *Reports* in hand, many Electors put two and two together. And it is Witz who finally wraps the subject up when he says: "Diplomatically the previous regime (Pope Paul 6's) sought to ease the plight of Roman Catholics by talking with the Russians, by backing left-wing regimes and by discouraging—even indirectly—all right-wing movements. In reality, this politique was trapped in the widening propaganda effort, as described in the *Liberation Report*." And, one American Cardinal observes to Cardinal Artel: "Many of the social policies and declarations of the American Bishops from 1965 on were—unknown to most of them—deeply colored by a pervasive plan to prepare for Marxization. The American Church has been used and bastardized in this process."

As the reading of these two *Reports* continues, new questions arise about the role of Franzus, and about his relationship with the Soviet masters of his country; and, inevitably, attention is focussed on the alliance between Franzus and Lynch on the one hand, and with Thule and his group, on the other hand.

For those reading the *Liberation Report* dealing with the left-wing doctrinal movement within the ranks of Roman Catholics, it is obvious that Thule is someone who by character and circumstance easily falls into the role of figurehead and leader in that movement. One thing is clear: Thule has had an extraordinary list of contacts and associations with non-Catholic bodies which, up to this time, have never seriously entertained any genuine idea of a close association, much less union, either with Rome or with any high-ranking official of Rome.

But Thule has changed all that! His strengh and his Achilles' heel in all this is his truly ardent desire to see a real union of Christians. Fond of saying that the post-Vatican Council spirit is a one-time thing and will never again be generated, Thule has been convinced that already the Holy Spirit has forged a new unity among Christians, and that only juridical structures and traditionalist mentalities impede that unity from becoming the guiding force in the quasi-ultimate form of the Church that Jesus founded.

Over a period of ten years, Thule, in his personal contacts, has established privately with many non-Catholic Christian leaders the bases on which that unity could be achieved. The purpose was not to attain a complete or even general conformity in belief and worship and governing Church structures.

Thule is and always has been too much of a realist to think that this could be achieved now or in the foreseeable future. Each Church, in fact, is to retain its present format, he has said, and its own formulation of belief.

The chief obstacle of everything in the *Liberation* plan is the Pope, the Bishop of Rome as the traditional head of the Roman Church—his primacy of teaching authority, his infallibility in teaching authority, and his primacy of governing jurisdiction.

Most of Thule's contacts in other churches have agreed that the Bishop of Rome should have—by force of mere historical longevity—a certain primacy of honor: That is, the Pope would be and should be accepted as the presiding Bishop (in Churches with an episcopal structure) or as presiding elder (in non-episcopally structured churches).

There would be no requirement to accept any Roman dogmas defined or accepted in the West after the first six Councils (the cut-off point would be around the end of the seventh century). This would rule out all Roman dogmas about the Papacy, about the Virgin, about the Eucharist, about the clergy (celibate and male), and about political liberties and personal property.

Thule has maintained close ties with many theologians in Europe and the Americans who have done pioneer work in the area of the beliefs that are acceptable on a wide scale to non-Catholic Christians.

In addition to all this, Thule has envisaged, with his non-Roman brothers as well as with the Progressivist theologians, the creation of a new Vatican Ministry, or *Congregation* as all ministries are called in Rome. It will be composed of an international team of theologians and will include non-Catholics. This body will have legislative and normative—that is, not merely advisory—power within the Church in dealing with doctrine and discipline. There will be, according to the new ecumenism of the Thule plan, a fresh effort to set up common modes of worship, the tendency and aim being to transform the Roman Catholic Mass ceremony into something acceptable to a wide range of non-Catholic believers. This is the type of open Church which is calculated to allow "the maximum liberty to the Spirit of Christ," to quote a phrase from the *Report.*

If this Church policy were wedded to the socio-political doctrine and action outlined in the Russian proposals, then it becomes a plan for Christianity to operate "free" of any "entrapment in outmoded social systems and decadent forms of the Church which have become ossified and unpopular and ineffectual."

The effect of the alliance between Franzus and Lynch and the Thule group becomes painfully clear in the light of these documents.

The two other *Secret Reports* are equally relevant in their own way. One concerns Vatican dealings with the Italian Communist Party (PCI). The other concerns the financial condition of the Vatican as well as projections of Vatican finances.

It is clear from the second of these *Reports* that the present Vatican Administration had tied Vatican finances to the fortunes of the United States economy and to the idea of a trilateral system—United States, Japan, Saudi Arabia—as the way in which the inflation and recession of the eighties is to be over-reached and survived.

Several Electors, notably the Asians, now underline the fact that the shift of Vatican investments begun in the late sixties and early seventies under the direction of the Italian financier, Michele Sindona, is not yet completed; that it is an ongoing affair. Four of the Asians go over to Bonkowski's apartment in order to get answers to some questions. Why the shift anyway? What was the fear?

Bonkowski has the reputation in the Roman Curia of knowing most things, but of having only rarely spoken about anything at any great length.

This time, however, he makes an exception. He points out that once already in this century the Holy See faced bankruptcy as an imminent possibility. By the late 1920s Vatican finances were in a sorry state. The first real audit in history of total Vatican wealth was carried out by Monsignore Dominic Mariana, who reported to Pope Pius 11 in 1928 that the Vatican was shaving very close to bankruptcy. A $1.5 million loan in twenty-year bonds arranged that same year by Cardinal Mundelein of Chicago (with Chicago Church property valued at several millions of dollars as collateral) staved off the feared bankruptcy; and in 1929 the Lateran Pact was signed with the Italian Government of Mussolini.

In that Pact, $90 million was granted to the Vatican by Mussolini's Government as indemnity for the properties which the Vatican had been deprived of by the Italians in 1870. This sum was confided for handling and investing to the almost genius-like mind of a man named Bernardino Nogara, He parlayed the sum into a huge financial empire which has conferred on the Vatican realizable assets more or less equal to the official gold and foreign exchange reserves of France, plus at least $2 billion of securities on the New York Stock Exchange, and a corporate wealth on the very sunny side of $20 billion. Between then and now, Vatican investments penetrated into every sector of the Italian economy as well as abroad.

By the beginning of the seventies it was clear that the economies of Europe were going downhill, and that politically Europe would be ready for Russian penetration toward the end of the decade. The Vatican had no intention of going bankrupt.

Then by 1973-74, Bonkowski goes on, it was clear that Saudi Arabia was on its way to exercising a super-power role in the fields of international finance and politics—all based on its unbeatable and seemingly inexhaustible sources of oil. United States policy in the meanwhile started to hew very closely to the rising role of Saudi Arabia. The United States no longer had any need to maintain a primacy of position and leadership in Western Europe. New markets must be sought and won in Africa and elsewhere.

"The other *Report* on dealings with the PCI and the Vatican," Bonkowski concludes, "has its relevance here. If, as is projected, the economy of Western Europe cannot be bolstered, and if the Vatican is to be closely associated with the trilateral combination of the United States, Japan and Saudi Arabia; and if, at the same time, the United States diminishes its interest and influence in Italy and Europe, then almost certainly—of course at the right time and never as a shock or surprise—the government of Italy will be partially peopled with Marxist ministers, and will eventually *be* Marxist not only in its ministerial composition but in its policies. But the Vatican remains, and shall remain in Italy Hence the discussions with the PCI."

"No," Bonkowski answers one remark, "it is not really schizophrenic; it only appears so, if one does not see the enormous shifts taking place in geopolitics."

The main items in the PCI's offer to the Vatican are simple and direct. If the Vatican will withdraw its traditional support—financial and moral—for the Demochristians (DC), and if it will go easy on official attacks on Communism as a system of economics, then when and if the PCI acquires preponderance and control in the Italian Government, the PCI will guarantee three main advantages for the Vatican: possession and power over its properties in Rome and throughout Italy; freedom to maintain and propagate its present financial plans and investments abroad; and freedom to teach and preach as its conscience dictates.

The Asians, who have seen all this before in the Far East, are satisfied that they understand what has happened. They know the process, once started, is irreversible. "Not pessimism," Ni Kan remarks. "Realism! Your Eminence." And they depart.

But there is a violent debate about all this among various Italian groups meeting. "I don't care if Angelico or anyone else says that 'the Communist hue will emerge from the European cauldron a pale shade of pink'—or *whatever* hue you wish to choose!" Nolasco exclaims to those around him in Masaccio's apartment. "They said that about the Chinese—how could the anciently cultured Chinese, how could *they* be Marxised. And about the gentle Cambodians. And the simple Laotians. And the sweet Vietnamese. And, believe me, today it's all a bloody, bloody, red, red, color! Why should the Europeans be any different?"

"How on earth can they imagine a Communist regime in Italy—specially if it is flanked by similar regimes in France, Spain, and Portugal, and backed up by a more westerly sphere of Russian influence affecting West Germany,

Switzerland, and the Benelux count.ies? How can they even *imagine* such an Italian Communist regime to respect *any* commitments?" Canaletto is incredulous. And his question is very practical.

"It sounds contradictory and foolhardy, I know," Bronzino responds, "but that is the way it most probably would turn out in such an hypothesis." He goes on: "We are realists. All the plans, you must remember, are just plans. There is a struggle going on right now. There is a crisis affecting everybody. It must be resolved. Someone is going to lose. Someone is going to win. If, as now seems likely, the PCI wins out—and Communist parties elsewhere win out—they too will be realists. Just as the hard-nosed Americans are realists and have decided to cut bait from Europe finally. After all, the masters of all Communists, the Russians, will only allow local Communist parties to take over aggressively when the time is ripe Now, they are going to estimate the ripeness of the time in purely economic terms—when it suits them best, when they need it. Not before that. Not later than that. As far as we can judge, this should be somewhere in the first five years of the next decade; between 1980 and 1985. Or thereabouts. It is very obvious that even in this configuration, the Russian dominated economies of Europe will need outside trading partners. And, as a financial investor of international stature, the Vatican has a role it can play in that configuration—it will be resident within a Russian orbit but have its financial sinews outside. . . . ."

By mid-evening, to Domenico's surprise and to the puzzlement of the Camerlengo and his associates, there has been very little coming and going between the various caucuses. Domenico is content with this, because for him it means that the Electors are making up their own minds on the basis of the new information supplied them.

The Thule-Franzus-Buff group appears only vaguely dissatisfied. For they feel that, on balance, the close association of Vatican political and financial policy with the United States will tell against those who oppose them, and will draw a massive Third World vote in their direction.

Everybody notes sedulously that the blacks and the Asians have remained very quiet on the whole. They have not been on the rounds seeing the Europeans or the Latin Americans.

By 10:45 P.M. still not much has happened. Angelico phones Domenico to get his feeling about it all. Angelico is nervous. "Sit tight," Domenico advises. "Don't do anything at all. They know where we are."

As the evening progresses, Buff and Lombardi and Franzus, particularly the latter, begin to hope for some reactions from the Electors. Franzus' name has come up again and again in the *Russian Initiative Report*, both as sounding-board used by the Russians, and as advisor to the members of the Vatican Secretariat of State who deal with Soviet Eastern Europe. And the tenor of his memoranda and messages to the Vatican Secretariat of State are all favorable toward the conclusion of some sort of agreement with the Russians. Near 11 o'clock, Buff and Lombardi set out to visit the main caucuses. They know that the blacks and Asians finished up in one caucus over in Makonde's apartment, so they head over there.

When they knock at Makonde's door they find that the African is in bed already. He insists, however, that they come in. He quickly dons a large, red dressing gown and slippers to match. Buff and Lombardi are somewhat mystified. Makonde tells them that the African-Asian caucus broke up about half an hour ago, the members deciding it was time to go to bed.

"None of us could see an alternative," Makonde concludes, as if accounting for the end of the caucus. "We realized that no Cardinal among us has an alternative. So, instead of wasting more time, we decided to retire."

"Alternative to what?" Buff and Lombardi ask almost simultaneously. The African looks at them both, extending both his arms, palms cupped upward.

"Here . . ." looking at his right hand, "We have the Conservative-Traditionalist. Here . . ." looking at his left hand, "we have the Progressivist. As are these two separate hands and arms of mine, both of them are attached to a body. Commands for them come from that body—directions, force, behavior, all from that body." He drops his arms to his knees. "Both are attached to a body of politics, finance, economics, governmental systems, lobbies, special interests, et cetera, et cetera, et cetera." Makonde repeats the words as if they were specific and loaded with significance. "And in between those two alternatives, Brothers, there is no other alternative. Only emptiness among us all. So now, what sort of a chance is that for our success? Must we decide to be capitalists or to be Communists, or at least to be the pawn of either—or of both, which is worse? Whether we like it or not?"

Buff and Lombardi rise, as Makonde rises. "So the Japanese Cardinal," Makonde continues in a half-cajoling, half-sleepy voice, "and the Philippine Cardinals, and the Indian Cardinals, and the Vietnam Cardinal, and the Oceanic Cardinals, and ourselves, we decided to wait and pray, Brothers. And sleep." He smiles like a big elder brother, as he shows them out.

"It's all right," Lombardi says to Buff as they walk away. "It's all right. We have an open field there."

"The next stop for them is at the large Third World caucus. Marquez is not there. Neither is Perez, nor Manuel. They are over with the Camerlengo. There are three older Cardinals (Navarro, Tacci, and Zubaran); three younger ones (Herrera, Sampere, and Mauderer); and, also, Ribera, LaMura and Teofilo.

As Buff and Lombardi enter, Ribera is being questioned about a certain

Father Roger Vekemans, a Belgian Jesuit, an information expert, who is cited as one of the sources for the *Liberation Report.*

"Didn't he get $5 million from the CIA in the 1960s to be used against the Marxists in Chile and elsewhere?" is one objection. Ribera waves aside all objections to Vekemans. He lists other sources for the Report—including Colombian Bishops Lopez Trujillo and Mario Revollo of Bogota, and Dario Castrillon of Pereira, among others.

"Furthermore," Ribera hurls the challenge back, "if you object to the way people like Vekemans and Lopez Trujillo work with politically involved laymen like Dr. German Bravo (former Colombian planner) or sociologist Dr. Nernando Bernal, or Dr. Rodrigo Escobar (director of ASOCANA, the Colombian sugar cane growers association) then why don't you also object, or didn't you object, to the close relationship between those 'liberation' theologians of yours with Chile's Marxist dictator, Salvador Allende? Or with Hortense, Allende's widow, who's such a great ally of Fidel Castro? Or with Orlando Letelier, whom we all know as Allende's propaganda minister and Castro agent in the United States until he was assassinated in 1977? Or with any of who knows how many other well-known Communist collaborators, workers, and fellow-travellers? Be careful!" Ribera warns them. "You will be hung by the same petard. And justly so."

"My Brothers," Lombardi is finally able to get a word in, "before we go to bed tonight, we would like to find out your reactions to the *Reports.*"

The Latin American tells him in plain terms. "It seems," they say, "that between the capitalist and United States-oriented Vatican policy and the Marxist-sympathizing attitude of many Roman Catholic clergymen, there is no choice—no alternative for the Church but to be torn in two by secular interests." Herrera adds the same note as Makonde a few moments before: "We Church leaders have run out of initiatives. Perhaps we never had any of our own. At least not for a very long time."

When Lombardi and Buff leave they are not feeling very happy now that they meet this second occurrence of the same vagueness.

Back in Buff's apartment, they find Thule with Marquez, Perez, and Manuel. As far as they can judge from Thule's account, the Camerlengo has no intention of taking any action whatever of a direct kind at tomorrow's meeting. "The only thing he was close-mouthed about," Marquez adds, "was the reaction of the Americans. Seems that the Americans have been studying the correspondence of the U.S.S.R.-Vatican. It has had its effect. What, I don't know. And the Camerlengo will not say. Would not say."

"Vague. All too vague for peace of mind."

Around midnight, Domenico telephones Angelico and asks him to step over to his apartment. When Angelico arrives there, he finds the Camerlengo, Lohngren, Ribera, Pellino, and Eck already in conference with Domenico. Angelico senses the silent dislike of the Camerlengo and others. He ignores it, but he has the clear impression that they have just been discussing him. Obviously, Domenico has called him over merely to include him in the meeting. This at least is a good sign. If the conversation had gone really badly against him, Angelico would not have been invited. In the same way, the fact that he accepted the invitation is a sign for the Camerlengo. Conclave convention forbids an aspiring and explicitly committed *papabile* to enter any group without identifying himself as such. Angelico does not, because he is not.

They fill Angelico in on the general poll they have taken. There is some unexpected spirit of independence—both of particular Electors and of individual groups of Electors. It must be reckoned with; it has surfaced. They cannot predict its direction. The Italians are, on the whole, very angry, feeling that the administration of Pope Paul 6 went much further than they were allowed to know in its approach and appeasement of the Marxists in Italy and in Russia. The French are apparently still very much on the left-wing, but are susceptible to any move by the Camerlengo. They have almost (but not quite) as much objection to Russian influence as they have to American influence. Neither the Germans nor the Spaniards are now in favor of a pan-European candidacy. The Eastern Europeans have an "I-told-you-so" attitude and a "we've-been-through-it-already" reaction to all talk of a Third World solution to the Conclave's problem. Ribera asserts that the Electors now realize the concrete issues. "And," the Camerlengo adds tartly, "one thing is now possible: a three-month Conclave with a rough-and-tumble deadlock and a completely unpredictable outcome."

There seems no way to gauge what will happen. Before long the general discussion dies down, and most of the group departs. The Camerlengo remains with Domenico.

The Camerlengo confides in Domenico about the security problems. We do not know, he explains, if the one man is aware of the fact—we suspect that he suspects; but anyway, he has some implant which records and transmits. No, he answers to Domenico's question. We plan to do nothing about it now—except to keep our mouths shut when speaking in his presence privately. To do anything more might endanger the man's life or the lives of several people in his own country and elsewhere.

"Now, as regards our second problem, I find it sad and, er, hard to admit this, but you were right. It is our young friend with the stutter." The Camerlengo is silent for a moment. Then he continues: "A matter of personal compromise, you understand, though as far as I can find out it involves, not the usual things that compromise a man, money or ..." the Camerlengo stumbles, looks sharply at Domenico and goes on, "but a matter of family security. Too much money invested in too many perilous places. Easily, too easily, destroyed. Old family, high connections ... that sort of thing. Y'know what I mean. Whatever it is, he can only send signals, nothing else. But even with mere signals—prearranged, of course—he can give the essence."

"Who is the recipient of those signals?"

"We only know the recipient lies south of this area. The Italians are looking into the lessee of an apartment off the Via della Conciliazione running down in a straight line from Saint Peter's Square. Somewhere down there. ..."

"And what shall we do now as a precaution."

"I want ..." the Camerlengo begins and then breaks off as his voice catches in his throat. He stands up and looks away examining a picture hanging on the wall. He is obviously profoundly concerned about the young Cardinal. He begins again: "I want no suffering for him—at least as little as possible. He has suffered enough. And he has much more to suffer ... a long life of it in front of him. Just make it impossible for him to do any damage. And in time for the Third Session tomorrow morning." He turns around to face Domenico. "Will Your Eminence talk with Ruzzo in the morning and arrange all that? Discreetly. Please!" Domenico nods. The other Cardinal leaves slowly and quietly and sadly.

By 1:00 A.M. all caucuses are over and all conversations are finished. For the first time in the long history of Conclaves, the Electors are all on an equal footing: Every one of them knows the inner reasons of state that have guided Vatican political policy in recent years. For the first time, also, the Electors are perfectly aware of the financial entanglements of the Vatican. They have as a body a very minute picture of the two dominant political influences playing within their ranks in the Conclave.

Perhaps it is all these factors that have produced the attitude with which most Electors retire this night. On the one hand, openness to all possibilities. No longer is any Conservative or Traditionalist or progressivist assured of a preponderance. On the other hand, a feeling of helplessness, of initiative lacking to them who should, above all others, have the God-given initiatives and drive of specially appointed messengers of the Gospel.

The Second Day

There are many early risers today. Thule, Domenico, the Camerlengo, Franzus, Angelico, Azande, are among the first to say their private Masses at 5:30 a.m.

By 6 o'clock, when the young Monsignore has been seated a bare five minutes at his desk, the Camerlengo arrives with Thule and Lohngren. They closet themselves in the inner office. The young Monsignore glances at his watch, then slips out and closes the outer door. He will have an early morning coffee with the priest-confessors.

Inside in the office, only one point is discussed: how to stop Angelico. In spite of Domenico's denial of any intention on his part to propose Angelico, or on Angelico's part to canvass for a nomination, the fear is that he will be nominated and will run as candidate. Too much has happened. All three Cardinals feel sure he will be put in nomination by Domenico and seconded by someone of Domenico's choosing. Before throwing their support in Thule's direction, the Camerlengo and Lohngren discuss the *Coalition Policy* with Thule. They have certain conditions: not so "open" a Church for non-Catholics as Thule proposes; a much slower and more cautious approach to the Marxists than Thule wishes. He agrees.

Then they discuss tactics. Thule's first idea is to create a long delay by organizing several speakers.

"It won't work, Eminence," the Camerlengo tells him. "Somewhere along the line, Domenico or one of his sympathisers may propose to elect their own candidate by acclamation. By then, he will have got all the Asians and Africans, most Europeans, perhaps even some of the Latin Americans. What then?"

"That's *it*, Brother!" Thule straightens up. "That's what *we* must do. We propose . . . I propose Yiu to be elected by acclamation. Buff seconds. My name is down already as first speaker. That's it, my Brother."

"Supposing they have the same idea?" the other men ask.

"No. It's not Domenico's way," Lohngren says soberly. "Besides, I think

Domenico is too respectful of proper procedure. No. It is Angelico I fear. If you can get your proposal and seconding through, and Angelico doesn't follow you—by the way is he marked down to speak? No? Well, then, if you get past that point, you should have no difficulty."

After a few minutes' further conversation, they break up. The Camerlengo has paperwork to get through concerning the Conclave—he still is Camerlengo. Thule seeks out Buff in order to alert him as to the plan. Lohngren has to go and talk with the other Germans and some of the North Americans.

Angelico and Azande have an appointment with Domenico for 7:30 a.m. Domenico is late. The other two sit in his apartment waiting for him. He arrives at 7:50 a.m. "Either of Your Eminences going to breakfast?" he asks them, as he walks in. Both visitors shake their heads. "Well then, let's get down to business. Here's the situation.

"There's going to be a rush acclamation, or an attempt at it." He looks at Azande. "By Thule and Buff." He stops, then adds: "Of Yiu, of course." Angelico draws a deep breath.

"Steady a moment," Domenico goes on. "I shall ask for special permission to speak. But—note it well—permission, not from the Presidents, but from the Conclave." He stops and looks at Angelico and Azande, appraising their reactions. "A rush acclamation job of our own."

"And then?" Angelico asks.

"Then," Domenico says slowly, "it is up to His Eminence here," turning his head around to look at Azande. Azande coughs and smiles a little sheepishly. The three are silent. Finally, Azande speaks.

"And what shall I recommend, Father?"

'Exactly what the situation demands, Eminence."

"But I have not prepared anything."

"Let me see: You have been an ordained priest, a Bishop, and a Cardinal for over twenty-five years. Yes, I guess, twenty-five years or more have either prepared Your Eminence for this moment or they have not. We are going to find out within an hour or two. Now Eminence . . ." Domenico says this to Azande as he glances at his watch, "if you will excuse us two, we have some private matters to discuss."

Azande rises, smiles at both of them, and leaves.

Angelico looks at Domenico and waits. Domenico is also waiting. He only says: "We will have a visitor at 8:15. When he leaves, you go with him. Apart from the bathroom, stick to him at every moment. If you cannot find room together at Mass, then when the Mass is over at about 9:40, meet him outside the Chapel and walk with him past my room and toward yours—as if you wished to pick up something for the Session but did not want to lose his company. Understood?"

At a few moments after 8:15, there is a light knock at the door. Domenico opens it. The young Cardinal with the stutter is there. "Good Morning, Eminence!" Domenico's voice is genial and friendly. Angelico stands up. "Angelico here is hungry, as I promised you! Now he will explain what I think exactly of the Progressivist theologians and about our prospects in Mainland China."

The Mass is a difficult experience for the young Cardinal. Again, as he gives a look around the Chapel, he senses the unity and the union of these men in spite of all their differences; or, rather their very differences seem to be the source of their unity. In front of him he recognizes Pellino with his continual shifting from knee to knee; Desai who is hunched over the pew, his head buried in his hands; the tremulous Sargent; the imperious figure of the arrogant Kirchner; Balboa, erect and slightly fierce; Dowd, the long Scotsman; Ni Kan, stiff and motionless. Each different, one from the other.

Looking over at the other side he runs his eye over a montage of faces: Domenico, Venturi, Lotuko, Lombardi, Vignente. Some invisible line of love, or at least of devotion to a cause, seems to run through them all, but to evade his own hand. All this is difficult enough for the young Cardinal. He feels alien.

His pain becomes acute when the Camerlengo raises the Consecrated Host, saying the ritual words: "Through Him, With Him, and in Him, there is for You, All-powerful Father, all glory and honor for ever and ever." For that instant, most of the Cardinals raise their eyes and look at the Host in the Celebrant's hands. The young Cardinal feels excluded from some happiness that the others share, even if they are not conscious of that sharing. And he remembers what was said to him as a young priest in a remote country parish years before. It was a suicide whom he tried to dissuade: "Father, yesterday or last year—I don't know when—I fell from the velvet dark of happy stars down into these senseless yet sense-lit days and noisome hours. I will have an end to it all now. I cannot go on like this."

As he walks with Angelico along the corridor and the warning bell rings, he says for no apparent reason and not in particular to Angelico: "I have a few important questions to ask you. But for the last hour, the heavens were sort of wiped out. Like a rough hand had banged all the doors shut. But let me drop into my own rooms. I will rejoin you at the door."

"Walk with me as far as my apartment," Angelico says easily, "it will take a second or two. Then you can drop off and catch up with me later." The young Cardinal acquiesces.

As they pass Domenico's door, they both see it open. Domenico and

Edouardo Ruzzo, the chief of security, are standing there. Ruzzo, Angelico thinks, is being very, very reverential and respectful. He does not look in the Cardinal's eyes. He has his eyes lowered and is looking intensely at the Cardinal's pectoral cross.

Domenico is all urbanity. "Eminence," he calls softly to the young Cardinal, "a moment of your time. Please!"

"We'll catch up with each other later at the bus," Angelico says, seeing his cue. The door of Domenico's apartment closes behind Domenico and Ruzzo and the young Cardinal.

THE THIRD SESSION

When the Cardinal Electors are assembled in the Upper Room, a quarter of an hour later, Domenico enters followed by the young Cardinal and by the Camerlengo. Probably no one even notices that the young Cardinal is no longer wearing his pectoral cross. All are calm, serious. All quietly take their places.

The Camerlengo starts the ritual for the election of the officials for this Third Session. Down on the Via della Conciliazone, two men sit at their silent console. As they will learn, there is no transmission.

In the Conclave, Bonkowski of Poland is chosen as President, to be assisted by Gellee of France and Kotoko of Africa, as co-Presidents. Scrutineers are Chera, Masaccio, and Motzu. Revisers are three Curial Cardinals: Uccello and two Frenchmen, Houdon and Lamy. *Infirmarii* are Bassano, Eakins, and Peale.

No sooner are the new Presidents seated, and Bonkowski has looked at the agenda, than he announces Thule's name as first speaker. Bonkowski attempts a light tone: "Your Eminences will be surprised to learn that our first speaker this morning will be the Most Reverend Lord Cardinal Thule." But no one laughs or even smiles. There is a deep hush as Thule stands up. He bends towards his table to get his notes.

At this precise moment Domenico chooses to rise and step out from the rows of Cardinals so as to stand in the center. "My Lord Presidents!" he speaks in a loud voice that carries to every corner. "My Lord Cardinals! In virtue of the ancient Conclave practice of *vox populi* (the voice of the people), I claim utter priority over all previously scheduled speakers!" Either by deliberate trick of voice, or because he really has mentally adopted such an attitude, his voice sounds like a back-bencher in the British House of Commons, or like a revolutionary jumping to his feet in the French Chamber of Deputies to upset the equilibrium, the status quo.

The effect is electrifying. Thule is frozen in his posture over his table. Bonkowski's mouth sags open. Every head is jerked around as if on invisible strings, as all eyes are on that one diminutive figure standing in the center of the Hall.

Every head except one: As soon as Domenico intervenes, the young Cardinal bends his head forward and covers his face with his hands. His shoulders are shaking. He, more than anyone here, knows what is happening now. And, if he has tears, it is not for himself, nor for what he must later suffer as penalty, but for the havoc unnecessarily created by him and by men like him. He and they have betrayed their Colleagues, sowing lies and ambiguities among honest men, playing on honest fears, abusing the zeal and hopes of many. A body of men who, by and large, wish the same thing have been confused and divided, one from the other, by clever tactics.

Everybody else is so stunned that the first reaction is silence, as though Domenico's words had been stones hurled into a well, and 118 men are waiting for the echo of their landing.

Then, in random cross fire, the reactions explode. Thule straightens and stands like a ramrod and starts speaking and gesticulating. Cardinals leap to their feet, faces fraught with rage, fear, confusion, disgust. Yelling, asking, objecting, shouting. Lombardi, Franzus, Buff, Marquez, Balboa, Lohngren, Delacoste, Manuel, Masaccio. The Camerlengo remains seated, but his hands grip the little table in front of him as if for support.

Domenico looks straight ahead at Bonkowski, his arms folded across his chest. Bonkowski rings his silver bell angrily and insistently, "My Most Reverend Lord Cardinals! My Most Reverend Lords! Please! My Lord Electors! Please! We will have silence! Please! My Lord Cardinals!"

But even as the turmoil and cries die down, a slow, steady quiet clapping of hands begins. Not loud. Not violent. Not quick. Just steady and in a regular beat. The Africans have started it. Garcia and another Spaniard take it up. Then Terebelski and Karewsky follow suit. Then Kinigoshi, Walker, Sargent, Witz, Kiel, the three Asians, two Frenchmen, and a whole host of Italians, Uccello, Riccioni, Canaletto, Maderno, Duccio, Lamennais, Bronzino, Nolasco, Pozzo. The Cardinals who had jumped to their feet to shout in protest are gradually silenced by the rhythmic hand-clapping and sink back on their chairs. The sound goes on and on, louder. Bonkowski consults with Gellee and Kotoko. Then, after a few more instants, he rings the silver bell gently and waits. The clapping fades slowly, then stops, almost as if on cue.

Bonkowski looks at Domenico who has not budged a muscle. "My Most Reverend Lord Domenico," he begins. But Buff is on his feet.

"Doubtless, My Lord Cardinal Domenico can cite historical precedents for this unexpected interruption? For us country cousins, Cardinals from the outer provinces, perhaps he will take the trouble to cite time and place and Conclave and Cardinal? Otherwise . . ." Buff leaves off significantly.

Bonkowski turns his head slowly to face the lone figure of Domenico standing in the center aisle. All eyes are on him again. "Sudden death for our clever friend," Marquez mutters half out loud.

In the expectant silence, Domenico unfolds his arms and draws from his sleeve a single sheet of paper. In that same raucous voice he thunders out a cascade of Conclaves, names, dates, times; and the phrase 'vox populi' recurs again and again. It is like a chorus line of support from past Conclaves.

"Conclave 31. 1471. The late afternoon. Cardinal Barbo invokes vox populi. Conclave 35. 1513. March 1. Early morning. Cardinal Backocz invokes vox populi. Conclave 40. 1549. December 5. Forenoon. Cardinal Salviati invokes vox populi. Conclave 53. 1621. January 28. Evening time. Cardinal Campori invokes vox populi. . . ." As the high voice of Domenico continues reading out numbers and names, the gentle hand-clapping starts again, low enough to allow his voice to be heard, loud enough to be heard as a background of support from Conclave 82. "Conclave 70. 1800. February 25. Cardinal Mattei invokes vox populi. . . ."

Bonkowski rings his silver bell. Domenico stops in the middle of recounting the example of vox populi in yet another Conclave ". . . Conclave 73. 1830. December 11. Forenoon. Cardinal Gaisrück. . . ." The rhythm of constant clapping also stops. Then it takes up again. Thule glances around the ranks of Cardinals as far as he can see—and the Presidents see as clearly as he does. Only one out of every eight or ten Cardinals is not clapping. The will of the majority is clear. Bonkowski rings his silver bell once more. There is silence.

"Most Reverend Electors, in view of the intervention of My Most Reverend Lord Domenico, I now declare he has the floor, and this according to the manifest will of the majority of you." There is a subdued murmur of assent.

Domenico places the sheet of paper back in his sleeve. He moves slowly up to the speakers' place. The silence is again so deep that by the time he rises from his brief prayer and faces the assembly, even those furthest from him can hear the soft rustling of his robes.

Domenico no longer has the "transcendant look" that his penitents and clients and students know so well. Instead, there is a great evenness, an equanimity, in his expression. At this moment what Domenico must do is reach every one of these Electors and bind them again in unity. But he must also point up the diverse motives that have divided them, in their fears and faults, into factions that have little to do with Jesus, or with the Church of Jesus.

He looks at the presiding Cardinals, smiles gently and bows: "Most Eminent and Reverend Lord Cardinal Presidents!" Then, turning: "My Most Beloved Brothers and Lord Cardinals." Domenico begins, his tone quiet now, his gaze ranging calmly from face to face. "I think there is not one Cardinal

Elector present here who has not suffered deeply in the last thirty-six hours."
He looks steadily at Makonde's darkling features. "Some have suffered
because they felt deeply slighted." Riccioni's frightened look is unlike his
confidence of the day before. "Some have suffered because a mortal fear was
let loose in their spirit." Thule is looking at him from beneath his bushy
eyebrows. "Others, because they banked all their hopes on one forceful twist
of events—or what they regarded as a twist of Providence, no doubt." On his
extreme left, Angelico is one of the few not looking at him. "A few because
they found whatever love they had for our Lord Jesus was severely deficient
in trust—that, in reality, they had trusted themselves, and of course, in the
painful crunch of crisis they felt themselves let down roughly." Domenico
can hardly restrain a smile as he sees the Camerlengo's studied expression, his
'holy indifference' as one Vatican wag put it. "Others still suffer because
nothing in our assembly has proceeded in an orderly fashion. Nothing in this
Conclave seems predictable or to be like past Conclaves." As his gaze travels
steadily from face to face and returns to the Presidents, he knows that in the
silence of this assembly, where only his words echo, by some alchemy of the
occasion, he is drawing concentration and attention up to where he stands.
He has them in the palm of his hand. He understands them. And their fears.

"In sum, my Beloved Colleagues," still in that level, quiet tone, "this is a
Conclave that has hurt everyone it touched." Domenico stops a moment.
"All of us." The three words seem to answer some doubt. Down the row on
his left hand, Cardinal Walker is praying to himself and is heard by his
neighbors as he says over and over again in a sort of controlled panic: "Lord
Jesus have mercy upon us. Tell him what to say. Lord Jesus have mercy on us
all. Tell him what to say. . . ."

Thule lifts his head and gives a quick glance at Franzus, then to Buff and to
Lynch. They look back and forth at each other, more in questioning than
anything else. The Africans, too, glance at one another and over to Yiu and
Ni Kan. There is a luminosity to their expressions that no word can convey.
Braun makes a small gesture to Bronzino. He hunches his shoulders
quizzically. Domenico knows how to read all the reactions. He is certain he
must give a focus to what so many in this assembly are suffering. And he must
throw a line of hope, must clinch their grasp of it, if he is to draw them along
with him where he wishes to go this day.

"Ah, well . . ." he continues, almost in a conversational tone, "I always told
those who came to me from time to time for consolation and encouragement,
that I myself would never be cast down or immobilized by failure, as long as I
suffered only what My Lord Jesus had suffered before me. I would only give
up trying, give up loving, I told them, the day I faced something Jesus had
not faced. That day has not yet come. For me. Or for us, my Venerable
Brothers.

"Is it not a fact," his voice is inflected now with a tiny note of pleading, "that for the first time since our Conclave began we are—as one heart and one mind—beginning to hear that ancient voice saying: 'I know. I know your hurt. I know all about hurting. Especially the hurt of failure.' Is it not so, my Brothers?" He takes a step backward and then forward. It is a mannerism of his.

"Let us not remain wallowing in our pain. Each one with his own. Let each examine his own conscience. Not so we may bleed, but so we can see without flinching how we have come to this impasse. And so we can see how we must move to escape from it. Let us ask ourselves about our major sins— our major sins as Churchmen. Let each of us ask: Have I consorted with those who wish the destruction of the Church?" Domenico's voice rises almost querulously at the end of each sentence. "Have I identified all my own ambitions with the glory of God? Have I too easily met the onslaught of barefaced barbarity—whether it be the comfort of corruption, or the lethal aims of the Church's enemies—with concessions? With smiles? Merely because I wished my accustomed life to continue a little longer? Merely because I did not want to step over the threshhold of hardship?

"Or is it force I relied upon? On those powerful sinews of gold and silver? On my beautiful friends? On the power of my position? And, as ultimate guardian, on the cunningly distributed nuclear tinderboxes of friendly powers? Our technological fix? Have I found it easier to sit with grandscale sinners and smile indulgently, and treat oleaginous officials with cooperative friendship? Have I found that easier, I mean, than to take a proper stand?"

Domenico has reeled off what is, in effect a litany of the faults besetting the chief factions in the Conclave drama. Many, if not all, feel Domenico may be building up to a name-by-name denunciation. Some Cardinals hold their breath. One or two gather up their papers, as if wishing they could leave. Some sit back as if waiting for the axe to fall. The silence is so concentrated one can almost touch it like velvet.

Until Domenico's next words, which come as sweetness to many: "And now for each of my weaknesses is there no way out? No way out but hard thinking and still harder deciding?

"My Brothers, there is an ancient voice speaking among us today. We need to listen to that voice. We need to. Because we must move forward. Because we must choose. Because we must act. And because our grace period is not of infinite duration, even though we serve a Lord whose grace is infinite." It is as though he has given every Elector a reprieve. All are listening to hear what their most trusted man thinks must be done.

"Haven't we all heard it? At one time or another? Do we not hear it now? And do we not know whose voice it is? We have an ancient proverb of this city which tells us: *Never is silence here. The voice of Rome is eternal.* That voice has nothing to do with our humanistic glory! Nor our Renaissance monuments, our libraries, our statuary, our frescoes, our palaces, our bureaucracy, our dignitaries, our power at the green-topped tables. No!

"No, my Brothers! I mean the real voice of Rome, the voice of our Lord present here!"

Then there is another abrupt change. Domenico's mood becomes downright cheerful, like someone setting out on a pleasant reminiscence of things beautiful and of certainties undoubted. "I remember, it was the morning after His Holiness Pope Paul had had his late night session with a certain financial gentleman and signed a bit of paper. I remember that morning, because that was the first time His Holiness made an open remark to me about that ancient voice.

"We discussed the whole demarche, of course—but that part of the discussion with His Holiness was only a springboard. We stood at one of the windows in his study and looked out over the Piazza of Saint Peter's, down at the Obelisk at its center, with the fountains playing around it in the sunlight." It is almost as though Domenico is looking magically through the solid walls and out across the roofs and on to the Piazza of St. Peter's where the Obelisk stands and the waters leap and fall splashing, gleaming. He seems to have the power to grant his listeners the same vision.

"His Holiness said that, whenever he had made a big decision, he always found a judgment on it mirrored around that Obelisk. I could have asked what judgment he found on the Sindona decision, but I didn't because that would have fractured the experience. Instead, we recalled how Emperor Caligula placed that Obelisk there about five or six years after Jesus was crucified in Palestine; and how Peter saw it upside down as he waited one evening for death and for Jesus; and how thousands of Christian men and women and children saw it as they waited for death and for Jesus.

"His Holiness turned away and sat down at his desk. Then he said, without my asking, that the judgment on him was hard, but not harsh. I remember nodding and quoting that old proverb: *Never in silence. The voice of Rome is eternal.* His Holiness looked at me, then, with that peculiar brusqueness of his, eyebrows raised, mouth clenched, chin jutting out. 'Even if I have not translated that voice correctly at times, Father, someone will. You! You translate it for us. For them. For all of us.' This was the essence of our conversation that morning."

Domenico is silent for a few seconds, caught in the strong emotion of memory. "Even though all of us hear that voice, many, perhaps most of us, can no longer understand it. Let me interpret then. In my own words. And let us put ourselves some hard questions.

"Is there any point in hiding the truth from ourselves? Isn't it the fact that we are dealing with life and death? Let us not fool ourselves. Yes surely, we are simple priests, sacred Cardinals; and we represent the spiritual interests, the supernatural values of believers.

"But is that the extent of our activity, the ambit of our effectve action? I ask you! My Brothers!

"Are we merely and only and exclusively clergymen processing birth, marriage, and funeral certificates across our desks, carefully elaborating descriptions of doctrine, devising new ways of fanning the piety of the faithful? Is that a complete and accurate and genuinely exhaustive account of our dealing with life and death? Who says that is us? Is that really us?" Domenico straightens up, his body rigid, his head flung back. He raises his hand and points at them all—points in accusation. His voice is hard. It rings loud around the hall. *"That is a lie!"* Domenico's lips close on that last Latin word, *mendacium,* as he spits it out distastefully, with sudden violence, unrelenting disgust portrayed in his face. "A lie, my Brothers!

"We know, we Cardinals who work in Rome, we all know the vast board on which we play the game of nations. And for what high stakes! And if any non-Curial Cardinal thinks that we spend our time blessing Holy Water and kneeling in adoration of statues and taking part in pious processions at orphanages; if any non-Curial Cardinal says, in other words, that he knows nothing of the full realities, he is either naive or he is deliberately turning a blind eye to the crude realities of our lives.

"No! Eminent Colleagues! Religion is big business, as the Americans say. And this affair of the Church of ours is the biggest of those businesses.

"And let none of you mistake my meaning. I am not saying that our financial structure is completely worldly; I am not saying our diplomatic participation is for purely secular objections. I am not saying our political clout is used for temporal glory. For none of that would be completely true. What I *am* asserting is that we are deeply engaged in the world of international finance; that we are definitely committed to the obligations and functions of secular diplomacy; that we are part and parcel of the socio-political community of nations and states. That is all.

"And I am stating all this not as a main conclusion, nor as something to stop at and consider. But, merely as a stage in the basic argument I wish to make with you. In other words, Eminent Brothers, you and I as Princes of this Church, as Most Eminent Cardinals of the Holy Roman Catholic and Apostolic Church, we are to be described and defined precisely and accurately as players on an international chessboard.

"When you think of that fact, think at the same time, of the middle-class housewife in Brooklyn, New York, or in Kansas City, Missouri, running her eye over the price of a pound of coffee. Or the little newly-married girl in Caracas, Venezuela, her baby in her arms, searching for a cheap tin of beef or some vegetables, perhaps. Or the slum-dwellers in London, Paris, or Palermo shivering for lack of heat because oil and coal and even wood are beyond their means. Or the swollen bellies of the babies in Bangladesh, or the beggars of Hong Kong, or the little children playing with roaches in Brazilian *barrios*, or the seven-year-old boys catching rats in the *favelas* in order to bring the meat home for dinner. ... Say to yourselves: Are we involved in these lives? Are we involved as *clergymen?* Or are we involved as political revolutionaries no different from all the others who carry guns and kill? No different, except that our candor must be less, for we serve a cause we cannot face or name when we kill.

"And then, when you think of the latest shipment of arms to Eastern Europe or West Africa, or the exclusivity of high-rise apartment houses in Rio de Janeiro and in Manhattan, or the pride and dominance of the Rome Hilton, the Pan Am building on the Champs Elysées, or the Watergate Complex in Washington, D.C., the Stock Exchange in Montreal, Canada ... say to yourselves: There, in each of those situations and places, we are involved deeply. Not as clergymen. Not as apostles of Jesus. But as businessmen. As corporation executives. As shareholders. As directors. As responsible for what happens. That is us.

"Or think of the flow of confidential information passing in the privileged circles, Hambros Bros. of London ... J. P. Morgan of New York ... Credit Suisse of Switzerland ... the Banco di Roma ... and the monopolist families of North America and Latin America ... and the financial dynasties of Europe and the Americas and the Far East ... and so on. Yes. Be sure. That is us. We are keenly interested. Deeply involved. Accepted players in that chessgame of nations. And if that were the nature of the game, we would be participating merely in a little human corruption.

"Again, this is not my conclusion. Only a stage in the argument. An accurate observation, and to be admitted! Without cavilling. That is us. Part of us. And, quite frankly, we do not, on the whole, participate in that game— in any of those games—merely for gain. No. Oh no! Our motives over all are pure. For we have learned the game well after sixteen hundred years apprenticeship and practice. The craft is ours—as much as any man's. And, to our credit, we have never taken the ultimate step: never has the economic and political and diplomatic power of the Church been used for the direct destruction of the Church of Jesus. But we have had, and we have still, our share of scoundrels, charlatans, and cheats. Simply put: of corruption.

"We do all that. We play that game. We move the pawns and the pieces around that board. We lose. We win. We make alliances. We break from traps.

"And we do all that because of a very ancient decision. Not one man's decision. Nor even one generation's decision—I mean one generation of Churchmen. You can point to this or that Churchman, Pope, Cardinal, clerical advisor. Yes. But no one in particular did it all.

"In fact, you will find that it was and is the result of a mentality that grew, first imperceptibly, and then quite openly. And it was not an economic decision, nor a political decision, nor even an intellectual decision.

"Here, my Brother, here is its subtlety. And, if we understand how and on what plane that decision was made, we will understand who was its prime mover and what the intentions were and are of that prime mover." Domenico pauses. He appears to be focusing on something far beyond the here and now of this assembly. His head is turned slightly to one side as if he were straining to listen. He stays like that for some seconds. Then he takes a few paces back and forth.

"I seem at this moment to hear the words of that ancient voice . . ." he stops pacing and looks at the farthest seated Cardinals, "we can wonder, even though we hear those words, we can wonder who among us will understand them still. And we can wonder if they will not be drowned out by the never-tiring voice of a most ancient enemy of ours with his hideous strength." And Domenico begins to recite in a low-pitched level tone:

I am the Light of divine salvation within a universe that I have made human. That universe was never a closed cosmos of material forces, of interlocking life structures, of weaving and webbing laws governing a material universe where not one particle escapes, and where all matter and energy interchange—shifting, dovetailing, expiring, reviving, transmuting, becoming, decaying, birthing.

Into that cosmos I came. I intervened. From outside it. And not according to its iron laws. Yet, not violating those laws. But transcending them.

And know that my intervention was an intervention by a completely different force. For I am not a new source of light. But Light uncreated. Not a loving being. But Love itself. Not a compassionate and saving force. But Compassion is my being. And Salvation is of my essence. All of this was incorporated into flesh and blood in a mother's womb. Into my flesh and blood. As baby's body, as a man's frame—his life, his actions, his promises, his death, his resurrection, his rule. Thus my being, the light of salvation. In this world, but not of this world.

Look what happened. Look how the Prince of this world with his hideous strength tries to tie me down! To explain me! To deal with me! At one moment, I am presented as the product of one brain hemisphere—analytical, digital, logical, discreet. At another moment, I am described as the product of another hemisphere—synthetic, mystical, affective. But I belong neither to Athens, nor to Jerusalem with its Bible and Passion. Yet within this human universe, I passed through Bible mind and Bible people, and through Athens and its child—the Western mind.

I am Love uncreated, uncreated Light. Light and Love that always were. Always will be. In all times. In all places. Belonging to each one intimately. But not limited by any time or place or system or theory. And, since the earliest days, the enemy has succeeded in tying me down.

Domenico ceases his monotone and waits for just a moment. Then he launches into a denunciation which mounts steadily in volume and emphasis to a crescendo until his whole body is shaking in the effort.

"I spoke a while ago of the chessboard and the worldwide game of pawn and dice we play. And play it we do. As well as any men. As successfully. As dismally. But let us not be stupid. The games of loans, investment banking, real estate, foreign credits, stocks and shares, corporate financing, portfolios, and all the myriad decisions in economics, industry, manufacturing, buying and selling, these are little games we play. Pettifogging checks and balances and giving and taking and destroying and creating. That is shadowplay. That is a shadow-game of the *real* game that is being played. The game of nations' souls, of salvation for men and women. *There* is the *real* game, my Brothers!

"And there we have been trapped! For our ancient adversary *knows* the board; and he plots his game one thousand years ahead. And now, our moves are made—and his. We face checkmate.

"If anything has frightened us all in this Conclave—hurt us all—it is that we feel trapped. We already hear the sardonic voice of that ancient enemy saying *'Checkmate! I got you to imagine that Uncreated Light was to be completely understood and made available in logic.'* Even so, my Brothers, we entrusted all we knew to scholastic philosophy. Aquinas made it all clear. And that was why Bonaventure tried to warn us when he called Aquinas the father of all the heretics. It was Aquinas who taught us to be rational even about faith.

"And there was more, my Brothers. That sardonic voice continues: *'I got you to imagine that Eternal Love itself could take sides in pettifogging games. To think you must compete in raw power. I got you to act as though Love saved by wealth, as though Love healed souls by armies, treasuries, chancelleries. You fell for it. It's too late now. Checkmate.'* Hear that sardonic cruelty, my Brothers," Domenico's face is flushed, his hands by his sides with fists closed. His voice rises, loud, clear, harsh.

"Look around you and listen and you will see and hear how accurate the voice of our enemy is, and how hard it is for us to hear the ancient voice of eternal light, of eternal and caring love. For our vocation is *not* of Light Eternal. Our method of government is *not* of Love Eternal. Our formulation of Light's knowledge is partial, provincial, out-of-date, blind. Our Cardinali-tial princedoms and our episcopal dignities have as much to do with the love and the light of the Lord Jesus, as the coins he paid in Caesar's tribute had to do with buying our salvation from the Devil and from the Devil's Hell and the Devil's sin.

"We meet as Princes. We think as brokers. We plot as career-men. We hate and despise. We are indignant and triumphalistic. We seek redress and revenge. We harbor grudges to be paid off in kind to those who oppose us. We undermine. We lord it over others. We walk proudly. We rely on wealth, on honeyed words.

"We accept a capitalist democracy which is unacceptable to God because it says all power is vested in the people—whereas we know from faith that all power is vested in God and passes from God to all those who have authority in our world—people or rulers.

"And, on the other side, a section of us is willing to throw in its lot with a socialist democracy that invests all power in the economic forces of history—and to the Devil with God and the people!

"And this, our Conclave? Do you think even this is exempt from critique or from influence? Do you? Honestly, do you, Brothers?

"Its very nature is that of a powerplay. Our purpose here is to balance bloc against bloc, interest with interest. To meet selfishness with selfishness, and patch together a working unity based on a power-broker's compromise. *Do ut des! Quid pro quo!* This for you. This for me. This for him. Nothing for them. A little bit here. A little bit there. And the power of Jesus is treated like a huge apple pie that all the greedy children must share. An inheritance that all the aspiring heirs must divide between them, each according to his own. These are the things that swing us hither and thither.

"What chance would Peter the Fisherman have here? For that matter, if Jesus were present and did not reveal his identity, would he get one vote from us, my Lord Cardinals? Of course not! And not because he was not a Cardinal. But because he had no faction behind him, could promise nothing.

"For, to tell the truth, we have two scales of value—we are torn apart by the disparity of rhythm in our very souls. And the life of our Church is cracking at the seams because the institution is filled with an unbearable inequality of vibrations. We are doomed as an institution. We were led off the path. We were hell-bent on winning. We looked to short-term victories—forty years, eighty years. And our adversary saw a victory looming up about two thousand years later. We did not see the strategy. We were occupied with tactics.

"So we made all the wrong moves on that chessboard. And now there is no saving what we have been building ever since the day Silvester talked with Constantine, and since Leo 3 kissed the foot of Charlemagne. No saving, I say. *No saving!*" The last two words are almost a scream, an old man's scream. Domenico is shaking all over, perspiration running down his face. He is weeping.

He pauses; and when he resumes, he succumbs for a moment to weariness. "You must forgive me, Brothers. Perhaps this is why Pope Paul said: 'The Church seems destined to die.' And if these tears flow freely, it is not for what we might have been, but for the deep pain we all must have at this moment, and in this Conclave."

Then, after a glance at the Presidents, he goes on. His voice still low, is vibrant and now burning anew with some powerful feeling. He speaks as if trying to pour out from himself all the force and violence he is undergoing. "Let no one, therefore, no one of us mistake or misapprehend what we are about, Eminent Brothers. What we are about to do today, now, in this final Conclave, is simply this: *to end the Church of Conclave!* Our job is to plot and plan *our own liquidation!* Not by summary execution. Not by unfaithful desertion. Not by craven stupidity. *But by our concerted will seeking the will of Jesus.* So that the Light we bear and the Love we claim to represent within this human universe shall be free! How shall both Light and Love be freed? How shall we deal with this deathly checkmate threat? For the threat of checkmate it is. . . ."

There is a sudden commotion down near where Thule is sitting. Domenico pauses, stands up straight, and drops his hands to his sides. He is silent.

"My Lord Cardinal Presidents! I rise to a point of order." It is Buff. He speaks in tone of controlled urgency. Dignified. His voice is silken and carefully correct. His tones are clear. A touch of detachment in his demeanor—almost haughtiness, as if all these proceedings were distasteful to him. "My Lord Cardinals, we are not proceeding constitutionally. My Most Eminent and Esteemed Brother, My Lord Cardinal Domenico, I feel, is going beyond the bounds of Conclave propriety. . . ."

Domenico's response is immediate. For the first time, his friends see the cold breath of sheer anger on his face. "If My Lord Buff were to spend a little more time studying the documents of the Church and not poring over letters from atheistic ministers and renegade bishops; if he spent his vacations with his colleagues and not among the neo-pagans of . . ." Buff glances at Thule appealingly. He cannot handle this attack and Domenico's unexpected rage all by himself. He has no defense against brutal confrontation.

Thule leaps to his feet. "My Lord Cardinal Presidents! In addition to advocating revolution in the College of Cardinals, My Lord Domenico is indulging in personal. . . ."

Domenico is after Thule in a flash. "Revolution! You! My Lord Thule! *You!*

You are the one who told a meeting of monks: 'I have come to preach strife in the world and war in the monasteries.' You, My Lord Thule! *You* are the one who told a public audience in France: 'Traditional Christianity is finished.' *You*, My Lord Thule, you. . . ."

"Will the Lord Cardinal President pardon my rising unbidden?" The voice is Franzus'. He is already standing, looking through his thick lenses at the Cardinal Presidents. He has that full echo in his voice that always betrays anger in a man no matter what language he is speaking. "It is not that we are afraid to go naked and unprotected into the world in order to preach. . . ."

Domenico is after him, too, as quickly as he can catch his breath. "You, My Lord Franzus, talk about walking naked? I don't know where Your Eminence intends to go with *that* opening thought. I tell you, My Lord Cardinal, my brother Cardinal, if all of us were as well protected as you have been, our desks and our altars and our baptismal fonts would be as thick in dust as those of your home diocese." Franzus flushes to the roots of his hair. The protection Domenico refers to is Franzus' constant companion, a Russian-appointed agent, who is always present. Nobody quite knows if this is Franzus' choice or something imposed on him. "Yes, my Lord Cardinal," Domenico goes on relentlessly, "you are protected. But God help you!" And before Franzus can reply, Domenico has another shot: "By the way, My Lord Cardinal, the next time you enter a private government clinic for a light operation, be sure to have yourself debugged before participating in further confidential conversations with Roman officials."

A sudden, audible, wave of puzzlement and nervousness sweeps over the Cardinals, heads turning from side to side, questioning looks and gestures, shoulders shrugged, a few whispered conversations. Franzus sinks back into his place. The presiding Cardinal is finally able to intervene. "My Lord Domenico will continue his address."

Domenico is eager to continue. "I would not have you think, my Brothers, that there is either hate or disgust or even anger in me today. Forgive me for any violation of fraternal charity. And may Jesus have mercy on my soul.

"It is just that we stand at the crossroads of history. We vote. But we must remember that the ballot paper will silently accept anything we write upon it. Only events will plague us. Only the Lord Jesus will judge us for the way we choose.

"In choosing, we must listen, listen, listen! For that same ancient voice is elentless, and we have very little time to take heed. In our real and undying faith, let us not fail to hear the word . . ." and Domenico resumes the "voice" of ancient Rome. All in the Conclave is silence, save for that curious, insistent monotone:

I can lose with equanimity all my monuments. It matters little if the robes of Jesus in Rome are destroyed or neglected. Let the Scala Sancta in the

Church of San Salvatore be torn out, if it comes to that. Let its marble be used for public latrines. Let the tanks of an enemy rumble into St. Peter's Basilica, as did the horses of the Spanish Army in 1527; as did the warriors of Attila and Genseric a thousand years before that. It does not matter. Let the mitres and croziers and tiaras and rings and crosses in my museums be sold as collateral or pillaged as booty. It does not matter. And let the Vicar of Jesus be a pilgrim as Jesus was, whose vicar the Pope now is. It does not matter. Let all such beauty, which is also mine, let it be dimmed and tarnished.

That is not your concern. You are not subject to history—there is no such thing really; nor are you subject to historical forces—these are concepts. History does nothing. It is the living human being that does something. And our history is nothing but the activity of men pursuing their purposes, individuals like you.

Individals are the determinants. And the future depends on your choice, your individual choice. You are not the creatures of systems or collectivities or aggregates or institutions. And the law of your lives and your achievement is not logic and not emotion. It is experience.

Experience tells you that you have to make an end to it all, in order to make a beginning. You must free me from the trammels you and your forebears in this Church have placed on me. Free me. Or else, I may have to destroy you, in order to make room for a more faithful generation who will not speak your language, will not think your thoughts, will not wear your dignities or your robes. But they will consent to offer to God that most acceptable sacrifice of the Lord Jesus in purity and in truth, all over this human universe! "From the rising of the sun," as the Hebrew Prophet wrote, "to the going down of the same," a pure offering.

"My Lord Cardinal Presidents, I thank you all." Domenico walks slowly to his place.

There is a short silence. No one of the Electors moves. Then the Cardinal President confers in whispers with his assistants. He stands. "We move that a balloting take place. We will vote as we should vote, first on policy, then on our candidate. The vote on policy is a choice between the formulation of My Lord Domenico and the formulation of My Lord Thule. Will their Eminences please assent or dissent to such a vote. First, those who assent." There is a moment's pause. Then, as a wave rippling onto a long curving shore, the *Ita's* sound. First from one Cardinal, another, another, all around the thrones. Then the *Ita's* finally die away. "Now, their Eminences who dissent," the President bids. There is no sound. No dissent.

"We shall proceed then to a balloting. And. . ." Bonkowski pauses. He looks down at his notes, then clears his throat. He speaks with gravity and emotion. "Not in virtue of my function as presiding Cardinal," he begins slowly, "but as one of you, my Most Eminent Brothers, permit me to add one short reflection." He looks around in query at the two rows of thrones and down to the far end.

"This seems to be an all-important moment in our history as a Conclave, when normal conventions can be mitigated. Personally, my Brothers, I have no use for the amnesia of our contemporaries or the futuristic doomsaying of our current prophets—I refer, of course, to no one here in our Conclave. We have time, the Lord's time. We have the secret of the only real time—not a vacuous eternity and not a dead past, but the sparkling instant that lies at the heartbeat of all human living. For this, for reminding us of this, we wish to thank My Lord Domenico . . ." there is a brief outburst of quiet handclapping. The President pauses a moment, nonplussed by the unexpected approval.

"It is the privilege of the Presiding Cardinal to call on any one of our number who, in his opinion, can properly set the tone and the mind of the Conclave in perspective. I have not yet exercised this prerogative. And this I wish to do now. Believe me, Brothers, it is not lightly or suddenly or at anyone else's bidding, but with deep conviction, that I now call on . . ." he looks around seeking that boyish face, and then finds it, "My Most Reverend Cardinal Lord Azande to address the Conclave on its task."

There are a few quiet voices of encouragement. *"Bravo* Azande!" *"Ita!"* Azande rises in a slightly awkward fashion and makes his way to the speaker's place. In his embarassment, he forgets to kneel at the Altar for the customary prayer. Facing the Electors, he looks shy, somewhat timid. But his voice is strong and resonant.

"I feel, my Most Eminent Colleagues, that my intervention may lack the necessary weight because of my junior years in the Sacred College." There are some cries of encouragement: *"Bravo!" "Avanti!"*

"I may lack clarity because, despite education and daily accustoming, I am not and cannot be of the Western mind. Even this language, as I use it, is a translation by my mind—my own—in itself alien to the mind of the great men who built the institutional Church and fashioned its language." He paces over toward one side, and turns around. There is a trace of quiet humor on his face.

"Many of you—all of you, perhaps—know that in the Sistine Chapel, which used to house every Conclave, Michelangelo covered the end-wall with the *Last Judgment.* And on the ceiling he portrayed the Prophets. Very few of you may know that Michelangelo inserted two self-portraits in his frescoes. He swings around and points as if they were all looking at the *Last Judgment.* The power of his imagination lifts the minds of his listeners with him.

"Look!" he says excitedly, pointing. "See that figure of one man groping his way out of his tomb: Jesus has summoned the dead to rise, according to the artist. Notice the ashen joy on the face of the man." Then, turning back to his listeners: "That's one of Michelangelo's self-portraits. In a sense, it is a portrait of me emerging into the light of some understanding, my Brothers." There is a rustle of approval, some pleasant murmurings of *"Bravo!" "Bene!"* Azande smiles boyishly, his angular features of mouth and chin expressing some mischevious trait in him.

As he walks back over toward the Presidents' table he looks up at the ceiling again, as if he were in the Sistine Chapel. He stops, seems to be searching, then exclaims: "Oh Yes! There he is! Jeremiah the Prophet!" There is a titter of laughter as the Cardinals anticipate the next comparison. "Michelangelo also put himself in Jeremiah's face.

"We think of Jeremiah as a prophet of doom, of sorrow, of laments over the ruins of Jerusalem. But, you know, my Brothers . . ." Azande's face has that casual brotherliness and cozy intimacy so natural to Africans, "Jeremiah is primarily the prophet, the announcer, of the New Covenant. And, if you permit, take me as an announcer, a proponent of a new covenant.

"First, as we say in Africa, let us get rid of the grass.

"To stand pat and hold on is no alternative for us: we would be as the Apostles still hiding in the Upper Room waiting for a Holy Spirit—who has already come!

"Alternatively, gradual and thoughtful change and adaptation is no alternative for us: The Church is already changed—in its people, and its spirit.

"So, should we step out and be like all the others, homogenize with all the others? Homologize our Church with theirs? No, that is no alternative for us either. What right have we to be like others? We have no rights. Only sacred *duties.*

"But still, could we not forge a socio-political alliance with populist—some democratic—elements and movements? Again, that is no alternative for us: We have had political alliances all the years of over sixteen centuries, and look where that has left us!

"But we must surely, indubitably, beyond the cavil of any sharp-eyed enemy, we must be rid of our present status. As financial giant. As diplomatic power. As beneficiaries and even as wielders of political interests. As real estate owners and operators. All that, we must get rid of.

"Why? Two reasons! One negative, one positive.

"The negative permits of no gentle treatment, Brothers. Ask around you. Walk disguised in the market place, in the parliaments of men, in their shops, their money exchanges, their clubs, their homes, their factories. Ask and you will blush. We are, according to them, the schizoid preachers. We celebrate divinity's love in the morning. We sit at Mammon's counting tables in the high noontide. We wander after hours along the boulevards of fine living in the domain of the 'beautiful people.'

"We operate—so they say, and they are correct—on the supposition that the gossamer substance of our faith and the metallic sheen of hard cash fertilize each other. We handle water and bread and wine, claiming that God's blessing impregnates one and that God's humanity and divinity transubstantiates the other two. But with the same consecrated hands we pocket the shekels of the Shylocks, and we deliver pocketfuls of votes to the chosen political party, and we steer contracts to the preferred clubhouse. That, my Brothers, is the negative reason.

"The positive reason is beautiful, consoling, encouraging." A smile wreathes around the angles of his face. "It is that we—and the Pope we elect—we, the Church, have within us a fund of spiritual enlightenment, an inexhaustible wealth, of moral authority! It is all there. But it is leashed in the toils of political commitment, of ruthless diplomacy, of moneying and bargaining and buying and selling and bartering. No amount of purple, my Brothers, no field of cloth-of-gold, no glistening ermine or perfumed ceremonies, no amount of human dignity can camouflage or make prettier to behold the fact that the *greatest* riches of our Church are caught in the poor trammels of worldliness.

"In the name of our triumphant Lord, have we not got something of our own? As My Lord Domenico said, have we not got an initiative all our own? Positively Christian, authentically Roman, Catholic, and Apostolic? Have we not the basis—the greatest basis—for a general policy to which we are all committed? To which our elected candidate must commit himself and his Church? *Must* commit his authority as Pope and as Christ's Vicar? And commit every ounce of energy the Church harbors?"

Suddenly, Azande is interrupted. All heads swing around as Thule is on his feet on the near right, and Vasari on the far left. Both Cardinals are signaling for permission to speak. Both have the question to ask—but for totally different reasons. Vasari fears for the old guard, Thule for what he sees as the vanguard of the near-future.

"My Lord Vasari!" It is the President.

"My Lord Cardinals! I think that My Most Eminent Lord, Cardinal Azande, owes us an actual list of concrete changes and proposals. We are not here to gather wool." Vasari is angry because he is frightened. Azande's hints and intimations are as fearful to him as are Thule's actual proposals.

Thule shrugs his shoulders, indicating by a hand motion that this also is his question, more or less.

Azande nods smilingly at Vasari. His mild and winsome manner is a perfect foil for the inherent harshness of his words. He speaks as if reciting a sweet and nostalgic poem of his youth in faraway Africa.

"On a certain day, at a certain hour, in a certain well-known part of the Vatican, by the instrumentality of a certain document duly signed, sealed, and delivered, and carried over television and radio in 25 languages, via satellite and by cable, to all the Continents of our world, through the written media and by simultaneous presentation of official versions of that document to all the bishops of all 2,700 dioceses, to all member governments of the United Nations, to all international organizations—governmental and non-governmental—let our candidate-Pope and his Sacred College of Cardinals inform the family of man precisely about the following initial measures which the Holy See and the Catholic Church is about to implement.

"Number One: the creation of an international, interdenominational, lay Trust Fund organization; and the legal transfer to its possession of all actual wealth—cash, securities, valuables, real estate, promissory notes—that at present belong legally and rightfully to the Holy See, to its agencies, to its representatives, at home and abroad."

Extraordinary! Already there is a silence that can only be described as dumfounded. Some Cardinals have craned forward in their seats, as if they feared to lose a word of what he is saying.

"National divisions of this international Trust Fund organization will be created for every sovereign state that requires this, according to its own national laws. But Churchmen will never again administer, decide upon, or allocate the wealth of this Church." By the time Azande reaches the end of this statement, the silence is shot through with emotions that are almost palpable. On the faces of Masaccio, Vasari, Ferro, there are looks of anger and consternation and bewilderment. They have been caught completely unawares. Lynch is biting his upper lip, gazing stolidly in front of him. Thule is obviously at sea—he does not quite know where Azande is going: it may be all in his favor; it may be against all he proposes. It is more radical than he and his group had ever contemplated.

The Camerlengo is like a man with all the blood drawn out of him. No longer dispassionate, detached, occupied with note taking, as has been his wont until this extraordinary moment, he is transfixed—eyes bulging, mouth held in a firm line; even his aquiline nose appears more curving than ever with the clenching of his lips.

Walker is the only one who seems more attentive to the looks on his fellow Cardinals' faces than to Azande. Walker seems to have understood at once all that Azande has said and not to be too surprised by a word of it.

"Number Two," Azande proceeds relentlessly in spite of the consternation he knows he has caused. "The termination of all diplomatic missions to the

Holy See from sovereign states and nations; and the simultaneous recall of all Vatican diplomatic missions accredited to sovereign governments and to international organizations." It would have seemed impossible for the shock of Azande first proposal to deepen; but his Number Two does it.

Still Azande has further to go.

"Number Three: Formal and legally drawn documents containing the official renunciation by the Holy See of all territorial possessions constituted juridically by the Lateran Treaty of 1929 between the State of Italy and the Holy See."

This is too much. Several muttered conversations have started. Cardinal Vasari does the extraordinary thing of rising and crossing over to talk with Angelico. Azande pauses. The Cardinal President, seemingly unruffled, rings his silver bell: "If the Eminent Cardinal will regain his seat, and their Eminences will give His Eminence, My Lord Azande, time, I am sure what remains for him to say will be of short duration." Vasari returns to his place.

Azande continues: "Number Four: The putting on notice of everybody concerned—governments, political organizations, financial groups, cartels, chancelleries, ministeries of foreign affairs—that henceforward the Holy See reserves the right—the duty—to criticize, to critique, to condemn, to approve, as it sees fit and as the principles of its faith dictate. Unencumbered by *any* motive arising out of political, financial, or diplomatic ties. *For there will be no such ties. Not ever again!* And that henceforth no one should be surprised by any such action that the Holy See may take without earthly fear, or hope, of earthly favor."

Now the Camerlengo is on his feet. Thule is on his feet. Vasari, Riccioni and Lynch too—all asking for permission to intervene. With all the dignity of the Camerlengo of the Universal Church, this senior official is most persistent in his request for "permission to question the Most Eminent and Esteemed Lord Cardinal, My Lord Azande." He obtains permission.

Glancing hurriedly at a pile of notes in front of him, the Camerlengo starts, his manner urgent and pressuring. "Will His Eminence explain what all this has to do with the *internal* condition of the Church? All these measures cover our *external* relations. And, beyond that, there are extraordinarily serious questions totally ignored by your, er, so-called proposal. For instance, who is to structure this supposed Trust Fund? How are we to be sure that another financial farce, worse than the Sindona affairs, would not result? What is to substitute for the diplomatic channels of communication with the various governments of the nations, if we wipe out our own diplomatic corps? And if we abrogate all treaty arrangements with the Italian State, what of the Vatican itself, to mention only the most obvious question? Has His Eminence any idea of what such vast restructuring involves?" Then he sits down with the air of a man dealing with madness, shaking his head.

Azande goes to his table and lifts two heavy files from it. He lifts them, saying simply: "The Camerlengo—and all of you, Eminent Brothers, for I will have it polycopied—will find here a very respectable skeleton blueprint of the processes of restructuring." He moves again to the center of the floor.

"As to the internal structure of the Church, my point Number Five (which I did not reach) outlines the general principle I would use in judging that. It is: that the Conclave will appoint, in conjunction with the election of a new Pope, a committee of seven or eleven or thirteen Cardinals. This Commission will prepare for the Holy Father certain preliminary documents within a couple of months. One document recommending revisions of all that the post-conciliar Commissions have decided about the Liturgy of the Mass and of the Sacraments." Thule shifts in his seat impatiently, perhaps angrily.

"A second document will contain the principles for a proposed restructuring of the Vatican and of the international structure of Church Government.

"A third document will list deviations from official doctrines, together with the names of the theologians, philosophers, writers, publicists, bishops, priests, and intellectuals involved in the active promulgation of those deviations, evident since the end of the Second Vatican Council in 1965. This document will also clarify the substance, meaning, and importance of such deviations, in terms of faith."

Thule is on his feet. He now must have the answer to one question. "On what basis, Eminent Brother, will the Church deal with the political and social problems and forces let loose on our world today?" Thule's leonine head is lifted in direct challenge.

Azande has expected this question—from Thule. He looks at the Cardinal, then at the other Electors, and then walks down the hall between the rows of Cardinals, all the while looking at the floor. He stops when he is opposite Thule, but it is at the Electors massed at the end of the hall that he looks. Then he turns and faces the whole assembly. When he speaks, the Electors hear the authority ringing in his voice, and feel the inner resolution of this young black whose grandparents were not even Christian.

"It would be easy, so easy—glib, that's the world—to answer the Most Eminent Lord Cardinal in his own words. After all ..." a quizzical smile spreads across his mouth, "My Lord Cardinal would have us trust those who have already killed, maimed, destroyed, imprisoned, executed, calumniated, persecuted the Church all over Europe and Asia." His voice becomes harsh in protest. "Trust the Maoists, Reverend Cardinal? Trust the KGB, Most Eminent Brothers? Trust that castrated Communist jackal, Kadar, Most Eminent Cardinal?" Thule is taken aback.

Then Azande's voice sinks back to normal. "So? I would be entitled to say: Let's trust in Our Lord!" He smiles in mock apology. "But that is not the answer. My answer is to deplore your poverty of alternatives, Eminent

Cardinal! You and everyone who has neglected one essential truth of our faith, and one irrefragable promise of our beloved Jesus Christ." He looks up toward Angelico's corner, and over to the Camerlengo, then to where Vasari sits.

"That truth and that promise are *one.*" He hits that word 'one' with high emphasis and repeats it: *"one!*

"Think Eminences! Imagine and recall to yourselves that day of all days! See Jesus conferring the power of the Keys on Simon Peter near Hermon. Look! Eminent Brothers! Look, each one of you, at that scene in your mind's eye. We all know it. We know the words by heart. In Latin. . . . In Greek. In our native languages. Yet," he looks all about him, he asks everyone there—everyone everywhere, "have we really grasped what those keys represent? What power is thereby given us?" He stalks up the aisle between the Cardinals again, musing as he goes.

"Somewhere along the line of our horizontal history on this globe, we lost hold of that vertical plumbline. We confused that power with the effects of money, of political sway, of military advantage, of cultural enrichment, of humanistic glory. And, to tell you the truth, as I see it, Eminent Brothers, I do not think there are ten men among us today who know what power in spirit is; and rarely has anyone of us seen it used in our day. And when it was used beneath our very eyes, did we recognize it for what it was? I doubt that. I doubt that.

"Let us meditate for one moment on that power. For what I propose in the name of the Eminent Cardinals who stand with me is that we remodel, refashion, refurbish all Papal and Vatican and Church activity, so that we rely *only* on that power. Only on *that* power."

There is a sudden, not disturbing, sound of approbation from the black Cardinals. It is strange but unwontedly exciting, deep, waving, drumlike. First from Makonde, then echoed down the right row by Chaega, Koi-Lo-Po, coming on the left from Lotuko, Nei Hao, Kotoko, Duala, Lang Che-Ning, Saleke, and echoing from the one black at the back of the assembly—Bamleke.

Coming from their chests and throats, the sound is a long, slow, resounding upbeat flow rising loud and high, then dropping off a cliff of sound to a very low and sustained basso tone. The sound is not molded into words. But it is inflected and modulated by an emotion so raw, so naked, so natural, so collective, so evident, that everyone understands. It is as if, to convey the experience of seeing a sunrise, the human throat formed sounds that conveyed not the idea of a sunrise, but the emotions aroused by a sunrise. It has a primordial quality that affects everyone, disturbing some, exciting others, making everyone sit up and look at Azande, who is smiling the smile of Africa at the black Cardinals, and they are smiling back at him and then at each other, and then at everyone else. This applause is a near-perfect expression of agreement, sympathy, and encouragement.

"This power," Azande's words command silence again, "this power, is not one of healing sick limbs, or seeing at a distance, or being in two places at the same time, or reading the secrets of the mind, or foretelling the future.

"This power is a force emanating from God, inhabiting those who are in God's grace. Power in spirit. And in the Keeper of the Keys and in his ministers and in the priests and in the people. This is a power that *resides* in them, that gives them moral authority—according to their grade in God's Kingdom of the Spirit.

"In Peter, whoever he be, the power is preeminent and forceful and unbeatable. With it, he can evoke the loyalty, the obedience, and the actions of all the faithful. He can literally oppose enemies and oppressors and all evil, and they cannot conquer him or the faithful or their faith.

"It would be easy to recall the example of Pope Leo the Great, alone, unarmed, walking out to meet Alaric the Hun and his sixty thousand warriors. Leo alone, by force of moral power, persuaded Alaric to turn away and not sack Rome. But that was 1500 years ago at least. And the distance in time makes the event unreal for us moderns.

"But we have modern examples nearer home. How, do you think, have the Poles survived with their Church intact in Stalinist Poland? Do you think they and their Church did that because of their bank balance? Or their stock investment? Or their real estate holdings? Their political clout? Their diplomatic influence? Not a bit of that! You know that better than I. Not a bit. Only because they held on to that power in spirit!

"How often in recent history has the Pope and the Vatican relied solely on that power? How often, relying on it alone, have they wielded it?

"And not the Pope only. Let us face the truth. For many of us Bishops, for thousands of priests, for millions of layfolk, this power-in-spirit, this moral authority has been obscured, disguised, transmuted, degraded. Above all, it has been confused with other things. We have become indentured as slaves to the fearful rigidities of a politico-economic system. And neither do we realize it, nor do we know how to get out of it. My God! Eminent Brothers, my God! And we rush to our brokers and our bankers and our realtors and our diplomats to solve our problems, instead of relying on the power of Christ. 'Ask of the Gods,' said Socrates, 'only for good things.' 'Ask for anything in my name,' said Jesus, 'and it shall be given to you.' Have we forgotten all that? Is it all a joke? An ancient story. May Jesus help us to let the scales fall from our eyes.

"And this is how confused we all are. We confound spiritual power with psychic energy. We confuse soul with psyche. We confuse God's inspiration with the irrational subconscious. Piety becomes behavioral psychology.

Theology bows to anthropology. Moral law and ethics are treated as nothing more than and nothing different from sociological quantification. We define human history with Lenin's chilling phrases and boil them down to 'Who has done what to whom?' We define divine salvation in Darwin's crass obliteration of spirit. And that boils down to 'What has become what?' Love is reduced to physical sex. The dignity of the mendicant is reduced to the claims of welfare recipients. Freedom is debased as the absence of any control. Liberty is transformed into resentment against any limit on behavior.

"The Sacrifice of the Mass is all but obliterated by the indignity of a 'holy meal.' Evil is equated with negative environmental factors; good is a refrigerator, a dishwasher, a TV set.

"The charity of Christ is confused with minority quotas; the works of mercy, with social activism; worship of God, with the fellowship of men and women sipping cocktails; unity and harmony, with majoritarian whims; civility, with no inflation; the fitness of things, with good plumbing; liberation, with more money; self-control, with the license to kill unborn babies; the dignity of man, with male sodomy; the emancipation of women, with Lesbianism; the truth, with repeated publicity of lies and half-lies and myths.

"And in this Conclave, the unbought grace of life stands in danger of being confused—for the last time—with financial subsidies from socialist governments.

"My God! Eminent Brothers, Oh, my God! Good Jesus! Where have we got to!" Azande's eyes are full of tears. His body is quavering. His fists are closing and opening. He stands silent and staring down the assembly for some instants.

Someone clears his throat in the absolute silence, as if he was about to say something out loud. The sound sets off a reaction. It comes without warning, but as if on cue. Some start clapping their hands. Then a few more. And a few more. The Camerlengo looks around quickly from one applauding Cardinal to another, alternately glaring and questioning with his eyes. The applause rises in volume. One Cardinal cries *"Bravo!"* Thirty cry *"Bravo!"* Already two have stood up, still clapping their hands and crying *"Bravo!"* Then all along the lines of seated Cardinals, Electors clamber to their feet dropping their papers on the little tables in front of the thrones, clapping, smiling, crying *"Bravo!" "Bravo!" "Azande!" "Magnifico!"* "Well said, Azande!" *Bravo!"* Some few remain seated—the Camerlengo, Lynch, Thule, Marquez, Manuel, Buff, Franzus. But they, too, rise after a few moments; and, if only as an act of consentient presence here, join the applause.

Some few Cardinals are weeping openly; one or two are seen shaking hands, as if together they had witnessed some scene or heard some words that together they had prayed and hoped for. Some pristine emotion has risen unbidden among these dignified and highly egotistical and personalistic men—career-men, bureaucrats, politicians, holy bishops, scholars, diplomats, men of the world. All know that as individuals, and as a College of Cardinals, they have suddenly seen some shining image, some shimmering ideal resting among them uninvited, winsome, the real object of their lives, and the highest object of the best moments of their spirit.

And, they know that that thin, angular, youthful black figure standing at the long table has been the occasion and the instrument for this experience.

"We see, Azande! Don't worry. We understand! We are with you, Azande! Azande has spoken for us all. The Holy Spirit has spoken from Africa! Azande! Jesus is with you, Azande! Azande!" The black Cardinal is trying to say something above the uproar. And some Electors start shushing the applause, waving their arms and hands: "Shhhh Shhhh! Brothers! Shhh! Let him speak!" The clamor dies down. All look at Azande. If anyone there had any doubts about Azande's ability to read an audience or to seize an opportunity, all such doubts are laid to rest. He looks steadily at the Electors on each side and down to the mass of Electors at the back of the assembly.

"Can we do it, my Brothers?" he finally says. "Can we do it still?"

There are several spontaneous cries. *"Ita!" "Ita!" "Ita!" "In nomine Cristi! Ita!"* (in the name of Christ, yes) *"Si volumus! Ita!"* (If we really want to, yes).

"If we really want to," Azande takes up the last exclamation, raising his own voice to be heard above the cries from the assembly. "If we have recourse to the Spirit of Jesus. Even if the whole human world were covered with concrete and all our lives were mechanized in steel and chrome, even so! Some day, somehow, our faith and our reliance on that Spirit would crack that cement. And through that solitary crack the flower of faith and true worship of the Risen Christ would blossom and grow. That gleaming inanimate machinery would be festooned in the glory of God's love. And over the bleak landscape of our human life would break the sunrise of the Resurrection! Believe it, my Brothers! Believe it! Believe it with the Apostles! With Peter! With Clement! With Leo! With Paul! With Pius! With all the saints! With the faithful! Believe it! Believe it and it shall be done!"

The tumult breaks out again. "We believe it!" "You are Peter!" "We believe it!" The clapping and cries of *"Bravo!"* ring through the Hall. Even the young Monsignore seated outside the door hears the noise. He rises, his face flushing with excitement. He thinks: A Pope has been chosen! He waits.

Behind the closed doors, the enthusiasm holds. Azande has no intention of letting it go. And what he now accomplishes takes no more than one minute. His energy is almost spent. His emotions are beginning to recede from him. But he knows what he must do. In a quick glance around the assembly, he takes it all in. There is, for the moment, a sea of affirmation and warmth— arms raised, eyes lit up with expectancy, voices echoing again and again.

And, in among those scarlet-clad figures with faces raised to Azande, there are the stock-still members of the opposition, a Thule, a Franzus, a Buff, their faces set, their eyes understanding more than their applauding colleagues. They, standing on the sidelines of this collective feeling, sense Azande's next move. But they are powerless to stop it.

"Brothers!" It is the first time that Azande raises his voice to the level of a proclamation. He raises both arms, palms facing outward to the assembly and gently motioning for silence. All the cries stop. Electors are held in the midflight of their aplause. "Brothers! Will you in your majority, will you declare the general policy I have outlined, will you give it the oldest form of Christian endorsement—your voice! your voices!" He pauses, then shouts in one loud triumphant cry: "*Ita!*"

For just a couple of seconds the whole assembly hangs there. And, suddenly, as one body it decides. It reacts.

Once more, it is the blacks who begin. Drawing out the first syllable of that affirmative *Ita*, they stay on it, prolonging the "ee" sound until one, seven, twenty, fifty, ninety, over one hundred voices have joined in. That "ee" has now become a full-throated fluency. As natural-born chorus leaders, the blacks raise the pitch of their voices while prolonging that sound. All instinctively understand that at a certain high point in that rising pitch the second syllable of *Ita* will come. All have their eyes on Azande who is in control. His hands, his eyes, the shape of his mouth as he forms that syllable "ee"—all his listeners are watching them. This assembly is now acting as one body.

Magically, when that second syllable comes, the majority of those voices hit it hard. And the young Monsignore—who has hastily summoned the priest-confessors, hears the tail-end of that rising "ee" capped by a thunderous and prolonged "*ta!*" Azande, on stage, holds his arms level and immediately cries out sharply "*Ita!*" The Cardinals repeat "*Ita!*" And then it is a row of twelve or fifteen *Ita*'s coming like the blows of a hammer driving home a nail already sunk deep into the wood.

Now, Azande has his last duty to perform. He raises his hands for silence. "Brothers! What are we waiting for? The Holy Spirit has spoken! We know our general policy. We need a Pope! We need a Pope! The Church needs a Pope! Jesus wills us to have a new Pope! Shall we not vote? Now? Here and now? Shall we not elect the successor to Peter and the Vicar of Jesus? Shall we? Does it seem good to the Holy Spirit and to us?"

There is one more resounding *Ita* followed by hand clapping. Azande looks around at the Presidents, then down to Domenico. The old man is sitting back motionless, his face drawn. But in his eyes, Azande reads: "Well done! Well done! Stop now. Get down." Azande turns, bows to the Presidents. As he walks to his place, the Cardinal President speaks. "Very Well, Eminent

Brothers. Your will is clear. The general policy as proposed by our Most Eminent Lord, My Lord Cardinal Azande, is official Conclave policy. We will proceed to a balloting and scrutiny. Will the Scrutineers, Revisers, and *Infirmarii* please come forward, so that we can distribute the ballot papers."

While the ballot papers are being distributed, two Cardinals leave their places. The young Cardinal with the stutter, unnoticed by many, goes over to Domenico and drops to his knees in front of the older man, his face in his hands. Those nearby see Domenico's lips moving, his right hand making the sign of the Cross. The Electors only surmise what is being transacted between the two. When the young Cardinal rises and goes back to his place, the Electors glance at his face and then look away hastily in pain and embarrassment. Most of them, priests though they are, have forgotten and cannot take the sight of a face that portrays the peculiar peace and that rather frightening strength of repentance done, of humiliation accepted, of love renewed. It is too much.

The other Cardinal is Thule. Stiff as a Rhinish oak, his face as immobile as an Alpine peak, large eyes reddened with feeling, Thule walks with a rare dignity and followed by 117 pairs of eyes. He stops in front of Azande who is already seated. Azande is about to rise for the older man. A flicker of Thule's gaze stops Azande, like a hand placed on the chest; and he sits there, his black face lifted up as he looks into Thule's eyes. Then, spontaneously, Azande clasps his own two hands together and raises them to Thule. Thule takes them into his own, bowing his head over them. Some word—short, gentle, whispered—passes between the European and the African. Then, slowly unhurried, as if he were walking in a total solitude of his own, Thule goes back to his place.

By **this** time, the ballots have been distributed. The Cardinal President takes off his glasses and looks at the assembly. "It is customary that the Cardinal presiding over what promises to be a definitive vote, has the privilege of saying a few unofficial words. I feel—as you all feel—that the agony of our choosing the next occupant of the throne of Peter should be ended as expeditiously and as efficiently and as easefully as possible. Now, in other words. And in fraternal union and peace." He looks around meditatively at his fellow Cardinals.

"The outside world will never understand it. But we have had moments of heart-rending experience in this Conclave, my Brothers. Something unique and precious has happened here to us. Eh?" He looks around again and receives nods of assent and smiles of encouragement. "The greatness of our Lord Jesus, I suppose, has passed in front of us, and we have touched the hem of his trailing glory. And grace has gone out from him to all of us.

"We have experienced that nameless breath of Jesus' inspiration blowing gently over our spirits. We, like other poor mortals, would not wish to examine its supiemacy too closely for fear of the demands it might make. And yet we are alone now. Absolutely alone with Jesus. We cannot afford to forget his presence. Much less pass it over in nonrecognition.

"We now choose for the highest of motives. There is no one of us here who has not been thoroughly informed of our situation. We are at the end of one road. Perhaps no one has been forced to see, as we have, how the presence and the power of Jesus, the good Lord of the Church, has for so long been invested with the toils of imperialism, financial strength, diplomatic panoply, cutural elitism, and personal ambitions. For so long!

"Yet there is not one of us now—no matter how worldly our hearts have been or become—who does not realize as perhaps never before that this presence and this power is among us men. But it is not of mankind. It is the only force uncontrollable and uncontrolled by men's power, by our sins and faults, and by the plots of the Evil One.

"We are the temporary holders of Roman power. We will bleed and die, each in his own way. But the heart of the Roman power rests safe in a guarantee of permanency. It will wreak its effects—dire and beautiful, by turns—effortlessly among men. And neither the evil nor the sanctity of Popes and Cardinals can violate or better that power, any more than the ravages of time can shatter it.

"What we can do, what we must do, what we are about to do now, is an awesome and terrible thing, my Brothers. For it is terrible and awesome to fall into the hands of the living God. And that is precisely where we have fallen. For this precious and fate-laden moment, we will stand outside of time, independent of space, as it were. And, as at Hermon, once again we will hear Jesus saying through us: 'You are Peter.' We can blaspheme—you know how! Or, we can bow to his will—you know how! We all know how!

"In marking his ballot, each one of us is touching the intimacy of the great mysterious Lord to whom each one of us will personally answer for what he does here today. And can our wait for that answering be long for any of us, my Brothers?" He lets his gaze travel over the faces. "A few years? A year? The Lord knows best. Praised be the Lord!"

He looks down at his notes, then folds them and places them in his briefcase. All the while, there is no movement or sound among the Electors. Then, quietly, he raises his right hand, gesturing with a forward motion of his outstretched fingers—the signal to begin.

Silence falls on the Conclave. One by one, each Cardinal bends over his writing table, takes a ballot paper, and opens it to write the name of the next Pope.

Selective Index